CANADIAN QUOTATIONS AND PHRASES

Canadian

QUOTATIONS
AND PHRASES

LITERARY AND HISTORICAL

Compiled by

Robert M. Hamilton

With an introduction by

Bruce Hutchison

McCLELLAND AND STEWART LIMITED

Publishers   Toronto

The Canadian Publishers

McClelland and Stewart Limited
25 Hollinger Road, Toronto 16

PRINTED AND BOUND IN CANADA BY
UNIVERSAL PRINTERS LTD., WINNIPEG

Contents

Introduction

Lacking better, we have got along pretty well in Canada so far on legends that are demonstrably untrue. Perhaps the legend of our national dumbness is the most widely believed and most deceptive of all. Canadians, it seems to be generally agreed, seldom say anything worth remembering. Hence, most of the Canadian sayings that deserve to be memorable are forgotten. We, being Canadian, ignore them in favor of foreign importations. The truthful legend of our inferiority complex is the exception that proves the rule.

The author of this book has made a unique contribution to our national life by proving how greatly it differs in one essential aspect from the accepted caricature. He has proved, in short, that Canadians have something to say and can say it in a fashion indigenous, pungent and unmistakably Canadian.

Even a glance through the quotations from Canadians, living and dead, will show the reader what a wealth of wisdom, wit, nobility and assorted Canadiana we have produced and left behind thoughtlessly in our brief march, without a marking stone to tell our followers to pause here and there for refreshment. The flowing wells and oases where the old caravans have rested are dried up as in a desert, which is quite imaginary. Mr. Hamilton has herewith tapped the wells lying deep in our nature, he has peopled the desert with the lively, articulate and misrepresented figures of our past.

The discerning reader, coming to this book with no knowledge of Canada, could form a pretty accurate picture of its history from the casual observations of its makers, large and small. All the great issues and causes on which the nation was founded and maintained are here, with the comments of the men who fought them. Conquest, rebellion, Confederation, war, peace, politics — all are suddenly illumined by their participants, speaking directly to us across the years. But something much more interesting, and perhaps in the end more important, emerges from these exhibits — they convey, as perhaps no other Canadian book has ever conveyed, the full texture and salty flavor of Canadian life.

The author probably had no such ambition when he began his laborious and, as it must have seemed, his almost hopeless task of assembling between two covers the final testament of the Canadian mind. Nevertheless, that is what he has achieved.

You cannot read the sayings of such diverse Canadians as Sam Slick, Sir John A., McGee, Carman, Dafoe and Bob Edwards without a mixture of bitter regret and heady pleasure — regret that so much lovely, earthy and glorious stuff has been lost in the pages of obscure books and deceased newspapers, and pleasure in an opulent discovery. Here, though only by quick hints, sly glances and monosyllables out of the side of the mouth, here is Canada, painted warts and all.

"A man," observes the first Canadian sage, Mr. Slick, "that has too many irons in the fire is plaguy apt to get some of 'em burnt." There is the solid practicality of Canada, the concentration on the day's work, the national scepticism. "There is no strength," says Joseph Howe, "where there is no strain; seamanship is not learned in calm weather; and born of the vicissitudes and struggles of life are the wisdom, the dignity and the consolations." There, if you will, is the philosophy of Canada, a nation built against every kind of strain, in defiance of all weathers. "Oh, I eat all I can," says Van Horne, "I drink all I can, I smoke all I can and I don't give a damn for anything." There (even among teetotalers and non-smokers) is the spirit of Canada from the days of birch bark to the days of jet airplanes.

The Canadian who loves his country will treasure this book not because the sayings of his people are wiser or wittier than those of other peoples — perhaps their average quality is inferior to some — but because they are so utterly Canadian. They touch his deep racial memory as sharply as the first news of winter, the report of maple sap flowing in the spring, the pictures of mountains, wheat fields and great rivers and all those other intimations which every Canadian receives not through his ears but in his heart.

The forgotten Canadians have tried to speak to us, they have said their say in passing and marched on, but we have seldom heard them. Now, for the first time, they speak to us as it were in a Canadian chorus. No, that is wrong; they never inflict their views on the listener, they do not deliver formal orations but speak casually, in disjointed but vivid sentences, as Canadians might speak at a street corner, around the stove of a country store or on a shady porch.

Let the reader seek a Canadian opinion on almost any subject, from death to drink, and he will find it here, conveniently arranged in alphabetical order. Better still, let him start at the beginning and read to the end. He is not much of a Canadian if he can lay this book down before he has finished every Canadian word of it.

Bruce Hutchison.

Preface

This book is designed mainly as a guide to what Canadians have said in the past about themselves or things Canadian, or from a Canadian point of view. I hope it may serve to some extent also as a supplement to the standard dictionaries of quotations, in which Canadians, for whatever cause, are conspicuous by their absence. It contains quotations and phrases from Canadian authors and sources on a variety of subjects, some of them exclusive to Canada, and also quotations from non-Canadians on subjects distinctly Canadian.

Most of the quotations and phrases gathered together here have been used time and again by writers and speakers. Some of them have been used in print, to my knowledge, only a few times. A small number of them have been selected by me from the context. This was done for one of two reasons; either I remembered seeing them quoted before, or I included them with the hope that they would be found useful. In a pioneer work of this kind I think there is something to be said in favour of this latter motive, if only in order to add body to the text, and, I hope, some worth.

A book of quotations, even as restricted as this one in its scope, can never be complete. I do not doubt that many good Canadian phrases and quotations have been inadvertently omitted from this collection. I have tried to make it fairly comprehensive and have searched far and wide with that in mind. Fortunately, out of the vast accumulation of print that has been built up in this country over the last two hundred years, bits and pieces have risen to the top through being unearthed and cherished and repeated. This process of perpetuation makes an otherwise impossible task feasible. The endeavour to bridge the gap between what was feasible and what might be successful constituted for me a challenge. Whether that challenge has been met can be measured only in terms of such qualities as inclusiveness, accuracy, selection, and so on, and ultimately is for the reader to decide.

I am uneasily aware that there are many gaps in this compilation. Whether this is because Canadians have not said anything memorable upon those subjects missing from this book, or because not enough Canadians consider those things worth repeating, I do not know. I prefer to conclude that this collection is a fair result of the labours of one person working more or less on his own, and that if much is lacking, much remains to be supplied by others. Therefore, if this book has some success in spite of its omissions, it might be worth improving. I shall be able to do this if readers and writers, librarians, teachers, journalists, speakers, indeed anyone alive to the possibility of increasing and enriching this body of our verbal heritage, are sufficiently concerned to send me their additions, criticisms, suggestions, remonstrances, corrections, and favourite quotations or phrases. All these I shall heartily welcome.

There has been almost no attempt made to improve or edit the text of these quotations. Words added for the sake of clarity have been placed within the conventional square brackets. Spelling follows the original wherever possible; where it was not possible, a few alterations and corrections have been made for the sake of consistency. In the notes appended to the quotations it will be observed that book titles and names of periodicals appear in italics, while titles of poems and essays appear within quotation marks.

Looking back over the five years during which this book was produced I recall with pleasure the kind cooperation of many friends, and strangers, who gave me assistance and encouragement. I am indebted to the following : Miss Agnes Coffey, Mr. Wilfrid Eggleston, Mr. Roger Graham, Mr. H. Pearson Gundy, Mr. F. A. Hardy, Miss Marjorie C. Holmes, Mr. Willard E. Ireland, Dr. W. Kaye Lamb, Mr. O. S. A. Lavallée, the late Dr. Alfred E. Lavell, Dr. Gerhard E. Lomer, Dr. A. R. M. Lower, Miss Isabel McLean, Mr. K. W. McNaught, Miss Lila McPhee, Miss Barbara Murray, Mr. Arthur L. Phelps, Mrs. J. B. Ringwood, Professor F. R. Scott, Mr. Alan Suddon, Miss M. E. Thompson, and Mrs. Frances Shelley Wees.

I am especially glad to acknowledge my debt to Dr. W. B. Bean, and Dr. W. W. Frances, whose extensive knowledge of Osler's writings was of much help ; to Mr. Daniel C. McArthur, who made many suggestions regarding the quotations of his father, Peter McArthur ; to Miss Elizabeth H. Morton, Executive Secretary of the Canadian Library Association, who was a constant source of stimulation and practical assistance ; to Mr. F. V. Stone of the Canadian Pacific Railway, and Mr. Walter S. Thompson, formerly of the Canadian National Railways, who were instrumental in gathering many of the railway nicknames ; to Professor F. H. Underhill, whom I fear I must have wearied by my numerous questions regarding the quotations of Goldwin Smith and Edward Blake ; to Miss Elizabeth Wallace, for her suggestions regarding Goldwin Smith ; to Miss Eileen Weber, for searching the New York Public Library quotations file ; and to my friend Bruce Peel, who gave freely of his wide knowledge of the West. The efficient assistance of Miss Audrey Gaylard in helping to prepare the index is appreciated. To Miss Martha Shepard, who read the proofs, made valuable criticisms and caught many errors, my debt is endless. For the rest of my life I shall be grateful to Mr. Bruce Hutchison for contributing the Introduction, which I immodestly confess is my favourite part of the book. Most importantly, the realization of this work is, to a great degree, a tribute to the patience and encouragement of my wife. This book is dedicated to her, to my mother, and to the memory of my late father.

R. M. H.

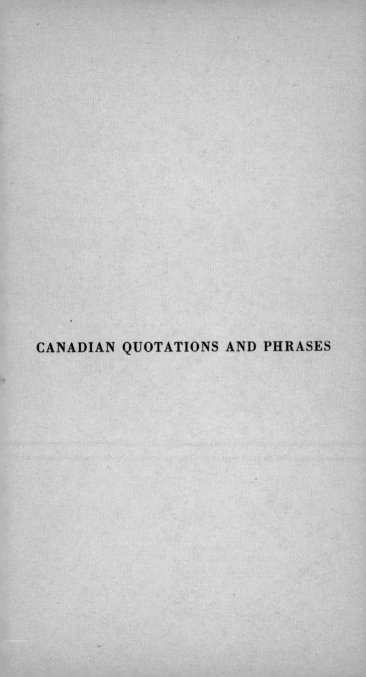

CANADIAN QUOTATIONS AND PHRASES

CANADIAN
QUOTATIONS AND PHRASES

A

ABILITY.

There is no field for ambition, no room for the exercise of distinguished talent in the provinces.

T. C. HALIBURTON, *Sam Slick*, 1840, 265, referring to the Maritimes.

You are as sharp as a needle.

T. C. HALIBURTON, *Nature and human nature*, 1855, I, 245.

It is wonderful what a personal interest the average man takes in discussions as to what constitutes genius.

PETER McARTHUR, *To be taken with salt*, 1903, 155.

If you haven't it in your head you must have it in your heels.

Proverb, Riverport, N. S.

People are always ready to admit a man's ability after he gets there.

ROBERT C. (BOB) EDWARDS, *Calgary Eye Opener*, Jan. 27, 1912.

Is not excellence in the ranks almost as rare as excellence in command?

GEORGE ILES, *Canadian stories*, 1918, 179.

ADVERTISING.

Braggin' saves advertisin'.

T. C. HALIBURTON, *Nature and human nature*, 1855, I, 206.

Trade follows the advertisement, not the flag.

JOHN A. COOPER, secretary, Can. Press Assoc., about 1896.

The best advertisement in the public eye is the show-ring award, and criticism.

JAMES BURNETT, *Farmer's advocate*, July 3, 1907.

The activating force which, harnessed to improvements in designing and manufacture, caused the old ways to be discarded and the new to become the rule, has been advertising.

H. E. STEPHENSON, C. McNAUGHT, *Story of advertising*, 1940.

ADVICE.

A man shows lack of nerve when he asks for advice and still more when he takes the advice that is given.

PETER McARTHUR, *To be taken with salt*, 1903, 152.

The difficulties were enhanced by an almost undue reliance of the Government on expert advice.

HAROLD A. INNIS, *History of the C.P.R.*, 1923, 91.

Advice is sought to confirm a position already taken.

Sir WILLIAM OSLER, in, Cushing: *Life of Osler*, 1926.

ALBERTA.

In token of the love which thou has shown

For this wide land of freedom, I have named

A province vast, and for its beauty famed,

By thy dear name to be hereafter known.

MARQUIS OF LORNE, Gov.-Gen., 1878-83, to his wife, H. R. H. Princess Louise Caroline Alberta, after a visit to the West.

Alberta or bust!

Sign on a caravan of American settlers who left Nebraska, May, 1900.

AMERICANS.

(See also: ANNEXATION;
CANADIAN-AMERICAN RELA-
TIONS; UNITED STATES)

The British can whip all the world
and we can whip the British.

T. C. HALIBURTON, 1836, *Sam
Slick*, ch. XXIII.

You must learn the American language, if you want to understand the
American people.

T. C. HALIBURTON, *Sam Slick*, 1838,
56.

The Yankees in the land abound
For Uncle Sam gets all around,
And with his push and grit and go
Is sure to make the country grow.

E. F. MILLER, in, *Grain growers
guide*, Sept. 20, 1911, 28.

We like the Americans we know, but
we do not like the United States.

ANON., quoted in *Can. and her
great neighbor*, ed. H. F. Angus,
1938.

You know, I don't believe I ever in
my life even thought to think about
Canada.

ANON., American woman to Arthur
Phelps. qu. in, *These United States*,
1941.

ANGER.

He flies right off the handle for
nothing.

THOMAS C. HALIBURTON, *Sam Slick
in England*, 1843, ch. 28.

A good temper must be kept cool to
retain its sweetness.

T. C. HALIBURTON, *Sam Slick's
wise saws*, 1853, I, 282.

For growl and cough and snarl are
the tokens of spendthrifts who know
not the ultimate economy of rage.

E. J. PRATT. "Silences", 1937.

ANIMALS.

(See also names of animals)

All critturs in natur' are better in
their own element.

THOMAS C. HALIBURTON, *Sam Slick*.

The silent pig is the best feeder, but
it remains a pig still, and hastens its
death by growing too fat.

T. C. HALIBURTON, *Nature and human nature*, 1855, I, 201.

By'n bye I'm close up by ze skunk.
I raise my axe on high.
When... up, kerplunk... zis damdam
skunk
He's tro something in my eye...

An' so I hunt ze skunk no more
For ze meat or for ze fur.
For she's smell so damdam bad
Jez Cris! I can't stan' her.

" Ze skunk", French-Canadian verse
of lumbering days; from "pub-
lishable" version *J. Amer. folklore*.
1944. 211.

The Caribou is a travelsome beast,
always in a hurry, going against the
wind. When the wind is west, all travel west; when it veers. they veer.

ERNEST THOMPSON SETON, *The
Arctic prairies*, 1911.

Ogopogo.

The Okanagan Lake, B.C., serpent
named by the Vancouver *Province*.
Aug. 24, 1926, p. 7; from the chorus of a popular song:

"I'm looking for the ogopogo, the
funny little ogopogo
His mother was an earwig, his father was a whale."

Caddy.

The Cadboro Bay, B.C., serpent
nicknamed from "Cadborosaurus"
by the Victoria *Times*, Oct. 17,
1933.

Pure blood domestic, guaranteed,
Soft-mannered, musical in purr,

The ribbon had declared the breed.
Gentility was in the fur.

E. J. PRATT, "The prize cat", 1937.

The young man looks at our abound-
ing Canadian wildlife, and thinks that
we have a precious heritage; the old
man looks back at his youth and mourns

for the vast numbers of wild things that now exist in a mere shadow of their former abundance; and whether young or old, we need to keep this matter constantly in mind, and be prepared to do our bit to hand on to our successors as full a measure as possible of the wildlife that we have enjoyed.

WILLIAM E. SAUNDERS, *Can. science digest*, Dec. 1937.

ANNEXATION.

(See also: CONFEDERATION: INDEPENDENCE; THE WEST; RECIPROCITY, 1911)

The Unanimous Voice of the Continent is Canada must be ours; Quebec must be taken.

JOHN ADAMS, 1776, after defeat of Montgomery at Quebec.

Canada, acceding to this confederation, and joining in the measures of the United States, shall be admitted into, and entitled to all the advantages of this Union: but no other colony shall be admitted into the same unless such admission be agreed to by nine states.

[U. S.] *Articles of confederation*, XI, Nov. 15, 1777.

The annexation of Canada this year as far as the neighborhood of Quebec, will be a mere matter of marching, and will give us experience for the attack of Halifax the next, and the final expulsion of England from the American continent.

THOMAS JEFFERSON, letter to Duane, Aug. 4, 1812.

Every man of sense, whether in the Cabinet or out of it, knows that Canada must at no distant period be merged in the American Republic.

Edinburgh rev., 1825, 290.

All Americans are unfortunately possessed with a vague notion, that Canada is somehow or other to fall into their hands without a war.

HENRY S. FOX, British minister to Washington, letter, Nov. 8, 1838.

Fifty-four-forty or Fight!

U. S. DEMOCRATIC PARTY, slogan, 1844, with reference to the boundary location between British Columbia and Oregon; agreement on forty-ninth parallel was reached by treaty, 1846.

No matter what the subject of complaint, or what the party complaining; whether it be alleged that the French are oppressing the British, or the British the French — that the Upper Canadian debt presses on Lower Canada, or Lower Canadian claims on Upper — whether merchants be bankrupt, stocks depreciated, roads bad, or seasons unfavourable — annexation is invoked as the remedy for all ills, imaginary or real.

LORD ELGIN, letter to Lord Grey. March 14, 1849.

I have no fear that the people of Upper Canada would ever desire to become the fag-end of the neighbouring republic.

GEORGE BROWN, Nov. 10, 1859, at Reform Convention, Toronto.

I should say that if a man had a great heart within him he would rather look forward to the day when, from that point of land which is habitable nearest to the Pole to the shores of the great Gulf, the whole of that vast continent might become one confederation of States.

JOHN BRIGHT, speech of 1861.

I do not believe it is our destiny to be engulfed into a Republican union, renovated and inflamed with the wine of victory, of which she now drinks so deeply — it seems to me that we have theatre enough under our feet to act another and a worthier part; we can hardly join the Americans on our own terms, and we never ought to join them on theirs.

T. D'A. McGEE, speech. "American relations and Canadian duties", Quebec, May 10, 1862.

If the Maritime Provinces would join us, spontaneously, to-day — sterile as they may be in the soil under a sky of steel — still their hardy population, their harbours, fisheries, and seamen, they would greatly strengthen and improve our position, and aid us in our struggle for equality upon the ocean. If we would succeed upon the deep, we must either maintain our fisheries or absorb the provinces.

E. H. DERBY, *Rept. to revenue commissioners*, U.S., 1866.

For the admission of the states of Nova Scotia, New Brunswick, Canada East and Canada West and for the organization of the territories of Selkirk, Saskatchewan and Columbia.

U. S. CONGRESS, July 2, 1886, wording of a Bill, H.R. 754.

The British North American colonies would in time, and probably at no very distant time, unite themselves to the group of states, of which they were already by race, position, commercial ties, and the character of their institutions, a part. No one could stand by the side of the St. Lawrence and doubt that in the end they would do this, but they would be left to do it of their own free will.

GOLDWIN SMITH, speech in England. 1866.

I can't help thinking that it would be a grand thing to see one Government rule from the Equator to the North Pole.

JOHN BRIGHT to Sir Charles Tupper, 1867, in London; Tupper, *Recollections*, 1914, 61.

The opening by us first of a North Pacific Railroad seals the destiny of British possessions west of the 91st. meridian. Annexation will be but a question of time.

U. S. SENATE, *Rept. on Pacific railroads*, Feb. 19, 1869, 1363.

Americans will not take any definite step; they feel that Canada must come into the Confederation, and will of herself. The American party in Canada is always at work.

RALPH W. EMERSON, remarks to William Allingham, Nov. 1872.

Mr. Smith has come into a peaceful community to do his best for the furtherance of a cause which means simply revolution.

TORONTO *Globe*, editorial Oct. 27, 1874 on Goldwin Smith.

Sharers in such a realm, heirs to such vast and varied privileges, Canadians are not for sale.

W. GEORGE BEERS, of Montreal, speech in Syracuse, Nov. 1883.

Nobody who has studied the peculiar methods by which elections are won in Canada will deny the fact that five or six million dollars, judiciously expended... would secure the return to Parliament of a majority pledged to the annexation of Canada to the United States.

NEW YORK *World*, 1890.

The day of annexation to the United States is past. Our future lies elsewhere.

STEPHEN B. LEACOCK, *Univ. mag.*, Feb. 1907, 140.

I am for it [the Reciprocity Agreement] because I hope to see the day when the American flag will float over every square foot of the British North American possessions clear to the North Pole.

CHAMP. CLARK, Speaker, in House of Reps., Washington, Feb. 14, 1911; *Cong. record*, 61st. Cong., 3rd sess., 2520.

Enter upon and prosecute from time to time such negotiations with the British Government as he may deem expedient for the annexation of the Dominion of Canada to the United States of America.

W. S. BENNET, Congressman from N.Y., in a resolution addressed to the President, Feb. 16, 1911.

We answer to a higher destiny.

SIR WILFRID LAURIER, on annexation, qu., *Willison's monthly*, 1928, 1.

Do not encourage any enterprise looking to Canada's annexation of the United States. You are one of the most capable governing peoples of the world, but I entreat you, for your own sakes, to think twice before undertaking management of the territory which lies between the Great Lakes and the Rio Grande. No, let us go

our own gaits along parallel roads, you helping us and we helping you.
WARREN G. HARDING, Pres. U. S., speech in Vancouver, July 26, 1923.

APPEARANCES.

As black as the devil's hind foot.
THOMAS C. HALIBURTON, *Sam Slick's wise saws*, 1853, ch. 5.

Many a feller looks fat, who is only swelled.
THOMAS C. HALIBURTON, *Sam Slick's wise saws*, 1853, ch. 24.

The higher the polish the more indurated you will find the substance.
T. C. HALIBURTON, *Sam Slick*, 1840, 210.

You are only what you are when no one is looking.
ROBERT C. (BOB) EDWARDS, *Calgary Eye Opener*, May 11, 1918.

APPLES.

The apple harvest time is here,
The tender harvest apple time:
A sheltering calm unknown at prime
Settles upon the brooding year.
BLISS CARMAN, "In apple time", 1888.

Art thou the topmost apple
The gatherers could reach,
Reddening on the bough?
Shall I not take thee?
BLISS CARMAN, *Sappho*, 1903.

ARCHITECTURE.

The orders of architecture baffle all description: every one builds his cottage or house according to his fancy, and it is not a difficult thing, in passing through the country, to tell what nation the natives of the houses "hail from", if we are aware of any of the whims and conceits that characterize them.
JOHN MACTAGGART, *Three years in Canada*, 1829, I, 308.

ARCTIC.
(See also: THE NORTH)

Doubtless there is a passadge.
WILLIAM BAFFIN, 1615, in *Voyages*, Hakluyt Society, 1881, 137, on the North West Passage.

This gloomy region, where the year is divided into one day and one night, lies entirely outside the stream of history.
W. W. READE, *Martyrdom of man*, III, 1872.

Not here! the white North has thy bones; and thou
Heroic sailor soul,
Art passing on thine happier voyage now
Toward no earthly pole.
LORD TENNYSON, inscription on monument to Sir John Franklin in Westminster Abbey, 1875.

The Eskimo has developed individual equality farther than we, he is less selfish, more helpful to his fellows, kinder to his wife, gentler to his child, more reticent about the faults of his neighbour than any but the rarest and best of our race.
VILHJALMUR STEFANSSON, in *Harper's monthly mag.*, Oct., 1908.

This Memorial is erected today to commemorate the taking possession for the Dominion of Canada of the whole Arctic Archipelago lying to the north of America from longitude 60 degrees west to 141 degrees west up to latitude 90 degrees north. Winter Harbour, Melville Island. C.G.S. *Arctic*. July 1st, 1909. J. E. Bernier, Commander.
JOSEPH E. BERNIER, *Report*, Ottawa, 1910, 194.

Capt. Joseph Elzear Bernier, Canada's master seaman, who has done everything but bring the North Pole home on deck.
C. H. J. SNIDER, in *Can. hist. rev.*, 1928, 74.

The inaccessible Arctic has disappeared overnight.
H. A. INNIS, in *Can. hist. rev.*, 1935, 200.

The whole history of the Canadian North can be divided into two periods — before and after the aeroplane.
H. L. KEENLEYSIDE, in *Can. geog. journal*, 1949, 167.

ARGUMENT.

To bung up a man's eyes ain't the way to enlighten him.
THOMAS C. HALIBURTON, *Sam Slick's wise saws*, 1853, ch. 4.

In order to carry on an argument you must descend to the other man's level.

> PETER MCARTHUR, *To be taken with salt*, 1903, 151.

Isn't it queer that only sensible people agree with you?

> ROBERT C. (BOB) EDWARDS, *Calgary Eye Opener*, Oct. 5, 1912.

. Never give 'em more than one barr'l to start with. But if they are foolish enough to ask for more, then give 'em the other barr'l right between the eyes.

> J. W. DAFOE, qu. in, G. V. Ferguson: *John W. Dafoe*, 1948.

ARMY.

(See also: DEFENCE; MILITIA; SOLDIERS; WAR; WAR DEAD)

Push on, brave York Volunteers!

> Popularly but incorrectly ascribed to General Isaac Brock before he fell at the battle of Queenston Heights, Oct. 13, 1812; a reference to the Third Regiment of York militia.

Our civilization, it seems to me, runs a risk of making us too effeminate. It admits the right of passive resistance, but it shudders overmuch at any man advocating the right (and sometimes the duty) of armed resistance to grievous wrong.

> SIR RICHARD CARTWRIGHT, speech to Young Liberal Club, Seaforth, Ont., Oct., 27, 1886.

Without drill there can be no discipline; without discipline there can be no cohesion; without cohesion, no success.

> COL. JAMES MASON, speech in Toronto, Dec. 28, 1900.

I do not believe in moral issues being settled by physical force.

> J. S. WOODSWORTH, speech in Winnipeg, June 4, 1916.

ART.

(See also: CULTURE)

The cold narrow minds, the confined ideas, the by-gone prejudices of the society are hardly conceivable, books there are none, nor music, and as to pictures! — the Lord deliver us from such! The people do not know what a picture is.

> ANNA JAMESON, on society in Toronto, 1837.

None o' your Potiphar's wives, or Susannahs, or sleepin' Venuses; such pictur's are repugnant to the high tone o' moral feelin' in this country.

> T. C. HALIBURTON, *Sam Slick*, 1838, 105.

An artist has more than two eyes, that's a fact.

> T. C. HALIBURTON, *Sam Slick's wise saws*, 1853, II, 18.

'The Discobolus is put here because he is vulgar,

He has neither vest nor pants with which to cover his limbs;

I, Sir, am a person of most respectable connections —

My brother-in-law is haberdasher to Mr. Spurgeon'.

O God! O Montreal!

> SAMUEL BUTLER, "A psalm of Montreal", 1875, written after a visit to the Montreal Museum of Natural History where he found a plaster cast of the Discobolus hidden in a store-room.

Stowed away in Montreal lumber room

The Discobolus standeth and turneth his face to the wall,

Dusty, cobweb-covered, maimed and set at naught,

Beauty cryeth in an attic and no man regardeth:

O God! O Montreal!

> SAMUEL BUTLER, "A psalm of Montreal", 1875.

Now ve vill make a nize leetle vatercolour. Ve vill put a round spot of red in the centre, so. Zat is ze sun. Now ve vill take some yellow, so, and some purple, so, and before you know it, ve haf a sky. Then ve put some trees on this side and some odders on the odder side, so. And then ve run a leetle vaterfall down the meedle, so;

and it is finished. Now you have seen
me make a vater-colour. It is very
simple. Make one yourself.

> O. R. JACOBI, to students at Ontario
> Soc. of Artists, Toronto, about
> 1875.

Half of art is knowing when to stop.
> J. A. RADFORD, *Can. mag.*, Dec.,
> 1893.

New Art, New Movements, and New
Schools,
All maimed and blind and halt!
And all the fads of the New Fools
Who cannot earn their salt.
> BLISS CARMAN, "Spring feeling",
> 1895.

If the artist were ungodly,
Prurient of mind and heart,
I must think they argue oddly
Who make shrines before his art.
> BLISS CARMAN, "To Raphael", 1896.

Said Life to Art — "I love thee best
Not when I find in thee
My very face and form, expressed
With dull fidelity,
But when in thee my craving eyes
Behold continually
The mystery of my memories
And all I long to be.
> CHARLES G. D. ROBERTS, "Life and
> art", 1901.

Art generalizes while science itemizes.
> PETER McARTHUR, *To be taken
> with salt*, 1903, 151.

If our artists and writers but realized
the truth the triumphs of science have
given them more glorious symbols.
Art is the only enduring expression of
science.
> PETER McARTHUR, *To be taken
> with salt*, 1903, 154.

An art is a handicraft in flower.
> GEORGE ILES, *Canadian stories*,
> 1918, 168.

Form may be of more account than
substance. A lens of ice will focus a
solar beam to a blaze.
> GEORGE ILES, *Canadian stories*,
> 1918, 167.

Never buy a picture that you do not
fall in love with, or it will always be
an incubus and a source of dissatisfac-
tion. The purchase of a picture, like
the selection of wife, can hardly be
done by proxy.
> SIR W. VAN HORNE, qu. in Vau-
> ghan: *Van Horne*, 1920, 268.

If he asks for bread, he is offered
a tombstone. I always suspect an artist who is successful before he is dead.
> JOHN MURRAY GIBBON, *Pagan love*,
> 1922.

The truest art, that which necessity
creates that beauty may live, civilization destroys.
> ARTHUR LISMER, in *Can. bookman*,
> Oct,. 1925, 160.

Tonight I give lecture to Art Students'
League. I want a picture of a horse
to show that animal is beautiful because
every part made for function, without
ornament. In Paris I would show
woman, but in Toronto I show a horse.
> ANON., French artist, qu. *Open
> house*, 1931, 93.

But how shall I hear old music?
This is an hour
Of new beginnings, concepts warring
for power,
Decay of systems — the tissue of art
is torn
With overtures of an era being born.
> F. R. SCOTT, "Overture", 1936.

If the world were not fundamentally
God's world, it could not grow artists.
The chaos could not blossom into poets
for its final flowers.
> JOHN MACNAUGHTON, *Essays*, 1946.

ASSOCIATIONS.

When men are prevented from discussing political matters openly, and
seeking in a fair and legitimate manner
the redress of what they regard as
grievances, they will naturally resort
to secret conclaves, and plots and con-
spiracies, and seek strength and redress
in organizations which the law knows
only to condemn.
> TORONTO *Globe*, June 22. 1871.

Man is a social, gregarious, and club-able animal and there is no doubt that the present is eminently an era of associations.

SIR RICHARD CARTWRIGHT, speech at Seaforth, Ont., Oct. 27, 1886.

Any association, organization, society or corporation, whose professed purpose or one of whose purposes is to bring about any governmental, industrial or economic change within Canada by the use of force, violence or physical injury, to person or property, or by threats of such injury, or which teaches, advocates, advises, or defends the use of force, violence or terrorism or physical injury to person or property, in order to accomplish such change, shall be an unlawful association.

CANADA. *Criminal code*, section 98, in force 1919-1936.

AUTHORS.

(See also: WRITERS)

We hope that Canadian editors will endeavour to do their best to encourage native talent. They should also pay for it.

Varsity, Jan. 23, 1886, edit.

Compiler, rhymer, author, advocate,
Writer of disquisitions on the State.
Analyst, sketcher, and what not, besides
Accoucher-general to the labouring scribes.

ALEXANDER C. STEWART, *The poetical review*, 1896, 8.

Fame, from a literary point of view, consists in having people know you have written a lot of stuff they haven't read.

ROBERT C. (BOB) EDWARDS, *Summer annual*, 1920, 57.

I have lived *for* poetry, but I have lived *by* prose.

CHARLES G. D. ROBERTS, d. 1943, favourite remark in his later years.

O Canada, O Canada, Oh can
A day go by without new authors springing
To paint the native purple, and to plan

More ways to set the selfsame welkin ringing?

F. R. SCOTT, "The Canadian Authors meet", *Can. forum*, Dec., 1935.

A great poet or author is a greater resource to his country in time of war than a battleship.

ROBERT J. C. STEAD, in, *Can. author*, Mar., 1943, 6.

AUTOMOBILES.

When I think of the motor-car silent and swift,
In the dark sky of transport, so long overcast,
I see in my vision a limitless rift
That heralds the dawn of the best things at last.
There is comfort and speed in the automobile
That none can deny, and no one gainsay;
Then I know that with me you will readily feel
How thankful I am that I'm living today.

PERCY H. PUNSHON, "The transition of transportation," 1911.

The trouble is that too often there is forty horsepower under the bonnet and one asspower at the wheel.

JOHN MACNAUGHTON, to D. D. Calvin, qu., *Queen's quart.*, 1933, 359.

AUTUMN.

Saw wood in Indian Summer.

Saying of pioneer Ontario farmers.

Autumn, like an old poet in a haze
Of golden visions, dreams away his days.

CHARLES SANGSTER, "The happy harvesters", 1860.

The Land had put his ruddy gauntlet on.
Of Harvest gold to dash in Famine's face.

ISABELLA V. CRAWFORD, "Malcolm's Katie", 1884.

On our Canadian climate I've little to say.

As I've lived in it many years and
cold days,
This present month. October, without strife,
Is the beautifullest I ever saw in
my life.
JAMES GAY, "On our climate",
[1885 ?]

The cornfields all are brown, and
brown the meadows
With the blown leaves' wind-heaped
traceries,
And the brown thistle stems that
cast no shadows,
And bear no bloom for bees.
ARCHIBALD LAMPMAN, "In October", 1888.

Miles and miles of crimson glories,
Autumn's wondrous fires ablaze;
Miles of shoreland red and golden,
Drifting into dream and haze.
WILFRED CAMPBELL, "Lake Huron".
1889.

And soon, too soon, around the cum-
bered eaves
Sly frosts shall take the creepers by
surprise,
And through the wind-touched redden-
ing woods shall rise
October with the rain of ruined leaves.
ARCHIBALD LAMPMAN, "September",
Harper's mag., Sept., 1893.

Thus without grief the golden days
go by,
So soft we scarcely notice how they
wend,
And like a smile half-happy, or a
sigh,
The summer passes to her quiet end.
ARCHIBALD LAMPMAN, "September",
Harper's mag., Sept., 1893.

There is something in the autumn
that is native to my blood —
Touch of manner, hint of mood;
And my heart is like a rhyme,
With the yellow and the purple and
the crimson keeping time.
BLISS CARMAN, "Vagabond song",
1894.

There is something in October sets
the gypsy blood astir:
We must rise and follow her.
When from every hill of flame

She calls, and calls each vagabond
by name.
BLISS CARMAN, "Vagabond song,"
1894.

Clothed in splendour, beautifully sad
and silent,
Comes the autumn over the woods
and highlands,
Golden, rose-red, full of divine remembrance,
Full of foreboding.
ARCHIBALD LAMPMAN, "Sapphics",
1899.

Of all Earth's varied, lovely moods,
The loveliest is when she broods
Among her dreaming solitudes
On Indian Summer days.
HELENA COLEMAN, "Indian Sum
mer", 1906.

The hound of the autumn wind is
slow,
He loves to bask in the heat and
sleep.
PETER McARTHUR, "An Indian wind
song", 1907.

AVIATION.

Bush pilot.
Term popular in the 1920's for
the men who flew transport airplanes into the North-West Territories.

But give me the air! Always the air!
The clean ways, and wings, wings.
To reach beyond accepted things,
And venture flights unendable!
TOM MacINNES, "Aspiration", 1910.

The Air Age faces mankind with a
sharp choice — the choice between
Winged Peace or Winged Death. It's
up to you.
W. A. BISHOP, *Winged peace*, 1944.
151.

B

BANKS AND BANKING.

The most efficacious and the most
immediate means which the Canadians
have to protect themselves against the
fury of their enemies. is to attack them
in their dearest parts — their pockets

— in their strongest entrenchments, the banks.

> LOUIS JOSEPH PAPINEAU, in Montreal *Gazette*, Dec. 11, 1834.

Whoever may get the milk, the Barings and Glyns will have the cream, that is certain.

> TORONTO *Globe*, Jan. 20, 1860.

We fear the Bank of Montreal has the Government in its power, and is disposed to play the tyrant.

> HAMILTON *Times*, qu., Toronto *Globe*, Oct. 30, 1867.

The tradition of Canadian banking is evolution and not revolution.

> C. R. FAY, in *Can. hist. rev.*, 1923, 186.

Montreal finance went into the west with the Bank of Montreal and to-day the old warfare of the embattled frontiersman against "the banks" and sound money, which Mackenzie fought in Upper Canada a century ago, is being waged on the last frontier by Mr. Aberhart.

> A. R. M. LOWER, in *Can. hist. rev.*, 1938, 209.

BEAUTY.

Ask a Northern Indian what is beauty, and he will answer: a broad, flat face; small eyes, high cheek-bones, three or four broad black lines across each cheek; a low forehead, a large, broad chin; a clumsy hook nose, a tawny hide, and breasts hanging down to the belt.

> SAMUEL HEARNE, *Journey from Prince of Wales Fort in Hudson's Bay*, 1795.

Make thou my vision sane and clear, That I may see what beauty clings In common forms, and find the soul Of unregarded things!

> CHARLES G. D. ROBERTS, "Prologue", 1893.

The medicine for heartache That lurks in lovely things.

> BLISS CARMAN, "Peony", 1916.

In mount or vale, throughout the changing year,

From all the by-ways of the world, I peer Into the secret places where they wind Almost beyond the utmost reach of mind, And beauty, beauty everywhere I find.

> ALBERT D. WATSON, "To worlds more wide", 1917.

Lord of the far horizons, Give us the eyes to see Over the verge of sundown The beauty that is to be.

> BLISS CARMAN, "Lord of the far horizons", 1925.

Beauty is always breaking on the reef That shelters righteousness with calm content; The stolid coast of commonplace belief Is shaken as the recreant surge is blent With patient granite. Crest on rebel crest Goes blazing up that ancient keep secure; Still the grey coast lifts its massive breast That loveliness may struggle — to endure.

> CHARLES BRUCE, "Surf", 1932.

This is the beauty of strength broken by strength and still strong.

> A. J. M. SMITH, "The lonely land", 1943.

Look well, who love all lovely things, The hour is, but the hour has wings.

> AUDREY A. BROWN, "All Fools' Day", 1948.

BEAVER.

For his crest, on a wreath argent sable, a beaver proper.

> Royal letter, Newmarket, 1632, by which King Charles I granted a coat of arms to Alexander, Viscount of Stirling, Lord Alexander of Canada; the first use of the beaver in Canadian heraldry.

If the pig had his rights, he would be our national emblem, instead of the beaver. What has the beaver done for us, anyway? The pig, on the other hand, sustained our fathers in their fight against the wilderness, and yet his name is a name of scorn.

> PETER MCARTHUR. *In pastures green*, 1915, 266.

BEES.

> The swarthy bee is a buccaneer,
> A burly velveted rover,
> Who loves the booming wind in his ear
> As he sails the seas of clover.
>
> BLISS CARMAN, "A more ancient mariner", 1890.

BEHAVIOUR.

(See also: CONDUCT OF LIFE; MANNERS)

Extremes nary way are none o' the best.

> T. C. HALIBURTON, *Sam Slick*, 1836, ch. XV.

He was legging it off hot foot.

> THOMAS C. HALIBURTON, *Sam Slick*, 1836, ch. XXIV.

My rule is to let everyone skin his own foxes.

> THOMAS C. HALIBURTON, *Sam Slick's wise saws*, 1853, Intro.

You won't take no for an answer.

> THOMAS C. HALIBURTON, *Sam Slick's wise saws*, 1853, ch. V.

Stick-in-the-mud.

> THOMAS C. HALIBURTON, *Sam Slick's wise saws*, 1853, 132.

I like to let every feller grind his own axe.

> THOMAS C. HALIBURTON, *Sam Slick's wise saws*, 1853, ch. XVI.

A critter who is a slave to his own rules is his own nigger.

> THOMAS C. HALIBURTON, *Sam Slick's wise saws*, 1853, ch. XXI.

> I will do this and that, and break
> The backbone of their large conceit,
> And loose the sandals from their feet,
> And show 'tis holy ground they shake.
>
> GEORGE F. CAMERON, "In after days", 1887.

By the time the average man has time and money to gratify his tastes, he hasn't any.

> ROBERT C. (BOB) EDWARDS, *Calgary Eye Opener*; attributed.

Don't meet trouble halfway. It is quite capable of making the entire journey.

> ROBERT C. (BOB) EDWARDS, *Calgary Eye Opener*, July 17, 1920.

A superiority complex quite often outlives the condition that brought it into existence.

> ARTHUR STRINGER, *The devastator*, 1944, 117.

BELIEF.

Suppose you do believe too much, it is safer than believing too little.

> T. C. HALIBURTON, *Nature and human nature*, 1855, II, 145.

Seein' is believin'.

> T. C. HALIBURTON, *Sam Slick's wise saws*, 1853, I, 41.

> I came upon a sudden door,
> Which gave me no reply;
> The more I questioned it, the more
> A questioner was I.
>
> BLISS CARMAN, "Behind the arras", 1895.

A superstition is a premature explanation that overstays its time.

> GEORGE ILES, *Canadian stories*, 1918, 168.

> But you came empty-handed, and your tongue
> Babbled strange tidings none could wholly trust.
> And if we half-believed you, it was only
> Because we would, and not because we must.
>
> CHARLES G. D. ROBERTS, "To a certain mystic", 1934.

We have swallowed all manner of poisonous certainties fed us by our parents, our Sunday and day school teachers, our politicians, our priests, our newspapers and others with a vested interest in controlling us.

> G. BROCK CHISHOLM, speech in Washington, D. C., Oct. 23, 1945.

Doubts are inseparable from life.

> JOHN MACNAUGHTON, *Essays*, 1946.

BILINGUALISM.

The Divinity could be invoked as well in the English language as in the French.

SIR WILFRID LAURIER, H. of C., *Debates*, 1877, 94.

I have no accord with the desire expressed in some quarters that by any mode whatever there should be an attempt made to oppress the one language or to render it inferior to the other; I believe that would be impossible if it were tried, and it would be foolish and wicked if it were possible.

SIR JOHN A. MACDONALD, H. of C., *Debates*, Feb. 17, 1890, 745.

The French Canadian father who today does not have his son learn English does not do justice to his child, for he forces him to remain behind in the struggle for existence.

SIR WILFRID LAURIER, H. of C., *Debates*, Feb. 17, 1890.

My children, be well up in French, but not *too* well up in English!

LOUIS LAFLÈCHE, Bishop of Three Rivers, Que. (1870-98). (trans.)

The soul of Canada is a dual personality, and must remain only half revealed to those who know only one language.

FRANK OLIVER CALL, *Spell of French Canada*, 1926.

If one knows his neighbour's tongue, he possesses the key of his house.

ABBÉ ARTHUR MAHEUX, *What keeps us apart?* 1944.

BIRDS.

No music in the sky, no chorus in the grove, in comparison with the feathered songsters of England — no lark, no linnet, no blackbird, no thrush, no nightingale, no robin but by name, chirp, chirp, chirp, chirp, and little of that.

ROBERT GOURLAY, attributed.

Swallow's nests in the barn keep away lightning.

Saying of pioneer Ontario farmers.

A beautiful bird seldom sings.

T. C. HALIBURTON, *Sam Slick's wise saws*, 1853, I, 313.

The Raven's house is built with reeds,
Sing alas and woe is me!
And the Raven's couch is spread with weeds
High on the hollow tree;
And the Raven himself telling his beads
In penance for his past misdeeds.
Upon the top I see.

THOMAS D'A. MCGEE, "The penitent raven, a nursery rhyme", 1858.

The red-bird pauses in his song,
The face of man aye fearing,
And flashes like a flame along
The border of the clearing.
The humming-bird above the flower
Is like a halo bending.

ALEXANDER MCLACHLAN, "Hall of shadows", 1874.

Never dost thou dream of sadness —
All thy life a merry madness,
Never may thy spirits sink —
Bobolink! Bobolink!

ALEXANDER MCLACHLAN, "Bobolink", 1874.

We have roamed the marshes, keen with expectation,
Lain at eve in ambush, where the ducks are wont to fly;
Felt the feverish fervour, the thrilling, full pulsation,
As the flocks came whirring from the rosy western sky.

BARRY STRATON, "Evening on the marshes", 1884.

On a sudden seven ducks
With a splashy rustle rise,
Stretching out their seven necks,
One before, and two behind,
And the others all arow,
And as steady as the wind
With a swivelling whistle go.

ARCHIBALD LAMPMAN, "Morning on the Lievre", 1888.

I watched the grey hawk wheel and drop,
Sole shadow on the shining world.

ARCHIBALD LAMPMAN, "After rain", 1895.

Shy bird of the silver arrows of song,
That cleave our Northern air so clear,
Thy notes prolong, prolong,
I listen, I hear:

"I — love — dear — Canada,
Canada, Canada."
> THEODORE H. RAND, "The White-
> throat", 1900.

Here beyond the silver reach in ringing wild persistence,
Reel remote the undulating laughter
of the loons.
> DUNCAN CAMPBELL SCOTT, "Spring
> on Mattagami", 1906.

From streams no oar hath rippled
And lakes that waft no sail,
From reaches vast and lonely
That know no hunter's trail,
The clamour of their calling
And the whistling of their flight
Fill all the day with marvel,
And with mystery, the night.
> PETER MCARTHUR, "Birds of pas-
> sage", 1907.

Blue on the branch and blue in the
sky,
And naught between but the breezes
high,
And naught so blue by the breezes
stirred
As the deep, deep blue of the Indigo
bird.
> ETHELWYN WETHERALD, "The indi-
> go bird", 1907.

Tecumseh watched the eagles
In summer o'er the plain,
And learned their cry, "If freedom
die,
Ye will have lived in vain!"
> BLISS CARMAN, "Tecumseh and the
> eagles", 1918.

Every man has his favourite bird.
Mine is the bat.
> ROBERT C. (BOB) EDWARDS. attrib-
> uted by Stubbs, Lawyers and lay-
> men, 1939, 180 ; Edwards' Summer
> annual, 1920, 67 : "The genial
> doctor's favourite hobby is orni-
> thology ; his favourite bird being
> the Bat".

What subtle alchemy dissolved the
night
And out of sheer invisibility
Extracted all its essence, setting free
One jet of ebon in expansive flight?
> ALBERT D. WATSON, "The crow",
> 1921.

Smoke-blue he is, and grey
As embers of yesterday.
Still he is, as death;
Like stone, or shadow of stone.
Without a pulse or breath,
Motionless and alone
There in the lily stems:
But his eyes are alive like gems.
> THEODORE G. ROBERTS, "The blue
> heron", 1926.

Jet crows cawing and cawing above,
Crows in the sky:
Is it a song they shout —
Or a warning cry?
> DOROTHY LIVESAY, "City wife",
> 1932.

No matter what the hour may be
Penguins are dressed to dine,
And have a gentle dignity,
Stuffy — but yet benign,
As though their minds dwelt much
on soup,
On walnuts, and on wine.
> VIRNA SHEARD, "Penguins", 1932.

Go out and hear the lark. The time
is at dawn.
> WILLIAM E. SAUNDERS, in London
> Free Press, 1939.

Look for birds with your ears.
> WILLIAM E. SAUNDERS, letter to
> R. G. Dingman, April 11, 1943.

BLAKE, EDWARD.

There are scores of earnest and able
young men in Canada who would
willingly range themselves under Mr.
Blake's leadership, were it not that
they are repelled by a manner as
devoid of warmth as is a flake of
December snow, and as devoid of
magnetism as is a loaf of unleavened
bread.
> JOHN C. DENT, The last forty years,
> II, 1882, 480.

Mr. Blake, on the other hand, was
constitutionally incapable of serving
loyally under anybody.
> SIR RICHARD CARTWRIGHT, Remin-
> iscences, 1912, 134.

We felt in the presence of genius and
would have been proud to serve to
the end, had he not drawn himself aloof.
> SIR WILFRID LAURIER, on Edward
> Blake, to O. D. Skelton, qu. in
> Skelton's Laurier, 1921, I, 224.

BOATING.

(See also : SCOTSMEN)

Faintly as tolls the evening chime,
Our voices keep tune and our oars
keep time.
Soon as the woods on shore look dim,
We'll sing at St. Anne's our parting
hymn.
Row, brothers, row, the stream runs
fast,
The Rapids are near, and the day-
light's past.

THOMAS MOORE, "Canadian boat
song", 1804.

BOOKS AND READING.

(See also: LITERATURE;
NEWSPAPERS AND THE
PRESS; WORDS)

We have beside us a mountain of
Books, Magazines, Pamphlets and Newspapers, that have been accumulating
for the last two months, unopened and
unread. Like a Turk, in the dim
twilight of his Harem, we scarcely
know which to choose...

JOSEPH HOWE, in *Novascotian*, May
2, 1833.

You may stop a man's mouth by a
crammin' a book down his throat, but
you won't convince him.

T. C. HALIBURTON, *Sam Slick*,
1836, ch. XXIV.

Human natur' — the best book a
man can study arter all, and the only
true one.

T. C. HALIBURTON, *Sam Slick*,
1838, 187.

What we hear with pleasure we
afterward read with diminished satisfaction.

T. C. HALIBURTON, *Sam Slick*,
1840, 263.

Never read a book, squire; always
think for yourself.

T. C. HALIBURTON, *The attaché*,
1843.

Some books are read in the parlour
and some in the kitchen, but the test of
a real genuine book is that it is read
in both.

THOMAS C. HALIBURTON, *Sam
Slick's wise saws*, 1853, ch. 19.

A fig for your scholar who puzzles
and looks,
And sees Nature's ways but in musty
old books!
Can Greek or can grammar, can
science or art,
Confer on a fool e'er a head or a
heart?

ALEXANDER MCLACHLAN, "I long
not for riches", 1856.

What was good enough for me is
good enough for my boys. They have
the Bible and the Toronto *Globe*, all
that I had, and that is enough for
them.

A story popular on the hustings
in Ontario after about 1860, always
followed by the rejoinder, "Well,
at any rate, you are giving them
both sides of the question".

They showed how contradictions
throng,
How by our weakness we are strong,
And how we're righted by the wrong.

ALEXANDER MCLACHLAN, "Compan-
ions in solitude", 1874.

People who have a taste for bathing
in a cesspool cannot be made much
dirtier by being allowed to do it. To
prosecute is to advertise; to advertise
is far the most effectual way of all.

GOLDWIN SMITH, *The Bystander*,
1880, 390, on the proposed banning
of Zola's works as immoral.

The bald truth is that Canada has
the money, but would rather spend it
on whiskey than on books.

ROBERT BARR, in *Can. mag.*, Nov.
1899, 5.

Only a maker of books can appreciate the labours of others at their
true value.

SIR WILLIAM OSLER, Address,
"Books and men", 1901.

Spend the last half-hour of the day in
communion with the saints of humanity.

SIR WILLIAM OSLER, *Montreal med.
jour.*, 1903, 771.

Biographies written by sons are, as
a rule, only one degree less contemptible
than those written by daughters.

ANON., in W. L. Grant and F.
Hamilton, *Principal Grant*, 1904.

It is easier to buy books than to read them and easier to read them than to absorb them.

> SIR WILLIAM OSLER, *Oslerisms* (Bean), 1905.

Divide your attention equally between men and books.

> SIR WILLIAM OSLER, "The student life", an address, 1905.

The classics are only primitive literature. They belong to the same class as primitive machinery and primitive medicine.

> STEPHEN B. LEACOCK, "Homer and humbug", *Century mag.* Oct. 1913.

After all, there is no such literature as a Dictionary.

> SIR WILLIAM OSLER, letter to students, Jefferson Med. Coll., 1914, qu. in Cushing, *Osler*, 238.

Money invested in a library gives much better returns than mining stock.

> SIR WILLIAM OSLER, attributed.

A good book has no ending.

> R. D. CUMMING, *Skookum Chuck fables*, 1915, 160.

A great book is a mine as well as a mint; it suggests and excites as much thought as it presents in finished form.

> GEORGE ILES, *Canadian stories*, 1918, 182.

Give me a book for use! If the margins are too wide, cut them down; if the covers are too clumsy, tear them off. If you buy a book as a work of art, put it in your cabinet and order a modern edition for reading.

> SIR W. VAN HORNE, to a book collector, qu. in Vaughan: *Van Horne*, 1920, 374.

That classic that the world has lost, The Little Book I Never Wrote.

> ROBERT W. SERVICE, "My masterpiece", 1921.

Men may fail to be heroes to their valets but they are more successful with their biographers.

> JOHN W. DAFOE, *Laurier*, 1922, 14.

I am what libraries and librarians have made me, with a little assistance from a professor of Greek and a few poets.

> B. K. SANDWELL, "The bibliothecary", 1928.

Bibliographies are always a surprise to the uninitiated.

> F. W. HOWAY, in *Can. hist. rev.*, 1929, 79.

Books worth reading are inspired by the ruthless, intolerant and cynical impulses.

> T. B. ROBERTON, in Winnipeg *Free Press*, Feb. 4, 1929.

I have seen a work in which on a single page there were fifteen notes relating to the same volume. It is all very thorough and sound but where does the public come in?

> G. M. WRONG, in *Can. hist. rev.*, 1933, 7.

One must say that a biography only becomes interesting and alive when the biographer is a partisan.

> F. H. UNDERHILL, in *Can. hist. rev.*, 1945, 69.

BORDEN, SIR ROBERT.

The Conservative party as such carries no indelible imprint from the man who for nearly a quarter of a century led it. He led it by going alongside. He was not a great partisan. He had no overwhelming and audacious bigotries.

> AUGUSTUS BRIDLE ("Domino"), *Masques of Ottawa*, 1921, 30.

His stature rises as the perspective lengthens but it has some way to go yet before justice is done him. I had many a heart to heart talk with him down the years, and after each of them I was in the habit of saying to myself : "Either he's a Grit in disguise or I'm a Tory".

> JOHN W. DAFOE, letter Sept. 16 1943, qu., *Can. hist. rev.*, 1944, 104.

BOUNDARIES.

And from the said lake [Mistassini], a line to run southward into 49 degrees north latitude... and that latitude to be the limit.

> HUDSON'S BAY CO., proposal made 1714, qu., in David Mills, *Rept. on boundaries of Ontario*, 173.

It scarcely requires a common geographical chart, to expose to universal contempt the fallacious boundaries prescribed to Canada.

> "PORTIUS", *Letter to the Earl of Shelburne*, 1783, 12.

The whole territory we were wrangling about was worth nothing.

> LORD ASHBURTON, on his participation in the Maine boundary dispute, 1843, qu., Greville, *Memoirs*, Pt. 2, I, 469.

What is a better boundary between nations than a parallel of latitude, or even a natural obstacle? — what really keeps nations intact and apart? — a principle. When I can hear our young men say as proudly, "our Federation," or "our Country," or "our Kingdom," as the young men of other countries do, speaking of their own, then I shall have less apprehension for the result of whatever trials the future may have in store for us.

> THOMAS D'A. McGEE, *Confederation debates*, Feb. 9, 1865, 145.

Even if all the territory Mr. Mowat asks for were awarded to Ontario, there is not one stick of timber, one acre of land, or one lump of lead, iron or gold that does not belong to the Dominion, or to the people who purchased from the Dominion Government.

> SIR JOHN A. MACDONALD, speech in Toronto, May, 30, 1882, on the Ontario boundary dispute with Manitoba.

The Dominion of Canada is not what it might have been if we had known what we now know at the time of the boundary negotiations with the United States; and there is no heavier charge, among all the heavy charges that may be brought against the British government in relation to the colonies, than that which arises from the ignorance and neglect that were shown...

> SIR CHARLES W. DILKE, *British Empire*, 1899, 35.

There is just one thing in which you excel Canada, I admit, and that is

with regard to your northern boundary, for, while you have the greatest nation under the sun as your northern boundary, we must admit we only have the north pole.

> CHARLES HOPEWELL, to an American, Empire Club speech, Dec. 7, 1911.

Three thousand miles of border line —
   nor fort nor armèd host
Of all this frontier neighbor-ground,
   from east to western coast;
A spectacle to conjure with! — a
   thought to stir the blood!
A living proof to all the world of
   faith in brotherhood.

> GUY W. BILSLAND, "Our border line", 1916.

Canada is bounded on the north by gold, on the west by the East, on the east by history, and on the south by friends.

> FRANCES SHELLEY WEES, "Geography lesson", 1937.

The "undefended frontier" was in reality defended by something stronger than bullets and bayonets, an aroused desire for self-sufficiency, adroitly fostered by those who could profit by such self-sufficiency.

> JOE P. SMITH, in *Can. hist. rev.*, 1940, 219.

Our frontier has long been immune from conflict, it is true, but it has suffered grievously from the effects of rhetoric. As a matter of fact, some of the realities have been obscured by the clouds of oratory which hang over this famous border. It has long been undefended, but realists have observed that the disparity of population has made armaments for one country futile and for the other superfluous.

> VINCENT MASSEY, *On being Canadian*, 1948, 115.

BOYS.

(See also: CHILDREN)

O Memory, take my hand today
   And lead me thro' the darkened bridge
Washed by the wild Atlantic spray
   And spanning many a wind-swept ridge
Of sorrow, grief, of love and joy,

Of youthful hopes and manly fears,
Oh, let me cross the bridge of years
And see myself again a boy!

WILLIAM H. DRUMMOND, "Child
thoughts", Oct., 1900.

The parent who could see his boy as
he really is, would shake his head and
say : "Willie is no good, I'll sell him."

STEPHEN B. LEACOCK, "The lot of
the schoolmaster", *Maclean's mag.*,
Sept., 1915.

Brother, little brother, your childhood
is passing by,
And the dawn of a noble purpose I
see in your thoughtful eye.
You have many a mile to travel and
many a task to do;
Whistle a tune as you go, laddie,
whistle a tune as you go.

LILIAN LEVERIDGE, "Over the hills
of home," 1918.

The best thing a boy can do is to
begin to collect. Let him collect something — I don't care what it is — and
you will find he begins to notice, and
from noticing he begins to classify
and arrange. Interest develops, and
wherever he goes there is nothing connected with his collection about which
he is not interested. The real education for a boy is simply a matter of
impressions.

SIR WILLIAM VAN HORNE, to S.
Macnaughtan, *My Can. memories*,
1920, 101.

BRAGGING.

Brag is a dog that everybody hates,
but nobody fears.

THOMAS C. HALIBURTON, *Sam
Slick's wise saws*, 1853, ch. 21.

As often as not it is the consciousness of a lack, not of a possession, that
prompts us to preach or to brag.

GEORGE ILES, *Canadian stories*,
1918, 173.

BRIBERY.

(See also: CORRUPTION)

The evil is in the low condition, or
rather total absence of honor & dignity
which make all classes, high & low,

accessible to bribery of every description.

SIR WILFRID LAURIER, letter to
Blake, July 10, 1882.

The foundation of party government
is bribery, is it not? Men are party
men for the spoils. They support the
government for the time for the sake
of the spoils. If a man "kicks" and
gives an independent vote against the
party he loses their patronage, does he
not? Is not bribery the corner stone
of party government?

Justice JOHN D. ARMOUR, in the
conspiracy case, *Queen v. Bunting* ; Toronto *Globe*, Dec. 5,
1884, 2.

We bribed them all, and generally
acquired nearly everything in sight.
We literally owned the Province. Public officials in Canada, so far as my
experience goes, do not have that
suspicious hesitancy in accepting money
that characterizes some officials in this
country. The Langevin crowd did not
scruple to take all they could get.

OWEN E. MURPHY, interview pub.
in *New York Times*, repub. in
Toronto *Globe*, Nov. 23, 1891;
Murphy was associated with Thomas McGreevy, a large railroad
contractor in Quebec.

Upon my word I do not think there
was much to be said in favour of the
Canadians over the Turks when contracts, places, free tickets on railways,
or even cash was in question.

SIR EDMUND HORNBY, *Autobiogra-
phy*, 1928, 90.

BRITISH COLUMBIA.

(See also: MOUNTAINS)

Island versus Mainland.

A familiar cry in the colonies of
Vancouver Island and British
Columbia before their union in
1866.

British Columbia, the land of golden
opportunities.

GEORGE BROWN, *Confederation
debates*, Feb. 8, 1865, 8.

Splendor sine occasu. (Splendour
without diminishment.)

Motto on provincial coat-of-arms.

The West beyond the West.
19th, century term for B.C.

Of all the conditions usually attached to a union of this colony with Canada, that of early establishment of railroad communication from sea to sea is the most important. If the railroad scheme is utopian, so is Confederation. The two must stand or fall together.

British Columbian, Feb. 2, 1870.

They won't secede, they know better.

EDWARD BLAKE, speech at Aurora, Ont., Oct. 3, 1874.

I think British Columbia a glorious province, a province which Canada should be proud to possess, and whose association with the Dominion she ought to regard as the crowning triumph of federation.

LORD DUFFERIN, speech in Victoria, Sept. 20, 1876.

It is war now between the Oriental and the Euro-Canadian for possession of British Columbia: the prize region of the whole Pacific.

TOM MACINNIS, *Oriental occupation of B.C.*, 1927, 7.

BRITISH COMMONWEALTH OF NATIONS.

(See also: BRITISH EMPIRE)

Nobody can imagine such an impossibility as a state of states or a cat of cats. The British Commonwealth of Nations is really nothing but a phrase — a very foolish phrase.

JOHN S. EWART, 1921, qu. in *Can. hist. rev.*, 1933, 140.

The unity of the British Commonwealth of Nations is at bottom a moral unity, and only in the exercise of a highly-refined political morality is there hope for its continuance.

ROBERT A. MCKAY. *Changes in legal structure of Commonwealth*, 1931.

We are supposed to be associated with the British Commonwealth of Nations, although no such thing exists. We are alleged to be a part of a third British Empire, although there never was more than one, and we have ceased to be part of it.

JOHN S. EWART, in *Can. hist. rev.*, 1933, 123.

Canada is the true architect of the present British Commonwealth of Nations.

BRUCE HUTCHISON, *Winnipeg Free Press*, Nov. 23, 1943.

The British Commonwealth has within itself a spirit which is not exclusive but the opposite of exclusive. Therein lies its strength. That spirit expresses itself in co-operation. Therein lies the secret of its unity. Co-operation is capable of indefinite expansion. Therein lies the hope of its future.

W. L. MACKENZIE KING, speech to British Parliament, May 11, 1944.

BRITISH EMPIRE.

(See also: BRITISH COMMONWEALTH OF NATIONS; CANADIAN-BRITISH RELATIONS; ISOLATION; UNION JACK)

The sun never sets on it.

T. C. HALIBURTON, *Sam Slick*, 1840, 273.

An allegiance like ours, that neither neglect nor indifference can extinguish, nor reward nor ridicule seduce, would win in the estimation of any other Government under Heaven but that of England, be considered above all praise and beyond all price.

T. C. HALIBURTON, speech in Glasgow, 1857.

We hold a vaster empire than has been!

SIR LEWIS MORRIS, "Song of Empire", written on occasion of Queen Victoria's jubilee, June 20, 1887; used as inscription on Canadian "All Red" postage stamp issued 1898 to commemorate adoption of Empire penny postage.

For myself I am a true Briton. I love the old land dearly. I am glad that I was born a British subject; a British subject I have lived for three score years and something more. I hope to live and die a British subject. I trust and hope that my children and my grand-children who have also been born British subjects will live their lives as British subjects, and as British subjects die.

> SIR OLIVER MOWAT, speech in Toronto, Feb. 18, 1891. (See: SIR JOHN A. MACDONALD, for a similar statement.)

If a day were ever to come when England was in danger, let the bugle sound, let the fires be lighted on the hills, and in all parts of the colonies, though we might not be able to do much, whatever we can do shall be done by the colonies to help her.

> SIR WILFRID LAURIER, speech, Imperial Institute, London, Eng., June 18, 1897.

The more I analyse the vital parts and the lusty members of this admirable political creation, with its nerves of steel and its rich blood, the more my admiration of England has grown. I was always glad enough to be a British subject, as most of my compatriots are, but now I experience the full pride in my British citizenship.

> HENRI BOURASSA, H. of C., *Debates*, Mar. 12, 1901.

A galaxy of free nations.

> SIR WILFRID LAURIER, speech in London Guildhall, July 11, 1902.

The most pressing need of the Empire is a new aristocracy in which the highest place will be accorded to those who inherit the spirit of great men rather than to those who inherit their blood.

> PETER MCARTHUR, *To be taken with salt*, 1903, 148.

It is an Empire not of force, or politics, but of mind, of literature, of ideals and tendencies, civil and social. As such it has no peer in history.

> GOLDWIN SMITH, Address at dedication of Goldwin Smith Hall, Cornell Univ., June 19, 1906.

The proper basis of the British Empire was that it was to be composed of a galaxy of nations under the British Crown.

> SIR WILFRID LAURIER, H. of C., *Debates*, Dec. 2, 1907.

The British Empire is a partnership of nations of equal status united in a partnership of consent.

> JOHN W. DAFOE, speech, Imperial Press Conference, Aug. 6, 1920.

It is possible to hold that not Chamberlain but Laurier, not Milner but Smuts, not the British Cabinet but the members of the Imperial Conferences, have been the true leaders into our present greatness.

> J. L. MORISON, *Can. hist rev.*, 1921, 194.

It is in many ways the most wonderful experiment in political relations that has ever been attempted. It is absolutely unique, unparalleled, unprecedented, in its structure and relationship.

> O. D. SKELTON, Can. club, Ottawa, Jan. 21, 1922.

As it was in Canada that the death blow to the old British Empire was struck, so it was in Canada that the New British Empire had its birth.

> W. R. RIDDELL, Empire Club speech, Apr. 25, 1929.

Six independent states are not an empire or a commonwealth. They are six kingdoms. And as they have the same King, their association is that of a Personal Union.

> JOHN S. EWART, Ottawa *Citizen*, Jan. 3, 1930.

When the remaining steps have been completed, the relations of the Six Kingdoms to one another will be that of a Personal Union. There will be no longer one dominant state and five subordinate states. All will be equal. And our people must learn what that means. They must become familiar with the idea of a divisible King, a King with several crowns, a King with several sets of advisers to whom he pays equal deference and by whom he is separately guided — possibly in conflicting directions.

> JOHN S. EWART, *Independence papers*, 1930, vol. 11, 337.

They little know of "empire" who only "England" know.

> W. P. M. KENNEDY, in *Can. hist. rev.*, 1935, 311. (*Cf.* Kipling: "What should they know of England who only England know?")

BRITISH NORTH AMERICA ACT, 1867.

(See also: CONFEDERATION; CONSTITUTION)

We are laying the foundation of a great State — perhaps one which at a future day, may even overshadow this country. But, come what may, we shall rejoice that we have shown neither indifference to their wishes, nor jealousy of their aspirations, but that we honestly and sincerely, to the utmost of our power and knowledge, fostered their growth, recognizing in it the conditions of our own greatness.

LORD CARNARVON, House of Lords, *Debates*, Feb. 19, 1867, col. 576b, on 2nd. reading of B. N. A. bill.

The object of the Act (the British North America Act) was neither to weld the provinces into one, nor to subordinate provincial governments to a central authority.

LORD WATSON, judgment, 1892, of the Privy Council.

The Statute of Westminster of 1931 is the logical outcome of the British North America Act of 1867. It was Sir John A. Macdonald who conceived the whole design at a time when scarcely anybody, including his own collegues, fully understood him; and his successors, Laurier, Borden and King, have merely put the increasingly less and less significant touches to a work which is now finished.

D. G. CREIGHTON, in *Can. hist. rev.*, 1945. 123.

BROWN, GEORGE.

After some five minutes' conversation in the *Globe* office with a hungry-looking, bald-headed individual in his shirt sleeves, and nails in mourning. I desired to see the Honourable Brown himself. Much to my surprise I found that he stood before me.

HORTON RHYS, *A theatrical trip for a wager*, 1861.

We acted together, dined at public places together, played euchre in crossing the Atlantic, and went into society in England together. And yet on the day after he resigned we resumed our old positions and ceased to speak.

SIR JOHN A. MACDONALD, after Brown's resignation from the Cabinet, Dec. 1865.

The great reason why I have been able to beat Brown is that I have been able to look a little ahead, while he could on no occasion forego the temptation of a temporary triumph.

SIR JOHN A. MACDONALD, letter to M. C. Cameron, Jan. 3, 1872.

I fancy that in his own home circle his presence has been a perpetual sunshine.

DANIEL WILSON, journal, April 23, 1880.

His nature was a rushing mountain stream;
His faults but eddies which its swiftness bred.

JOHN W. BENGOUGH, on the death of George Brown, May 9, 1880.

BUFFALO.

Plains provisions.
Red River colony term for buffalo meat, early 19th. century.

The Running of the Buffalo.
The phrase for the summer hunt of the buffalo by the Hudson's Bay Co., 1820 to 1860.

And, lo! before us lay the tameless stock,
Slow wending to the northward like a cloud!
A multitude in motion, dark and dense —
Far as the eye could reach, and farther still,
In countless myriads stretched for many a league.

CHARLES MAIR, *Tecumseh*, 1886.

One stride he took, and sank upon his knees,
Glared stern defiance where I stood revealed,
Then swayed to earth, and, with convulsive groan,
Turned heavily upon his side, and died.

CHARLES MAIR, "The last bison", 1890.

BUSINESS.

(See also : INDUSTRY ;
TRADE)

Around his store, on spacious shelves
arrayed
Behold his great and various stock
in trade.
Here, nails and blankets side by
side are seen;
There, horses' collars, and a large
tureen;
Buttons and tumblers, fish-hooks,
spoons and knives,
Shawls for young damsels, flannel
for old wives;
Woolcards and stockings, hats for
men and boys,
Mill-saws and fenders, silks and
children's toys;
All useful things and, joined with
many more,
Compose the well-assorted country
store.

OLIVER GOLDSMITH, "The rising
village", 1825.

I know of no money-making business
in Canada except the Law, Store Keeping, Tavern Keeping, and perhaps I
may add horse dealing.

JOHN LANGTON, letter to his
brother, Oct. 21, 1844.

Depend upon it, our commercial
embarassments are our real difficulty.
Political discontent properly so-called,
there is none.

LORD ELGIN, dispatch, winter,
1848; qu. in Walrond, ed., *Letters
of Elgin*, p. 70.

Punctuality is the soul of business.
THOMAS C. HALIBURTON, *Sam
Slick's wise saws*, 1853, ch. 3.

Canada is not one market but four,
widely separated from each other, and
each of them sparse in itself.

GOLDWIN SMITH, *Canada and the
Can. question*, 1891, 284.

We will now get all we can out of
the people of Canada.

Attributed to directors of Grand
Trunk Railway, about 1922; qu.,
Vaughan, *Van Horne*, 207.

Every successful enterprise requires
three men — a dreamer, a business-
man, and a son-of-a-bitch.

PETER MCARTHUR, a favorite epigram coined about 1904 after
failure of his jointly-published
The Daily Paper in England.

Dear Doctor: I have not received a
reply to my former letter. Let me
assure you that the machinery of the
Union Trust Company requires oil.
Please turn on the tap. We need the
surplus of the I. O. F. Yours sincerely,
George E. Foster.

GEORGE E. FOSTER, a private letter
read by J. A. Macdonald, editor
of the *Globe*, in a campaign address,
North Toronto, Oct. 6, 1908.

The history of Canada since Confederation — the outcome of a politico-
commercial, or a commercio-political
conspiracy, if consequences are any
indication of motive — has been a
history of heartless robbery of both
the people of the Maritimes and of the
Prairie Sections of Canada by the Big
'Vested' Interests — so called from the
size of their owners' vests — of the
politically and financially stronger
Central Provinces.

E. A. PARTRIDGE, *A war on poverty*,
[1925?] 77.

Most prudent people hesitate to do
business with their relatives. When the
necessity arrives, the results are seldom
a stimulant of family affection. Each
kinsman expects the other by reason
of his kin to make kindly concessions.

WALTER FENTON, *Queen's quart.*,
1932, 716.

It has been difficult not to be
impressed by the fact that the corpo-
rate form of business not only gives
freedom from legal liability, but also
facilitates the evasion of moral responsibility for inequitable and uneconomic
practices.

ROYAL COMMISSION ON PRICE
SPREADS, *Report*, 1934.

The history of much of North America
might be termed the history of the
rivalry of New York and Montreal.

A. R. M. LOWER, *N. A. assault on
Can. forest*, 1938, 58.

The patriotic way for the true French Canadian to live is to save and become a small proprietor. English methods are not ours. The French became great by small savings and small business.

> Roman Catholic curé, qu. by E. C. Hughes, *French Canada in transition*, 1943, 151. (trans.)

C

CABINET MINISTERS.

If I had my way, they should all be highly respectable parties whom I could send to the penitentiary if I liked.

> SIR JOHN A. MACDONALD, to Sir Richard Cartwright, about 1870, qu., Cartwright, *Reminiscences*, 304.

It is the function of Ministers — we know it, and I do not quarrel with it — to say nothing that can be caught hold of, nothing in advance of the popular opinion of the day, to watch the current of that opinion, and when it has gathered strength, to crystallize it into Acts of Parliament. That is the function of a Liberal Minister. The function of a Tory Minister is to wait till he is absolutely forced to swallow his own opinions.

> EDWARD BLAKE, speech at Aurora, Ont., Oct. 3, 1874.

Give me better wood and I will make you a better cabinet.

> SIR JOHN A. MACDONALD, a reply sometimes made to criticisms of his choice of cabinet ministers.

I have been represented as a Protestant minister; there was not one of the canvassers of the honourable gentlemen opposite that did not represent to the people that I was not a Minister of the Crown, but that I was a Protestant minister.

> SIR WILFRID LAURIER, H. of C., *Debates*, Feb. 11, 1878, on his personal defeat in Drummond-Arthabaska by-election.

The time has come, I think, when we must choose men for their qualifications rather than for their locality.

> SIR JOHN A. MACDONALD, letter to J. A. Chapleau, June 6, 1888.

We fought like blazes.

> JOSEPH I. TARTE, on ministers in Sir Wilfrid Laurier's government; Tarte was a minister, 1896-1902.

I notice that a lot of commonplace men get into cabinets nowadays.

> FRANK B. CARVELL, retort to Martin Burrell, Minister of Agriculture, when he voiced his doubt that Carvell would ever become a minister, H. of C., *Debates*, 1916.

CANADA.

> (See also: CANADIANS; FUTURE; INDEPENDENCE; NATIONALITY; UNITY, *etc.*)

Not less large than Canada.

> RABELAIS, *Pantagruel*, 1548, Bk. iv, ch. 2; (N'estoit moins grand que de Canada.)

You know that these two nations [France and England] are at war for a few acres of snow, and that they are spending for this fine war more than all Canada is worth.

> VOLTAIRE, *Candide*, 1759, ch. 23. (trans.)

[Pitt] divided his propositions thus, either to retain all Canada, Cape Breton, and exclude the French from their fishing on Newfoundland, and give up Guadeloupe and Gorée, or retain Guadeloupe and Gorée with the exclusion of the French Fishery on Newfoundland, and give up some part of Canada, and confine ourselves to the Line of the Lakes... He did not talk of one of them as sine qua nons.

> DUKE OF NEWCASTLE, letter to Hardwicke, Dec. 3, 1760.

...His Most Christian Majesty cedes and guarantees to his Britannick Majesty, in full right, Canada...

> From the TREATY OF PARIS, Feb. 10, 1763.

I wish the British Government would give you Canada at once. It is fit for nothing but to breed quarrels.

> ALEX. BARING (Lord Ashburton), to John Q. Adams, U.S. ambassador, London, 1816.

The Kingdom of Canada.

Originated by SIR JOHN BEVERLEY ROBINSON, 1822; later adopted by SIR JOHN A. MACDONALD in first draft of British North America Act, 1867; mss. in Macdonald's hand-writing in Public Archives.

Canada must neither be lost nor given away!

WILLIAM IV, at the time of the Maine boundary dispute.

Feller Citizens, this country is goin' to the dogs hand over hand.

T. C. HALIBURTON, *Sam Slick*, 1836, ch. XXXI.

Advancing quietly; old differences settling down, and being fast forgotten; public feeling and private enterprise alike in a sound and wholesome state; nothing of flush or fever in its system, but health and vigour throbbing in its steady pulse: it is full of hope and promise.

CHARLES DICKENS, *American notes*, 1842.

The nursing mother of half a continent.

TORONTO *Globe*, Dec. 10, 1861.

Four nations welded into one
    with long, historic past,
Have found, in these our western
    wilds, one common life at last.
Through the young giant's mighty
    limbs that stretch from sea to sea
There runs a throb of conscious life,
    of waking energy;
From Nova Scotia's misty coast
    to far Pacific shore,
She wakes, a band of scattered homes
    and colonies no more,
But a young nation, with her life
    full beating in her breast,
A noble future in her eyes,
    the Britain of the West.

AGNES M. MACHAR (*Fidelis*), "Dominion Day, 1879", in, *Can. monthly*, III, 9.

O Child of nations, giant-limbed,
    Who stand'st among the nations
    now
Unheeded, unadorned, unhymned,
    With unanointed brow, —
How long the ignoble sloth, how long

The trust in greatness not thine own?
Surely the lion's brood is strong
    To front the world alone!

CHARLES G. D. ROBERTS, "Canada", January, 1885; ("O Child of nations.")

It is a goodly land; endowed with great recuperative powers and vast resources as yet almost undeveloped; inhabited by populations moral and religious, sober and industrious, virtu-ous and thrifty, capable and instructed — the decendants of a choice immigra-tion, of men of mark and courage, energy and enterprise, in the breasts of whose children still should glow the sparks of those ancestral fires.

EDWARD BLAKE, To the Members of the West Durham Reform Convention, Feb. 6, 1891.

God bless our mighty forest-land
    Of mountain, lake and river,
Whose loyal sons, from strand to
    strand,
    Sing "Canada Forever".

AGNES M. MACHAR, "A song for Canada", 1899.

Up Along.

Term for Canada used by fishermen of Newfoundland.

It is the brightest gem in the Crown of the British Empire.

SIR WILFRID LAURIER, speech in London, Eng., July 1, 1902; originally appears as a reference to freedom in a poem by R. HEBER, in, *Pietas universitatis Oxoniensis*, 1761: "The brightest jewel in the British crown".

I am one who believes in Canada first and the Empire next.

W. F. MCLEAN, H. of C., *Debates*, Feb. 11, 1907. (See also, POLI-TICAL PHRASES: "Canada first".)

Canada has given and taken all along the line for nigh on three hundred years, and in some respects is the wisest, as she should be the happiest, of us all.

RUDYARD KIPLING, *Letters to the family*, 1908.

O Canada! our home, our native land!
True patriot-love in all thy sons
     command.
With glowing hearts we see thee rise,
The true North strong and free,
And stand on guard, O Canada,
We stand on guard for thee.

R. STANLEY WEIR, "O Canada",
1909.

O Canada! Dominion of the North,
How vast the path whereon thy sun
     rides forth!

GRANT BALFOUR, "Canada", 1910.

Canada is a country without a soul.

ANON., American friends qu. by
Rupert Brooke, Letters from America, 1916, 49.

Canada is a live country, live, but not,
like the States, kicking.

RUPERT BROOKE, Letters from
America, 1916, 83.

Historically, Canada is a by-product
of the United States.

ARTHUR MACMECHAN, Can. hist.
rev., 1920, 348.

This country is much more than a
chain of wheat fields, and gold mines,
and pulp-wood forests; it is more even
than the union of nine separate provinces: it is the expression of certain
ideas.

VINCENT MASSEY, Can. club, Ottawa, Jan. 20, 1924.

Land of the matchless march of lake
     and stream!
Land of the virile seasons!

WILSON MACDONALD, "Ode on the
Diamond Jubilee of Confederation",
1927.

Her [Canada's] power, her hopes,
her future guarantee the increasing
fellowship of the Nordic races of the
East and the West; in fact, no state, no
country, no band of men can more
truly be described as the linchpin of
peace and world progress.

WINSTON CHURCHILL, Saturday
evening post, Feb. 15, 1930, 51.

My country, last across the world
     To leave tradition's night,
Strong hater of her seers is she,
     And worshipper of might.

WILSON MACDONALD, "Sea shore
and compline," 1935.

The real reason for Canada's tardy
growth is to be found partly in her
spiritual dependence on Great Britain,
which has often paralyzed her energies,
but to a far greater extent in her
geographical proximity to the United
States.

JOHN MACCORMAC, Canada; America's problem, 1940, 200.

Canada is a secondary and second-rate
country without much depth of experience: everyone admits that — too
freely, sometimes.

A. R. M. LOWER, in Can. hist. rev.,
1941, 12.

No one knows my country, neither
the stranger nor its own sons. My
country is hidden in the dark and teem-
ing brain of youth upon the eve of its
manhood. My country has not found
itself nor felt its power nor learned its
true place. It is all visions and doubts
and hopes and dreams. It is strength
and weakness, despair and joy, and the
wild confusions and restless strivings
of a boy who has passed his manhood
but is not yet a man.

BRUCE HUTCHISON, The Unknown
country, 1942, 3.

CANADIAN-AMERICAN
BEHAVIOUR.

(See also: AMERICANS;
ANNEXATION; DEFENCE; PO-
LITICAL PHRASES; RECIPRO-
CITY; UNITED STATES)

It is authors of silly books, editors of
silly papers, and demogogues of silly
parties that keep us apart.

T. C. HALIBURTON, Wise saws,
1853, ch. 26.

The policy which the United States
actually pursue is the infatuated one
of rejecting and spurning vigorous and
ever-growing Canada, while seeking to
establish feeble states out of decaying
Spanish provinces on the coast and
islands of the Gulf of Mexico. I shall
not live to see it, but the man is already
born who will see the United States
mourn over this stupendous folly.

WILLIAM H. SEWARD, Cruise to
Labrador, 1857.

That shot fired at Fort Sumter, on the 12th of April, 1861, had a message for the north as well as for the south... That shot fired at Fort Sumter was the signal gun of a new epoch for North America, which told the people of Canada, more plainly than human speech can express it, to sleep no more except on their arms.

THOMAS D'A. McGEE, speech in Legislative Assembly, 1861.

The clover lifts its trefoil leaves to the evening dew, yet they draw their nourishment from a single stem. Thus distinct, and yet united, let us thrive and flourish.

JOSEPH HOWE, speech in Detroit, Aug. 14, 1865.

War will come some day between England and the United States and India can do us yeoman's service by sending an army of Sikhs, Ghoorkas and Belochees &c, &c, across the Pacific to San Francisco and holding that beautiful and immoral city with the surrounding California as security for Montreal and Canada.

SIR JOHN A. MACDONALD, letter to J. S. Maine, Calcutta, April 9, 1867.

Remember, Canada lives cheek by jowl with the United States.

SIR RICHARD CARTWRIGHT, to Lord Carnarvon, Colonial Secretary 1874-8.

I am a subject of the British Crown, but whenever I have to choose between the interests of England and Canada it is manifest to me that the interests of my country are identical with those of the United States of America.

SIR WILFRID LAURIER, speech in Boston, Nov. 17, 1891.

It is far more to Canada's advantage than ours to be on good terms with us. Lord Salisbury, in a private conversation the other day, compared her to a coquettish girl with two suitors, playing one off against the other. I should think a closer analogy would be to call her a married flirt, ready to betray John Bull on any occasion, but holding him responsible for all her follies.

JOHN HAY, U. S. ambassador to London, letter to John W. Foster, Dec. 27, 1897.

The best and most effective way to maintain friendship with our American neighbours is to be absolutely independent of them.

SIR WILFRID LAURIER, H. of C., Debates, July 30, 1903.

I remember, and you remember also, that since the abolition of the Reciprocity Treaty in 1866, we have sent delegation after delegation to Washington to obtain Reciprocity. We are not sending any more delegations.

SIR WILFRID LAURIER, speech to Can. Manufacturers Assoc., Montreal, Nov. 6, 1901; see also his speech in Toronto, qu., Toronto Globe, April 2, 1907, p. 2.

There will be no more pilgrimages to Washington. We are turning our hopes to the old motherland.

SIR WILFRID LAURIER, attributed remark on the Fielding budget of April 22, 1907.

There may be a spectacle perhaps nobler yet than the spectacle of a united continent, a spectacle which would astound the world by its novelty and grandeur, the spectacle of two peoples living in amity side by side for a distance of 4,000 miles, a line which is hardly visible in many quarters, with not a cannon, with not a gun frowning across it, with not a fortress on either side, with no armament one against another, but living in harmony, in mutual confidence, and with no other rivalry than a generous emulation in commerce and the arts of peace.

SIR WILFRID LAURIER, H. of C., Debates, Mar. 7, 1911.

So long as Canada remains a part of the British Empire, Canada's position, geographically, is such that she must be either a hostage or a link of union between Great Britain and the United States.

SIR RICHARD CARTWRIGHT, speech in Toronto, Aug. 29, 1911.

Canada is the greatest country under the Stars and Stripes.

JAMES A. MACDONALD, editor Toronto Globe, speech in Massey Hall to Assoc. Clubs of America, 1914.

Shake! cries a voice from the mountain;
Shake! shouts a voice from the mine;
Shake! Let the hands of brothers Meet over the Boundary Line.

CLIVE PHILLIPPS-WOLLEY, "A Christmas greeting", 1917.

Nobody knows better than the historian how much courage it still takes to tell the truth about American-Canadian relations, and how near the surface these antiquated but latent prejudices are still to be found.

CHESTER MARTIN, in *Can. hist. rev.*, 1937, 10.

Economically the story is one story and politically it is either less or more than two.

S. MORLEY SCOTT, in *Can. hist. rev.*, 1938, 378.

Children of a common Mother. — Brethren dwelling together in peace and unity.

South and north inscriptions on Peace Arch at Blaine, Wash., on B. C. border, erected 1946.

CANADIAN-BRITISH RELATIONS.

(See also: DIPLOMACY; ENGLAND; FOREIGN RELATIONS; FRENCH-CANADIANS; INDEPENDENCE; SOVEREIGNTY; WAR)

Whenever the "British yoke" becomes burthensome to ¸North America it will be broken like a pack-thread, and I would be one of the first to break it.

JOSEPH HOWE, letter to Lord Falkland, April 9, 1846.

I trust that for ages, for ever, Canada may remain united with the mother country. But we are fast ceasing to be a dependency, and are assuming the position of an ally of Great Britain. England will be the centre, surrounded and sustained by an alliance not only with Canada, but Australia, and all her other possessions; and there will thus be formed an immense confederation of freemen, the greatest confederacy of civilized and intelligent men

that has ever had an existence on the face of the globe.

SIR JOHN A. MACDONALD, speech Legislative Assembly, April 19, 1861.

Instead of looking upon us as a merely dependent colony, England will have in us a friendly nation — a subordinate but still a powerful people — to stand by her in North America in peace or in war.

SIR JOHN A. MACDONALD, *Confederation debates*, 1865, 44.

I hope to live to see the day, and if I do not, that my son may be spared to see Canada the right arm of England — to see Canada a powerful auxiliary of the Empire — not, as now, a cause of anxiety and a source of danger.

SIR JOHN A. MACDONALD, H. of C., *Debates*, May 3, 1872, on the Washington treaty.

Take up your freedom; your days of apprenticeship are over.

The Times (London), editorial on Canada and the San Juan water arbitration award, Oct. 30, 1872; advice often summarized as "cut the painter"; see Tennyson quotation below.

And that true North, whereof we lately heard
A strain to shame us "keep you to yourselves;
So loyal is too costly! friends — your love
Is but a burthen; loose the bonds and go."
Is this the tone of empire? here the faith
That made us rulers?

LORD TENNYSON, epilogue to "Idylls of the King"; written November, 1872, after reading a "villainous" editorial in *The Times* on Canada, Oct. 30, 1872.

Those who dislike the colonial connection speak of it as a chain, but it is a golden chain, and I for one, am glad to wear the fetters.

SIR JOHN A. MACDONALD, H. of C., *Debates*, Mar. 30, 1875, 981.

I believe... that everything that extends the liberties of Canadians, everything that accords to Canada and her statesmen greater breadth of view in the management of their own affairs, is more likely to conduce to the advancement of Imperial interests and greatness than any curbing policy that keeps us down to the grindstone.

ALEXANDER MACKENZIE, H. of C., *Debates*, April 21, 1882.

Why should we waste money and men in this wretched business? England is not at war, but merely helping the Khedive to put down an insurrection, and now that Gordon is gone, the motive of aiding in the rescue of our countrymen is gone with him. Our men and money would therefore be sacrificed to get Gladstone and Co. out of the hole they have plunged themselves into by their own imbecility.

SIR JOHN A. MACDONALD, letter to Tupper, Mar. 12, 1885.

Colonies are destined to become nations, as it is the destiny of a child to become a man. No one, even on the other side will assume that this country, which will some day number a larger population than Great Britain is forever to remain in its present political relations with Great Britain. The time is coming when the present relations of Great Britain and Canada must either become closer or become severed altogether.

SIR WILFRID LAURIER, H. of C., *Debates*, 1888, I, 363.

The silken chain which binds the Dominion and the Mother-land together.

J. CASTELL HOPKINS, *Can. mag.*, Dec., 1893, 171.

A Nation spoke to a Nation,
A Queen sent word to a Throne:
"Daughter am I in my mother's house,
But mistress in my own.
The gates are mine to open,
As the gates are mine to close,
And I set my house in order,"
Said our Lady of the Snows.

RUDYARD KIPLING, "Our Lady of the Snows, 1897", London *Times*, April 27, 1897.

Make us the half-way house of the empire.

GEORGE M. GRANT, letter to Sir Wilfrid Laurier, Feb. 25, 1899,

referring to the Pacific cable project.

If we were to be compelled to take part in all the wars of Great Britain, I have no hesitation in saying that... sharing the burden, we should also share the responsibility. Under that condition of things, which do not exist, we should have the right to say to Great Britain: If you want us to help you, call us to your councils.

SIR WILFRID LAURIER, H. of C., *Debates*, Mar. 13, 1900.

Imperialism means that the British Empire is one and that her interests are one, and that what makes the British Empire great makes Canada great; that if Britain falls Canada falls; that if Canada is hurt the Empire is hurt; that if you strike a blow at the Empire you strike Canada.

GEORGE W. ROSS, speech at Niagara, Aug., 1901.

I stand in the first place for the British Empire against the world, and within the British Empire I stand first for Canada.

SIR ROBERT BORDEN, a frequent declaration, 1905-12; also July 25, 1930, in support of R. B. Bennett, "The British Empire first and, within the British Empire, Canada first".

Natural growth is better than revolution; partnership between Canada and Great Britain is in the interests of both; the political tie between Canada and Great Britain leads to the working of educative influences between the two countries; it will lead to Canada's bearing her share of Britain's burdens.

GEORGE M. WRONG, *Can. nationalism and the Imperial tie*, 1909.

Let there be no dispute as to where I stand. When Britain's message came, then Canada should have said: "Ready, aye ready; we stand by you." I hope the time has not gone by when that declaration can yet be made. If that declaration is made, then I will be at the back of the government.

ARTHUR MEIGHEN, address, Toronto Business Men's Conservative Club, Sept. 22, 1922, after the "Chanak affair"; see speech by Laurier, H.

of C., *Debates*, Spec. session, 1914, 10, for earlier and similar use of the phrase "Ready, aye ready".

I am for the British Empire next to Canada, the only difference being that some gentlemen are for the United States before Canada. I am for the British Empire after Canada.

RICHARD B. BENNETT, H. of C., *Debates*, May 6, 1930.

CANADIAN NATIONAL RAILWAYS.

(See: RAILWAYS)

CANADIAN PACIFIC RAILWAY

(See also: RAILWAYS; TRANS-PORTATION)

With the construction of the railway the country will be populated by Englishmen; without it by Americans.

TORONTO *Globe*, Mar. 23, 1870.

I am confident that a bushel of wheat will never go to England over an all-rail route from Saskatchewan to the seaboard.

EDWARD BLAKE, speech at Aurora, Ont., Oct. 1874.

Two streaks of rust across the wilderness.

EDWARD BLAKE, attributed reference to the future of the Canadian Pacific.

Until this grand work is completed, our Dominion is little more than a "geographical expression".

SIR JOHN A. MACDONALD, letter to Sir Stafford Northcote, May 1, 1878.

I shall not be present; I am an old man, but I shall perchance look down from the realms above upon a multitude of younger men — a prosperous, populous, and thriving generation — a nation of Canadians, who will see the completion of the road.

SIR JOHN A. MACDONALD, speech at Hochelaga depot on return from Europe after negotiating for completion of the Railway, Sept. 27, 1880.

It will never pay for its axle-grease.

EDWARD BLAKE, attributed. Also attributed to Sir Richard Cartwright, George W. Ross, and the Liberal Party leaders, all of whom were in opposition to Tupper's proposals to help finance the Railway, especially during the years 1880-81. Ross (*Getting into Parliament*, 1913, 118) uses the phrase as a summation of his attitude.

Well, boys, he'll do it. Stay over till tomorrow. The day the Canadian Pacific busts, the Conservative party busts the day after.

JOHN HENRY POPE, winter 1883, to Van Horne and other C.P.R. officials, after persuading Sir John A. Macdonald to extend another loan to the company.

"How High We Live," said the Duke to the Prince, "on the Canadian Pacific Railway".

Advertising slogan adopted by Van Horne, 1890.

Cutting a melon.

Term used about 1898 to signify a supposed financial "deal" whenever the C.P.R. applied for an increase in its capital stock.

Wise Men of the East
Go West by the C.P.R.

SIR WILLIAM VAN HORNE, advertising slogan adopted about 1890.

Since we can't export the scenery, we shall have to import the tourists.

SIR WILLIAM VAN HORNE, about 1895.

Come to Alberta and go into partnership with the Canadian Pacific.

C. P. R., slogan, 1908.

No Crop, no Payment!

C. P. R. slogan in the West, about 1908.

The Great Colonizer.

A reference to the Railway in recognition of its efforts in western land settlement.

No single work of any man in any part of the world at any period of the world's history has so obviously and directly contributed to the making of a nation as the transcontinental railway in Canada.

C. P. LUCAS, *Greater Rome and greater Britain*, 1912, 119.

Be it understood the C.P.R., Clifford Sifton and the Almighty comprise the Trinity of Canada, ranking in importance in the order named.

ROBERT C. (BOB) EDWARDS, *Calgary Eye Opener*; attributed.

CANADIANS.

(See also: FRENCH-CANADIANS; NATIONALITY; PATRIOTISM; THE NORTH, etc.)

Both on account of the feudal system and the aristocratic government, a private man [is] not worth so much in Canada as in the United States; and, if your wealth in any measure consist in manliness, in originality and independence, you had better stay here.

HENRY THOREAU, *Excursion to Can.*, 1850, advice to Americans.

North American Chinamen.

Pre-Confederation, British Columbia term used to describe the "Canadians" who were unpopular because of their thriftiness.

We are ourselves an American people geographically and commercially, though we retain our British connection; our situation is continental, and our politics, in the large and best sense, must needs be continental.

THOMAS D'A. McGEE, speech in London, Ont., Sept, 26, 1861.

I am not one of those who thank God I am a Nova Scotian merely, for I am a Canadian as well.

JOSEPH HOWE, speech in Halifax, Aug. 13, 1864, to leaders of Confederation from the Canadas.

One individual chooses Tuponia and another Hochelaga, as a suitable name for the new nationality. Now I would ask any member of this House how he would feel if he woke up some fine morning and found himself, instead of a Canadian, a Tuponian or a Hochelagander.

THOMAS D'A. McGEE, *Confederation debates*, Feb. 9, 1865, 126;

Tuponia is from "The United Provinces of North America".

Canadians desire to be a power on the American continent, and to make their influence felt from the Atlantic to the Pacific.

SIR GEORGE E. CARTIER, Jan., 1869, speech in London, Eng.

Four millions of Britons who are not free.

EDWARD BLAKE, speech at Aurora, Ont., Oct., 1874.

As long as I live, as long as I have power to use in the service of my country, I shall repel the idea of changing the nature of its different elements. I want the marble to remain the marble; I want the granite to remain the granite; I want the oak to remain the oak; I want the sturdy Scotchman to remain the Scotchman; I want the brainy Englishman to remain the Englishman; I want the warm-hearted Irishman to remain the Irishman.

SIR WILFRID LAURIER, speech, Arichat, N. S., Aug. 15, 1900. (trans.)

We first saw light in Canada, the land beloved of God;
We are the pulse of Canada, its marrow and its blood;
And we, the men of Canada, can face the world and brag
That we were born in Canada beneath the English flag.

PAULINE JOHNSON, "Canadian born", 1903.

We in Canada are trustees for the British race. We hold this land in allegiance, we hold it in development, for our brothers, who are the sons of those who won it for us.

F. B. CUMBERLAND, Empire Club speech, Toronto, 1904.

Our fathers came to win us
This land beyond recall —
And the same blood flows within us
Of Briton, Celt, or Gaul —
Keep alive each glowing ember
Of our sireland, but remember
Our country's Canadian
Whatever may befall.

WILLIAM H. DRUMMOND, "Canadian forever", 1905.

Little Canadians.

From "Little Englanders"; a term used early 20th. century to describe nationalists.

Friends have I found in far and alien places,
Beauty and ardour in unfamiliar faces,
But first in my heart this land I call my own!
Canadian am I in blood and bone!

CHARLES G. D. ROBERTS, "These three score years", 1927.

If I were English, Canada
Should love me like the deuce,
But I was born in Canada
So what the hell's the use.

WILSON MACDONALD, "Song of a bloody Canuck", 1931.

My roots are in this soil,
Whatever good or bad, what vain hope or mighty triumph lies in you,
That good or bad, that destiny is in me.
Where you have failed, the fault is on my head.
Where you are ignorant or blind or cruel, I made you so.
In all your folly and your strength I share,
And all your beauty is my heritage.

GWEN PHARIS (RINGWOOD), "Oh Canada, my country", written 1940; qu., A. R. M. Lower, *Colony to nation*, 1946, 561.

We Canadians are a worthy, thrifty people, perfectly safe and constituting no problem to the countries in control of our destinies: we are therefore uninteresting.

A. R. M. LOWER, in *Can. hist. rev.*, 1941, 8.

For we are young, my brothers, and full of doubt, and we have listened too long to timid men.

BRUCE HUTCHISON, *Unknown country*, 1942.

If I were to offer, not a definition, but a working description of an alert Canadian citizen just now, I could say he is one (man or woman) increasingly aware of being North American in the continental sense without being American in the national sense.

ARTHUR L. PHELPS, speech at Univ. of New Brunswick, Feb. 18, 1947, *Community and culture*, 10.

CAPITALISM.

(See also: ECONOMICS)

The capitalistic system has grown up and it is in use because, and only because, the experience of mankind has proven it to be the best way of doing what has to be done.

SIR CLIFFORD SIFTON, speech, about 1925, qu., Dafoe, *Sifton*, 510.

We believe that the social realization of the Kingdom of God is not compatible with the continuance of the capitalistic system, and we think the Church should now uncover fearlessly the anti-social and unchristian basis of that system and declare unremitting war upon it.

TORONTO CONFERENCE, United Church of Canada, resolutions, 1933.

CARTIER, Sir GEORGE E.

I am an Englishman speaking French.

SIR GEORGE E. CARTIER, a saying of his later years. In 1858, Cartier was introduced to Queen Victoria and he told Her Majesty that a Lower Canadian was "an Englishman who speaks French".

Cartier was as bold as a lion. He was just the man I wanted. But for him Confederation could not have been carried.

SIR JOHN A. MACDONALD, Jan. 29, 1885, to his secretary Joseph Pope, after unveiling statue of Cartier in Ottawa.

CARTIER, JACQUES.

In the sea-port of Saint Malo 'twas a smiling morn in May
When the Commodore Jacques Cartier to the westward sail'd away;
In the crowded old Cathedral all the town were on their knees
For the safe return of kinsmen from the undiscover'd seas;

And every autumn blast that swept
o'er pinnacle and pier
Filled manly hearts with sorrow and
gentle hearts with fear.

THOMAS D'A. McGEE, "Jacques
Cartier", 1858.

CHARACTER.

Climate, locality and occupation, form
or vary character, but man is the same
sort of critter everywhere.

T. C. HALIBURTON, *Nature and
human nature*, 1855, II, 386.

It's the bad that's in the best of us
Leaves the saint so like the rest of us!
It's the good in the darkest-curst of us
Redeems and saves the worst of us!
It's the muddle and hope and
madness;
It's the tangle of good and badness;
It's the lunacy linked with sanity
Makes up, and mocks, humanity!

ARTHUR STRINGER, "Humanity",
1920.

The real test of character is in
surprise. It is the unforeseen crisis,
the sudden calamity, the unexpected
shock, when the man is off guard,
which shows truly what he is.

A. MacMECHAN, R.S.C., *Trans.*,
1926, II, 3.

CHARITY.

He clothed the needy, the hungry
fed,
Pitied the erring, the faltering led,
Joyed with the joyous, wept with the
sad,
Made the heart of the widow and
orphan glad,
And never left for the lowliest one
An act of kindness and love undone...

PAMELIA V. YULE, "Littlewit and
Loftus", 1881.

How read you the Scriptures? What
say they? These three with the
world now abide,
Hope, charity, faith, and the greatest is charity — blessed above
all.
Our hands should be fruitful and
open. The field for our giving
is wide,

And blessing shall follow the gifts,
though the power to give may
be small.

BARRY STRATON, "Charity", 1884.

Thou askest not to know the creed,
The rank or name is naught to
thee;
Where'er the human heart cries
"Help!"
Thy kingdom is, O Charity!

MARY MORGAN, "Charity", 1887

The hardest lesson of all to learn is
that the law of the higher life is only
fulfilled by love, i.e. charity.

SIR WILLIAM OSLER, "The master
word in medicine", in, *Montreal
med. jour.*, 1903.

Charity is infinitely divisable. He
who has a little can always give a
little.

PETER McARTHUR, *To be taken
with salt*, 1903, 156.

Remain the well-wrought deed in
honour done,
The dole for Christ's dear sake, the
words that fall
In kindliness upon some outcast
one —
They seemed so little: now they are
my All.

JOHN McCRAE, "Upon Watts' picture *Sic transit*", 1919.

Hard hearts and soft heads generally go together.

JOHN MACNAUGHTON, *Essays*, 1946

CHEESE.

We have seen thee queen of cheese
Lying quietly at your ease,
Gently fanned by evening breeze,
Thy fair form no flies dare seize.

JAMES McINTYRE, the Cheese Poet,
"Ode on the mammoth cheese",
1884.

Then let the farmers justly prize
The cows for land they fertilize,
And let us all with songs and glees
Invoke success into the cheese.

JAMES McINTYRE, "Lines read at a
dairymen's supper", 1889.

CHILDREN.

(See also: Boys; Girls)

Now to this very day, when'er you see
A baby well contented, crying "Goo!"
Or crowing in this style, know that
it is
Because he then remembers in great
joy
How he in strife, all in the olden
time,
Did overcome the Master, conqueror
Of all the world. For that, of crea-
tures all,
Or beings which on earth have ever
been
Since the beginning, Baby is alone
The never yielding and invincible.

GLOOSCAP, Micmac legend, N. S.
and Newfoundland; anglicized
version.

Why, I guess I wasn't brought up
at all. I just growed up.

T. C. HALIBURTON, *Sam Slick*,
1836, chap. XII.

The Indians apparently have no idea
of correcting or restraining their children; personal chastisement is unheard
of. They say that before a child has
any understanding there is no use in
correcting it; and when old enough
to understand, no one has a right to
correct it.

ANNA B. JAMESON, *Winter studies*,
1837.

Boys are mothers' sons. It's only
gals who take after their father.

T. C. HALIBURTON, *Nature and
human nature*, 1855, I, 361.

Not in science, not in art,
Hides the balm for the poor heart :
We are bound, until made free
By the great humility!
Knowledge is the tree of woe. –
All your fathers found it so:
All philosophy is vain —
Be a little child again.

ALEXANDER MCLACHLAN, "Fate",
1856.

We are weakest
When we are caught contending with
our children!

CHARLES HEAVYSEGE, *Saul*, 1857.
pt. 3.

Childhood alone is glad. With it
time flees
In constant mimes and bright fes-
tivities

CHARLES HEAVYSEGE, poem no. IV,
in *Jephthah's daughter*, 1865.

They lingered on the middle heights
Betwixt the brown earth and the
heaven;
They whispered, "We are not the
night's,
But pallid children of the even".

WILFRED CAMPBELL, "The dreamers", 1889.

There's two of twins — oh, it must
be fun
To go double at everything,
To holler by twos, and to run by
twos,
To whistle by twos and to sing!

JEAN BLEWETT, "The boy of the
house", 1897.

Ah! Why have I lost the eyes of
childhood?

ADJUTOR RIVARD, *Chez nous*, 1914
(trans.)

They think more of the future of
their children than the past of their
grandparents.

ARTHUR HAWKES, on Anglo-Cana-
dians, in, *The birthright*, 1919, 88.

A woman never stops to consider
how very uninteresting her children
would be if they were some other
woman's.

ROBERT C. (BOB) EDWARDS, *Calgary Eye Opener*, Aug. 9, 1919.

The Stork Derby.

The competition in human fecun-
dity resulting from the terms of
the will of Charles Vance Millar,
died Oct. 31, 1926, who bequeathed
$500,000 to the Toronto woman
who bore the most children during
10 years after his death. The
claims of four women, each with
nine children, were accepted, and
two others received settlements.

Aye, child by wistful child they
turned
Where dull the yellow street-lamps
burned,

And for a breath they caught the gleam,
And for a moment dreamed the dream.

ARTHUR STRINGER, "The children's theatre", 1929.

The Quints.

A popular abbreviation of quintuplets as applied to the Dionne sisters, born at Callander, Ont., May 28, 1934.

The most important thing in the world today is the bringing up of children.
C. BROCK CHISHOLM, speech in Washington, D.C., Oct. 23, 1945.

That freedom, present in all children and known as innocence, has been destroyed or crippled by local certainties, by gods of local moralities, of local justice, of personal salvation, of prejudice and hate and intolerance — frequently masquerading as love — gods of everything that would destroy freedom to observe and to think and would keep each generation under the control of the old people, the elders, the shamans, and the priests.
G. BROCK CHISHOLM, speech in Washington, D.C., Oct. 23, 1945.

Two weeks here in the sun and air
Through the charity of our wealthy citizens
Will be a wonderful help to the little tots
When they return for a winter in the slums.
F. R. SCOTT, "Social notes: Summer camp", 1945.

Are you Canada's child?
Do you wander her meadows, gather her bright flowers,
Do you walk her grey streets, follow her winding roads on your way to school?
Are you Canada's child?
FRANCES SHELLEY WEES, "Canada's child", 1947.

CHILDREN'S RHYMES.

(*Note.* See: Laura Durand, "Play rhymes of the Dominion" in Toronto *Globe*, Nov. 13-Dec. 18, 1909, and, *Journal of American folklore*,

1918, p. 1 - 179. The following are samples of local variants.)

Awkum bawkum
Curious kawkum,
Ellikum bellikum bony bus,
If you'd a been where I'd a been,
You'd a been out.
(Ottawa, Ont.)

Eny, meny, hippery dic,
Delia, dolia, dominic,
Hoachy poachy, noma noachy,
Te, tan, tush,
Ugly, bugly, boo,
Out goes you.
(Thamesville, Ont.)

Inty, minty, figgity, feg;
El, del, domen, egg,
Urky, purky, stone and rock;
Ann, dan, tush.
(Carleton Place, Ont.)

Kaiser Bill went up the hill,
To see the boys in France.
Kaiser Bill came down the hill
With bullets in his pants.
(Recited during war of 1914-18.)

One-ery, two-ery, dickery-dee,
Alabo, crackabo, tender-lea;
Twin, twan, just began,
Twiddle, twaddle, twenty-one.
O-u-t spells out.
(Perth, Ont.)

One-zol, two-zol, zig-zol sam,
Bob-tail vinegar, tiddle-um-a-tan,
Harum scarum, virgum marum,
Tee, taw, tum.
O-u-t spells out.
(Toronto, Ont.)

CHRISTMAS.

Bright shines the sun across the drifts,
And bright upon my Christmas gifts;
They brought Him incense, myrrh, and gold,
Our little Lord who lived of old.
MARJORIE PICKTHALL, "A little child's song of Christmas", 1913.

Give each new day its own good cheer
All other days apart,
And every day throughout the year
Keep Christmas in your heart.
ALBERT D. WATSON, "Christmas", 1914.

Glory to God, this wondrous morn,
On earth the Saviour Christ is born.

BLISS CARMAN, "Bethlehem," December, 1928.

A child who believes in Santa Claus, who really and literally believes, because his daddy told him so, that Santa comes down all the chimneys in the world on the same night has had his thinking ability permanently impaired if not destroyed.

G. BROCK CHISHOLM, Ottawa, 1945; qu., *MacLean's mag.*, Jan. 1, 1946, 44.

THE CHURCH.

The habits and opinions of the people of Canada were, in the main, averse from the absolute predominance of any single church.

LORD STANLEY, letter to Bagot. Oct. 8, 1841.

We early freed ourselves from the incubus of a State Church.

EDWARD BLAKE, speech at Aurora, Ont., Oct. 3, 1874.

The crisis time of the nation is the crisis time of the church.

WESTMINSTER, edit., April 2, 1898.

Not endowments, property, support of the clergy, and a share in the government of a province or of its municipalities are the essential points in an establishment, after all, but rather beliefs, doctrine, discipline, forms of worship and of orders.

A. H. YOUNG, in *Can. hist. rev.*, 1934, 351.

More people would go to church if it weren't exactly the proper thing to do.

ROBERT C. (BOB) EDWARDS, *Calgary Eyeopener*, Mar. 9, 1918.

CIRCUMSTANCES.

(See also: EXISTENCE)

Circumstances alter cases.

T. C. HALIBURTON, *The old judge*, 1849, ch. 15.

Some weak, luckless wretches ever seem

Flying before the hounds of circumstance,
Adown the windy gullies of this life.

CHARLES HEAVYSEGE, *Saul*, 1857.

Truly, circumstances alter cases; but circumstances do not change principles.

EGERTON RYERSON, *Story of my life*, 1883.

When schemes are laid in advance, it is surprising how often the circumstances fit in with them.

SIR WILLIAM OSLER, "Internal medicine as a vocation", 1897, in *Aequanimitas*.

CITIES AND TOWNS.

The greatest country I ever struck. There are hundreds of towns and cities between Winnipeg and Moosejaw, and it takes a rich man to own the ground under his shoes in those places. Wherever there's a siding that's a town; and where there's a siding and a tank, that's a city!

ANON., C.P.R. conductor to E. B. Osborn, on the 1881 land-fever in the West.

Lurid and lofty and vast it seems;
It hath no rounded name that rings
But I have heard it called in dreams
The City of the End of Things.

ARCHIBALD LAMPMAN, "The city of the end of things", *Atlantic monthly*, Mar., 1894.

Two towns stand on the shores of the lake less than a mile apart. What Lloyds is to shipping, or the College of Surgeons to medicine, that they are to the Wheat. Its honour and integrity are in their hands; and they hate each other with the pure, poisonous, passionate hatred which makes towns grow.

RUDYARD KIPLING, *Letters to the family*, 1908, on Fort William and Port Arthur.

Our country will grow and prosper only if the clamour of the great cities does not dominate the traditional voice that rises from the fields, only if the plough continues to be recognized as the most essential and the most fruitful instrument of production.

GEORGE BOUCHARD, *Other days, other ways*, 1928, 149.

CITIES AND TOWNS — NICKNAMES, etc.

Armstrong, B. C. — The Celery City.

Bassano, Alta. — Best in the West by a Dam Site.

Brandon, Man. — The Wheat City. — Gateway to the North. — Vires acquirit eundo — (motto: She acquires strength in her progress.)

Brantford, Ont. — The Telephone City. (Alexander G. Bell invented the telephone here, 1874) — Industria et perseverentia. (motto)

Brockville, Ont. — The City of the Thousand Islands. — You are a Stranger in Brockville Only Once.

Calgary, Alta. — The City of the Foothills.

Carlyle, Sask. — Where they Grow WHEAT. (1910)

Charlottetown, P. E. I. — The Cradle of Confederation. (From the conference held in 1864 by delegates of the Maritime Provinces to discuss union, and at which delegates from the Canadas attended.)

Chatham, Ont. — The Maple City. — Canada's Southland City. — Greges, agricultura et commercium — (motto: Herds, crops and commerce.)

Cornwall, Ont. — The Factory Town. — The Friendly Town.

Dundas, Ont. — The Valley Town.

Edmonton, Alta. — The Crossroads of the World. — The Friendly City. — The Gateway to the North. — The Oil Centre of Canada. — Industry, Energy, Enterprise. (motto)

Fort Erie, Ont. — The Gateway to Canada.

Fort William, Ont. — The Golden Gateway From the Great West. — The Twin Cities. (With Port Arthur.) — A posse ad esse. (motto : From possibility to actuality.)

Fredericton, N. B. — The Celestial City. — Fredericopolis silvæ filia nobilis. (motto)

Galt, Ont. — The Manchester of Canada.

Granby, Que. — The Princess of the Eastern Townships.

Guelph, Ont. — The Royal City. (Guelph was the name of the reigning family at time of founding by John Galt, 1827; incorporated, 1877.) — The Main Street of Ontario. — Fides, Fidelitas, Progressio. (motto)

Halifax, N. S. — The Gateway to the Dominion. (See also: HALIFAX, N. S.)

Hamilton, Ont. — The Ambitious City. (From R. J. MacGeorge, *Count or Counterfeit,* 1858: "the ambitious and stirring little city".) — The Birmingham of Canada. (Pamphlet title, pub. 1893.)

Ingersoll, Ont. — The Cheese Town of Canada.

Kamloops, B. C. — The Hub of the Interior.

Kelowna, B. C. — The Orchard City.

Kingston, Ont. — The Limestone City. — The Derry of Canada. (About 1860, when the Orangemen were predominant.) — Pro Rege, Grege, Lege. (motto: For the King, for the Community and for the Law.) (See also: KINGSTON, ONT.)

Kitchener, Ont. — The Industrial City.

Leamington, Ont. — The Sun Parlour of Canada. (Coat of arms.) — The Sunshine Town.

Lethbridge, Alta. — The City of Opportunity. — The Windy City. — Ad Occasionis Januam. (motto: The gateway to opportunity.)

London, Ont. — The Forest City.

Medicine Hat, Alta. — The Chicago of Western Canada. — The Gas City of Canada. — The Hat. — The Hub of the West. — The Place Where the Weather Comes From. (After the establishment of the weather station, 1910.) — — The town that was born lucky. (Kipling, 1907.) — Enterprise. (motto)

Mitchell, Ont. — The Town Worth Living In.

Moncton, N. B. — The Bend. (Before 1855.) — The Hub of the Maritimes. —Resurgo. — (motto: We / They rise again.)

Montreal, Que. — The Metropolis. — Concordia Salus. (motto)

Moose Jaw, Sask. — The Friendly City. (1908)

Nanaimo, B. C. — The Gateway to Vancouver Island. — The Hub of Vancouver Island.

Nelson, B. C. — The Queen City of the Kootenays.

New Westminster, B. C. — The Royal City. (Incorporated 1860)

Niagara Falls, Ont. — The Honeymoon Centre of the World. — The Power City of the World.

North Battleford, Sask. — The Rising Star of Northern Saskatchewan. (1911)

North Bay, Ont. — The Gateway City.

North Sydney, N. S. — The Bar Town. (From a harbour sand bar.) — Goathill. (From Chapel Hill, a goat pasture.)

North Vancouver, B. C. — The Ambitious City. — The City of Homes and Industry. — Industry, Progress. (motto)

Oliver, B. C. — The Cantaloupe City.

Oshawa, Ont. — The Motor City of Canada. — Nulli Secundus. (motto)

Ottawa, Ont. — The Washington of the North. (Laurier, 1893) — Advance. (motto, 1844) (See also: OTTAWA, ONT.)

Owen Sound, Ont. — The Scenic City. — Arbor Virga Fuit. — (motto: The tree was once a sapling.)

Peterborough, Ont. — The Electric City. (The first to have incandescent street lighting.) — The Lift Lock City. — Nature Provides, Industry Develops. (motto)

Port Arthur, Ont. — The Gateway to the West. — The Twin · Cities. (With Fort William)

Portage La Prairie, Man. — The Hub of Central Manitoba. — The Plains City. — The Prairie Gateway City.

Preston, Ont. — The Hub of Waterloo Country.

Prince Albert, Sask. — The Capital of Saskatchewan's Top Two-Thirds. Gateway to the North, — The Pivot of the Saskatchewan Northland. — Esse quam videri. (motto)

Quebec, Que. — The Ancient Capital. — The Gibraltar of America. (See also: QUEBEC CITY)

Regina, Sask. — Pile of Bones. (Official name; see Lt. Gov. Dewd-

ney, Can. *Sess. paper 25B*, June 30, 1882, so-called from the accumulated bones of the buffalo; name changed to Regina by Princess Louise in autumn, 1882.) — The Queen City of the Plains. — Floreat Regina. (motto) (See also: REGINA, SASK.)

Saint Boniface, Man. — The Cathedral City. — The Holy City. (From Whittier, "Red River voyageur".) — The Industrial Section of Greater Winnipeg. — Salus a cruce. (motto) (See also: SAINT BONIFACE, MAN.)

St. Catharines, Ont. — The Garden City of Canada. — Industry and Liberality. (motto) — St.Catharines, city of the host of flowers. (From Lampman, "Niagara landscape", 1900.)

Saint John, N. B. — The Loyalist City. (From the 3,000 U. E. Loyalists who landed May 18, 1783; city incorporated May 18, 1785.) — O fortunati quorum jam mœnia surgunt. (motto from Virgil: O fortunate are the people whose walls are even now arising.)

St. Mary's, Ont. — The Stone City.

Sarnia, Ont. — Canada's Chemical Centre.

Saskatoon, Sask. — The Hub City. — The Hub City of the Hard Wheat Belt. (1908) — Saskatchewan's City of Opportunity. (slogan) — "We thought of Minnetonka for a name, but found some Saskatoon berries and that settled it". (John N. Lake, Temperance Colonization Co., on the founding, Aug. 20, 1882.)

Shawinigan Falls, Que. — The City of Light. (La Ville Lumière.) — Age quod agis. (motto: Do well what you do.)

Sherbrooke, Que. — The Queen City of the Eastern Townships. — Onward. (motto)

Stratford, Ont. — The Classic City. — Industry, Enterprise. (motto)

Sudbury, Ont. — The Hub of the North. — Industry, Enterprise, Integrity. (motto)

Sydney, N. S. — Down Where the East Begins. — The Pittsburgh of Canada. — The Steel City.

Thorold, Ont. — The Town of Seven Locks. (From the Welland Canal.) — Where the Steamships Climb the Mountain.

Toronto, Ont. — The Athens of the Dominion. — The Belfast of America. — The Choral Capital of North America. — The City of Churches. (1890) — Hog Town. — The Queen City. — Toronto the Good. (1890; from campaigning of Women's Temperance Union.) — Tory Toronto. — Industry, intelligence, Integrity. (motto adopted 1835 by William Lyon Mackenzie, the first mayor.) (See also: TORONTO, ONT.)

Trail, B. C. — The Smoky City.

Truro, N. S. — The Hub of Nova Scotia.

Vancouver, B. C. — Canada's Golden Gate. (1912) — From Stumps to Skyscrapers. (1936) — Gas Town. (From Captain John "Gassy Jack" Deighton, builder of a hotel on Burrard Inlet, 1867.) — The Gateway to the Orient. (1906) — The Lion-Guarded City. (1925) — Queen of the Coast. (From E. Pauline Johnson, "A toast".) — The Sunset City. — The Terminal City. — By land and sea we prosper. (motto) (See also: VANCOUVER, B. C.)

Verdun, Que. — The Bedroom of Montreal. — The Pay as You Go City. (From its excellent financial state.)

Vernon, B.C. — The Hub of the North Okanagan.

Victoria, B. C. — The City of Gardens. — Semper Liber. (motto: Always free.)

Wallaceburg, Ont. — The Glass Town.

Waterloo, Ont. — The Hartford of Canada. — Stability. (motto)

Wesmount, Que. — The Holy City.

Weston, Ont. — The Hub of York County. — Equal Justice to All. (motto)

Windsor, Ont. — The Automotive Capital of the British Empire. — The Most Southerly City in Canada. — The Sun Parlour of Canada. — Per mare per terras. (motto)

Winnipeg, Man. — The Chicago of the Canadian West. (1880) — The Gateway City. — The Gateway of the Canadian West. (1912) — The Peg. — Commerce, Prudence, Industry. (motto) (See also: WINNIPEG, MAN.)

Yorkton, Sask. — The Parkland's Trading Centre.

CITIZENSHIP.

All we have to do is, each for himself, to keep down dissensions which can only weaken, impoverish and keep back the country; each for himself do all he can to increase its wealth, its strength and its reputation; each for himself — you, and you, gentlemen, all of us — to welcome every talent, to hail every invention, to cherish every gem of art, to foster every gleam of authorship, to honour every acquirement and every gift, to lift ourselves to the level of our destinies, to rise above all low limitations and narrow circumscriptions, to cultivate that true catholicity of spirit which embraces all creeds, all classes and all races, in order to make of our boundless province, so rich in known and unknown resources, a great new Northern nation.

THOMAS D'A. McGEE, speech in Quebec City, 1862.

As we are now, the words, "I am a Canadian" derive their force from the fact that they are equivalent to saying, "I am a British subject".

TORONTO *Globe*, 1865, qu., *Can. hist. rev.*, 1929, 127.

I am a Nova Scotian by birth and a Canadian by act of Parliament.

ALFRED JONES, M.P. for Halifax 1888.

We are full Canadian citizens, but we are much more than Canadian citizens — we are citizens of the whole Empire.

NEWTON W. ROWELL, Burwash lecture, Toronto, 1922.

We hear much these days of education for citizenship, but the only real and effective education for citizenship lies in its actual practice.

FRED LANDON, Can. Hist. Assoc., *Rept.*, 1937, 86.

CIVIL SERVICE.

(See also: PATRONAGE)

The price of a commission in the government service is the free exercise of a glib tongue, deftness in canvassing, unscrupulousness in everything.

Canadian Monthly, Nov., 1876, 443.

Every government selected for the civil service their own friends, and no one could object to it.

SIR JOHN A. MACDONALD, H. of C. *Debates*, Apr. 27, 1878, 2229.

The Civil Service of the country, though not the animating spirit, is the living mechanism through which the body politic moves and breathes and has its being. Upon it depends the rapid and economical conduct of every branch of your affairs; and there is nothing about which a nation should be so particular as to secure in such a service independence, zeal, patriotism and integrity.

LORD DUFFERIN, speech to Agricultural and Arts Association, Toronto, Sept. 24, 1878.

A refuge for people who, by reason of their indolence or lack of intelligence, could not succeed in other employment.

CANADA, *Report*, 1880.

The permanent conviction had forced itself on the party members that there was not room for the entire male population of the country in the civil service.

J. E. COLLINS, *Canada under admin. of Lorne*, 1884, 211.

If you have any ambition; if you expect to make any headway in the world; if you place any value on your initiative, then, for Heaven's sake, steer clear of the Civil Service. If you want to become part of a machine by which you move along, without exercising your initiative, then the Civil Service is the proper place for you.

DONALD SUTHERLAND, H. of C., *Debates*, May 10, 1918, 1740.

The iniquitous examination system and the whole vertical system of promotions is the central core from which a stream of mediocrity seeps into our whole federal administration.

W. L. GRANT, in *Univ. Toronto quarterly*, 1934, 438.

He was educated at Lévis College, studied law for a time, then went into business, and finally took refuge in the Civil Service.

ENCYCLOPEDIA OF CANADA, 1935, II, 35.

CLASSES.

(See also: THE PEOPLE)

The upper classes don't know one half the virtue that's in the middlin' and lower classes; and they don't know one half the integrity and good feelin' that's in the others; and both are fooled and gulled by their own noisy and designin' champions.

T. C. HALIBURTON, *Sam Slick*, 1836, ch. XVIII.

The upper-crust folks.

T. C. HALIBURTON, *Sam Slick*, 1838, 53.

We have here no traditions and ancient venerable institutions; here, there are no aristocratic elements hallowed by time or bright deeds; here, every man is the first settler of the land, or removed from the first settler one or two generations at the furthest; here, we have no architectural monuments calling up old associations; here, we have none of those old popular legends and stories which in other countries have exercised a powerful share in the government; here, every man is the son of his own works.

THOMAS D'A. McGEE, *Confederation debates*, Feb. 9, 1865, 146.

We have no aristocracy but of virtue and talent, which is the only true aristocracy, and is the old and true meaning of the term.

THOMAS D'A. McGEE, *Confederation debates*, Feb. 9, 1865, 146.

I believe in the true aristocracy of energy, learning, ability, and integrity; an aristocracy whose marks and titles are found in the earnest efforts of a man to do his duty and to excel in its discharge; and whose distinctions are such as a free people themselves confer by the expression of their confidence, by mandates to the great council of the country, by selection for high offices of public trust, by the commission to regulate the affairs, to guide the high destinies of the people among whom they live. That is the aristocracy and the only aristocracy which is suited to our day and country.

EDWARD BLAKE, qu., Ross, *Patriotic recitations*, 183.

There is only one class on the plains, and that is the working class. Here and there you meet a gentleman of leisure, but he is called a tramp.

HOWARD A. KENNEDY, *New Canada*, 1907.

Power in politics is not found in Parliament but in the country, prior to the election. Politics only exist where there are classes, and any action taken by a class in defence of its interest is political action. Hence you cannot define any particular action as political, but any action used to control political power in order to utilize it for the benefit of that class — that is political action, and it matters not what method it takes.

JACK KAVANAGH, speech at Western Labour Conference, Calgary, Mar. 13, 1919.

Class organization is the only road along which civilization can travel to safety. I believe in that as I believe in God.

HENRY WISE WOOD, *Western independent*, Oct. 29, 1919.

The root conflict of interest within our national society is not fundamentally sectional or geographical at all, *i. e.*, it is not between the central provinces and the outlying provinces. It is a class conflict, between the small class which controls the sources of wealth and power and the other classes which are exploited by them.

F. H. UNDERHILL, *C. J. E. P. S.*, 1935, 402.

CLEAR GRITS.

(See also: LIBERAL PARTY)

Him! We don't want him, we only want men who are clear Grit.

DAVID CHRISTIE to George Brown, late in 1849, when discussing the

platform and members of the advanced Reformers. The term "Clear Grit" was soon afterward applied by the *Globe* to the new party, but it had been in use for years without reference to politics and was used by T. C. Haliburton in *Sam Slick*, 1836.

All sand and no dirt, clear grit all the way through.

DAVID CHRISTIE, attributed, 1849. Also ascribed to Peter Perry, Malcolm Cameron, and William McDougall, all active in the formation of the Clear Grit party which took form at a convention at Markham, Ont., March, 1850.

A little miserable clique of office-seeking buncombe-talking cormorants who met in a certain lawyer's office in King Street, and announced their intention to form a new party on "Clear Grit" principles.

TORONTO *Globe*, Jan. 8, 1850.

"Clear grit" is pure sand without a particle of dirt in it.

ALEXANDER MACKENZIE, to C. H. McIntosh, editor of the Strathroy *Despatch*, from a platform in an election campaign, West Middlesex, 1867.

CLIMATE.

(See also: PRAIRIES; WEATHER; WINTER)

I fear that I have not got much to say about Canada, not having seen much; what I got by going to Canada was a cold.

HENRY THOREAU, *Excursion to Can.*, 1850.

There can be but little doubt that the greater part of the vast region included under the name of British America is doomed to everlasting sterility on account of the severity of its climate.

LIPPINCOTT's *Gazetteer*. 1866.

The climate of Manitoba consists of seven months of Arctic winter and five months of cold weather.

NORTHERN PACIFIC RAILWAY Co., *Settler's guide to the North-west*, N. Y., 1882. Refuted in, Can., Dept. of Agric., *Canadian North-*

*west; climate and productions; a
misrepresentation exposed*, Ottawa,
1883.

The climate is most trying to tramps.
> GEORGE M. GRANT, address to
> Canadian Club, N. Y., 1887.

A country of dry frost in winter, and
of fruitful heat in summer, with numerous delightful climates in between —
this is the rising nation, Canada.
> WILFRED CAMPBELL, *Canada*, 1907,
> 1.

The stimulation of the climate may
lead the Westerner to overmuch action
and to make large drafts upon his
future with confidence, but what he has
done is so wonderful that he has reason
in venturing upon wide horizons.
> SIR R. FALCONER, speech, *The
> quality of Canadian life*, 1917.

CLOTHES.

It makes little difference; Canada is
useful only to provide me with furs.
> MADAME DE POMPADOUR, 1759, on
> being told of the fall of Quebec.

So sneer not at words, for experience
    taught me
That sensitive worth is so easily
    hurt;
And honour in patches this parable
    brought me:
The meanest of men often wear
    the best shirt.
> J. R. RAMSAY, *Win-on-ah*, 1869.

Ladies are to wear low-necked
dresses, without Court trains, and
gentlemen are to be in full dress.
Ladies, whose health will not admit
of their wearing low-necked dresses
may, on forwarding to the A.D.C. in
waiting, a medical certificate to that
effect, wear square cut dresses.
> E. G. P. LITTLETON, Military
> Secretary to Lord Lorne, Gov. Gen.,
> Montreal, 1878, proclamation on
> vice-regal drawing-room.

Let him wear brand-new garments
    still,
Who has a threadbare soul, I say.
> BLISS CARMAN, "The mendicants,"
> 1894.

What of all the colours shall I
bring you for your fairing,

Fit to lay your fingers on, fine
    enough for you?
Yellow for the ripened rye, white
    for ladies' wearing,
Red for briar-roses, or the skies'
    own blue?
> MARJORIE PICKTHALL, "The green
> month", 1913.

If a girl has a pretty face, no man
on earth can tell you what kind of
clothes she has on.
> ROBERT C. (BOB) EDWARDS, *Cal-
> gary Eyeopener*, Oct. 5, 1918.

I knew him well. He was a vest
A gleam of shirt, a round of collar,
Felt hat, suit coat, pants neatly
    pressed.
None cared if he were dunce or
    scholar.
He was of shoes with shining lace,
Fur overcoat with each November.
There may, perhaps, have been a
    face —
His clothes are all that I remember.
> ALAN CREIGHTON, "Mr. Clothes",
> 1939.

CLOUDS.

In steady fleets serene and white,
The happy clouds go on.
> ARCHIBALD LAMPMAN, "April in
> the hills", 1896.

Clouds like far turrets in a dream
Stand baseless in the summer sky.
> ARCHIBALD LAMPMAN, "At the
> ferry", 1896.

COAL.

The Coal Trade — Dirty work makes
clean money, our stomachs need never
be empty while the bowels of the earth
are full.
> N. S. PHILANTHROPIC SOC., toast,
> Nov. 1, 1836.

"Then look at the beeowells of the
airth; only think of the coal; and
it's no use a-talkin', that's the only
coal to supply us that we can rely on.
Why, there ain't nothin' like it. It
extends all the way from Bay of Fundy
right out to Pictou through the Province, and then under all the Island
of Cape Breton; and some o' them
seams are the biggest, the thickest,

and deepest ever yet discovered since the world began. Beautiful coal it is too.

> T. C. HALIBURTON, *The clockmaker*, 1838.

Canada is a country with coal-fields at both ends and the railways in between.

> ANON., about 1900.

COLLEGES AND UNIVERSITIES.

From this college every blessing may flow over your country. May it continue to dispense them to the latest ages! Let no jealousy disturb its peace; let no lukewarm indifference check its growth!

> EARL OF DALHOUSIE, at laying of corner stone of Dalhousie College, Halifax, May 22, 1820.

A college education shows a man how devilish little other people know.

> T. C. HALIBURTON, *Sam Slick's wise saws*, 1853, I, 53.

Baldwin's bill converted King's College into the University of Toronto, an absolutely Godless institution according to the pietists.

> JOHN LANGTON, letter, Nov. 12, 1856.

The colleges with us are a hotbed of conservatism.

> SIR WILFRID LAURIER, letter to Blake, July 10, 1882.

Oil thigh na Banrighinn gu brath! Cha Gheill! Cha Gheill! Cha Gheill!

> Queen's University yell, adopted 1891; composed by ALFRED E. LAVELL and Messrs. F. A. McRæ, D. Cameron, and McLean; see, *Queen's journal*, Nov. 8, 1946; trans.: "The House of Learning of the Queen forever, Never yield! Never yield! Never yield!"

On the old Ontario strand, my boys,
Where Queen's for evermore shall stand,
For has she not stood
Since the time of the flood,
On the old Ontario strand?

> Chorus of students' song (*Songbook*, 1903); originally an American college song, adopted by

Victoria College (Cobourg, Ont.) with wording of the last line "On the banks of the old Raritan"; later adopted by Queen's.

If I had had a university education, I should probably have entered upon the path of literature and acquired distinction therein.

> SIR JOHN A. MACDONALD, qu. by Sir Joseph Pope, *The day of Sir John A. Macdonald*, 1915, 6.

If I were founding a university I would found first a smoking room; then when I had a little more money in hand I would found a dormitory; then after that, or more probably with it, a decent reading room and a library. After that, if I still had more money that I couldn't use, I would hire a professor and get some textbooks.

> STEPHEN B. LEACOCK, "Oxford as I see it", *Harper's mag.*, May, 1922.

A university in which professors are overawed by political, social or sectarian influence cannot aspire to an honourable position in the Commonwealth of Learning. Just as we measure the progress of democratic government by its freedom from the spoils system, so that faithful servants are not dispossessed whenever a new party comes into power, so we can measure the rank and stability of a university by the security given to a professor to pursue and expound his investigations without being compelled to justify himself to those who differ from him.

> SIR ROBERT FALCONER, *Academic freedom*, 1922.

Our boys and girls must be taught
Right ideas from the start.
There is a great danger
In independent thought —
We'll have none of it here,
No fear!

> A. J. M. SMITH, "College $pirit", 1925.

Honoris causa — some one said,
  and all the seers and scholars
Rose up in reverent array and bowed
  the knee to dollars.

> WILSON MACDONALD, "Convocation", 1932.

The distinction about old McGill is the men who are not there.

> STEPHEN B. LEACOCK, *My discovery of the West*, 1937, 138.

Dalhousie College was an idea prematurely born into an alien and unfriendly world, deserted by its parents, betrayed by its guardians, and throughout its minority abused by its friends and enemies alike.

> D. C. HARVEY, *Intro. hist. of Dalhousie Univ.*, 1938.

The university must deny the finality of any of the conclusions of the social sciences. It must steadfastly resist the tendency to acclaim any single solution to the world's problem at the risk of failing to play its role as a balancing factor in the growth of civilization. The Marxist solution, the Keynesian solution, or any solution, cannot be accepted as final if the universities are to continue and civilization is to survive.

> HAROLD A. INNIS, *Pol. econ. in the modern state*, 1946, 141.

COLONIES AND COLONIALISM.

> See also: CANADIAN-BRITISH RELATIONS; IMPERIALISM; LITERATURE, CANADIAN)

There is no field in a colony for a man of talent and education.

> T. C. HALIBURTON, *Sam Slick*, 1838, 183.

These wretched colonies will all be independent too in a few years and are a millstone round our necks.

> BENJAMIN DISRAELI, letter to Lord Malmesbury, Aug. 13, 1852, respecting Newfoundland fisheries.

I am no more against Colonies than I am against the solar system. I am against dependencies, when nations are fit to be independent.

> GOLDWIN SMITH, *The Empire*, 1863, 123.

Great Britain must presently reach the condition of shaking hands with her colonies instead of expecting them to touch their hats to her.

> PETER MCARTHUR, *To be taken with salt*, 1903, 158.

This colonial status is a worn-out, by-gone thing. The sense and feeling of it has become harmful to us. It limits the ideas, and circumscribes the patriotism of our people. It impairs the mental vigour and narrows the outlook of those who are reared and educated in our midst.

> STEPHEN LEACOCK, *University mag.*, 1907, 133.

It is hardly too much to say that in some quarters there is a surviving colonialism which cannot forget that the British connection once involved colonial subordination, and would willingly demonstrate independence of Britain by avowing dependence upon the United States.

> R. G. TROTTER. in *Inter-American quart.*, Jan., 1940.

COMMUNISM.

> The good still moveth towards the good:
> The ill still moveth towards the ill:
> But who affirmeth that we will
> Not form a nobler brotherhood
> When communists, fanatics, those
> Who howl their *"vives"* to Freedom's name
> And yet betray her unto shame,
> Are dead and coffined with her foes.
>
> GEORGE F. CAMERON, "In after days", 1887.

The evidence proves that the Communist Party of Canada is a member of the Communist International of Russia and that instead of determining its own policies, purposes, teachings and aims, it adopted and adopts those of the Communist International, and, therefore, whatever are the policies, purposes, teachings and aims of the Communist International are also automatically those of the Communist Party of Canada.

> SIR WILLIAM MULOCK, 1931, Ontario Appeal Court judgment on conviction of Tim Buck.

The Padlock Law.

> A popular name for the Québec act of 1937 aimed at curbing Communist activities.

Communism is the most subtle of all evils, because its appeal is made in the name of freedom, and it marches under the banners of Freedom. Its appeal is to the masses, whom it promises to deliver from their chains. It speaks in the name of enlarged opportunity and increased security. It is, in reality, none of these. The immediate purpose of Communism is the complete control of the individual in the name of the state. Its ultimate aim is world domination. Beneath its mask are concealed the secret police, slave labour, and the concentration camp.

> W. L. MACKENZIE KING, speech at National Liberal Convention, Ottawa, 1948.

CONDUCT OF LIFE.

(See also: BEHAVIOUR; DEEDS AND DOING; DUTY; SUCCESS)

A man that has too many irons in the fire is plaguy apt to get some of 'em burnt.

> T. C. HALIBURTON, *Sam Slick*, 1836, ch. XXXII.

Support what is right, oppose what is wrong; what you think, speak; try to satisfy yourself, and not others; and if you are not popular, you will at least be respected; popularity lasts but a day, respect will descend as a heritage to your children.

> T. C. HALIBURTON, *Sam Slick*, 1838, 35.

By work you get money, by talk you get knowledge.

> T. C. HALIBURTON, *Sam Slick, wise saws*, 1853, I, 270.

Providence requires three things of us before it will help us — a stout heart, a strong arm, and a stiff upper lip.

> THOMAS C. HALIBURTON, *Sam Slick's wise saws*, 1853, ch. 13.

Give and take, live and let live, that's the word.

> THOMAS C. HALIBURTON, *Sam Slick's wise saws*, 1853, ch. 27.

If thou wouldst truly win
The race thou art pursuing,
Heed well the voice within.

> CHARLES SANGSTER, "The dreamer", 1860.

There is no strength where there is no strain; seamanship is not learned in calm weather, and born of the vicissitudes and struggles of life are the wisdom, the dignity, and the consolations.

> JOSEPH HOWE, address, Ottawa Y.M.C.A., Feb. 27, 1872.

Illusion makes the better part of life.
Happy self-conjurors, deceived, we win
Delight and ruled by fancy live in dreams.

> NICHOLAS F. DAVIN, "An epic of the dawn", 1884.

It's not what a man profess;
It's what a man possess.

> JAMES GAY, "Barnum and Gay", [1885?].

We are here to add what we can *to*, not to get what we can *from*, Life.

> SIR WILLIAM OSLER, address, "Doctor and nurse", June 4, 1891.

Have little care that Life is brief,
And less that Art is long.
Success is in the silences
Though Fame is in the song.

> BLISS CARMAN, "Envoy", in, *Songs from vagabondia*, 1894.

No fidget and no reformer, just
A calm observer of ought and must.

> BLISS CARMAN, "Joys of the road", 1894.

An open hand, an easy shoe,
And a hope to make the day go through.

> BLISS CARMAN, "Joys of the road", 1894.

A simple love, and a simple trust,
And a simple duty done,
Are truer torches to light to death
Then a whole world's victories won.

> WILFRED CAMPBELL, "Afterglow", 1899.

Not to be conquered by these headlong days,
    But to stand free; to keep the mind at brood
On life's deep meaning, nature's altitude
Of loveliness, and time's mysterious ways;
At every thought and deed to clear the haze

Out of our eyes, considering only
    this,
What man, what life, what love,
    what beauty is.
This is to live, and win the final
    praise...

> ARCHIBALD LAMPMAN, "Outlook",
> *Living age*, Mar. 14, 1903.

You may learn to consume your own
smoke... Learn to accept in silence the
minor aggravations, cultivate the gift
of taciturnity and consume your own
smoke with an extra draught of hard
work, so that those about you may not
be annoyed with the dust and soot of
your complaints. More than any other
the practitioner of medicine may illus-
trate the second great lesson, that
we are here not to get all we can out
of life for ourselves, but to try to make
the lives of others happier... And the
third lesson you may learn is the
hardest of all — that the law of the
higher life is only fulfilled by love, i.e.,
charity.

> SIR WILLIAM OSLER, "The master-
> word in medicine", address at Univ.
> of Toronto, 1903.

Alter the golden rule — what you do
not like when done to yourself, do
not do to others.

> SIR WILLIAM OSLER, *Oslerisms*
> (Bean), 1905.

By far the most dangerous foe we
have to fight is *apathy* — indifference
from whatever cause, not from a lack
of knowledge, but from carelessness,
from absorption in other pursuits,
from a contempt bred of self-satis-
faction.

> SIR WILLIAM OSLER, address,
> "Unity, peace and concord", 1905.

I soon discovered that if I ever
accomplished anything in life, it would
be by pursuing my object with a persistent determination to attain it. I had
neither the training nor the talents to
accomplish anything without hard work,
and fortunately I knew it.

> GEORGE STEPHEN, Lord Mount
> Stephen, on receiving the freedom
> of the city of Aberdeen, Scotland,
> 1911.

There's very little honey
These days for any man:

Take it where you find it!
Taste it while you can!

> TOM MACINNIS, "Now then",
> 1918.

As for you who stand on the threshold of life, with a long horizon open
before you for a long career of usefulness to your native land, if you
will permit me, after a long life, I
shall remind you that already many
problems rise before you. Let me tell
you that for the solution of these
problems you have a safe guide, an
unfailing light, if you remember that
faith is better than doubt and love is
better than hate.

Banish doubt and fear from your
life. Let your souls be ever open to
the promptings of faith and the gentle
influence of brotherly love. Be adamant
against the haughty, be gentle and
kind to the weak. Let your aim and
purpose, in good or ill, in victory or
defeat, be so to live, so to strive, so to
serve, as to do your part to raise ever
higher the standard of life and of
living.

> SIR WILFRID LAURIER, speech
> to Ontario Liberal Club convention,
> London, Oct. 11, 1916.

Oh, I eat all I can; I drink all I
can; I smoke all I can; and I don't
give a damn for anything.

> SIR WILLIAM VAN HORNE, qu. in
> Vaughan *Van Horne* 1920, 272.

Behold a marvel! — He that stays
At the utmost fringes of his days,
He only a centre hath always.

> WARWICK CHIPMAN, "Immortality",
> 1930.

CONFEDERATION.

> (See also: BRITISH NORTH
> AMERICA ACT, 1867; CONFED-
> ERATION, FATHERS OF; GOV-
> ERNMENT, etc.)

A general union of all the Provinces
might in my opinion be so modified as
to regenerate British North America
but a partial union appears to me
pregnant with evil.

> JOHN STRACHAN, Letterbook, Mar.
> 10, 1839, Ontario Archives.

We desire free trade among all the
Provinces, under our national flag,

with one coin, one measure, one tariff, one Post Office. We feel that the courts, the press, the educational institutions of North America, would be elevated by union; that intercommunication by railroads, telegraphs and steamboats would be promoted; and that, if such a combination of interests were achieved wisely and with proper guards, the foundations of a great nation, in friendly connection with the mother country, would be laid on an indestructible basis.

JOSEPH HOWE, letter to George Moffatt, May 8, 1849.

Resolved: — That whether protection or reciprocity shall be conceded or withheld, it is essential to the welfare of this colony, and its future good government, that a Constitution should be framed in unison with the wishes of the people, and suited to the growing importance and intelligence of the country, and that such Constitution should embrace a union of the British North American Provinces on mutually advantageous terms, with the concession from the Mother Country of enlarged powers of self-government.

BRITISH AMERICAN LEAGUE, Proc., Nov. 3, 1849.

Resolved, that the union of confederation of the British Provinces on just principles, while calculated to perpetuate their connection with the parent State, will promote their advancement and prosperity, increase their strength and influence, and elevate their position.

JAMES W. JOHNSTONE, Conservative leader of the Opposition, resolution passed in N.S. Legislature, 1854.

See what an empire is here, surely the best in climate, soil, mineral, and other productions in the world, and peopled by such a race, as no other country under heaven can produce. No, Sir, here are the bundle of sticks; all they want is to be united.

THOMAS C. HALIBURTON, Nature and human nature, 1855.

That in view of the rapid development of the population and resources of Western Canada, irreconcilable difficulties present themselves to the maintenance of that equality which formed the basis of the Union of Upper and Lower Canada, and require this House to consider the means whereby the progress which has so happily characterized this province may not be arrested through the occurrence of sectional jealousies and dissensions. It is therefore the opinion of this House that the Union of Upper and Lower Canada should be changed from a Legislative to a Federative Union by the subdivision of the province into two more divisions, each governing itself in local and sectional matters, with a general legislature and government for subjects of national and common interest...

SIR ALEXANDER T. GALT, resolution moved in House of Assembly, July 7, 1858 (Votes and proc., 513).

That a general confederation of the Provinces of New Brunswick, Nova Scotia, Newfoundland and Prince Edward Island with Canada and the Western Territories, is most desirable, and calculated to promote their several and united interests, by preserving to each Province the uncontrolled management of its peculiar institutions, and of those internal affairs, respecting which differences of opinion might arise with other members of the Confederation, while it will increase that identity of feeling which pervades in possessions of the British Crown in North America.

SIR ALEXANDER T. GALT, resolution moved in House of Assembly, Toronto, July 7, 1858.

Is this federation proposed as a step towards nationality? If so, I am with you. Federation implies nationality. For colonial purposes only it would be a needless incumbrance.

GEORGE SHEPPARD, at convention of Upper Canada Reformers, Toronto, Nov., 1859.

I do place the question on the grounds of nationality. I do hope there is not one Canadian in this assembly who does not look forward with high hope to the day when these northern countries shall stand out among the nations of the world as one great Confederation... Who does not feel that to us rightfully belong the right and the duty of carrying the blessings of civilization throughout those boundless regions, and making our own country the highway of traffic to the Pacific?

> GEORGE BROWN, speech to Reform Convention, Toronto, Nov., 1859.

The only feasible scheme which represents itself to my mind as a remedy for the evils complained of, is a confederation of all the provinces. In speaking of a confederation, I must not be understood as alluding to it in the sense of the one on the other side of the line, for that has not been successful...

> SIR JOHN A. MACDONALD, speech in the Legislature, April 19, 1861.

Let the dog return to his vomit rather than Canada to division. In conclusion, I am pleased to think the day is rapidly approaching when the Provinces will be united, with one flag above our heads, one thought in all our bosoms, with one Sovereign and one constitution.

> JOSEPH HOWE, speech in Halifax to leaders of Confederation from the Canadas, Aug. 13, 1864.

Who will oppose — who are now opposed to our union? Only those who have a vested interest in their own insignificance.

> THOMAS D'A. McGEE, "Prospects of the Union", remarks at Halifax, Aug. 14, 1864.

This question has now assumed a position that demands and commands the attention of all the colonies of British America. There may be obstructions, local prejudices may arise, disputes may occur, local jealousies may intervene, but it matters not — the wheel is now revolving and we are only the fly on the wheel; we cannot delay it — the union of the colonies of British America under the Sovereign is a fixed fact.

> SIR JOHN A. MACDONALD, speech in Halifax, Sept. 12, 1864.

The Botheration Scheme.

> JOSEPH HOWE, anti-Confederation letters, in Halifax *Morning Chronicle*, Jan. 11 - Mar. 2, 1865.

Messrs Tupper, Archibald and McCully, when the deed is done, may escape to Canada and stifle, as Arnold did, the reproofs of conscience amidst the excitements of a wider sphere and of more lucrative employment. But what is to become of the poor dupes who have been their accomplices in this dark transaction? Nineteen-twentieths of them will live and die at home, and all their lives must behold the averted faces of their indignant countrymen; and creep at last to dishonoured graves in the bosom of the province they have betrayed, to poison the worms that consume them beneath the soil to which they were untrue.

> JOSEPH HOWE, "The Botheration Papers" no. 9, 1865.

Some entertained the opinion that it was unnecessary to have British North American confederation to prevent absorption into the vortex of American Confederation. Such parties were mistaken.

> SIR GEORGE CARTIER, *Confederation debates*, Feb. 7, 1865, 55.

Events stronger than advocacy, events stronger than men, have come in at last like the fire behind the invisible writing to bring out the truth of these writings and to impress them upon the mind of every thoughtful man who has considered the position and probable future of these provinces.

> THOMAS D'A. McGEE, *Confederation debates*, Feb. 9, 1865, 127, on the previous advocates of federation.

We are in the rapids and must go on.

> THOMAS D'A. McGEE, *Confederation debates*, Feb. 9, 1865, 134.

By its slender and elongated form, the rainbow would afford a perfect representation of the geographical configuration of Confederation. By its lack of consistence — an image without substance — the rainbow would represent aptly the solidity of our Confederation.

> HENRI G. JOLY, *Confederation debates*, Feb 20, 1865, 354.

Prince Edward Island will have to come in, for if she does not we will have to tow her into the St. Lawrence.

> THOMAS D'ARCY McGEE, 1865, attributed.

Little Boy: "Father, what country do we live in? Father: "My dear son, you have no country, for Mr. Tilley has sold us all to the Canadians for eighty cents a head."

ANDREW R. WETMORE, New Brunswick election, March, 1865, imaginary dialogue between himself and his son told in his anti-Confederation speeches.

We are sold for the price of a sheepskin.

JOSEPH HOWE, speeches in Nova Scotia, 1866. In the *Novascotian*, Aug. 13, 1866, he wrote that a visit of Tupper and Archibald to Ottawa to arrange a license system for American fishermen was really to sell the Nova Scotians for eighty cents a head, the per capita amount of the grant to Nova Scotia on entering Confederation. T. C. Haliburton, *Old judge*, 1849, ("Sheepskins and politics") uses the phrase, "Are you going to sell your country for a sheepskin?"

If the Imperial Government should refuse our prayer, we shall then have to appeal to another nation to come to our aid.

MARTIN WILKINS, Attorney-General, N. S. House of Assembly, 1867, in an anti-Confederation speech.

We need above everything else the healing influence of time.

THOMAS D'A. McGEE, speech in House of Commons, April 5, 1868; on agitation in Nova Scotia for repeal of Confederation.

We will compel them to come in and accept this union, we will compel them by our fairness, our kindness, our love, to be one with us, in this common and this great national work.

THOMAS D'A. McGEE, speech, House of Commons, April 5, 1868; on agitation in Nova Scotia for repeal of Confederation.

Confederation is only yet in the gristle, and it will require five years more before it hardens into bone.

SIR JOHN A. MACDONALD, letter to Sir John Rose, March 5, 1872.

The immediate causes of Canadian Confederation were clearly enough the deadlock in the Canadian Parliament.

GOLDWIN SMITH, *Can. monthly*, Aug., 1872, 172; also, "The Father of Confederation was Deadlock", *The Bystander*, April 1883, 86; also, "Whoever may claim to the parentage of Confederation — and upon this momentous question there has been much controversy — its real parent was Deadlock", *Canada and the Can. question*, 1891, 143.

Awake, my country, the hour is great with change!

CHARLES G. D. ROBERTS, "Ode for the Canadian Confederacy", 1880.

A great opportunity was lost in 1867 when the Dominion was formed out of the several provinces. This remarkable event in the history of the British Empire, passed almost without notice.

SIR JOHN A. MACDONALD, letter to Lord Knutsford, July 18, 1889.

I have devoted my career to the realization of an idea. I have taken the work of Confederation where I found it when I entered political life, and determined to give to it my life, and nothing will deter me from continuing to the end in my task to preserve at all price our civil liberty.

SIR WILFRID LAURIER, speech before Club National, Montreal, Dec. 30, 1896. (trans.)

Confederation is a compact, made originally by four provinces but adhered to by all the nine provinces who have entered it, and I submit to the judgment of this house and to the best consideration of its members, that this compact should not be lightly altered.

SIR WILFRID LAURIER, H. of C., *Debates*, 1907.

In the hearts and minds of the delegates who assembled in this room on Sept. 1, 1864 was born the Dominion of Canada.

———

Providence being their guide
They builded better than they knew.

Inscription on plaque erected 1917, unveiled July 1927, in Legislative chamber, Charlottetown; the quoted lines are from MILTON, *Paradise lost*, book xii, and EMERSON, "The problem" (adapted).

I believe in the Canadian Confederation.

> SIR LOMER GOUIN, speech in Legislative Assembly, Quebec, Jan. 23, 1918.

When McGee became its preaching friar from Sarnia to Halifax it was changed into a gospel rich in personal values and shot through with faith in personal redemption.

> W. P. M. KENNEDY, in *Can. hist. rev.*, 1925, 167.

Confederation itself, it will now be conceded, was almost a miracle.

> CHESTER MARTIN, in *Can. hist. rev.*, 1937, 1.

Lacking materials out of which to reconstruct the story, or to discover how the scheme had come to be, historians have, almost to our own day, complacently accepted the stork theory of confederation.

> W. M. WHITELAW, in *Can. hist. rev.*, 1938, 126.

Federation in 1867 became the instrument for westward expansion. It was the political expedient for bringing the West under the control of the St. Lawrence Valley.

> R. G. RIDDELL, in *Can. hist. rev.*, 1940, 270.

CONFEDERATION, FATHERS OF

The Fathers of Confederation.

> Term applied to the 33 delegates at the Quebec conference, October, 1864.

Among the Ministers I made many friends — John (usually called Jack) Macdonald, Sir Francis Hincks, Sir William [sic] M'Nab, Cartier, Brown a journalist, and several others. All able men with unlimited powers of consuming champagne.

> SIR EDMUND HORNBY, (1854), *Autobiography*, 1928, 64.

If Macdonald is entitled to be called the Father of Confederation it would appear that Alexander Hamilton has some claim to be designated as its grandfather.

> W. B. MUNRO, *Amer. influences on Can. govt.*, 1929, 20.

Statesmen they were by every fair test; but they were politicians too — politicians resourceful and not too scrupulous.

> J. W. DAFOE, in *Can. hist. rev.*, 1932, 52.

[Thomas] Dalton has been called the godfather of Confederation, as he was one of the first Colonial writers to urge a federation of the provinces.

> R. CARD, in *Can. hist. rev.*, 1935, 177.

The intentions of the Fathers of Confederation... have in fact been largely frustrated by judicial decision, especially those of Lord Haldane, who might very suitably be termed the Step-father of Confederation.

> E. FORSEY, *C. J. E. P. S.*, 1936, 596.

THE CONQUEST, 1759.

Happy Laurentia, to thy farthest shore,
Lavish of life, a chosen band she led;
And to those royal towers her standard bore,
Whence fell Oppression, Gallic tyrant, fled.

> W. H. REYNALL, in, *Pietas universitatis Oxoniensis...*, 1761.

He who has conquered by force has only half vanquished his enemy.

> FRANÇOIS-XAVIER GARNEAU, about 1826, to the English clerks in the office of Archibald Campbell, a Quebec notary.

The statement that has been made so often that this is a conquered country is *à propos de rien*. Whether it was conquered or ceded, we have a constitution now under which all British subjects are in a position of absolute equality having equal rights of every kind — of language, of religion, of property and of person. There is no paramount race in this country; we are all British subjects, and those who are not English are none the less British subjects on that account.

> SIR JOHN A. MACDONALD, H. of C., *Debates*, Feb. 17, 1890, 745.

A happier calamity never befell a people than the conquest of Canada by the British arms.

> FRANCIS PARKMAN, attributed.

CONSCRIPTION, MILITARY.

The volunteers themselves found how ineffective the voluntary system was, and how unfairly it worked. While they were not only undergoing the hardships and dangers of campaigning, but were also suffering financial loss, their stay-at-home fellow-countrymen, whom they were defending, were making money and were at ease in Zion.

> ANON., 1870, in *Can. hist. rev.*, 1923, 101.

We have never ceased to say that a tax-of-blood is the logical and inevitable consequence of the principles and acts imposed by the two parties who have in turn ruled this country. The germ of Conscription was contained in the volunteer expedition to South Africa.

> HENRI BOURASSA, in *Le Devoir*, May 29, 1917. (trans.)

We will resist Conscription and we will not have Conscription, not because we are cowards, but because we have received from God and the King the mission of making of this country a prosperous land and not one of exile and misery.

> HENRI BOURASSA, speech in Montreal, June 7, 1917. (trans.)

The basic principle of the State is compulsion. This is fundamental in its entire organization. It runs through every system of law, both civil and criminal, through practically all the conventions of society; without it law, order, system and organization could not exist.

> SIR JAMES LOUGHEED, Senate *Debates*, Aug. 3, 1917, on Conscription.

If, in reference to the very difficult question of service overseas, anyone can conceive of a policy which is better calculated to serve the national interest, than the one the government has formulated, and which is clearly and concisely expressed in the words: "Not necessarily conscription, but conscription if necessary," I shall be first to advocate its acceptance.

> W. L. MACKENZIE KING, H. of C., *Debates*, July 7, 1942, 4011; probably adapted from editorial, Toronto *Star*, June 11, 1942.

CONSERVATISM.

The Conservative, who defends his country's old institutions, may do much good, as he also may do much evil, if he be obstinate in maintaining abuses, which have become intolerable.

> SIR WILFRID LAURIER, speech to Club Canadien, Quebec, June, 1877. (trans.)

Conservatism and old fogeyism are totally different things; the motto of the one is, "Prove all things, and hold fast that which is good," and of the other, "Prove nothing, but hold fast that which is old".

> SIR WILLIAM OSLER. "Importance of post-graduate study" in *Lancet*, 1900.

CONSERVATIVE PARTY.

> (See also: CANADIAN PACIFIC RAILWAY; POLITICAL PARTIES)

Never did we see such an assemblage of long-visaged Tories. They appeared as if they were following the hearse of conservatism to the grave.

> BATHURST COURIER, Feb. 5, 1836, on the departure of Sir John Colborne from Toronto.

The party nowhere — damned, everlastingly damned.

> SIR JOHN A. MACDONALD. 1854, qu. in letter by A. Campbell, Pub. Arch. of Can., *Macdonald papers*, March 8, 1855.

So pray do become true blue at once: it is a good standing colour and bears washing.

> SIR JOHN A. MACDONALD, to Sir Alexander T. Galt, letter, Nov. 2, 1857.

It is well known, sir, that while I have always been a member of what is called the Conservative party, I could never have been called a Tory, although there is no man who more respects what is called old-fogey Toryism than I do, so long as it is based upon principle.

> SIR JOHN A. MACDONALD, speech in St. Thomas, 1860.

The heart of the average Tory is deceitful above all thengs and desperately wecked.

> ALEXANDER MACKENZIE, Prime Minister, speech at Clinton, Ont., July 5, 1878.

If I could only go to the country I would sweep the Grits into the sea.

> SIR JOHN A. MACDONALD, to his friends, 1877-8; qu., Biggar, *Anecdotal life*, 167.

We say no matter what your antecedents are, whether you are an old Tory, a Baldwin Reformer, or whatever you were in the past, if you honestly and conscientiously agree with us and our policy for the country in the future, we stretch out to you the right hand of fellowship and greet you as a Liberal-Conservative or a Conservative-Liberal.

> SIR JOHN A. MACDONALD, qu., *Willison's monthly*, 1927, 84.

If there is one thing to which the Conservative party has been true in the past; if there is one thing to which I hope it will be true in the future. it is the unity of the races in Canada.

> ROBERT L. BORDEN, speech in Ottawa, Mar. 1, 1901.

In Quebec the Conservative Party is a pretty lively corpse.

> J.-G.-H. BERGERON, speech in Toronto, Dec. 14, 1905.

Failing principles the Conservatives fell back on personalities.

> STEPHEN LEACOCK, *National rev.*, Jan., 1909.

Looking again to the future, and bringing up the past only to shed its light, let me say: There will be more danger on the side of the party itself than on the side of the leader you will choose. Even here at this Convention the supreme consideration is not: who shall be the leader of the party? The supreme consideration is: what manner of party shall he have to lead?

> ARTHUR MEIGHEN, speech at Winnipeg Conservative Convention, Oct. 10, 1927.

For a long time the Conservatives had a corner on superiority and. for a long time, a corner on patriotism. I mean one's devotion to one's country was always an open question, unless one is a Conservative and an Anglican. If you are a Conservative, a Methodist and an Orangeman, you can get by.

> AGNES MACPHAIL, speech to Canadian Club, Toronto, Mar. 4, 1935.

The Conservative Party must stand for all that its name implies. The word "Conservative" suggests stability and security at a time when the whole world longs for stability and security. The word implies sound business methods as opposed to radical experiments. In a world gone mad the word "Conservative" offers hope of common sense and orderly progress. It is a word which carries into the realm of practical politics the Biblical injunction "prove all things; hold fast that which is good".

> GEORGE DREW, speech in Toronto, April 17, 1940.

CONSTITUTION.

That it is desirable to give the Canadians a constitution in every respect like the constitution of Great Britain, I will not say, but I earnestly hope that they will enjoy as much of our laws and as much of our constitution as may be beneficial for that country, and safe for this.

> LORD NORTH, H. of C. (London), *Debates*, 1774, 248. ed. by Cavendish.

You know my enthusiasm respecting the constitution of England. Every encomium I ever read in its favour is short of my idea of its perfection;... of all modes of government I pronounce it to be the best.

> CHIEF JUSTICE WM. SMITH, letter to B. Watson, Oct. 24, 1788 (Pub. Arch.)

This province is singularly blessed. not with a mutilated Constitution. but with a Constitution which has stood the test of experience, and is the very image and transcript of that of Great Britain.

> JOHN GRAVES SIMCOE, Lieut.-gov., at close of first Upper Canada legislature session, Oct. 15, 1792.

So much for the wisdom of giving a British Constitution to men who can neither read nor write, and who are mulish, enough to refuse and kick at those who ought to lead.

LORD DALHOUSIE, letter, May 5, 1822.

Preserve the balance of the constitution for your life.

T. C. HALIBURTON, *Sam Slick*, 1838, 58.

You may change constitutions for ever, but you cannot change man.

T. C. HALIBURTON, *Sam Slick*, 1840, 264.

We want not only the Constitution, but as regards the administration of our local affairs, the whole Constitution and nothing but the Constitution.

ROBERT BALDWIN, speech to Reform Association, Mar. 25, 1844; the motto of the Brockville *Gazette* (1828 - 32) was, "The Constitution, the whole Constitution, and nothing but the Constitution".

Not one hair's breadth farther do we go, or desire to go: but not with one hair's breadth short of that will we ever be satisfied.

ROBERT BALDWIN, reference to the English constitution, on objects of the Reform Association, founded, Toronto, 1844.

In framing the constitution care should be taken to avoid the mistakes and weaknesses of the United States system, the primary error of which was the reservation to the different states of all powers not delegated to the general government. We must reverse this process by establishing a strong central government to which shall belong all powers not specially conferred on the provinces. Canada, in my opinion, is better off as she stands than she would be as a member of a confederacy composed of five sovereign states, which would be the result if the powers of the local governments were not defined. A strong central government is indispensable to the success of the experiment we are trying.

SIR JOHN A. MACDONALD, speech at Quebec Conference, Oct. 11, 1864.

The ink was scarcely dry upon our Constitution when we began to think constitutionally. We began to think federally.

G. W. ROSS, Empire club speech, May 12, 1905.

As I advance in years I appreciate the more the wisdom of that British Constitution under which I was born and brought up, and under which I have grown old, which has given to the various portions of the Empire their separate free governments.

SIR WILFRID LAURIER, address at Tercentenary Celebration, Quebec, 1908.

Canada stands practically alone in modern, self-governing, democratic countries in her inability to change her constitution in accordance with what may be the development of political thought.

SIR CLIFFORD SIFTON, in *Can. hist. rev.*, 1922, 9.

Preposterous as it may seem, no one knows where the constitution begins or ends.

H. McD. CLOKIE, in *C.J.E.P.S.*, 1942, 1.

CO-OPERATIVES.

There are still moments at meetings of Canadian agriculturalists when one feels that co-operation is a veneer; when the women are in the room the apprehension vanishes.

C. R. FAY, *Co-op. at home and abroad*, 1924.

True co-operation is wrung out of the bitter need of the weak.

H. MICHELL, in *C.J.E.P.S.*, 1937, 410.

CORRUPTION.

(See also: BRIBERY; PATRONAGE)

Down with Rolph and Malcolm Cameron. We can stand anything else — we can stand Toryism, we can stand Sir Allan McNab and John A. Macdonald, but we cannot stand Rolph. Corrupt may be Sir Allan McNab and steeped to the chin in Toryism, and

John A. Macdonald may be following in his footsteps, a budding Tory at least — they are not bad fellows, however, for Tories — but put down Rolph and Cameron.

> TORONTO *Globe*, during election 1851; Rolph and Cameron were Clear Grits.

They have Walpoles in the ministry, not Pitts; the government is steeped to the very lips in infamy; they are tainted with corruption, collectively and individually, both in their public and private characters. All honour has gone from them, and all loyalty even to one another; and the only bond by which they are held together now is the bond of common plunder.

> SIR JOHN A. MACDONALD, speech on address from the throne, Legis. Assembly, 1854; origin of the phrase, "steeped to the lips in corruption".

Corruption pervades every tissue of our society.

> SIR WILFRID LAURIER, letter to Blake, Dec. 7, 1881.

Another mistake which our leaders make is this — they seem to think the people are pure. It is a great mistake; they are as corrupt as the government that represents them at Ottawa. Until the Reformers can score one against Sir John by superior low cunning, they will be beaten at the elections.

> CONSTANT READER, in the Toronto *Globe*, May, 1882.

The name of Peter McGonigle will ever stand high on the roll of eminent confiscators.

> ROBERT C. (BOB) EDWARDS, *Calgary Eyeopener*, Oct. 6, 1906.

I shall allow no man to make an attack on me or my character without retorting. I shall discuss the character of Honourable members opposite whether they be Ministers or private members and their connection with wine, women and graft.

> GEORGE W. FOWLER, H. of C., *Debates*, Feb. 19, 1907, in answer to remarks by Duncan Ross, M.P.; this led subsequently to the resignation of a cabinet minister.

Men, as a rule, do not and cannot rise above the level of their general environment; and under our form of party government, if one side becomes corrupt, more especially if after proof of its corruption it is successful for a time, it is pretty certain to corrupt a great many of the other side also, or at any rate to lower the whole tone of public life.

> SIR RICHARD CARTWRIGHT, *Reminiscences*, 1912, 199.

Graft is still graft even if you call it a commission.

> ROBERT C. (BOB) EDWARDS, *Calgary Eye Opener*; attributed.

COURAGE.

A brave man is sometimes a desperado. A bully is always a coward.

> T. C. HALIBURTON, *Sam Slick's wise saws*, 1853, I, 105.

Be hooted and hissed by the mob,
From pillar to post be driven.
Be sneered at by every snob:
Of such is the kingdom of heaven.

> ALEXANDER MCLACHLAN, "Cowardice", 1900.

Strong for the red rage of battle;
sane, for I harry them sore;
Send me men girt for the combat,
men who are grit to the core.

> ROBERT SERVICE, "The law of the Yukon", 1907.

There are times when it requires more courage to stand still than to go forward.

> JOHN OLIVER, when premier of B. C., 1918-27.

If there were no cowards there would be no bullies.

> GEORGE ILES, *Canadian stories*, 1918, 170.

Courage, cleanliness, charity:
Hold by these to the end of the tether,
For only these may lead us free:
We who are all in the mud together.

> TOM MACINNES, "Ballade of virtues", 1918.

COWS.

And the ladies dress in silk
From the proceeds of the milk,
But those who buy their butter,
How dear it is, they mutter.
JAMES McINTYRE, "Oxford cheese
makers song", 1884.

When potatoes were in blossom,
When the new hay filled the mows,
Sweet the paths we trod together,
Bringing home the cows.
CHARLES G. D. ROBERTS, "Bring-
ing home the cows", 1893.

Their bodies glisten sharply red,
With shaggy brow and curving horn,
Large waggling ear, grass-bending
head.
With dainty hoof and solemn lurch
They munch along their quiet search.
ALAN CREIGHTON, "Pastoral", 1936.

CRITICS.

And still in the honest working world
With posture and hint and smirk,
These sons of the devil are standing
by
While Man does all the work.
They balk endeavor and baffle reform,
In the sacred name of law;
And over the quavering voice of Hem,
Is the droning voice of Haw.
BLISS CARMAN, "Hem and Haw,"
1895.

Bow down, ye scribes, before the
mighty *Week*,
Malicious vendor of the base critique,
Lean Egoist, that claims the right
divine
To whip the slavish scribblers into
line.
ALEXANDER C. STEWART. *The poetical review*, 1896, 20; Goldwin Smith
was editor of the *Week*.

The Critic, Sir, the Critic is to blame
Who with insulting clemency misuses
One rule for home, and one for
foreign, muses.
L. A. MACKAY, "And spoil the
child", 1931.

True feeling is critical as well as
honest thought.
JOHN MACNAUGHTON, Essays, 1946.

THE CROWN.

(See also: THE KING;
STATUS)

The Crown must consent to carry the
government on by means of those in
whom the representative members have
confidence.
LORD DURHAM, *Report*, 1839.

Disguise it how you may, the idea
that underlies this plan is this, and
nothing else — that we are to create
here a something — kingdom, vice-
royalty or principality — something
that will soon stand in the same
position towards the British Crown
that Scotland and Ireland stood in
before they were legislatively united
with England; a something having no
other tie to the Empire than the one
tie of fealty to the British Crown.
CHRISTOPHER DUNKIN, *Confederation debates*, 1865, 527.

It must be remembered the sovereign holds a two-fold position; that the
sovereign is not only the first branch
of the legislature, and as such has
a right to inquire into such matters,
but is also the head of the executive
and is the executive. The crown
governs the country; the crown chooses
its own ministers, and this house has
no control, and the Senate has no
control over the crown in this respect,
except in deciding whether they have
confidence in the ministers chosen.
SIR JOHN A. MACDONALD, H. of
C., *Debates*, Nov. 3, 1873.

The Crown is the supreme executive
in the United Kingdom and in all
the Dominions, but it acts on the advice
of different Ministries with different
constitutional units; and under Resolution IX of the Imperial War Conference, 1917, the organization of the
Empire is to be based upon equality
of nationhood.
SIR ROBERT BORDEN, Memorandum
circulated on behalf of the Dominion Prime Ministers, at the Paris
peace conference, Mar, 12, 1919.

CULTURE.

(See also: ART)

I'm sick of refinement, I'm weary of
art,

I hate all refinement that withers
the heart;
Away with your dandies your crea-
tures of steam,
With nothing but buttons where
hearts should have been.

ALEXANDER MCLACHAN, "I long not
for riches", 1856.

How utterly destitute of all light
and charm are the intellectual conditions of our people and the institutions
of our public life! How barren! How
barbarous!

ARCHIBALD LAMPMAN, in *The
Globe*, Feb. 27, 1892.

We forget that the measure of the
value of a nation to the world is
neither the bushel nor the barrel, but
mind; and that wheat and pork, though
useful and necessary, are but dross in
comparison with those intellectual pro-
ducts which alone are imperishable.

SIR WILLIAM OSLER, "Teacher and
student", 1892, in *Aequanimitas*.

Culture is the consciousness of truth
expressed in conduct. Good form
appears to be the accumulated weariness of centuries expressed in a
general air of boredom.

PETER MCARTHUR, *To be taken
with salt*, 1903, 149.

With the Greek, let us measure our
contribution to civilization in what we
give to the humanities. With the He-
brew, let us believe that God continues
to work through the centuries and
that He may work for continents as
well as men. With the founder of
our faith, let us believe that all life
is sacred and all human life but the
reflected image of the Divine.

W. L. MACKENZIE KING, speech
"Culture and religion", 1914.

French culture in Canada rested on
twin factors: the vitality of ancestral
traditions coupled with isolation.

MARIUS BARBEAU, *Quebec*, 1936.

Let any English-speaking Canadian
sit down in his corner and divest himself of whatever is American in origin
and impulse and culturally and intel-
lectually he'll look like a half-skinned
rabbit.

ARTHUR PHELPS, *These United
States*, 1941.

To be truly and productively cultivated three things are necessary, and
three only. The first is to appropriate
all the heritage of the past (or at least
as much of it as can be compassed):
the second is to see the present as it
really is, unobscured by prejudice and
wishful thinking; the third is frankly
to speak forth one's findings in one's
own idiom — which may be national
or continental or even imperial, but
which in our present state of development is most likely to be sectional.

A. S. P. WOODHOUSE, in *Univ.
Tor. quart.*, April 1941, 350.

CUSTOM.

When a custom can and ought to
be follered, foller it. When it can't,
set your own compass and steer your
own course.

T. C. HALIBURTON, *Sam Slick's
wise saws*, 1853, II, 146.

The morality of convention cannot be
overvalued. It is based on consideration for others, and that is the beginning of morality. There is a religion
in ritual itself, and ritual is not monarchical, it is human and everlasting.

GILBERT PARKER, *Tarboe*, 1927.

D

DAY.

And with one foot on the water,
And one upon the shore,
The Angel of Shadow gives warning
That day shall be no more.

JOHN G. WHITTIER, "Red River
voyageur", 1854.

The pensive afterthoughts of sundown
sink
Over the patient acres given to peace;
The homely cries and farmstead noises
cease,
And the worn day relaxes, link by
link.

CHARLES G. D. ROBERTS, "Where
the cattle come to drink", 1896.

Lovely the day, when life is robed in
splendour,
Walking the ways of God and
strong with wine:

But the pale eve is wonderful and
tender,
And night is more divine.
> Marjorie Pickthall, *The drift of
> pinions*, 1913.

The day is done, done, done. The
day is done.
> Duncan Campbell Scott, "The
> end of the day", 1935.

DEATH.

(See also: Immortality;
War Dead)

Let the dead be, we don't often
inherit their talents or their money;
and if we did, why should we be
answerable for their follies?
> T. C. Haliburton, *Sam Slick's
> wise saws*, 1853, II, 140.

Arrived this day at the canyon at
10 a.m. and drowned running the canoe
down. God bless my poor wife.
> J. Carpenter, of Toronto, an Over-
> lander going to the Cariboo, B. C.,
> entry in his diary, Sept. 30, 1862,
> before losing his life in the rapids
> of the Grand Canyon, Fraser River.

Never yet did the assassin's knife
reach the core of a cause or the heart
of a principle.
> Thomas D'A. McGee, speech in
> Montreal, on the death of Lincoln,
> 1865.

The flesh that I wore chanced ever
to be
Less of my friend than my enemy.
So bury it deeply — strong foe,
weak friend —
And bury it cheaply — and there it
ends.
> Isabella V. Crawford, "His clay",
> in Toronto *Evening telegram*, Oct.
> 22, 1884.

As for me, I'm time-weary,
I await my release.
Give to others the struggle,
Grant me but the peace;
And what peace like the peace
Which Death offers the brave?
What rest like the rest
Which we find in the grave?
> Nicholas F. Davin, "An epic of
> the dawn", 1884.

Dear friend, I know this world is
kin,
And all of hate is but a breath:
We all are friends, made perfect in
Our near relationship by death.
> George F. Cameron, "Death",
> 1887.

Death always carries with it an in-
credible sense of pain; but the one
thing sad in death is that which is
involved in the word separation —
separation from all we love in life.
> Sir Wilfrid Laurier, H. of C.,
> *Debates*, June 8, 1891.

The hands were wrinkled; the face
was cold; the body was wet; the man
was drowned and dead.
> Gilbert Parker, *Pierre and his
> people*, 1892.

Bury me early in the morning, that
only my friends may take the trouble
to get up in time to follow me to the
grave.
> Sir Matthew Baillie Begbie, a
> few days before his death at
> Victoria on June 11, 1894.

The wind of death that softly blows
The last warm petal from the rose,
The last dry leaf from off the tree,
To-night has come to breathe on
me.
The wind of death, that silently
Enshroudeth friend and enemy.
> Ethelwyn Wetherald, "The wind
> of death", 1896.

So often have I met death face to
face
His eyes now wear the welcome of
a friend's.
> Frederick G. Scott, "Dion", 1899.

For you, as once of old you came,
at last
Would surely come, and with unfaltering faith
Lead me beyond the dominance of
death.
> Francis Sherman, "The house of
> night" 1899.

As a rule, man dies as he had lived,
uninfluenced by the thought of a future
life.
> Sir William Osler, *Science and
> immortality*, 1904.

Master, I've filled my contract,
  wrought in Thy many lands;
Not by my sins wilt Thou judge
  me, but by the work of my hands.
Master, I've done Thy bidding, and
  the light is low in the west.
And the long, long shift is over...
  Master, I've earned it — Rest.

> ROBERT SERVICE, "Song of the wage-
> slave", 1907.

Nothing is to me more odious than
the pageantry of death.

> GOLDWIN SMITH, *Reminiscences*,
> 1910, 46.

Too dear for death to dim, or life
cast down.

> MARJORIE PICKTHALL, "Vale", 1916.

Call no man happy till he dies.

> SIR WILLIAM OSLER, *Diary*, Aug.
> 31, 1917, on the death of his son
> killed in action.

All now is over,
The dream is done.
Fasten the cover,
Shut out the sun.
Farewell to lover,
To rival, to friend,
To sorrow, to splendour,
To earth's weird wonder,
For this is the end.

> WILFRED CAMPBELL, "Requiem",
> 1918.

We must all in the graveyard lie:
  This is the last of certainties:
Strange horizons some descry,
  That to the masses are fantasies:
But take your choice of theories
To meet an end so villainous,
  In this at least each one agrees:
This World of our goes ruinous.

> TOM MACINNES, "Ballade of woe-
> ful certainties", 1918.

Out of the winds' and the waves'
  riot,
  Out of the loud foam,
He has put in to a great quiet
  And a still home.

> MARJORIE PICKTHALL, "Ebb tide",
> 1923.

Easily to the old
Opens the hard ground:
But when youth grows cold,
  And red lips have no sound,
Bitterly does the earth

Open to receive
And bitterly do the grasses
In the churchyard grieve.

> WILSON MACDONALD, "Exit", 1926.

Without a hail at parting
Or any colors shown,
My friend has gone aboard her
For the Isles of the Unknown.

> BLISS CARMAN, "Passing strange,"
> 1929.

This is the sheath, the sword drawn;
  These are the lips, the Word
  spoken;
This is Calvary toward dawn;
  And this is the third day token —
The opened tomb and the Lord gone:
  Something Whole that was broken.

> A. J. M. SMITH, "Beside one
> dead", 1938.

I said that he fell straight to the ice
  where they found him,
And none but the sun and the in-
  curious clouds have lingered
Around the marks of that day on
  the ledge of the Finger,
That day, the last of my youth, on
  the last of our mountains.

> EARLE BIRNEY, "David", 1942.

DEEDS AND DOING.

> (See also: PEOPLE; SUC-
> CESS; WORK)

He put his foot in it.

> T. C. HALIBURTON, *Sam Slick*,
> 1838, 123.

If a bear comes after you, Sam, you
must be up and doin' or it's a gone
goose with you.

> THOMAS C. HALIBURTON, *Sam
> Slick in England*, 1843, ch. XVIII.

Pretty is as pretty does.

> THOMAS C. HALIBURTON, *Sam
> Slick's wise saws*, 1853, ch. VI.

There is a way of doin' everything,
if you only know how to go about it.

> THOMAS C. HALIBURTON, *Sam
> Slick's wise saws*, 1853, ch. XXVII.

As far as I can judge, not much
good can be done without disturbing
something or somebody.

> EDWARD BLAKE, speech at Aurora,
> Ont., Oct. 3, 1874.

The men who save the world are those who work by rule of thumb; who do the day's work by the day's light and advance on chaos and the painful dark by inches; in other words, the practical men.

> GOLDWIN SMITH, *The Onlooker*; attributed.

To know just what has to be done, then to do it, comprises the whole philosophy of practical life.

> SIR WILLIAM OSLER, *Montreal med. jour.*, 1897, 186.

I praise Thee for my will to strive.
I bless Thy goad of discontent.

> CHARLES G. D. ROBERTS, "The aim", 1903.

My orders are to fight.
    Then if I bleed, or fail,
Or strongly win, what matters it?
    God only doth prevail.

The servant craveth nought
    Except to serve with might.
I was not told to win or lose —
    My orders are to fight.

> ETHELWYN WETHERALD, "My orders", 1907.

Highest thought is ever told in deeds.

> PETER MCARTHUR, *The prodigal*, 1907, 22.

Just have one more try — it's dead easy to die,
It's the keeping-on-living that's hard.

> ROBERT W. SERVICE, "The quitter", 1912.

If all the kind deeds never done
    Should blossom into flower,
The earth would be a paradise
    This very hour.

> ALBERT D. WATSON, "This very hour", 1913.

Man makes all his first inventions in the most complex way possible, and it takes him years before he can hit on the simple and obvious way of doing things.

> PETER MCARTHUR, "In pastures green", 1915, 87.

The biggest things are always the easiest to do because there is no competition.

> SIR WILLIAM VAN HORNE to S. Macnaughtan, *My Can. memories*. 1920, 109.

A man can always find time to do a thing if he has the inclination.

> ROBERT C. (BOB) EDWARDS, *Summer annual*, 1920, 35.

DEFENCE.

> (See also: CANADIAN-AMERICAN RELATION; ENGLAND; ISOLATION; MILITIA)

I will answer out of the mouths of my cannon.

> FRONTENAC, 1690, at Quebec, reply to an envoy, prior to defeating Phipps.

Let but the rash intruder dare
    To touch our darling strand,
        The martial fires
        That thrilled our sires
Would flame throughout the land.

> CHARLES SANGSTER, "Song of Canada", 1860.

The reciprocal duties of subject and Sovereign are not attenuated by distance, but, on the contrary, are often enhanced, since they are cherished against the relaxing influence of such distance. Those who talk, therefore, of it being unreasonable to expect the Empire to defend Canada, forgot that Canada *is* the Empire in North America.

> THOMAS D'A. MCGEE, speech in House of Assembly, Mar. 27, 1862; his conclusion was, "The lion must bear the lion's share".

Canadian vigilance must sleep no more except upon its arms. We have burst into a new era — the halcyon has fled to other climes and latitudes — the storm and peril are daily visible in our horizon.

> THOMAS D'A. MCGEE, speech in House of Assembly, Quebec, Mar. 27, 1862.

What men love best they defend
best; what they truly believe in, for
that they will bravely die.

> THOMAS D'ARCY MCGEE, "A plea
> for a British American nationality,"
> in, *British American mag.*, Aug.,
> 1863.

You have sent young men to guard
your frontier. You want a principle to
guard your young men, and thus truly
defend your frontier.

> THOMAS D'A. MCGEE, in Legis-
> lative Assembly, Feb. 9, 1865.

Strong arms shall guard our cherished
   homes
When darkest danger lowers,
And with our life-blood we'll defend
    This Canada of ours,
      Fair Canada,
      Dear Canada,
    This Canada of ours.

> JAMES D. EDGAR, "This Canada
> of ours", 1870.

Beside the dark Utawa's stream two
   hundred years ago,
A wondrous feat of arms was
   wrought, which all the world
   should know;
'Tis hard to read with tearless eyes
   that record of the past
It stirs the blood and fires the soul
   as with a clarion's blast.
What though no blazoned cenotaph,
   no sculptured columns tell
Where the stern heroes of my song,
   in death triumphant, fell;
What though beside the foaming
   flood untombed their ashes lie —
All earth becomes the monument of
   men who nobly die.

> GEORGE MURRAY. "How Canada
> was saved", 1874, a ballad on the
> fight between Dollard des Ormeaux
> and the Indians on the Ottawa
> River, in 1660.

Much of its property is not worth
stealing; but all the more will it hold
on with grim tenacity to all that is
worth anything.

> GEORGE M. GRANT, on Canada,
> speech to Can. Club, N. Y., 1887.

Sometimes the best method of defending one's self is to attack, and in that
case Canadian soldiers might be sent
to Spain, and it is quite certain that
they might legally be so despatched to
the Iberian Peninsula.

> SIR WILFRID LAURIER,, interview,
> qu., in Toronto *Globe*, Oct. 4, 1899.

The secret of Imperial defence is
Imperial dispersion.

> T. ARNOLD HAULTAIN, in, *The
> monthly rev.*, June, 1903.

The first duty of a free citizen is to
be prepared to defend his country.

> DONALD A. SMITH (Lord Strath-
> cona), letter to Sir Frederick
> Borden, 1907, on contributing
> $250,000 for the encouragement of
> military training.

We are loyal to the British Crown
and will defend the Empire in Canada
with the last drop of our blood, but
we are free and independent and no
one — not Laurier or even His Majesty
— has the right to ask us to go beyond
our shores.

> HENRI BOURASSA, speech at Ste.
> Rose, Sept. 6, 1911. (trans.)

I would like you to remember that
those who are or who become responsible for that Empire defence must, in
the very nature of things, have some
share in that policy which shapes the
issues of peace and of war. I would
like you to understand that Canada
does not propose to be an "adjunct"
even of the British Empire, but, as
has been well and eloquently expressed,
to be a greater part in a greater whole.

> SIR ROBERT BORDEN, speech at
> Royal Col. Inst., London, Eng.,
> July 10, 1912.

As far as fighting goes, I prefer to
do mine here, and if I have to shed
my blood I prefer to shed it here where
I know it will be for freedom.

> F. J. DIXON, speech in Winnipeg,
> May 27, 1917.

Firm stands the red flag battle-blown,
And we shall guard our own,
Our Canada,
From snow to sea,
One hope, one home, one shining des-
   tiny!

> MARJORIE PICKTHALL, "Star of the
> north", 1926.

Beware the northerner, the barbarian, who comes in as a thief and, undaunted, sleeps with his boots in the bed of the princess, whose name is Culture!

> MARIUS BARBEAU, in *Can. hist. rev.*, 1932, 417.

We are Canadians here and we don't want any peregrinating Imperialists to dictate our defence policies... We in Canada can take care of our policies, defence and others.

> IAN MACKENZIE, Minister of National Defence, in answer to a statement by Viscount Elibank in Toronto, August 19, 1936.

I believe that if war must come again, Great Britain is our first line of defence, yours and ours — perhaps our only external line.

> ARTHUR MEIGHEN, speech in Cleveland, Nov. 13, 1937.

Let us not be stampeded; let us do our duty by this little nation of 10,000,000 and trust in God.

> RAOUL DANDURAND, Senate *Debates*, 1937, 16, on defence against German militarism.

The Dominion of Canada is part of the sisterhood of the British Empire. I give to you assurance that the people of the United States will not stand idly by if domination of Canadian soil is threatened by any other Empire. We can assure each other that this hemisphere, at least, shall remain a strong citadel wherein civilization can flourish unimpaired.

> FRANKLIN D. ROOSEVELT, speech in Kingston, Ont., Aug. 18, 1938.

We, too, have our obligations as a good friendly neighbour, and one of them is to see that, at our instance, our country is made as immune from attack or possible invasion as we can reasonably be expected to make it, and that, should the occasion ever arise, enemy forces would not be able to pursue their way, either by land, sea, or air to the United States, across Canadian territory.

> W. L. MACKENZIE KING, speech at Woodbridge, Ont., Aug. 21, 1938.

In strength together we will stand, Defending our beloved land, ___ This Canada of ours; And never shall it cease to be A nation where all men are free In harmony from sea to sea, This Canada of ours.

> PERCY J. PHILIP, "This Canada of ours", 1945.

DEMOCRACY.

> (See also: GOVERNMENT; LIBERTY; MONARCHY; THE PEOPLE)

The Democracy which shall make government the organ of public reason, and not of popular passion or of demagogism which trades upon it, is yet in the womb of the future.

> GOLDWIN SMITH, *Schism in the Anglo-Saxon race*, 1887, 17

Democracy and science do not go to Canossa.

> GOLDWIN SMITH, *Reminiscences*, 1912, 395.

Democracy is a system of thought even more than a system of government.

> BENJAMIN A. GOULD, *War thoughts of an optimist*, 1915.

Clericalism and democracy are mutually exclusive terms. For clericalism implies that the mass of ordinary people possess insufficient wisdom to direct their own destinies and need the guidance of superior persons who, of course, are the clerics. Thus it comes that every extension of democratic government is gall and wormwood to clericalism.

> MANITOBA *Free Press*, Feb. 21, 1916.

I hold it to be true that you cannot make a real democracy out of ignorant people. The preliminary to making a democracy if the word is to mean anything, is that your people shall be educated.

> G. M. WRONG, Can. club, Ottawa. Dec. 8, 1916.

Democracy is rarely beautiful in its working, for the many still refuse to be refined, restrained and artistic.

G. M. WRONG, R. S. C., *Trans.*, 1917, Sec. II, 63.

The Kingdom of Heaven and perfect democracy are synonymous terms.

HENRY WISE WOOD, *Grain Growers' Guide*, Dec. 11, 1918, 35.

Democracy may be simply defined as the people in action.

HENRY WISE WOOD, *Grain Growers' Guide*, July 2, 1919, 7.

Democracy is the consensus of opinion of the majority of the people crystallized into law.

J. J. MORRISON, *Farmer's sun*, July 31, 1919, 3.

If any one ever had any doubt as to the existence of a Divine Provider, the operation of democratic institutions is sufficient to dispel that doubt, as nothing short of Divine Power could hold together such elements of chaos.

CHARLES J. DOHERTY (d.1931) qu., *Standard dict. Can. biog.*, 1934, 154.

No form of government makes greater demands upon the intelligence and sacrificial service of its citizens than does democracy.

H. J. CODY, Can. club, Ottawa, Dec. 15, 1919.

In Canada, democracy has been even more of a condition and less of a theory than it has been in the United States.

A. R. M. LOWER, in Can. Hist. Assoc., *Report*, 1930, 67.

Democracy has made half truths and even lies its coins in controversy. It has given the demagogue a field for his own profit and we may wonder if it has a balance of truth in its favour.

GEORGE M. WRONG, in *Can. hist. rev.*, 1933, 7.

Democracy is a great institution, but on account of the men thrown up sometimes, its institutions are very often in a perilous position.

ALEX. J. McPHAIL, *Diary*, 1940, 88.

There is no greater farce than to talk of democracy. To begin with, it is a lie; it has never existed in any great country.

HENRI BOURASSA, in *Le Devoir*, Feb. 11, 1943. (trans.)

Democracy, as measured by the franchise, came to Canada almost by stealth, certainly not as an army with banners.

W. L. MORTON, Can. hist. assoc., *Rept.*, 1943, 73.

DESIRE.

(See also: PASSION)

Come where the urge of desire availeth,
And no fear follows the children of men;
For a handful of dust is the only heirloom
The morrow bequeaths to its morrow again.

BLISS CARMAN, *"Wanderer"*, 1893.

O wild, dark flower of woman,
Deep rose of my desire,
An eastern wizard made you
Of earth and stars and fire.

CHARLES G. D. ROBERTS, "The rose of my desire", 1903.

Starving, savage, I aspire
To the red meat of all the world:
I am the Tiger of Desire!

TOM MACINNES, "The tiger of desire", 1918.

DESPAIR.

Upward, around, and downward I explore,
E'en to the frontiers of the ebon air;
But cannot, though I strive, discover more
Than what seems one huge cavern of despair.

CHARLES HEAVYSEGE, "The stars", 1865.

I curse him, and he leers; I kick him, and he whines;
But he never leaves the stone at my door.

Peep of day or set of sun, his
  croaking's never done
Of the Red Wolf of Despair at my
  door.
> BLISS CARMAN, "The red wolf",
> 1893.

DESTINY.

(See also: FATE)

With light and with darkness
  We're compassed about;
The clearer our vision,
  The darker our doubt.
The knot of our destiny
  Will not undo;
The bars of our prison
  We cannot get through.
> ALEXANDER McLACHLAN, "A
> dream", 1856.

We are either on God's side or evil's,
We are either perjured or true —
And that, which we set out to do
  in the first place.
That must we do.
> WILFRED CAMPBELL, "Our dead",
> 1923.

There is no such thing as free-will;
destiny rules.
> CHARLES MAIR, a letter written
> shortly before his death in 1927.

DIPLOMACY.

Britain has lost more by the pens of
her state officials than she has won by
the sword.
> TORONTO *Globe*, Mar. 26, 1858.

I am greatly disappointed at the
course taken by the British Commissioners. They seem to have only one
thing in their minds — that is, to
go to England with a Treaty in their
pockets, — no matter at what cost to
Canada.
> SIR JOHN A. MACDONALD, letter
> to Tupper, April 1, 1871, on
> Washington Treaty negotiations.

The history of the diplomatic service
of England, as far as Canada is concerned, has been a history of error,
blunder, wrong, and concession.
> EDWARD BLAKE, H. of C., *Debates*,
> 1882, 1074.

All that Canada owes to Great Britain is a great deal of Christian forgive-
ness.
> SIR RICHARD CARTWRIGHT, attri-
> buted; see his speech, H. of C.,
> *Debates*, Mar. 14, 1888, p. 156:
> "I do not think for my part, that
> we are under any deep debt of
> gratitude to English statesmen,
> that we owe them much, unless,
> per chance, it may be the duty, as
> Christian men, to forgive them for
> the atrocious blunders which mark-
> ed every treaty, or transaction, or
> negotiation that they have ever had
> with the United States where the
> interests of Canada were con-
> cerned".

British diplomacy has cost Canada
dear.
> CHARLES W. DILKE, *Problems of
> Greater Britain*, 1890, 64.

We have suffered on the Atlantic, we
have suffered on the Pacific, we have
suffered on the Lakes, we have suffered
wherever there has been a question to
be discussed between British diplomats
and foreign diplomats.
> SIR WILFRID LAURIER, speech
> in Toronto, Sept. 26, 1907.

We've got to bring this thing to a
head. I will take sight unseen any
resolution which the Canadian delegate
will propose.
> FIORELLO H. LAGUARDIA, in U. N.
> Social and Humanitarian Affairs
> Comm., Lake Success, N. Y., 1946.

DISCIPLINE.

Discipline is the Foundation of Character and the Safeguard of Liberty.
> SIR WILLIAM VAN HORNE, Boy
> Scout motto suggested to Sir Sam
> Hughes; qu., Vaughan, *Van Horne*,
> 1920, 357.

DOCTORS.

It's my theory that more folks die
of the doctor than the disease.
> THOMAS C. HALIBURTON, *Sam
> Slick's wise saws*; 1853 ch. XI.

The desire to take medicine is perhaps the greatest feature which distinguishes man from animals.

> SIR WILLIAM OSLER, address, "Recent advances in medicine", Baltimore, Feb. 22, 1891.

There are only two sorts of doctors: those who practise with their brains, and those who practise with their tongues.

> SIR WILLIAM OSLER, "Teaching and thinking", in, *Montreal med. jour.*, 1895.

Errors in judgment must occur in the practice of an art which consists largely in balancing probabilities.

> SIR WILLIAM OSLER, *Teacher and student*, 1897.

The great republic of medicine knows and has known no national boundaries.

> SIR WILLIAM OSLER, *Johns Hopkins hosp. bull.*, 1897, 161.

Ole Docteur Fiset of Saint Anicet,
Sapré tonnerre! he was leev long tam!
I'm sure he's got ninety year or so,
Beat all on de Parish 'cept Pierre Courteau,
An' day affer day he work all de sam'.

> WILLIAM H. DRUMMOND, "Ole Docteur Fiset", 1898.

Observe, record, and publish.

> SIR WILLIAM OSLER, qu., in Cushing, *Osler*, 1925.

The practice of medicine is an art, not a trade; a calling, not a business; a calling in which your heart will be exercised equally with your head.

> SIR WILLIAM OSLER; attributed.

As little as possible and as much as necessary.

> DR. THOMAS S. CULLEN, a favorite answer to patients who asked what he planned to do in surgical operations.

In the United States a Canadian doctor has a position of special prestige. I have been told — I need hardly say by a Scot — that you occupy in the States very much the position that a Scotchman does in England.

> LORD TWEEDSMUIR, speech, conf., Ontario Medical Assoc., London, May 27, 1936.

DOGS.

Je suis un chien qui ronge lo
En le rongeant je prends mon repos
Un temps viendra qui nest pas venu
Que je morderay qui maura mordu.
(I am a dog that gnaws his bone,
I couch and gnaw it all alone.
The time will come, which is not yet,
When I'll bite him by whom I'm bit.)

> Inscription in stone set over doorway of a house at the end of Buade St., near Mountain Hill, Quebec City, once occupied by Nicolas Philibert, merchant, killed in a quarrel by Le Gardeur de Repentigny, 1748. The translation is by William Kirby, the author of *The golden dog*, 1877, a novel based on the above.

Every dog has his day in this world.

> T. C. HALIBURTON, *The attaché*, 2nd. ser., 1844, vol. II, 26.

Like a good sportin'-dog, if I did beat round the bush, I always put up the birds.

> THOMAS C. HALIBURTON, *Sam Slick's wise saws*, 1853 ch. X.

A good dog is so much a nobler beast than an indifferent man that one sometimes gladly exchanges the society of one for that of the other.

> SIR WILLIAM BUTLER, *Wild north land*, 1872.

Newfoundland dogs are good to save children from drowning, but you must have a pond of water handy and a child, or else there will be no profit in boarding a Newfoundland.

> H. W. SHAW (Josh Billings), lecture at San Francisco, 1885.

"I am Death, I only offer
Peace — the long day done,
Follow me into darkness."
"Welcome! Friend, lead on;
Only spare my dog, let something
Grieve when I am gone!"

> CHARLES P. MULVANY, in *Can. birthday book*, 1887, 28.

Never trust a man whose dog has gone back on him.

> ROBERT C. (BOB) EDWARDS, *Calgary Eye Opener*, Feb. 19, 1910.

Every dog wonders why the other dog was born.

> R. D. CUMMING, *Skookum Chuck fables*, 1915, 158.

DOMINION.

He shall have dominion also from sea to sea, and from the river unto the ends of the earth.

> PSALMS, 72nd., verse 8. Sir Leonard Tilley is credited with using this verse in 1867 as the source of the official word *dominion* in designation of the Canadian Confederation; see, a letter by his son, L. P. D. Tilley to G. S. Holmstead, June 28, 1917 in the Public Archives, Ottawa. Origin of the legend on the Canadian Coat of Arms: *A mari usque ad mare.* — From sea to sea.

And His Dominion shall be from sea even to sea, from the river even to the ends of the earth.

> ZECHARIAH, ch. 9, verse 10; sometimes cited as the source for the word *dominion*, and for the Canadian motto. (See entry, above.)

His Majesty's Dominion in British North America.

> SIR EDMUND HEAD, 1858, qu., Can. Hist. Assoc., *Report*, 1929, 14; an early instance of the use of the word *dominion*.

On reading the above [letter] over I see that it will convey the impression that the change of title from Kingdom to Dominion was caused by the Duke of Buckingham. This is not so. It was made at the instance of Lord Derby, then [1867] foreign minister, who feared the first name would wound the sensibilities of the Yankees.

> SIR JOHN A. MACDONALD, letter from Rivière-du-Loup to Lord Knutsford, July 18, 1889.

We are called a dominion, although we have become a kingdom. We are said to be a confederation, although we are a federation.

> JOHN S. EWART, *Can. hist. rev.*, 1933, 123.

DRINKING.

Fire water.

> Term (trans.) used by Indians to describe brandy given them in exchange for furs; good liquor blazed up when poured on a fire, diluted liquor quenched it.

Paradise for them is to get drunk.

> MONTCALM, *Journal des campagnes*, Aug. 29, 1757, on the Indians. (trans.)

We have upwards of one hundred licensed houses and perhaps as many more which retail spirituous liquours without license; so that the business of one half of the town is to sell rum and the other half to drink it.

> ANON. resident of Halifax, N.S., 1760; qu., Sabine, *Report on the principle fisheries*, Washington, 1853, 62.

He drank like a fish.

> THOMAS C. HALIBURTON, *The old judge*, 1849.

Those who drink but water will have no liquor to buy.

> THOMAS C. HALIBURTON, *Sam Slick's wise saws*, 1853, ch. II.

We have an old sayin', "Only what I drink is mine".

> THOMAS C. HALIBURTON, *Sam Slick's wise saws*, 1853, ch. XXIII.

Here's a ho, boy!

> A drinking term popular in the West, 19th. century; in the early days the commonest form of cup was a buffalo horn; the signal to attack in the great buffalo hunts was the cry of "Ho!"

It would almost take a line of packet ships running between here and San Francisco to supply this Island with grog, so great a thirst prevails among its inhabitants.

> *The Royal emigrant's almanac.* (Mss. in B. C. Archives; ref. to Vancouver Island, 1853.)

It will be long ere the poor,
  Will learn their grog to shun.
While it's raiment, food and fire,
  And religion all in one.

> ALEXANDER MCLACHLAN, "We live in a rickety house", 1861.

The Curse of Canada.

> GRIP, Feb. 28, 1874, cartoon on whiskey, by J. W. Bengough.

For though within this bright se-
ductive place
My dollars go not far,
I never more shall see them face
to face,
When they have crossed the bar.

> BLISS CARMAN, "Crossing the bar," 1895.

A club is a place where a gentleman can get drunk respectably.

> PETER MCARTHUR, *To be taken with salt*, 1903, 154.

Bacchus hasn't a ghost of a chance against a good backing of Scotch Pres-
byterianism.

> SIR WILLIAM OSLER, *Oslerisms* (Bean), 1905.

When one is driven to drink he usually has to walk back.

> ROBERT C. (BOB) EDWARDS, *Cal-
gary Eye Opener*, Aug. 4, 1906.

The ability to take a drink and let it alone takes constant practice.

> ROBERT C. (BOB) EDWARDS, *Cal-
gary Eye Opener*, Feb. 19, 1910.

Whiskey drowns some troubles and floats a lot more.

> ROBERT C. (BOB) EDWARDS, *Cal-
gary Eye Opener*, April 3, 1915.

We write upon the drink question with almost pontifical authority.

> ROBERT C. (BOB) EDWARDS, *Cal-
gary Eye Opener*; attributed.

Their lordships think that the decision in *Russell* v. *the Queen* can only be supported today... on the assumption of the Board [the Privy Council], appa-
rently made at the time of deciding the case of *Russell* v. *the Queen*, that the evil of intemperance at that time amounted in Canada to one so great and so general that at least for the period [1882] it was a menace to the national life of Canada so serious and pressing that the National Parliament was called on to intervene to protect the nation from disaster. An epidemic

of pestilence might conceivably have been regarded as analogous.

> LORD HALDANE, *Appeal Cases*, 1925, 412.

DURHAM, LORD.

I would fain hope I have not lived altogether in vain. Whatever the Tories may say, the Canadians will one day do justice to my memory.

> LORD DURHAM, on his death-bed at Cowes, July, 1840.

The work he accomplished was greater than the man.

> LORD TWEEDSMUIR, in *Can. hist. rev.*, 1939, 117.

DURHAM REPORT, 1839.

Nothing can be better than the states-
manlike tone and the temper of this masterly document, and it would be impossible to rate too highly the influence it is likely to exercise.

> *The Examiner* (Lond.), Feb. 10, 1839.

The *Report* will be a most valuable textbook for Colonial Reforms in time to come — it has sapped the very foundation of our wretched Colonial system.

> *The Spectator* (Lond.), Feb. 16, 1839.

It is a farrago of false statements and false principles... the most fatal legacy that could have been bequeathed to our American colonies.

> *Quarterly Review*, Mar., 1839, 505.

Lord Durham's plan is *English*, and directly tends to raise a nation of equal and prosperous freemen; the plan of his opponents is *Russian* and directly tends to produce a few arro-
gant, insufferable nobles, and a multi-
tude of wretched, insulted slaves.

> KINGSTON *Upper Canada Herald*, May, 1839.

French Canada of 1839 deliberately set itself to falsify Lord Durham's prophecy and who will say that it has not succeeded?

> CHESTER MARTIN, in *Can. hist. rev.* 1939, 184.

DUTY.

This bent, this work, this duty —
    for thereby
God numbers thee, and marks thee
    for His own:
Careless of hurt, or threat, or praise,
    or pelf,
Find it and follow it, this, and
    this alone!

ARCHIBALD LAMPMAN, "Salvation",
1900.

However anxious I may be to be
gracious and civil, I don't care a damn
for any one when a matter of duty is
involved.

LORD DUFFERIN, letter to Lord
Kimberley, 1873.

If he has to, he will not,
    He will if he mustn't;
He does if he shouldn't
    And should if he doesn't.

ALBERT D. WATSON, "Who is it?",
1908.

E

ECONOMICS.

Hewers of wood and drawers of
water.

A Biblical phrase frequently used
to describe the Canadian economy
during the 19th. century ; first
used by William Lyon Mackenzie,
speech at Streetsville, Ont., 1836.

Political causes alone seldom produce
serious discontent, unless they affect
injuriously the economic condition of
the people.

SIR WILFRID LAURIER, H. of C.,
Debates, April 5, 1888.

I challenge any man to prove, or
even assert with any degree of authority
or knowledge that any banking institution, any wholesale house, or any
department store, no matter how large,
ever added one new dollar to the
wealth of the realm; but the farmer who
tills the soil and sells one bushel of
wheat or grows a bullock for the
market adds to the wealth of the
nation.

SIR RODMOND ROBLIN, speech,
Manitoba Grain Growers' Convention, Winnipeg, 1906.

It's called political economy because
it has nothing to do with either politics
or economy.

STEPHEN B. LEACOCK; attributed.

The economist can, of course, give
us the facts. That is his job. He is a
good cartographer, but a bad pilot.
There were plenty of crises in the
nineteenth century, when cold-blooded
economic fact would have been the end
of us if there had not been some
vision to interpret it.

VINCENT MASSEY, Can. Club, Ottawa, Jan. 20, 1924.

More than any country in the world,
Canada is the result of political, not
economic forces.

JOHN W. DAFOE, Canada: an
American nation, 1935.

Our economists have played the
humble self-imposed role of minor
technicians, never questioning the
major purposes of the capitalist system
in which they found themselves... happy
in their unambitious way as the intellectual garage-mechanics of Canadian
capitalism.

F. H. UNDERHILL, in C.J.E.P.S.,
1935, 404.

All these new-fangled doctrines, when
you examine them closely, have nothing
inside them but some withered fallacy
or some loose and livid lunacy.

ARTHUR MEIGHEN, speech to
McGill Graduates' Society, Montreal, 1935.

The dole is a condemnation of our
economic system. If we cannot abolish
the dole, we should abolish the system.

R. B. BENNETT, radio address, Jan.
2, 1935.

If an economist becomes certain of
the solution of any problem, he can be
equally certain that his solution is
wrong.

H. A. INNIS, qu., Dalhousie rev.,
1936, 226.

I know a very tiresome Man
Who keeps on saying, "Social Plan,"
    At every Dinner, every Talk,
    Where Men foregather, eat and
        walk,

No matter where, — this Awful Man Brings out his goddam Social Plan.

STEPHEN B. LEACOCK, *Hellements of hickonomics*, 1936.

This is the end of an economic era. Capitalism will never again work in the old way. The only system which can work hereafter is the system controlled and guided by the state.

W. D. HERRIDGE, speech in Sydney, N. S., Sept. 27, 1937.

There can be no betterment in the standard of living by any distribution of unearned money. Nothing but a distribution of goods needed by humanity can help the standard of living, and these goods must first be brought into being. You cannot Beveridge a country into prosperity any more than a lawyer can make his client rich by drawing up his Will.

ARTHUR MEIGHEN, speech in Vancouver, Oct. 21, 1943.

EDMONTON, ALTA.

Edmonton is as big as Chicago, but it isn't all built up yet.

ANON., early 20th. cent.; answer to an American visitor who asked the size of the city.

EDUCATION.

(See also: COLLEGES AND UNIVERSITIES; STUDENTS; TEACHERS)

Although the Canadian Peasants are far from being a stupid race, they are at present an ignorant people, from want of instruction — not a man in five hundred can read; perhaps it has been the policy of the clergy to keep them in the dark, as it is a favourite tenet with the Roman Catholic priests that ignorance is the mother of devotion.

HUGH FINLAY, letter to Evan Nepean. Under-Secretary of State, Home Dept., London, 1784.

The attention paid to education in the United States is the grand secret of their power and the most indissoluble bond of their union.

WILLIAM LYON MACKENZIE, in *Colonial advocate*, Jan. 22, 1829.

Until lately, it was denied that *intelligence* was a desirable quality in the great body of the people; and as *intelligence* is power, such is an unavoidable opinion in the breasts of those who think that the human race ought to consist of two classes — one that of the *oppressors*, another that of the *oppressed*. But, if education be to communicate the art of happiness; and if Intelligence consists of knowledge and sagacity; the question whether the people should be educated is the same with the question whether they should be happy or miserable.

WILLIAM LYON MACKENZIE. *Catechism of education*, 1830, 24.

For a long time there have been complaints that the education given in our seminaries does not fully correspond to the needs of the century, that it is too much turned towards the study of ancient languages and old theories.

LE CANADIEN, Jan. 8, 1836. (trans.)

The true purpose of education is to cherish and unfold the seed of immortality already sown within us ; to develop, to their fullest extent, the capacities of every kind with which the God who made us has endowed us.

ANNA JAMESON, *Winter studies and summer rambles*, 1838.

By education, I mean not the mere acquisition of certain arts, or of certain branches of knowledge, but that instruction and discipline which qualify and dispose the subjects of it for their appropriate duties and appointments in life, as Christians, as persons in business, and also as members of the civil community in which they live.

EGERTON RYERSON, *Rept. on system of instruction for U. C.*, 1847.

I am in favour of national school education free from sectarian teaching, and available without charge to every child in the province.

GEORGE BROWN, election address, Haldimand election, 1850.

National education. — Common school, grammar school, and collegiate free from sectarianism and open to all on equal terms. Earnest war will be waged with the separate school system, which has unfortunately obtained a footing.

> Toronto *Globe*, Oct. 1, 1853, statement of policy.

The best of colleges — a farmer's fireside.

> Joseph Howe, on his own education; qu., in G. M. Grant, *Joseph Howe*, 1906, 33.

Catholic electors who do not use their electoral power in behalf of separate schools are guilty of the mortal sin; likewise persons who do not make the sacrifice necessary to secure such schools or send their children to mixed schools.

> André de Charbonnel, Bishop of Toronto, pastoral letter, 1856.

What, after all, is education but a subtle, slowly-effected change, due to the actions of the externals — of the written record of the great minds of ation; in G. M. Grant, *Joseph ious surroundings of nature and art, and of the lives, good or ill, of our fellows? — these alone educate us, these alone mould the growing mind.

> Sir William Osler, "The leaven of science", in *Univ.* [of Penn.] *med. mag.*, 1894.

If every day in the life of a school could be the last day but one, there would be little fault to find with it.

> Stephen B. Leacock, *College days*, 1923, 32.

The critical test of the value of our educational systems is the attitude of adults to their own mental growth.

> R. C. Wallace, *A liberal education*, 1932.

Scholars who love minutiæ deny everything.

> Stephen B. Leacock, speech to Can. Pol. Sci. Assoc., 1933.

Scholarship is the frontier of the mind.

> J. B. Brebner, *Scholarship for Can.*, 1945.

EFFICIENCY.

One trouble with being efficient is that it makes everybody hate you so.

> Robert C. (Bob) Edwards, *Calgary Eye Opener*, Mar. 18, 1916.

ELECTION FUNDS.

The fight goes bravely on... We have expended our strength in aiding outlying counties and helping our city candidates. But a big push has to be made on Saturday and Monday for the East and West divisions... We therefore make our grand stand on Saturday. There are but half a dozen people that can come down handsomely, and we have done all we possibly can do, and we have to ask a few outsiders to aid us. Will you be one?

> George Brown, letter to a Toronto banker, Senator John Simpson, August 15, 1872; the "big push" letter.

Immediate, private. I must have another ten thousand — will be the last time of calling. Do not fail me; answer today.

> Sir John A. Macdonald, Aug. 26, 1872, telegram to J. J. C. Abbott, legal adviser to Sir Hugh Allan who had been granted a charter for construction of the Canadian Pacific Railway.

This evil is the bane of democracy; it is the nightmare of every man in public life who is anxious to give service to the State.

> Sir Clifford Sifton, in *New Era*, 1917.

Gratefulness is always regarded as an important factor in dealing with democratic governments.

> John Aird, Jr., President, Beauharnois Corp., investigation evidence, 1931, 823.

ELECTIONS.

> (See also: Parliamentary Representation; Political Slogans; Voting)

The more broken heads & bloody noses there is the more election like.

> David W. Smyth, 1792, in *John Askin papers*, ed. M. Quaife, 1928, I, 427.

Nothin' improves a man's manners like an election.

> T. C. Haliburton, *Sam Slick*, 1836, ch. XV.

Elections cannot be carried without money. Under an open system of voting, you can readily ascertain whether the voter has deceived you. Under vote by ballot, an elector may take your money and vote as he likes, without detection.

> JOHN H. CAMERON, speech in H. of C., April 21, 1874.

If you buy a man to stay at home, you can always tell whether he has kept his bargain or not.

> EDWARD BLAKE, speech at Aurora, Ont., Oct. 3, 1874.

It is not for me, mes enfants, to tell you for which party you should vote, but I would have you remember that the place on high [pointing to the heavens] is *bleu,* while the other [pointing downward] is *rouge.*

> Rev. Ignace Langlais, curé of St. Hilarion, Qué., to his congregation during the Charlevoix by-election campaign, January 1876 ; attributed, but denied in evidence given before the Superior Court, Aug. 8, 1876. [*Charlevoix election case* ; printed *evidence for the Defence*], same date, p. 41. *Bleus* and *rouges* are popular names in Quebec for the Conservatives, and Liberals respectively.

An election is like a horse-race in that you can tell more about it the next day.

> SIR J. MACDONALD, qu. in, Pope: *Memoirs of Sir J. A. Macdonald,* II, 202; said before the election of 1882.

The great mass of the electors are ignorant, & a great majority of them never read, & remain as much in the dark as to what is going on in this country as if they were residing in Europe.

> SIR WILFRID LAURIER, letter to Edward Blake, July 10, 1882.

I know an old lady in Toronto who solemnly assured me that her Conservative cow gave two quarts of milk more each day than it had done before the elections.

> SIR JOHN A. MACDONALD, speech in Ottawa; attributed.

Elections are not won by prayers alone.

> JOSEPH I. TARTE, statement, 1896.

I do not know, but Mr. Gibbons told us that the friends of Mr. Hyman having fought two elections and won fairly and having been deprived of the seat by unfair and fraudulent methods, came to the conclusion that they would fight the enemy with the devil's fire.

> SIR WILFRID LAURIER, H. of C., *Debates,* Nov. 23, 1906, 38.

Wolves, it is said, hunt in packs; the lion hunts alone. The way of the lion was the way of Sir John Macdonald. Today the lion is dead, and all the furious howlings of the wolves do not carry one-tenth of the weight of the roar of the lion.

> SIR WILFRID LAURIER, speech at Strathroy, Sept. 19, 1908, on Sir Robert Borden's campaigning with a phalanx of provincial premiers.

With every change of government in Canada we are made into a nation over again.

> SIR JOHN WILLISON (d. 1927) attributed as said at the close of his life.

EMIGRATION.

(See also: IMMIGRATION)

Emigration to the United States is the fear of the hour. It is indeed going on to an extent truly alarming and astonishing.

> WILLIAM RYERSON, April, 22, 1838, qu., Hodgson, *Life of E. Ryerson,* 1883, 184.

Emigrate ye Canadians! If England will not treat you with decency, shake the dust from your feet, cross the border and build up a home where tyranny does not dare show its head.

> CINCINNATI *News,* quoted in Cobourg *Plain speaker,* July 28, 1838.

In one sense and that no secondary one, all men have been emigrants or

sons of emigrants since the first sad
pair departed out of Eden.

> THOMAS D'A. McGEE, speech,
> House of Assembly, Quebec, May
> 10, 1862.

Here and there, by the trees half-
hidden,
We catch a glimpse of some pleasant home ;
And the thought springs up to the
lips unbidden,
"O why should Canada's children
roam?"

> EDWARD H. DEWART, "Summer
> rambles", 1869.

An exodus to the United States is
going on from all the Provinces.

> GOLDWIN SMITH, *The Bystander*,
> May, 1880, 234. The term "The
> Exodus" was popularly applied to
> the movement of Canadian people
> to the U. S.; see, Laurier's speech,
> H. of C., *Debates*, April 5, 1881,
> for another example.

They will do better away.

> A common remark in Prince
> Edward Island, about 1882, by
> parents referring to their children
> who had gone to the United States.

Canada's story begins in Lamentations and ends in Exodus.

> A popular witticism of the 1880's.

There is scarcely a farmhouse in
the older provinces where there is not
one empty chair for the boy in the
United States.

> TORONTO *Mail*, 1887.

The Americans may say with truth
that if they do not annex Canada,
they are annexing the Canadians.
They are annexing the very flower of
the Canadian population, and in the
way most costly to the country from
which it is drawn, since the men whom
that country has been at the expense
of breeding leave it just as they
arrive at manhood and begin to
produce.

> GOLDWIN SMITH, *Canada and the
> Can. question*, 1891, 233.

Pioneering young Canadians must
have found that the inertia of their
entrenched elders had drained Canadian life of colour, zest, adventure,
and the stimulation which comes from
free-ranging experimentation in ideas,
in material enterprises, and in the arts.
It must have been because they could
not feel in Canada the sense of sharing
in something more than the defence
of things as they are that they left
their country seeking "lots more of
something else".

> JOHN B. BREBNER, *Scholarship
> for Canada*, 1945, 8.

ENEMIES.

Grant me, God, that in the battle,
For a moment we may meet;
Let mine be the sword to send him
Staggering to Thy judgment seat.

> ALEXANDER McLACHLAN, "Hamil-
> ton's address", 1856.

Here lies the man I could have
wished for friend!
How shall I atone for injuring him
of old?

> CHARLES HEAVYSEGE, *Saul*, 1857.

Humanity has but three great enemies: fever, famine and war; of these
by far the greatest, by far the most
terrible, is fever.

> SIR WILLIAM OSLER, Address,
> "Study of the fevers of the South",
> Atlanta, May 6, 1896.

Next a worthy friend, honour a
worthy foe.

> SIR RICHARD CARTWRIGHT, qu.,
> *Standard dict. Can. biog.*, 1934, 103.

The question before Canada is not
what she thinks or pays, but what an
enemy may think it necessary to make
her pay. If she continues wealthy and
remains weak she will surely be
attacked under one pretext or another.

> RUDYARD KIPLING, *Letters to the
> family*, 1908.

Take up our quarrel with the foe
To you from failing hands we throw
The torch: be yours to hold it high.
If ye break faith with us who die,
We shall not sleep, though poppies
grow
In Flanders' fields.

> JOHN McCRAE, "In Flanders'
> Fields", ("We shall not sleep")
> *Punch*, Dec. 8, 1915, 468.

There is no earthly hope for a man who is too lazy to acquire enemies.

ROBERT C. (BOB) EDWARDS, *Calgary Eyeopener*, June 15, 1918.

A man always remembers his enemies, but he sometimes forgets his friends.

ROBERT C. (BOB) EDWARDS, in his *Annual*, 1922, 80.

ENGLAND.

(See also: BRITISH EMPIRE)

England would be better off without Canada; it keeps her in a prepared state for war at a great expense and constant irritation.

NAPOLEON I, in, *Diary of P. Malcolm at St. Helena*, Jan. 11, 1817.

Your triumphant election on the 16th and ejection from the Assembly on the 17th must hasten the crisis which is fast approaching in the affairs of the Canadas, and which will terminate in independence and freedom from the baneful domination of the mother country and the tyrannical conduct of a small and despicable faction in the colony.

JOSEPH HUME, letter to W. L. Mackenzie, Mar. 29, 1834; ("The baneful domination" letter.)

I, therefore, need scarcely state my firm belief that the prosperity of Canada depends upon its permanent connection with the Mother Country, and that I shall resist, to the utmost, any attempt (from whatever quarter it may come) which may tend to weaken that union.

SIR JOHN A. MACDONALD, letter "To the Free and Independent Electors of Kingston", Oct. 5, 1844; his first political address.

I have been possessed... with the idea that it is possible to maintain on this soil of North America, and in the face of Republican America, British connection and British institutions, if you give the latter freely and trustingly. Faith, when it is sincere, is always catching.

LORD ELGIN, letter to Cumming Bruce, Sept. 1852.

We were and are willing to spend our last men and our last shilling for our mother country.

SIR ALEXANDER T. GALT, speech in Cornwall, Mar. 2, 1866.

Canada is ready to join the mother country in her offensive and defensive league, to sacrifice her last man and her last shilling in defence of the Empire and the flag of England.

SIR JOHN A. MACDONALD, speech in London, Eng., Jan. 4, 1886.

The lilies withered where the Lion trod.

OLIVER WENDELL HOLMES, "Francis Parkman", Nov., 1893.

England, England, England,
Girdled by ocean and skies,
And a power of a world and the heart of a race,
And a hope that never dies.

WILFRED CAMPBELL, "England", 1899.

If you ask me as a French-Canadian why I am deeply attached to Great Britain, it is because I find in her institutions and under her flag all the protection I need. It is because she has been in the world the nurse of liberty. She has understood better than any other nation the art of government.

RODOLPHE LEMIEUX, speech in Toronto, March, 1905.

O mighty Soul of England, rise in splendour
Out of the wrack and turmoil of the night,
And as of old, compassionate and tender,
Uphold the cause of justice and of right.

FREDERICK G. SCOTT, "To England", May, 1926.

She is part of you, heart of you — England, England —
Till you answer the trumpet-call of God.

AUDREY ALEXANDRA BROWN, "The pilgrims", 1937.

This, this is Britain, bulwark of our breed,

Our one sure shield against the
hordes of hate.
Smite her, and we are smitten; wound
her, we bleed.
Yet firm she stands and fears no
thrust of fate.

CHARLES G. D. ROBERTS, "Canada
speaks of Britain", 1940.

ENGLISHMEN.

(See also: LABOUR; UNION
JACK)

Bishop Taché has been here and has
left for the Red River... He is strongly
opposed to the idea of an Imperial
Commission, believing, as indeed, we
all do, that to send out an overwashed
Englishman, utterly ignorant of the
country and full of crochets, as all
Englishmen are, would be a mistake.

SIR JOHN A. MACDONALD, letter
to Sir John Rose, Feb. 23, 1870.

Is there a man who can forget that,
when the constitutional voice was useless, when our representations and our
remonstrances remained for years and
years unanswered, and when the peasants of St. Denis took up arms and faced
the veterans of Waterloo, their commander was not a Canadian, but an
Englishman named Wolfred Nelson ?
And, three days afterwards, when these
same peasants were swept with the
leaden hail at St. Charles, can it be
forgotten that the man who again led
them was an Englishman named Thomas S. Brown?

SIR WILFRID LAURIER, speech
in Quebec, 1877.

While the Frenchman wants you to
have his opinions, the Englishman wants
you to have opinions of your own.

SIR WILFRID LAURIER, speech
in Montreal, May 19, 1884. (trans.)

The Englishman respects your opinions; but he never thinks of your
feelings.

SIR WILFRID LAURIER, speech
in Montreal, May 19, 1884. (trans.)

I owe it to the cause of truth to
declare that the hostility towards us
which we have been given to understand exists in the mother-country has
never existed, at least not to the degree

that has been pictured. The English
people are free enough to have no
fear of the comparative freedom of
the colonies. The English government
has never wanted to rule slaves. Who
speaks of the English people, and of
every class of population connected
with them, speaks of independence and
constitutional liberty.

THOMAS J. J. LORANGER, speech
of June 27, 1884.

An Englishman's social standing
seems to depend on the number of people he can afford to despise.

PETER MCARTHUR. *To be taken
with salt*, 1903, 157.

The average Englishman has so deep
a reverence for antiquity that he would
rather be wrong than be recent.

PETER MCARTHUR. *To be taken
with salt*, 1903, 157.

Lord Dundonald, in his position, is
charged with the organization of the
Militia, but he must take counsel
here when organizing a regiment.
He is a foreigner — no — [Some
hon. members. "No, no."] I had
withdrawn the expression before
Hon. gentlemen interrupted. He is not
a foreigner, but he is a stranger.

SIR WILFRID LAURIER, H. of C.,
Debates, June 10, 1904, 4620, on
the dismissal of Lord Dundonald,
General Officer Commanding Canadian Militia.

He's a son of dear old England, he's
a hero, he's a brick;
He's the kind you may annihilate
but you can never lick.

ROBERT J. C. STEAD, "The son of
Marquis Noddle", 1917.

The Anglo-Saxon has never had too
many friends.

A. R. M. LOWER, in *Can. hist. rev.*,
1931, 59.

EXPERIENCE.

I guess I warn't born yesterday.

T. C. HALIBURTON, *Sam Slick*,
1836, ch. XV; also, "I have some
wrinkles on my horn, for I warn't
born yesterday". *Sam Slick's wise
saws*, 1853, ch. VII.

They know by experience, and not by books; and experience is everything; it's hearin', and seein', and tryin'; and arter that, a feller must be a born fool if he don't know.

> T. C. HALIBURTON, *Sam Slick*, 1836, ch. XXXII.

The value of experience is not in seeing much, but in seeing wisely.

> SIR WILLIAM OSLER, "The army surgeon", 1905.

EYES.

I put my clothes on as quick as a wink.

> THOMAS C. HALIBURTON, *Sam Slick's wise saws*, 1853, ch. VII.

For the sake of two
Sad eyes and true,
And the old, old love
  So long ago.
> BLISS CARMAN, "Why", 1893.

In a moment the pirates were all around us, rolling their eyes, gnashing their teeth, and filing their nails.

> STEPHEN B. LEACOCK, "Soaked in seaweed", 1911.

In their eyes I have seen
the pin-men of madness in marathon
  trim
race around the track of the stadium
  pupil.
> P. K. PAGE, "The stenographers", *Can. forum*, Sept. 1942.

F
FACES.

A long face is plaguy apt to cover a long conscience.

> T. C. HALIBURTON, *Sam Slick*, 1836, ch. XXIV.

I love the face of every man
Whose thought is swift and sweet.
> ARCHIBALD LAMPMAN, "Amor vitæ", 1899.

From the dark pane
As I draw near,
I see the silent, the invisible face
Disappear.
> MARY QUAYLE INNIS, "Haunted", 1939.

FACTS.

Facts are stranger than fiction.

> T. C. HALIBURTON, *Sam Slick's wise saws*, 1853, I, 5.

I often wish that I could rid the world of the tyranny of facts. What are facts but compromises ? A fact merely marks the point where we have agreed to let investigation cease. Investigate further and your fact disappears.

> BLISS CARMAN, *Atlantic monthly*, May, 1906.

Some men spoil a good story by sticking to the facts.

> ROBERT C. (BOB) EDWARDS. *Calgary Eye Opener*, Jan. 25, 1919.

Facts never collide; in their long procession there is always harmony from the first movement to the last.

> ARTHUR MEIGHEN, Senate, *Debates*, April 28, 1932.

FAILURE.

> (See also: CONDUCT OF LIFE; OPPORTUNITY; SUCCESS)

You can't get blood out of a stone, you know.

> THOMAS C. HALIBURTON, *Sam Slick's wise saws*, 1853, ch. IV.

A miss is as good as a mile.

> THOMAS C. HALIBURTON, *Sam Slick's wise saws*, 1853, ch. XXVII; from earlier usage.

We sneer and we laugh with the
  lip — the most of us do it,
Whenever a brother goes down
  like a weed with the tide;
We point with the finger and say —
  Oh, we knew it! We knew it!
But, see! we are better than he
  was, and we will abide.
> GEORGE F. CAMERON, "The way of the world", 1887.

And, through the gathering gloom,
  the silent rage
Of years undone came from the sea
  of death

To meet me there — and Time was
lost to me
With all its wealth of opportunity.
> WILLIAM E. MARSHALL, "Failure",
> 1894.

Here the high failure, not the level
fame,
Attests the spirit's aim.
> CHARLES G. D. ROBERTS, "The
> unknown city", 1907.

And each forgets, as he strips and
runs,
  With a brilliant, fitful pace,
It's the steady, quiet, plodding ones
  Who win in the lifelong race.
And each forgets that his youth has
fled,
  Forgets that his prime is past,
Till he stands one day, with a hope
that's dead
  In the glare of the truth at last.
> ROBERT W. SERVICE, "The men that
> don't fit in", 1907.

The things that come to the man
who waits are seldom the things he
waited for.
> ROBERT C. (BOB) EDWARDS, Cal-
> gary Eye Opener, Jan. 27, 1912.

One of the worst stings of defeat is
the sympathy that goes with it.
> ROBERT C. (BOB) EDWARDS, Cal-
> gary Eye Opener, June 8, 1912.

The man who never tried has no
sympathy for the one who tried and
failed.
> ROBERT C. (BOB) EDWARDS, Sum-
> mer annual, 1920, 27.

Much have we tried, and little done;
Much have we dreamed, and little
won;
And back into the Gloom we lapse,
Confronted by the old Perhaps.
> ARTHUR STRINGER, "The age end",
> 1929.

There is no search when nothing is
left to seek,
Nothing to find when what was found
is lost,
Nothing to lose when what is lost
was all.
> ROBERT FINCH, "Over", 1943.

Forgive us, who have not
Been whole or rich as fruit;

Who, through the eyes' lock enter
A point beyond the centre
To find our balance shot...
Our blueprint was at fault.
> P. K. PAGE, "Forgive us, who
> have not been whole", 1947.

FAITH.

Faith wanting, all his works fell
short.
> CHARLES HEAVYSEGE, Saul, 1857.

Nothing in life is more wonderful
than faith — the one great moving
force which we can neither weigh in
the balance nor test in the crucible...
To each one of the religions, past or
present, faith has been the Jacob's
ladder.
> SIR WILLIAM OSLER, in, Brit. med.
> jour., June 18, 1910.

Who builds, but sits not on his
throne,
Lest the king come, to him alone
The immortal Kingdoms shall be
known.
> WARWICK CHIPMAN, "Immortality",
> 1930.

Fearfully the mind's hands dig
In the débris of thought, for the
lovely body of faith.
> F. R. SCOTT, "Recovery", 1945.

FAME.

(See also: HEROES)

Fame I will have, but it must be
alone.
> THOMAS SIMPSON, letter from Fort
> Garry, 1840.

Who the devil cares for a monument
that actilly desarves one?
> T. C. HALIBURTON, The attaché,
> 2nd. ser., 1843, II, 19.

I dreamed a dream when the woods
were green,
And my April heart made an April
scene,
  In the far, far distant land.
That even I might something do
That should keep my memory for
the true,
  And my name from the spoiler's
hand.
> THOMAS D'ARCY MCGEE. "A frag-
> ment", 1869.

To have done this is to have lived,
    though fame
Remember us with no familiar name.
    ARCHIBALD LAMPMAN, "The largest
    life", *Atlantic monthly*, Mar., 1899.

There are many kinds of fame, but
the best of all fame is the lustre and
distinction whose immediate results
mean the amelioration of the suffering
of mankind.
    ARTHUR MEIGHEN, speech in Otta-
    wa, Feb. 13, 1923, on Dr. Banting.

It is strange how the memory of
a man may float to posterity on what
he would have himself regarded as the
most trifling of his works.
    SIR WILLIAM OSLER, in, Cushing:
    Life of Osler, 1926.

The moral is, if you wish to be
famous, write a book about yourself,
and be sure to leave everybody else
out of the story.
    A. S. MORTON, *Under Western
    skies*, 1937.

FAMILY.

Family trees are apt to be ques-
tionable about the roots.
    SIR WILLIAM VAN HORNE, to Lady
    Nicholson, 1909.

I have been too busy all my life to
cast a thought so far back as my
grandfather.
    SIR W. VAN HORNE; attributed.

FARMS AND FARMING.

                (See   also: SETTLERS;
                WHEAT)

Let us go back to our farming for
this must be our goal. That is the
first mine for which we must search,
and it is of better worth than the
treasures of Atahualpa.
    MARC LESCARBOT, *Hist. of New
    France*, 1606, ed. Grant, 1907, II,
    317. (trans.)

Let this be held the farmer's creed:
For stock seek out the choicest breed
In peace and plenty let them feed;
Your hands sow with the best of seed
Let it not dung nor dressing want
And then provisions won't be scant.
    WEST RIVER (N.S.) FARMING Soc.,
    motto, 1817.

While the poor peasant, whose labor-
    ious care
Scarce from the soil could wring
    his scanty fare,
Now in the peaceful arts of culture
    skilled,
Sees his wide barn with ample trea-
    sure filled.
    OLIVER GOLDSMITH, "The rising
    village", 1825.

A shining plough makes a full mow.
    Saying of pioneer Ontario farmers.

Plant corn when oak leaves are as
big as a squirrel's ear.
    Saying of pioneer Ontario farmers.

When the Spring comes, and the fields
are dry enough to be sowed, they all
have to be ploughed, cause fall rains
wash the lands too much for fall
ploughin. Well the ploughs have to be
mended and sharpened, cause what's
the use of doin that afore its wanted.
Well the wheat gets in too late, and
then comes rust, but whose fault is
that? Why the climate to be sure, for
Nova Scotia aint a bread country.
    T. C. HALIBURTON, *Sam Slick*,
    1836, 172.

Put him to the PLOUGH, the most
natural, the most happy, the most
innocent, and the most healthy employment in the world.
    T. C. HALIBURTON, *Sam Slick*,
    1836, ch. XXVI.

Make a farmer of him, and you will
have the satisfaction of seeing him an
honest, an independent, and a respectable member of society; more honest
than traders, more independent than
professional men, and more respectable
than either.
    T. C. HALIBURTON, *Sam Slick*,
    1836, ch. XXVI.

When grasshoppers are so plenty as
to make pastures poor, gobblers grow
fat.
    THOMAS C. HALIBURTON, *Sam
    Slick's wise saws*, 1853, ch. VI.

Kind heaven speed the Plough!
And bless the hands that guide it;
    God gives the seed —
    The bread we need,
Man's labour must provide it.
    CHARLES SANGSTER, "The happy
    harvesters," 1860.

Up, be stirring, be alive!
Get upon a farm and thrive!
He's king upon a throne
Who has acres of his own!

ALEXANDER MCLACHLAN, "Acres of
your own", 1874.

His only joy since when a boy
    Has been to plod and moil,
Until his very soul itself
    Has grown into the soil.

ALEXANDER MCLACHLAN, "Neighbor John", 1874.

Manurin', ploughin', drainin', seedin',
All farmin's to be done by readin'!
O Lord! O Lord! it makes me mad,
When every striplin' of a lad,
And every edicated ass,
Who scarce knows growin' wheat
    from grass,
Must teach the likes o' me to farm,
Wi' Latin names as long's my arm;
Them critters teach the likes o' me?
Who farmed ere they could reach
    my knee,
Ain't it presumption? — Gee Buck
Gee!

ALEXANDER MCLACHLAN, "Old
Canada", 1874.

None ever saw such crops as these,
So great the yield of oats and pease;
Fifty bushels to the acre
Makes us grateful to our maker.

JAMES MCINTYRE, "Big crops of
1891".

Bring me one of your students who
has taken a degree and gone back
to the farm and I shall be proud to be
allowed to shake his hand.

GOLDWIN SMITH (d. 1910), to his
secretary, T. A. Haultain.

City people envy the farmer — but
not to such an extent that they take
advantage of the continuous opportunities to be one.

ROBERT C. (BOB) EDWARDS, Calgary Eye Opener, Aug. 12, 1912.

Contented women, good chances for
the education of the children, and a
reasonably richly developed social life
are in the long run of immensely more
consequence than conveniences for
growing crops. The place of the latter
is to minister to the former. What
shall it profit a country to be called,

or to be, the Granary of the Empire
if it lose the soul of happy rural life?

CANADA. ROY. COMM. ON INDUSTRI-
AL TRAINING, Rept., 1913, II, 1912.

Farming is one of the finest occu-
pations in the world if taken in moderation.

PETER MCARTHUR, In pastures
green, 1915, 93.

The Farmers' Parliament.
    Term in common use about 1915 for
    annual conventions of the Saskat-
    chewan Grain Growers' Association
    at which political problems were
    debated.

Then come our friends, good and true
With good of all the world in view;
The die is cast, it's up to you
    Organize! O organize!

Song of Alberta farmers, about
1920.

The farmers of the prairie lands are
    massing in their might,
Exulting in a Principle, a Cause for
    which they fight;
The sacred cause of Justice, the
    establishment of right,
And Equal Rights to all.

"The day of right", a song of
the Prairie farmers, about 1920.

Yus farmers want to keep your boys
at home. Don't let them go up to the
city; keep them on the farm, — the
temptations is more pure.

A SENATOR, speech at Pakenham,
Ont., election campaign of 1921.

To be born on a farm is the greatest
good that can befall a human being.
To live on a farm and enjoy all that it
has to offer is the greatest good that
can be attained by poet or a philosopher.

PETER MCARTHUR, Around home,
1925, 182.

How many perfumes come and go,
    but they
Are half-forgotten in the dew-wet
    day;
On mountain, mere, on hillside sand
    or sod,
There is no smell this side the fields
    of God
Like new-mown hay.

ROBERT K. KERNIGHAN, "Perfume
of the sods", 1925.

FATE.
(See also: DESTINY; FUTURE)

Doubt not, nor dread the greatness
of thy fate.
> CHARLES G. D. ROBERTS, "Ode for
> the Canadian Confederacy", 1880.

Inexorably decreed
By the ancestral deed,
The puppets of our sires,
We work out blind desires,
And for our sons ordain
The blessing or the bain.
> CHARLES G. D. ROBERTS. "Origins",
> 1896.

Well, if that's our fate,
I would rather go down with those
I love
Than float among those I hate.
> TOM MACINNES, "Choice", 1918.

FATHERS.

For thirty years he was my instruc-
tor, my playfellow, almost my daily
companion. To him I owe my fondness
for reading, my familiarity with the
Bible, my knowledge of old colonial
and American incidents and characteristics. He left me nothing but his
example and the memory of his many
virtues, for all that he ever earned was
given to the poor. He was too good
for this world; but the remembrance
of his high principles, his cheerfulness,
his child-like simplicity, and truly
Christian character, is never absent
from my mind.
> JOSEPH HOWE, on the death of his
> father, Dec. 27, 1835.

With a full knowledge of all that has
passed, and all the consequences that
have flowed from a day of weakness,
I will say that an honester man does not
breathe the air of heaven; that no
son feels prouder of his father than
I do to-day; and that I would have
submitted to the obloquy and reproach
of every act, not fifteen years, but
fifty — ay, have gone down to the
grave with the cold shade of the world
upon me, rather than that one of his
gray hairs should have been injured.
> GEORGE BROWN, speech in Legis.
> Assembly, 1858, on his father.

Your fathers are but silly fools,
Old relics of a past age,

No wonder they can't comprehend,
This go-ahead, this fast age.
> ALEXANDER MCLACHLAN, "Young
> Canada", 1861.

The name of Father, ever will it be
A name of music, true and sweet to
me.
Behind the years, far back in childhood's day,
The name recalls my human trust
and stay.
> GRANT BALFOUR, "Father", 1910.

And never more my father's voice
Comes with insistent tone;
And I, alas! am all too free
To tread my path alone.
> JAMES E. CALDWELL, "Peccavi",
> 1913.

My son, honor thy father and thy
mother by improving upon their example.
> GEORGE ILES, Canadian stories,
> 1918, 182.

FEAR.

A bully is always a coward.
> THOMAS C. HALIBURTON, Sam
> Slick's wise saws, 1853, ch. IV.

Dream of that constable, his name
is Fear, he'll be at your heels till
you die.
> THOMAS C. HALIBURTON, Sam
> Slick's wise saws, 1853, ch. IV.

We build our little life by hour,
by day;
God wakes — and winks a million
years away;
He will have patience though ten
thousand years
Have brought us still no further than
our fears.
> ANNIE C. DALTON, "Flame and
> adventure", 1924.

Fear is a permanent curse in a
democratic world.
> G. M. WRONG, in Can. hist. rev.,
> 1933, 8.

FENCES.

It's no use to make fences unless
the land is cultivated.
> T. C. HALIBURTON, Sam Slick,
> 1836, ch. XVI.

It's a high fence that can't be scaled,
and a strong one that can't be broke
down.

> THOMAS C. HALIBURTON, *Nature
> and human nature*, 1855, I, 65.

FENIANS.

Weed out and cast off these rotten
members, who, without a single governmental grievance to complain of in
Canada, would yet weaken and divide
us in these days of danger and
anxiety.

> THOMAS D'A. McGEE, speech
> in Montreal, 1865.

We are a Fenian brotherhood, skilled
in the arts of war,
And we're going to fight for Ireland,
the land that we adore;
Many battles have we won, along
with the boys in blue,
And we'll go to capture Canada,
for we've nothing else to do!

> Fenian battle song, 1866.

Shout! Shout! Shout! ye loyal
Britons!
Cheer up, let the rebels come,
For beneath the Union Jack
We will drive the Fenians back,
And we'll fight for our beloved
Canadian home.

> THOMAS WILSON, marble-cutter, of
> Brampton, Ont., 1866; sung to the
> tune of "Tramp, tramp, tramp, the
> boys are marching."

In Toronto one extreme is made
auxiliary to the other; Orangeism has
been made the pretext of Fenianism,
and Fenianism is doing its best to
justify and magnify Orangeism.

> THOMAS D'A. McGEE, 1858, *Irish
> position*, 1866, 15.

The Fenian snake is scotched but
not killed... it may revive at any moment.

> SIR ALEXANDER T. GALT, speech on
> the Budget, June 26, 1866.

The Fenians would indeed have
proved the invaluable, though involun-
tary benefactors of Canada, if the only
experience derived from their foolish
proceedings had been the proofs of
warm attachment exhibited by Cana-

dians universally for the land of their
birth or adoption.

> PATRICK MacDOUGALL, *Report on
> militia*, 1866, in *Sessional papers*,
> 2, no. 4.

FINANCE.

Our railway speculations have provided a very efficient issue which will
prevent us dying of plethora.

> JOHN LANGTON, letter, April 17,
> 1856.

Bankruptcy is when you put your
money in your hip pocket and let your
creditors take your coat.

> ROBERT C. (BOB) EDWARDS, *Cal-
> gary Eye Opener*; attributed.

With respect to giving moneys out
of the federal treasury to any Tory
government in this country for these
alleged unemployment purposes, with
these governments situated as they are
today, with policies diametrically opposed to those of this government, I
would not give them a five-cent piece.

> W. L. MACKENZIE KING, H. of C.,
> *Debates*, Unrev., Apr. 3, 1930.

Provincial subsidies are a tangle of
opportunism and necessity.

> A. W. BOOS, *Financial arrange-
> ments*, 1930.

Our whole war effort, both militarily
and economic, at home as well as
overseas, depends upon finance.

> W. L. MACKENZIE KING, radio
> broadcast, Oct. 31, 1939.

Canada joined the large collection
of countries that keep pushing ahead
of them a heavy National Debt; all the
best countries have unredeemable
national debts.

> A. R. M. LOWER, *Colony to nation*,
> 1946, 468.

The modern governmental budget is,
and must be, the balance wheel of
the economy. Its very size is such that
if it were permitted to fluctuate up and
down with the rest of the economy,
instead of counter to the swings of
economic activity, it would so exaggerate booms and depressions as to be
disastrous.

> DOUGLAS C. ABBOTT, speech, Nov.,
> 1949.

FISHING.

These waters plenty fish afford,
    The perch, and pike, and cat;
And there the spotted salmon swims,
    And sturgeon stored with fat.
    The Methodist Magazine, 1828,
    74.

The Fisheries — Banks which always
discount — the wealth we draw from
them need never be repaid.
    N. S. PHILANTHROPIC SOC., Toast,
    Nov. 1, 1836.

Well, here go the fisheries.
    SIR JOHN A. MACDONALD, May 8,
    1871, to Hamilton Fish when sign-
    ing the Treaty of Washington.

Lurked in their watery lairs the
    trout,
But, silver and scarlet, I lured them
    out.
Wary were they, but warier still
My cunning wrist and my cast of
    skill.
    CHARLES G. D. ROBERTS, "The trout
    brook", 1893.

Never can tell when the bass is a-
    coming,
    Never can tell when he's going
    to bite;
First thing you know your reel will
    be humming,
    Strike him quickly and hold him
    tight.
    WILLIAM H. ELLIS, *Wayside weeds*,
    1914.

Oh, this is the place where the fish-
    ermen gather
    With oilskins, boots and capeanns
    battened down ;
All sizes of figures with squid-lines
    and jiggers
    They congregate here on the squid-
    jiggin' ground.
    A. R. SCAMMELL, "Squid jigging-
    ground", a Newfoundland song.

The weather for catching fish is that
weather, and no other, in which fish
are caught.
    W. H. BLAKE, *Brown waters*, 1915,
    29.

The science of fishing can be had
from books; the art is learned by the
catching and the losing of fish.
    W. H. BLAKE, *Brown waters*, 1915.

My fish this year have cost me only
fifty dollars a pound.
    WEIR MITCHELL, quoted in J. M.
    Clarke, *L'Ile Percée*, 1923.

All the big fish in the sea were lost
at the gunnel.
    Newfoundland saying; qu., Devine.
    Folklore of Nfld., 1937.

FLAG.
              (See also: UNION JACK)

All those subordinate matters which
foster a sentiment on union should be
studiously attended to — their flag
should be a modification of that of
England — the Union Jack with a
difference of some kind.
    SIR EDMUND HEAD, memo. on
    gov't. to Lord Grey, 1851, qu.,
    Can. Hist. Assoc., *Report*, 1928, 25.

I hope that the people of the United
States and Great Britain will always
remain true to those great principles
on which their institutions are founded,
and that their flags may wave together
in beauty and harmony in many a distant land, the one bearing on it that
emblem of the might of the Creator, the
starry heavens, which express His infinite power, and the other emblazoned
with the emblem of God's greatest work,
the redemption of man.
    ALEXANDER MACKENZIE, Prime
    Minister, speech in Saint John,
    N. B., 1876.

Canadians waved the flag but Canada
buttoned her pocket.
    ALAN SULLIVAN, *Blantyre — alien*,
    1914.

FLATTERY.

Almost anybody will take any amount
of it.
    SIR JOHN A. MACDONALD, to Sir
    Joseph Pope, his secretary, about
    1880.

FLOWERS.

Erect and towering to the skies,
    Shaggy and rough to sense,
He stares with round expanded face
Full on the sun's meridian rays,
    Picture of impudence.
    JACOB BAILEY, "A farewell", 1779;
    a reference to the sunflower.

The otter of roses is stronger than the rose, and a plaguy sight more valuable.

> T. C. HALIBURTON, *Sam Slick*, 1836, ch. XXXIII.

If folks will let the roses alone, the thorns will let them be.

> THOMAS C. HALIBURTON, *Sam Slick's wise saws*, 1853, ch. XVII.

Over the shoulders and slopes of the dune
I saw the white daisies go down to the sea,
A host in the sunshine, an army in June,
The people God sends us to set our heart free,

The bobolinks rallied them up from the dell,
The orioles rallied them out of the wood;
And all of their singing was, 'Earth, it is well!'
And all of their dancing was, 'Life, thou art good!'

> BLISS CARMAN, "Daisies", 1894.

Green against the draggled drift.
Faint and frail and first,
Buy my northern bloodroot
And I'll know where you were nursed!
Robin down the logging road whistles. "Come to me!"
Spring has found the maple-grove, the sap is running free,
All the winds of Canada call the ploughing-rain.
Take the flower and turn the hour, and kiss your love again!

> RUDYARD KIPLING, "The flowers", 1895.

Give us the flowers now and you need not bring any to our funeral.

> ROBERT C. (BOB) EDWARDS. *Calgary Eye Opener*, Jan. 28, 1905.

The rose was given to man for this:
He, sudden seeing it in later years,
Should swift remember Love's first lingering kiss
And Grief's last lingering tears.

> ISABELLA VALANCY CRAWFORD, "Rose". 1905.

Surely no nobler theme the poet chants
Than the soft science of the blooming plants.

> STEPHEN LEACOCK, verses written in 1909, in, *College days*, 1923, 57.

She has a deep hid virtue
No other flower hath.
When summer comes rejoicing
A-down my garden path,
In opulence of colour,
In robe of satin sheen,
She casts o'er all the hours
Her sorcery serene.

> BLISS CARMAN, "Peony", 1916.

We are the roadside flowers,
Straying from garden grounds,
Lovers of idle hours,
Breakers of ordered bounds.

> BLISS CARMAN, "Roadside flowers", 1916.

FOOD.

A house must have solid foundation, but a dinner a soft one.

> T. C. HALIBURTON, *Nature and human nature*, 1855, II, 21.

More people are killed by over-eating and drinking than by the sword.

> SIR WILLIAM OSLER, *Oslerisms* (Bean), 1905.

Frankly, I don't give a dam
For taste of things too long denied!
Very sick and tired I am
Of this our mutton that once was lamb!

> TOM MACINNES, "Villanelle of mutton", 1918.

We are thankful for these and all the good things of life. We recognize that they are a part of our common heritage and come to us through the efforts of our brothers and sisters the world over. What we desire for ourselves we wish for all. To this end may we take our share in the world's work and the world's struggles.

> J. S. WOODSWORTH, grace before meat, in *The first story of the Labor Church*, 1920.

FOOLS.

(See also: WISDOM AND UNWISDOM)

Old fellers always think young ones fools; but young fellers sometimes know old ones is fools.

T. C. HALIBURTON, *Sam Slick*, 1840, 216.

You were always a fool and always will be to the end of the chapter.

THOMAS C. HALIBURTON, *Sam Slick in England*, 1843 ch. II.

People have no right to make fools of themselves, unless they have no relations to blush for them.

T. C. HALIBURTON, *Sam Slick's wise saws*, 1853, II, 65.

The vanity of fools is the wisdom of the wise.

T. C. HALIBURTON, *Sam Slick's wise saws*, 1853, II, 121.

What this country wants more than anything else is a fool-killer.

SIR W. VAN HORNE, 1891; qu., in Vaughan; *Van Horne*, 1920, 205.

There is hope for the man who can occasionally make a spontaneous and irrevocable ass of himself.

PETER MCARTHUR, *To be taken with salt*, 1903, 153.

Ceremony was invented by a wise man to keep fools at a distance.

ROBERT C. (BOB) EDWARDS, *Calgary Eye Opener*, May 6, 1916.

People always laugh at the fool things you try to do until they discover you are making money out of them.

ROBERT C. (BOB) EDWARDS, *Calgary Eye Opener*, May 31, 1919.

The fool takes things as they come, but the wise guy lets a good many of them pass on.

ROBERT C. (BOB) EDWARDS, *Summer annual*, 1920, 74.

A fool is a man who is not addicted to your own brand of folly.

ROBERT C. (BOB) EDWARDS, *Calgary Eye Opener*; attributed.

FOREIGN RELATIONS.

(See also: CANADIAN-BRITISH RELATIONS; STATUS)

We could not be freer than we are now, for we have no foreign policy to complicate things, and no army to provide.

TORONTO *Globe*, 1874.

You rule yourselves as fully as any people in the world, while in your foreign affairs, your relations with other countries, whether peaceful or warlike, commercial or financial, or otherwise, you may have no more voice than the people of Japan.

EDWARD BLAKE, speech at Aurora, Ont., Oct. 3, 1874.

The Suez Canal is nothing to us, and we do not ask England to quarrel with France or Germany for our sakes.

SIR JOHN A. MACDONALD, letter to Sir Charles Tupper, in London, Mar. 12, 1885.

Not only are we free to manage our domestic concerns, but, practically, we possess the privilege of making our own treaties with foreign countries, and in our relations with the outside world, we enjoy the prestige by a consciousness of the fact that behind us towers the majesty of England.

SIR JOHN A. MACDONALD. "To the electors of Canada", Feb. 7, 1891.

What have we to do with the affairs of South Africa? What interests have we in the Transvaal? Why should we take the money and the blood of the taxpayers of this country to squander them in these far-away regions?

LA PATRIE (Montreal), Oct. 10, 1899. (trans.)

Canadians are becoming weary of negotiating with Washington through London, and of the solemn and elaborate farces called arbitration which for one hundred and twenty years have been robbing Canada to enrich the United States.

Daily Mail, (London, Eng.) despatch from its Toronto correspondent, Oct., 1903.

What did we care for the Boer or what did we care for a few aliens in that country? That was not the thought. Britain needed help, or if she didn't need help she would take it.

> GEORGE W. Ross, speech, Empire Club, Toronto, May 12, 1905.

In matters between Canada and other countries, Canada should arrange her own affairs.

> W. L. MACKENZIE KING, H. of C., *Debates*, April 21, 1921.

France lives and France is free. and Canada is the nobler for her sacrifice to help free France to live.

> ARTHUR MEIGHEN, address at The-lus Military Cemetery, Vimy Ridge, at unveiling of Cross of Sacrifice, July 3, 1921.

Foreign policy is simply an extension of domestic policy.

> O. D. SKELTON, speech, Can. Club, Ottawa, Jan. 21, 1922.

Our external relations are enveloped in what might be called a highly luminous but cloudy halo.

> S R CLIFFORD SIFTON, in *Can. hist. rev.*, 1922. 11.

We are fortunate both in our neigh-bours and in our lack of neighbours.

> W. L. MACKENZIE KING, H. of C., *Debates*, June 18, 1936.

One cannot help feeling that, al-though collective security represents a conviction in so far as the Canadians are concerned, it is only a conviction *de luxe.*

> ANDRÉ SIEGFRIED, *Canada*, 1937.

Canada is a sovereign nation and cannot have dictated to her, by Great Britain, the United States or any other, the attitude she is to adopt in world affairs.

> LORD TWEEDSMUIR, speech in Mont-real, Oct. 12, 1937.

We have a habit of continually worrying about the problems of other countries in order to keep from worrying about our own.

> H. A. INNIS, in *Conf. on Can.-Amer. affairs*, 1939, 133.

FORESTS.

> (See also: LUMBERING; TREES)

The thickness of the wood and greatness of Forrests doe hinder the Sunne from warming the ground.

> *Purchas his pilgrims* (1606), 1905, XVIII, 275.

Dread swell of sound! loud as the gusts that lash
The matted forests of Ontario's shore
By wasteful steel unsmitten.

> WILLIAM WORDSWORTH, "The River Duddon", sonnet XIII, 1820.

Talk not of old cathedral woods
Their Gothic arches throwing,
John only sees in all those trees
So many saw-logs growing.

> ALEXANDER McLACHLAN, "Neighbor John", 1874.

And in the distance, far apart,
As if to shame man's proudest art,
Cathedral arches spread;
While yonder ancient elm has caught
A glory past the reach of thought
Upon his hoary head.

> ALEXANDER McLACHLAN, "October", 1874.

Into the stilly woods I go.
Where the shades are deep and the wild-flowers blow.
And the hours are dreamy and lone than song,
And the power of silence is greater than song,
Into the stilly woods I go.
Where the leaves are cool and the wild-flowers blow.

> WILFRED CAMPBELL, "A wood lyric", 1899.

The wild witchery of the winter woods.

> WILFRED CAMPBELL, "Under the wild witchery of the winter woods", 1922.

Save The Forests!

> NEW BRUNSWICK government slo-gan, 1924.

FREE SPEECH.

I believe you realize the value in the interests of true liberty of a free utterance before his fellow country-men, of the distinctive opinions held by a public man.

EDWARD BLAKE, speech at Aurora, Ont., Oct. 3, 1874.

It is to our own convictions, right or wrong, that we must after all be true. To put forward opinions we do not hold, or ignore difficulties we cannot solve, or deny or conceal the tenden-cies and results of policies we under-take to propound, would be dishonest and unworthy.

EDWARD BLAKE, To the Members of the West Durham Reform Conven-tion, Feb. 9, 1891.

FREE TRADE.

It is in vain to suppose that a free-trade system will be beneficial to a new and struggling colony which has nothing to export but raw materials. It is rather calculated to enrich an old commonwealth, whose people by their skill and labour make such raw materials valuable, and return them for consumption. The result of the system has been that the suppliers of the raw material at last become hewers of wood and drawers of water to the manufacturers.

ABRAHAM GESNER, *Industrial re-sources of N. S.*, 1849.

[Alexander Mackenzie] thinks that Free Trade is the Bible, the catechism, the creed and the paternoster of the political belief of Canada.

SIR JOHN A. MACDONALD, H. of C., *Debates*, 1870, 1202.

Our adversaries wish to present to you an issue as between the present tar-iff and absolute free trade. That is not the true issue. Free trade is, as I have repeatedly explained, for us im-possible; and the issue is whether the present tariff is perfect, or defective and unjust.

EDWARD BLAKE, Address to the electors of West Durham, May 23, 1882.

I invite the most ardent free trader in public life to present a plausible solution of this problem, and I contend that he is bound to do so before he talks of free trade as practicable in

Canada... The thing is removed from the domain of practical politics.

EDWARD BLAKE, speech at Mal-vern, East York, Jan. 22, 1887.

Assuming that absolute free trade with the States, best described as commercial union, may and ought to come, I believe that it can and should come only as an incident, or at any rate as a well-understood precursor of political union, for which indeed, we should be able to make better terms before than after the surrender of our commercial independence.

EDWARD BLAKE, To the Members of the West Durham Reform Con-vention, Feb. 6, 1891.

I may say that on principle I am a very strong free-trader. I have been fed and educated on free trade doc-trines, but doctrines do not always apply to facts.

SIR CLIFFORD SIFTON, letter to J. Fleming, Mar. 13, 1897.

We had a Free Trade party once. The Liberal Party before the advent of the golden silence of office was a Free Trade party.

F. J. DIXON, *Grain growers' guide*, Sept. 9, 1915.

FREEDOM.

(See also: INDEPENDENCE; LIBERTY)

I'm on my way to Canada,
That cold and dreary land;
The dire effects of slavery
I can no longer stand...
Farewell, old master,
Don't come after me,
I'm on my way to Canada
Where coloured men are free.

"Away to Canada", American slave song; in, *Voice of the fugit-ive*, Sandwich, Ont., 1851.

I felt as one, who being awhile confined
Sees drop to dust about him all his bars: —
The clay grows less, and, leaving it, the mind
Dwells with the stars.

GEORGE F. CAMERON, "Standing on tiptoe", 1885.

True greatness is the struggle to be
free,
And he who would be truly great
must bear
A thorny heart for lovely Freedom's
sake.

> THOMAS B. P. STEWART, "Lines
> to my mother", 1887.

Who wooed the west to win the east,
And named the stars of North and
South,
And felt the zest of Freedom's feast
Familiar in his mouth.

> CHARLES G. D. ROBERTS, "Epitaph
> for a sailor buried ashore", 1893.

I scorn your empty creeds, and bend
my knee
    To none of all the gods adored
    by men;
I worship nothing, that I may be free!
    "Mayhap," said one; "you kneel
    to freedom then."

> ARTHUR STRINGER, Epigrams, 1896.

Freedom breeds loyalty. Coercion
always was the mother of rebellion.

> SIR WILFRID LAURIER; attributed.

Canada is a nation. Canada is free,
and freedom is its nationality. Although
Canada acknowledges the suzerainty of
a sovereign power I am here to say
that independence can give us no more
rights than we have at the present day.

> SIR WILFRID LAURIER, speech,
> London, Eng., June 18, 1897.

It is our proud boast that Canada
is the freest country in the world. It
is our boast that in this country liberty
of all kinds, civil and religious liberty,
flourish to the highest degree.

> SIR WILFRID LAURIER, address at
> Tercentenary Celebration, Quebec,
> 1908.

Praise for faith in freedom
Our fighting fathers' stay,
Born of dreams and daring,
Bred above dismay.

> BLISS CARMAN, "In the day of
> battle", 1916.

Crowd back the hills and give me
room,
    Nor goad me with the sense of
    things;
Earth cramps me like a narrow
tomb,

Your sunlight is too dense for
wings;
    Away with all horizon bars;
    Push back the mountains and the
    stars.

> ALBERT D. WATSON, "Soul-lifted",
> 1920.

Since you who walked in freedom
And the ways of reason fought on
our front,
We foresee the plot is solvable, the
duel worthy.

> EARLE BIRNEY, "For Steve", 1945.

FRENCH CANADIANS.

(See also: BILINGUALISM;
UNITY; VOYAGEURS)

Nothing will satisfy the licentious
fanaticks trading here, but the expulsion of the Canadians who are perhaps
the bravest and the best race upon the
Globe, a race, who could they be in-
dulged with a few of the priviledges
which the law of England deny to
Roman Catholicks at home, would soon
get the better of every national antip-
athy to the conquerors and become
the most faithful and most useful set
of men in the American empire.

> GOV. JAMES MURRAY, letter to Lords
> of Trade, Oct. 29, 1764.

I glory in having been accused of
warmth and firmness in my protecting
the King's Canadian Subjects and
doing the utmost in my Power to gain
to my Royal Master the affection of that
Brave, hardy people.

> GOV. JAMES MURRAY, letter to Lord
> Shelburne, Aug. 20, 1766.

Barring Catastrophe shocking to
think of, this Colony must to the end
of Time, be peopled by the Canadian
Race.

> SIR GUY CARLETON, in despatch
> to Lord Shelburne, Nov. 25, 1767.

I think there is nothing to fear from
them, while we are in a state of
prosperity, and nothing to hope for
when in distress.

> SIR GUY CARLETON, letter to Lord
> Germain, Sept. 28, 1776.

Our language, our institutions, and
our laws.

> LE CANADIEN (Montreal), motto,
> 1806. (trans.)

We shall be the France of America afore long — the grand nation — the great empire. It's our destiny — everything foretells it.

T. C. HALIBURTON, *Sam Slick*, 1838, 153.

Whatever may happen, whatever government shall be established over them, they can see no hope for their nationality...

LORD DURHAM, *Report*, 1839, ed. Lucas, 1912, 291.

There can hardly be conceived a nationality more destitute of all that can invigorate and elevate a people, than that which is exhibited by the descendants of the French in Lower Canada, owing to their retaining their peculiar language and manners. They are a people with no history, and no literature.

LORD DURHAM, *Report*, 1839, ed. Lucas, 1912, 294.

I have little doubt that the French, when once placed, by the legitimate course of events and the working of natural causes, in a minority, would abandon their vain hopes of nationality.

LORD DURHAM, *Report*, 1839, ed. Lucas, II, 307.

If we would make them civilised and free men, we must put them on an equality with the rest of the population, and we must have them speak the language and be partakers of those institutions, which are the language and institutions of every free man in North America.

CHARLES BULLER, Gt. Brit., *Hansard*, 3rd. ser., 1839, vol. 48, 1202.

If ever this country should cease one day to be British, the last gun fired in defence of British sovereignty in America will be that of a French Canadian.

ETIENNE-PASCAL TACHÉ, speech on militia, Legislative Assembly, Montreal, April 24, 1846; varies. See: *La Minerve*, 27 avril, 1846, p. 2: "Si jamais ce pays cesse un jour d'être britannique, le dernier coup de canon tiré pour le maintien de la puissance anglaise en Amérique le sera par un bras Canadien."

You may perhaps *Americanize*, but depend upon it, ...you will never *Anglicize* the French inhabitants of the province. Let them feel, on the other hand, that their religion, their habits, their prepossessions, their prejudices if you will, are more considered and respected here than in other portions of this vast continent, who will venture to say that the last hand which waves the British flag on American ground may not be that of a French Canadian?

LORD ELGIN, dispatch to Lord Grey, May 4, 1848.

The truth is you British Canadians never can forget that you were once supreme... No man in his senses can suppose that the country can for a century to come be governed by a totally unfrenchified government. If a British Canadian desires to conquer, he must "stoop to conquer". He must make friends of the French without sacrificing the status of his race or religion. He must respect their nationality. Treat them as a nation and they will act as a free people generally do — call them a faction and they become factious.

SIR JOHN A. MACDONALD, letter to Brown Chamberlin, June 21, 1856.

I would say this, to their honour and credit, that if today Canada is a portion of the British Empire, it is due to the conservatism of the French Canadian clergy.

SIR GEORGE CARTIER, *Confederation debates*, Feb. 7, 1865, 59.

Here we sit today seeking amicably to find a remedy for constitutional evils and injustice complained of — by the vanquished? No, sir, — but complained of by the conquerors! Here sit the representatives of the British population claiming justice — only justice; and here sit the representatives of the French population, discussing in the French tongue whether we shall have it.

GEORGE BROWN, *Confederation debates*, Feb. 8, 1865, 85.

For my part, I am not afraid of the French Canadian majority in the future Local Government doing injustice, except accidentally; not because I am of the same religion as themselves; for origin and language are barriers stronger to divide men in this world than is religion to unite them.

THOMAS D'A. McGEE, *Confederation debates*, Feb. 9, 1865, 143.

Attachment to the soil is the secret of the future greatness of the French Canadian people. We hear a great deal of nationality, but I tell you that the race which will triumph in the future will be that which has held the soil.

SIR GEORGE CARTIER, speech at Rimouski, Aug. 7, 1870. (trans.)

French Canada is a relic of the historical past preserved by isolation, as Siberian mammoths are preserved in ice.

GOLDWIN SMITH, *Political destiny of Canada*, 1878, 10.

So long as there are French mothers the language will not die.

SIR WILFRID LAURIER, H. of C., *Debates*, Mar. 16, 1886, 180.

In Barrie, last election, I pointed out, in a few simple words, that the great danger which overshadowed Canada was the French national cry, this bastard nationality, not a nationality which will take us in as we will take them in, but a nationality which begins and ends with the French race — which begins and ends with those who profess the Roman Catholic faith, and which now threatens the dismemberment of Canada.

D'ARCY McCARTHY, speech at Stayner, Ont., July 12, 1889.

With courage, with perseverance, with union, with effort, and above all with a constant devotion to our religion and our language, the future must be ours. Sooner or later, marching on together, we shall arrive at the position of a great nation. The logical conclusion of my work can only be this — One day we shall be Catholic France in America.

N. - H. - E. FAUCHER DE SAINT-MAURICE, *La question du jour*, 1890. (trans.)

We are loyal to the great nation which gave us life. We are faithful to the great nation which gave us liberty.

SIR WILFRID LAURIER, speech in Paris, 1897.

If Britain is ever in danger — nay, I will not say that — if Britain is ever on trial, I, a Canadian of French origin, will be the first to go to the people and call upon them to assist with all our might.

SIR WILFRID LAURIER, speech in Cobalt, Ont., Sept. 18, 1912.

French by descent and affection, we are British by allegiance and conviction.

RODOLPHE LEMIEUX, Canadian Club speech, Toronto, 1914.

It was there that she heard her Voice, the Voice of Quebec, 'half the song of a woman and half the sermon of a priest.' "Strangers have surrounded us," the voice says, "barbarians they seem to us, they have taken almost all the power, they have taken almost all the money, but in the land of Quebec nothing has changed. Nothing shall change, for we are here to bear witness. This is the only clear idea we have of ourselves and our destinies, to persist, to keep our identity. And we have kept our identity; perhaps centuries in the future the world will turn to us and say: 'These people come from a race that does not know how to die'."

LOUIS HÉMON, *Maria Chapdelaine*, 1916. (trans.)

Canada is today British because French Canadians refused to have it something else.

W. H. MOORE, *The clash*, 1918, 278.

It is one of the paradoxes of history that, had Canada been more completely anglicized in 1776, it would probably today be a part of the United States.

GEORGE M. WRONG, *Can. hist. rev.*, 1922, 72.

The habitant is the true Canadian for he has no other country.

RAMSAY TRAQUAIR, *Atlantic mo.*, 1923, 823.

The French Canadian in a real sense is the truest Canadian. He has lived on the soil for three hundred years, and the family ties with another world have long been broken. To Canada alone does he feel attached, for England conquered him and France first deserted him and then travelled a political and spiritual road his clergy has taught him to abhor. He sees no hope coming from without; he knows he must build up his own resources.

F. R. SCOTT, *Canada today*, 1938, 72.

The disturbing factor to the French Canadians is not the British Crown but British policy.

W. BOVEY, *French Canadians*, 1938.

If the Great Powers stubbornly insist on clinging to the old concept of nationalism — which is out-dated now — peoples who have not found nationalism a happy experience may be the only ones who can give the world the fresh solution that it needs. I suspect that the coming people in the Americas may be the French Canadians.

ARNOLD TOYNBEE, *World review*, Mar. 1949, 12.

FRIENDS.

Indeed, my friend you bite very hard!

DUKE OF RICHMOND, August, 1819, at Richmond, Ont., to the pet fox from which he contracted hydrophobia.

An intemperate advocate is more dangerous than an open foe.

T. C. HALIBURTON, *Sam Slick*, 1836, chap. XXIV.

No one hates like him that has once been a friend.

T. C. HALIBURTON, *Sam Slick*, 1838, 209.

A comrade neither glum nor merry.

BLISS CARMAN, "Joys of the road", 1896.

In the life of a young man the most essential thing for happiness is the gift of friendship.

SIR WILLIAM OSLER, introd. to *Life of Pasteur*, 1911, by Vallery-Radot.

It is well that there is no one without a fault for he would not have a friend in the world.

ROBERT C. (BOB) EDWARDS, *Calgary Eye Opener*, Dec. 11, 1915.

I bow not down to any book,
No written page holds me in awe;
For when on one friend's face I look
I read the Prophets and the Law!

ROBERT NORWOOD, "After the order of Melchisedec", 1917.

Whether at sea or whether on shore,
Or at the job or over the wine,
Whether on two legs, whether on four —
All good fellows are friends of mine!

TOM MACINNES, "Ballade of friends", 1918.

A friend who knows your secret holds a mortgage on your peace of mind.

ROBERT C. (BOB) EDWARDS, *Calgary Eye Opener*, Dec. 25, 1920.

I have some friends, some honest friends,
And honest friends are few;
My pipe of briar, my open fire,
A book that's not too new.

ROBERT W. SERVICE, "I have some friends", 1921.

The difference between a friend and an acquaintance is that a friend helps where an acquaintance merely advises.

ROBERT C. (BOB) EDWARDS, *Calgary Eye Opener*, Aug. 20, 1921.

In all my wending
I've seen no sight
So full of friending
As you, eyebright!

GEORGE HERBERT CLARKE, "*Eyebright*", 1930.

Friend o' mine in the year oncoming
I wish you a little time for play
And an hour to dream in the eerie gloaming
After the clamorous day.

L. M. MONTGOMERY, "Friend o' mine", in *Good housekeeping*, Jan. 1936.

FROGS.

Breathers of wisdom won without a
    quest,
Quaint uncouth dreamers, voices high
    and strange;
Flutists of lands where beauty hath
    no change,
And wintry grief is a forgotten
    guest;
Sweet murmurers of everlasting rest.
    ARCHIBALD LAMPMAN, "The frogs",
    1888.

For the unrest of passion here is
    peace,
And eve's cool drench for midday
    soil and taint.
To tired ears how sweetly brings
    release
This limpid babble from life's un-
    stilled complaint.
    CHARLES G. D. ROBERTS, "Frogs",
    1893.

Nobody but a Canadian can really
appreciate frogs. As a musical instrument they do not exist in other
countries, and it is as a musical
instrument that they are of value in
the expression of beauty in Canada.
    B. K. SANDWELL, speech, Can.
    Club, Ottawa, Mar. 13, 1920.

Quaint and low, like some remote
    bassoon,
    Across the marsh there came a
    muffled croon,
And all alone one melancholy frog,
Squat on the butt of a sunken log,
    Solemnly did serenade the Moon:—
In tone so low, and quaint — like
    the quaint bassoon.
    TOM MACINNES, "The moonlit
    wheat", 1923.

FUR TRADE.

The most obvious Benefit acquired
by the Cessions made to your Majesty
is the Fur & Skin Trade of all the
Indians in North America.
    THE LORDS OF TRADE, to the King,
    June 8, 1763.

Fortitude in distress.
    Motto of the BEAVER CLUB, Mont-
    real, founded, 1775, by the part-
    ners of the North West Company.

Philanthropy is not the object of
our visits to these Northern Indians.
    GEORGE SIMPSON, of the Hudson's
    Bay Co., 1821, Journal, Athabasca
    dept., ed. by Rich, 1938.

The feudal state of Fort William is
at an end; its council chamber is
silent and deserted; its banquet-hall
no longer echoes to the burst of loyalty, or the 'auld world' ditty; the
lords of the lakes and forests have
passed away.
    WASHINGTON IRVING, Astoria, 1836,
    on the Nor'Westers.

Colonization and the fur trade could
not exist together.
    SIR GEORGE CARTIER and WILLIAM
    MCDOUGALL, communication on
    acquiring the property of the Hud-
    son's Bay Company addressed to
    Sir F. Rogers, London, Feb. 8,
    1869.

FUTURE.

    (See also: DESTINY; NATION-
    ALITY)

Mankind lives on promises.
    THOMAS C. HALIBURTON, Sam
    Slick's wise saws, 1853, ch. XI.

An ounce of prevention is worth a
pound of cure.
    THOMAS C. HALIBURTON, Sam
    Slick's wise saws, 1853, ch. XV.

I never draw on to-morrow. It is
like anticipatin' one's income makin'
the future bear the expenses of the
past.
    T. C. HALIBURTON, Sam Slick's
    wise saws, 1853, II, 106.

Deep, infinite deeps before us,
    Ruin riding in the wind,
Cloudy curtains hanging o'er us,
    And eternities behind.
    ALEXANDER McLACHLAN, "A
    dream", 1856.

Every radiant winged Tomorrow
    hidden in the distant years,
Has its poise of joy and sorrow, has
    its freight of hopes and fears.
Every hour upon the dial, every
    sand-grain dropped by Time,

Quickens man, by useful trial, for his march to the Sublime.

CHARLES SANGSTER, "A poet's love", 1856.

Our Northern rising nationality has an example field before it — a brilliant future in the distance.

ALEXANDER MORRIS, Hudson's Bay, 1858.

I look a little ahead.

SIR JOHN A. MACDONALD, the reason given for his defeat of George Brown.

To these objections, I answer, that though theoretical today, our future will be practical tomorrow; that I do not, and never did, place myself in the position of a preacher of loyalty; that I preach rather security, I preach precaution, I preach self-preservation.

THOMAS D'A. McGEE, "The future of Canada", a lecture delivered in St. Lawrence Hall, Toronto, Nov. 26, 1863.

It may be doubted whether the inhabitants of the Dominion themselves are as yet fully awake to the magnificent destiny in store for them, or have altogether realised the promise of their young and hardy nationality. Like a virgin goddess in a primæval world, Canada still walks in unconscious beauty among her golden woods and by the margin of her trackless streams, catching but broken glances of her radiant majesty as mirrored on their surface, and scarcely recks as yet of the glories awaiting her in the Olympus of nations.

LORD DUFFERIN, speech in Belfast, June 11, 1872, after appointment as Governor-General.

It is not our poverty of land or sea, of wood or mine, that shall ever urge us to be traitors. But the destiny of a country does not depend on its natural resources. It depends on the character of its people.

GEORGE M. GRANT, From ocean to ocean, 1873.

The future of Canada, I believe depends very largely on the cultivation of a national spirit.

EDWARD BLAKE, speech at Aurora, Ont., Oct. 3, 1874.

In a world apart, secluded from all extraneous influences, nestling at the feet of her majestic Mother, Canada dreams her dream, and forebodes her destiny — a dream of ever-broadening harvests, multiplying towns and villages, and expanding pastures, of constitutional self-government. and a confederated Empire; of page after page of honourable history, added as her contribution to the annals of the Mother Country and to the glories of the British race.

LORD DUFFERIN, speech in City Hall, Winnipeg, Sept. 29, 1877.

Of one thing you may be sure, that the country you call Canada and which your sons and your children's children shall be proud to call by that name, will be a land of power among the nations.

MARQUIS OF LORNE, speech in Winnipeg, 1881.

Be Canadians and the future is yours.

LOUIS FRÉCHETTE, qu., Can. leaves, 1887, 131.

O Falterer, let thy past convince
Thy future, — all the growth, the gain,
The fame since Cartier knew thee, since
Thy shores beheld Champlain.

CHARLES G. D. ROBERTS, "Canada", 1887.

I hope that when another century has been added to the age of Canada it may still be Canada, and that its second century shall like its first be celebrated by Canadians, unabsorbed, — numerous, prosperous, powerful, and at peace. For myself, I should prefer to die in that hope than to die President of the United States.

SIR OLIVER MOWAT, speech at Niagara-on-the-Lake, July 16, 1892.

The floodtide is upon us that leads to fortune; if we let it pass it may never recur again. If we let it pass, the voyage of our national life, bright as it is today, will be arrested in the shallows.

SIR WILFRID LAURIER, H. of C., Debates, July 30, 1903.

We cannot look into the future; we cannot foresee the destiny of Canada; but, sir, on this we rest well assured: that Canada has not been led through the perils and difficulties of its chequered career, that six million people have not been placed in command of the northern half of this continent with all its vast resources, that we shall occupy an ignoble and insignificant position amongst the nations of the earth.

> Sir Clifford Sifton, July. 1904, at Winnipeg Exibition.

Thus stands the question of the future of Canada. Find for us something other than mere colonial stagnation, something sounder than independence, nobler than annexation, greater in purpose than a Little Canada. Find us a way.

> Stephen B. Leacock, *Univ. mag.*, Feb., 1907, 141.

Canada should define her own citizenship, Canada should make her own treaties, Canada, eventually, should select her own chief magistrate, be he king or president. I have no hesitation in laying this down as my belief in regard to Canada's future and her connection with the Empire.

> W. F. Maclean, H. of C., *Debates*, Feb. 11, 1907.

We should try to arrange ourselves so that we will appear as plausible as possible to posterity.

> R. D. Cumming, *Skookum Chuck fables*, 1915, 157.

Posterity pays our debts but repudiates our excuses.

> Robert C. (Bob) Edwards, *Calgary Eye Opener*, Feb. 8, 1919.

I have in my veins all the sweet unrest of the wild places,
And if you toss me aside I will come hither again on the morrow;
For I am a force that you cannot deny;
I am an offering that you finally must accept
For I am the herald of new things in a new land.

> Wilson MacDonald, "Out of the wilderness", 1926.

In time of prosperity prepare for trouble.

> Sir Clifford Sifton, letter to his son, Harry, Feb. 9, 1929.

What seek we to repair this piteous time?
Our answer lies within us, and our star;
We have to-morrow what today we are.

> Warwick Chipman, "The millenium", 1930.

It would be well to bear in mind that the present of today was the future of yesterday and that it is what it is because of the human actions, the human decisions from yesterday. Therefore the future will be what we make it.

> John W. Dafoe, speech. Toronto, Empire Club, Jan. 30, 1936.

One thing I will not do, and cannot be persuaded to do, is to say what Canada will do in regard to a situation that may arise at some future time and under circumstances of which we now know nothing.

> W. L. Mackenzie King, speech in Toronto, Aug. 8, 1939.

G

GEOGRAPHY.

(See also : Precambrian Shield; Thompson, David.)

Geographically we are bound up beyond the power of extinction.

> Thomas D'A. McGee, speech in St. John, N. B. 1863.

Geography and treaties have united to make [Canada's] unification difficult.

> George M. Grant, address, Canadian Club, N. Y., 1887.

You cannot legislate against geography.

> Sir Wilfrid Laurier, speech at Somerset, Que., Aug. 2, 1887. (trans.)

Those who are not of it bear this testimony, that once Canada was to them a mere geographical expression; now they know it not only as a great Colony of the crown, but all, save in name, a nation.

> G. MERCER ADAM, *Sir John Macdonald*, 1891, xvii; the phrase "a mere geographical expression" was used by Laurier, speech at Joliette, Aug. 17, 1911.

Canada is a country of enormous distances.

> SIR JOHN WILLISON, *Railway question in Canada* (pam.), 1897; also, "A country of such magnificent distances", E. B. Osborn, *Greater Canada*, 1900, 105.

The Barrens.

> A common name for the Arctic regions and the northern part of the Canadian Shield.

Did you fight geography to make a Confederation? Then fight geography to keep a Confederation.

> GEORGE E. FOSTER, speech in North Toronto, April 17, 1911.

In Canada man is making a nation in defiance of geographical conditions.

> W. L. GRANT, in, *Geographical jour.*, Oct., 1911.

That the present Canada is not a natural geographical unit is an undeniable fact.

> OSCAR D. SKELTON, *The railway builders*, 1916, 28.

In the beginning was geography.

> W. STEWART WALLACE, in *Can. hist. rev.*, 1920, 139.

Let us sing in a song together:
Mattawa, Napanee,
Manitowaning, Ottawa,
Nipissing, Ville Marie.
Missanabie, Manitoulin,
  (Whisper them soft and low)
Espinola, Michipicoten,
Iroquois, Orono.

> WILSON MACDONALD, "Singing words", 1934.

If some countries have too much history we have too much geography.

> W. L. MACKENZIE KING, H. of C., *Debates*, June 18, 1936.

Rose on the map, with flakes as lakes of blue;

Fretted with rivers and provincial boundaries;
Straight at the base and jagged at the top —
The east-west dream mocks the northwest fact.

> GUY GLOVER, "Canadian poem", 1947.

GIRLS.
(See also: CHILDREN)

A good darter and a good housekeeper is plaguy apt to make a good wife and a good mother.

> T. C. HALIBURTON, *Sam Slick*, 1838, 84.

Canadian girls are so pretty it is a relief to see a plain one now and then.

> MARK TWAIN, notebook written on a trip to Montreal, Nov., 1881.

How in the end, and to what man's desire
Shall all this yield, whose lips shall these lips meet?
One thing I know: if he be great and pure,
This love, this fire, this beauty shall endure;
Triumph and hope shall lead him by the palm:
But if not this, some differing thing he be,
That dream shall break in terror; he shall see
The whirlwind ripen, where he sowed the calm.

> ARCHIBALD LAMPMAN, "A forecast", 1888.

Avoid wine and women — choose a frecklefaced girl for a wife; they are invariably more amiable.

> SIR WILLIAM OSLER, *Oslerisms*, (Bean), 1905.

There's a girl at Calabogie, an' another at the Soo
An' with sparkin' and colloguin', I've been foolish with the two.

> WILLIAM H. DRUMMOND, "Marriage", 1908.

I honour the girls who choose instead
The ancient duties, day by day,
As wives and mothers and makers of bread:
Good women give themselves away.

> TOM MACINNES, "Ballade of good women", 1918.

The daughters were pleasant and pious and more useful than both.

J. L. MACDOUGALL, *History of Inverness county, N. S.*, 1922.

Last night in a land of triangles,
I lay in a cubicle, where
A girl in pyjamas and bangles
Slept with her hands in my hair.

TOM MACINNES, "Zalinka", 1923.

Many a man in love with a dimple makes the mistake of marrying the whole girl.

STEPHEN B. LEACOCK; attributed.

THE GLOBE (TORONTO).

(See also: BOOKS AND READING)

When we commence with a man we never let him go until we finish him.

ANON., quoted by Egerton Ryerson, letter in *The Leader*, July 12, 1863.

No journal ever did more to poison the heart of society; the most virulent of party organs, the most scandalous of society papers would not have wrought practically so much harm.

GOLDWIN SMITH, *The Bystander*, Jan., 1883, 77.

There were probably many thousand voters in Ontario, especially among the Scotch settlers (who always formed the backbone of the Liberal party in that province), who hardly read anything except their *Globe* and their Bible, and whose whole political creed was practically dictated to them by the former.

SIR RICHARD CARTWRIGHT, *Reminiscences*, 1912, 9.

GOD.

A knowledge of God is the foundation of all wisdom.

T. C. HALIBURTON, *Sam Slick*, 1840, 258.

We worship the spirit that walks unseen
Through our land of ice and snow:
We know not His face, we know not His place,
But His presence and power we know.

THOMAS D'A. MCGEE, "The Arctic Indian's faith", 1858.

Let me see
Some portion of the truths that tend
By slow gradations up to Thee.

CHARLES SANGSTER, "Mystery", 1860.

God has many bests.

JOHN M. KING, Manitoba College, 1883-1899; frequently quoted by J. S. Woodsworth.

For long ago, when the world was making,
I walked through Eden with God for guide;
And since that time in my heart forever
His calm and wisdom and peace abide.

BLISS CARMAN, "Wanderer", 1892.

Der Kaiser auf der Vaterland
Und Gott on high, all dings gommand.
Ve two, ach, don'd you understandt?
Meinself — und Gott.

ALEXANDER MACGREGOR ROSE [GORDON], "Kaiser & Co.", later called "Hoch der Kaiser"; in, Montreal *Herald*, Oct., 1897.

Lord of my heart's elation
Spirit of things unseen,
Be thou my aspiration
Consuming and serene!

BLISS CARMAN, "Lord of my heart's elation", 1903.

The great world's heart is aching, aching fiercely in the night,
And God alone can heal it, and God alone give light;
And the men to bear that message, and to speak the living word,
Are you and I, my brothers, and the millions that have heard.

FREDERICK C. SCOTT, "Our duty", 1909.

I took a day to search for God,
And found Him not. But as I trod
By rocky ledge, through woods untamed,
Just where one scarlet lily flamed,
I saw His footprint in the sod.

BLISS CARMAN, "Vestigia", *Harper's mag.*, 1921.

Between ourselves I must confess
Tho I may talk somewhat of God
Yet I have found no God, unless —
God is a state of consciousness.

TOM MACINNES, "Unless", 1923.

The Spirit of God works through the human mind in accordance with psychological laws, not otherwise.

> FREDERICK H. DuVERNET, *Out of a scribe's treasure*, 1927.

God judges us by what we would become,
By the direction, not the distance gained;
Of all our shortcomings He knows the sum,
Where we have failed, and what we have attained.

> H. ISABEL GRAHAM, *Saint Ignace*, 1935.

GOOD AND EVIL.

(See also: SIN; VIRTUE)

Good and evil seldom come where they are expected.

> T. C. HALIBURTON, *Sam Slick's wise saws*, 1853, I, 243.

Innocence is not suspicious, but guilt is always ready to turn informer.

> THOMAS C. HALIBURTON. *Sam Slick's wise saws*, 1853, ch. XV.

A good man who goes wrong is just a bad man who has been found out.

> ROBERT C. (BOB) EDWARDS, *Calgary Eye Opener*, Sept. 22, 1917.

These moralists are growing over-nice:
Surely, my friend, some need there is for spice!
The salt and pepper of impropriety —
I would not call it vice.

> TOM MacINNES, "*Protest*", 1918.

Say if you choose there is naught but good:
Harden your heart and soften your brain:
Say wrong is right misunderstood:
Close your eyes to filth and pain:
Swear all is right and all is sane,
And all correct from days primeval:
And then — well, then what will you gain?
No man knoweth the end of evil.

> TOM MacINNES, "*Ballade of evil*", 1918.

GOVERNMENT.

(See also: BRIBERY; THE CROWN; GOVERNOR-GENERAL; INDEPENDENCE; PARLIAMENT; POLITICS; PUBLIC OPINION)

It has been the cant of time immemorial to make mystery of the art of government. The folly of the million, and the cunning of the few in power, have equally strengthened the reigning belief; but it is false, deceitful and ruinous.

> ROBERT GOURLAY, *Statistical account of U. C.*, 1822, II, 390.

The representative system is become the desire of all civilized nations, because it promises to nations a powerful lever to extirpate abuses; because it affords a popular efficacious action which penetrates into all parts of administration, and influences, in a salutary manner, all its agents, from the Sovereign to the lowest officer, recalling them continually to their destination, which is the peace and welfare of nations.

> LOUIS JOSEPH PAPINEAU, speech. Montreal West election, Aug. 11. 1827. (trans.).

The hour approaches in which the electors of Upper Canada are to decide whether a few factious and aspiring men shall yet a little longer mar the happiness of its inhabitants. or whether an honest and intelligent House of Assembly composed of our most deserving inhabitants will go hand in hand with the King and his excellent ministers in perfecting our political institutions and bestowing on us that free government which, although it is not happiness, is, when wisely employed, a sure means of procuring all the prosperity mankind can reasonably look for.

> WILLIAM LYON MACKENZIE, Address to the Reformers of Upper Canada. Toronto, Sept., 1834.

Government is founded on the authority, and is instituted for the benefit, of a people; when, therefore, any Government long and systematically ceases to answer the great ends of its foundation, the people have a natural right given them by their

Creator to seek after and establish such institutions as will yield the greatest quantity of happiness to the greatest number.

Declaration of Toronto Reformers, Aug., 1837.

Government, both in theory and practice, resides with the people.

T. C. Haliburton, *Sam Slick*, 1838, 52.

May our government never degenerate into a mob, nor our mobs grow strong enough to become our government.

T. C. Haliburton, *Sam Slick*, 1838, 138.

Not government merely, but society itself seems to be almost dissolved; the vessel of the State is not in great danger only, as I had been previously led to suppose, but looks like a complete wreck.

Lord Durham, letter to Glenelg, Aug. 9, 1838.

The government of the country *must* be carried on. It *ought* to be carried on with vigour. If that can be done in no other way than by mutual concessions and a coalition of parties, they become necessary. And those who, under such circumstances assume the arduous duties of becoming parties to them, so far from deserving the opprobrium that is too frequently and often too successfully heaped upon them, have, in my opinion, the strongest claims upon public sympathy and support.

Robert Baldwin, letter to Francis Hincks, Sept. 22, 1854.

Self-government would be utterly annihilated if the views of the Imperial Government were to be preferred to those of the people of Canada. It is therefore the duty of the present government distinctly to affirm the right of the Canadian legislature to adjust the taxation of the people in the way they deem best, even if it should unfortunately happen to meet the disapproval of the Imperial ministry. Her Majesty cannot be advised to disallow such acts, unless her advisers are prepared to assume the administration of the

affairs of the colony, irrespective of the views of its inhabitants.

Sir Alexander Galt, dispatch, Can. Sess. paper no. 38, 1860.

If coalition between two parties means that for the sake of emolument or position they sacrifice principle, then coalition government ought not to receive the confidence of the people. But if it means the junction of a number of men, who, forgetting old quarrels which have been wiped out, and who instead of raking up the ashes after the fire of dissension had burned away, finally extinguished it, and refused to prolong discord — then I say that coalition is the act of true patriots.

Sir John A. Macdonald, speech, 1861; qu., Biggar, *Anecdotal life*, 180.

Happily political institutions kill as seldom as they cure.

Goldwin Smith, *Lectures on modern history*, 1861, 20.

Retrenchment is the immediate duty, the duty of the day and the hour, — but the government must lead as well as save, it must march as well as fortify, it must originate plans for the future, as well as correct the errors of the past.

Thomas D'Arcy McGee, speech in Ottawa, Oct. 14, 1862.

Peace, order and good government.

British North America Act, 1867, sect. 91; also, Unemployment Relief Act, 1934, sect. 2.

Whereas, it is admitted by all men, as a fundamental principle, that the public authority commands the obedience and respect of its subjects. It is also admitted that a people, when it has no Government in preference to another, to give or to refuse allegiance to that which is proposed.

Proclamation of the Provincial Government of the Northwest, Dec. 8, 1869, signed by John Bruce and Louis Riel.

For the honour of the country, no government should exist which has a shadow of suspicion resting upon it, and for that reason I cannot give it my support.

> DONALD A. SMITH (Lord Strathcona) H. of C., *Debates*, Nov. 5, 1873, on the "Pacific Scandal".

Canada is a hard country to govern.

> SIR JOHN MACDONALD, a favourite saying. Also used by Laurier, see his letter to John Willison, March 7, 1905, "This is a difficult country to govern".

Our form of government is a representative monarchy.

> SIR WILFRID LAURIER, speech in Quebec, June, 1877, before the Club Canadien. (trans.)

The only conceivable basis for government in the New World is the national will; and the political problem of the New World is how to build a strong, stable, enlightened and impartial government on that foundation.

> GOLDWIN SMITH, *Political destiny of Canada*, 1878, 57.

I do not believe that any nation has now attained, and I doubt whether any nation ever will attain, such a point of morality, as to be able to govern other nations for the benefit of the governed.

> GOLDWIN SMITH, "The last Republicans of Rome", in *Lectures and essays*, 1881.

Nothing, it would seem, could be more comical than a man paid by a Government for opposing its measures and striving to turn it out.

> GOLDWIN SMITH, in London *Spectator*, Dec. 2, 1905, on the Opposition.

A people for high dreamings meant, But damned by too much government.

> WILFRED CAMPBELL, in Campbell and Martin, *Canada*, 1907, 45.

Phipps, if you had a secretary you could govern the universe.

> NICHOLAS F. DAVIN, to R. W. Phipps, Ont. Superintendent of forestry, on agreeing with his statement that he could govern Canada as well as Sir John A. Macdonald; qu., Willison, *Reminiscences*, 1919, 52.

Is not our whole system of government built upon the principle that all political power is vested in the people at large?

> MANITOBA *Free Press*, June 18, 1914, 13.

How different the story of the world's relations would be today had the Brute, in the name of the State, not been permitted to control the Man.

> W. L. MACKENZIE KING, *Industry and humanity*, 1918, 114.

Federal government appears to me to be the only possible one in Canada because of our differences of race and creed, and also because of the variety and multiplicity of local needs in our immense territory.

> SIR LOMER GOUIN, in *Quebec and Confederation*, ed. by Savard, 1918, 124.

A Government upon the defensive is a Government in distress.

> SIR JOHN WILLISON, *Reminiscences*, 1919, 31.

The people of Canada get better government than they deserve.

> SIR JOHN WILLISON, *Reminiscences*, 1919, 279.

Group government.

> A term used to describe the form of government advocated by Henry Wise Wood, especially in his speech at Crossfield, Oct. 21, 1919.

I claim that we have come to a period in the history of our country when we must decide once and for all which shall prevail — profits or human welfare.

> JAMES S. WOODSWORTH, H. of C., *Debates*, Mar. 14, 1922.

It is not the business of the Government to maintain the people — it is the business of the people to maintain the Government.

> JOHN OLIVER, Premier of British Columbia, 1918-27.

It is commonplace that Canada has been the laboratory of the British Empire; a place where theories of government have had their first practical test; where, upon the breakdown of theories, other policies have been suggested and applied.

JOHN W. DAFOE, in, *Great Britain and the Dominions*, 1927, 178.

The way to get things out of a government is to back them to the wall, put your hands to their throats, and you will get all they have.

AGNES MACPHAIL, speech to Southern Progressive Assoc., Regina, Sask., 1927.

One-man Government.

W. L. MACKENZIE KING, H. of C., *Debates*, Mar. 16, 1931, a reference to R. B. Bennett, Prime Minister.

The whole structure of our national life must be built upon the thought that everything that is good we seize upon and everything that is bad must be rejected.

R. B. BENNETT, speech at Newmarket, 1933, in *Can. problems*.

In our day any citizen who tried to follow intelligently all the public affairs and the public elections of his township, his country, his municipality, his school board and his sanitary district, his Province and his Dominion, his Empire and his League of Nations, would have no time for anything else.

STEPHEN B. LEACOCK, presidential address, Can. Pol. Sci. Assoc., 1934.

Governments begin to die as soon as they gain power, and finally the popular will is accomplished when a government is defeated — it being only incidental that the opposing party is placed in the seats of the mighty.

R. J. MANION, *Life is an adventure*, 1936, 266.

The genius of the British peoples for political association consists perhaps not so much in a power of constructing good institutions as in the invincible habit of worshipping what they have constructed. This makes even a bad organization work well.

P. E. CORBETT, *C.J.E.P.S.*, 1933, 114.

It is not easy to govern a country, part of whose people are more British than the King and part more Catholic than the Pope.

A. R. M. LOWER, *Colony to nation*, 1946, 417.

There are only two kinds of government — the scarcely tolerable and the absolutely unbearable.

JOHN W. DAFOE, qu. in George V. Ferguson, *John W. Dafoe*, 1948, 59.

GOVERNMENT, RESPONSIBLE.

(See also : POLITICAL PHRASES)

If the Canadians are to be deprived of representative government, it would be better to do it in a straightforward way, than to attempt to establish a permanent system of government on the basis of what all mankind would regard as mere electoral frauds. It is not in North America that men can be cheated by an unreal semblance of representative government, or persuaded that they are out-voted, when, in fact, they are disfranchised.

LORD DURHAM, *Report*, 1839.

One event after another has occurred, calculated to impair confidence in the excellence of what by courtesy has been called Responsible Government.

GEORGE SHEPPARD, in Toronto *Globe*, 1859, qu., *Can. hist. rev.*, 1935, 246.

The winning of responsible government a century ago was neither a Colonial victory or a British defeat. It was the triumph of both British and Colonial reformers over conservatism, reaction and timidity on both sides of the Atlantic.

GEORGE W. BROWN, in *Can. hist. rev.*, June, 1942.

GOVERNOR-GENERAL.

If that system be continued, some colonist will, by and by, or I am much mistaken, hire a black fellow to horsewhip a Lieutenant-Governor.

JOSEPH HOWE, speech in N. S. Assembly, Feb. 20, 1846; a reference to Lord Falkland who denounced Howe's friends, including the Speaker, to the Colonial Office in a dispatch later made public.

A Governor-General should be something more than a drill-sergeant, or a schoolmaster.

TORONTO *Globe*, Oct. 13, 1860.

I would rather be the proprietor of the *Globe* newspaper for a few years than be governor-general of Canada, much less a trumpery little province.

GEORGE BROWN, letter to his family, May 13, 1864.

My only guiding star in the conduct and maintenance of my official relations with your public men is the Parliament of Canada — in fact, I suppose I am the only person in the Dominion whose faith in the wisdom and in the infallibility of Parliament is never shaken.

LORD DUFFERIN, speech in Halifax, Aug. 8, 1873.

I cannot describe to you the feeling of loneliness without peace, and of dull oppression which weighs upon the spirits of a person in my position.

LORD DUFFERIN, letter to Carnarvon, Oct. 2, 1874.

[The Governor General is like] the humble functionary we see superintending the working of some complicated mass of chain-driven machinery. This personage merely walks about with a little tin vessel of oil in his hand and he pours in a drop here and a drop there, as occasion or the creaking of a joint may require, while his utmost vigilance is directed to no higher aim than the preservation of his wheels and cogs from the intrusion of dust, grits, or other foreign bodies.

LORD DUFFERIN, speech at National Club, Toronto, Jan. 12, 1877.

I admit the responsibility of the Ministers for every utterance made by the Governor-General respecting public affairs, or which has any bearing on public affairs.

ALEXANDER MACKENZIE, H. of C., *Debates*, Mar. 1, 1877, 375.

The King who reigns and does not govern is represented by a Governor-General who does the same, and the Governor-General solemnly delegates his impotence to a puppet Lieutenant-Governor in each province. Religious Canada prays each Sunday that they may govern well, on the understanding that heaven will never be so unconstitutional as to answer her prayer.

GOLDWIN SMITH, *Canada and the Can. question*, 1891, 147.

We had far rather that he should speak his mind than that he should waste our time — and his own — in telling us how exceedingly green our grass is, and how much better we are than other people he has ever had the good fortune to meet

TORONTO *Star*, May 2, 1905.

For nearly five years I have endeavoured in my public utterances to call the attention of the people to the importance of keeping before them high national and Imperial ideals. For nearly five years I have, quite conscious of my constitutional limitations, walked the tight-rope of platitudinous generalities and I am not aware of having made any serious slip.

LORD GREY, speech to Canadian Club, Winnipeg, Oct. 13, 1909.

I hope that my colleagues and I shall not be found wanting in respect or indeed in admiration for the wide military experience of Your Royal Highness and the high position which you hold as a Field-Marshal in His Majesty's Forces. It would appear to us that the matters under consideration do not call so much for the exercise of military skill or the application of military experience as the consideration of international law and the exercise of the common-place quality of common sense.

SIR ROBERT BORDEN, letter to Duke of Connaught, Gov.-Gen., Aug. 4, 1916.

The Governor-General of today is little more than a convenient peg on which to hang our system of government.

R. MACGREGOR DAWSON, *Principle of official independence*, 1922, 218.

We don't want any more Mintos. We don't want any more Greys. We certainly don't want any more Byngs. I sometimes wonder if we want any more of 'em at all, but we really do.

JOHN W. DAFOE, to George V. Ferguson, Mar. 21, 1927.

GRAVEYARDS.

We'll bury old Guibord
In the consecrated ground...
Guibord's coffin weighs exactly forty
tons.

> Montreal ditty, (trans.) Joseph
> Guibord was under excommuni-
> cation when he died 1869, and was
> not buried until 1875, because of
> opposition from the Church.

Unaltering rest their perfect being
cloaks —
A thing too vast to hear or feel or
see —
Children of Silence and Eternity,
They know no season but the end
of time.

> ARCHIBALD LAMPMAN, "In Beech-
> wood cemetery", 1900.

Just think! some night the stars
will gleam
Upon a cold grey stone,
And trace a name with silver beam,
And lo! 'twill be your own.

> ROBERT W. SERVICE, "Just think",
> 1912.

Cometh the night. The wind falls
low,
The trees swing slowly to and fro;
Around the church the headstones
grey
Cluster like children strayed away
But found again and folded so.

> JOHN McCRAE, "The night cometh",
> 1913.

Long years ago they went to take
their rest
Beneath the spreading trees on yonder
hill —
The field they cleared for use at
God's behest,
And where the quiet tenants of his
will
Are undisturbed of any joy or ill.

> WILLIAM E. MARSHALL, "Brook-
> field", 1914.

Stony fields and lonely roads,
Meagre hamlets, very lean,
And most prosperous graveyards
Lying all between.

> KATHERINE HALE, "Northern grave-
> yards," 1923.

GREATNESS.

Being great is apparently a very
pleasant pastime.

> PETER McARTHUR, *To be taken
> with salt*, 1903, 148.

We shall not be great simply because
we have a productive soil and natural
resources; we shall be great only if
we have our quota of great engineers,
great authors, great orators, great
sculptors and painters, great statesmen
and great journalists.

> W. F. OSBORNE, Can. Club, Mont-
> real, Jan. 27, 1919.

GROWTH.

To grow may mean to outgrow, to
be charged with inconstancy as infertile
ground is left for pastures new.

> GEORGE ILES, *Canadian stories*,
> 1918, 177.

All God's word is but one word 'grow'.

> PETER McARTHUR, "The priest of
> Amen-Ra", (unpublished), qu. in
> W. A. Deacon, *Peter McArthur*,
> 1923, 122.

H

HALIFAX, N. S.

> (See also: CITIES AND TOWNS
> — NICKNAMES)

Hell or Halifax.

> The alternative destination of the
> United Empire Loyalists on their
> expulsion from New England, about
> 1783.

Into the mist my guardian prows put
forth,

Behind the mist my virgin ramparts
lie,
The warden of the Honour of the
North,
Sleepless and veiled am I!

> RUDYARD KIPLING, "The song of
> the cities — Halifax", 1896.

Dear, dingy, old Halifax,

> CHARLES DUDLEY WARNER, qu., *Can.
> mag.*, 1899, 289.

Halifax sits on her hills by the sea
In the might of her pride, —

Invincible, terrible, beautiful, she
   With a sword at her side.
     E. PAULINE JOHNSON, "Guard of
     the Eastern gate", 1903.

HAPPINESS.

Happiness is rather a negative than a
positive term in this world, and
consists more in the absence of some
things than in the presence of others.
     THOMAS C. HALIBURTON, *The old
     judge*, 1849, ch. V.

He's great who's happy anywhere.
     CHARLES HEAVYSEGE, qu., *Can.
     birthday book*, 1887, 100.

Happiness lies in the absorption in
some vocation which satisfies the soul.
     SIR WILLIAM OSLER, *Doctor and
     nurse*, 1891.

Therefor is joy more than sorrow,
   foreseeing
The lust of the mind and the lure
   of the eye
And the pride of the hand have their
   hour of triumph,
But the dream of the heart will
   endure by and by.
     BLISS CARMAN, "Wanderer", 1893.

A nameless and unnatural cheer,
A pleasure secret and austere.
     ARCHIBALD LAMPMAN, "In Novem-
     ber", 1895.

Because the tardy gods grew kind.
Unrest and care were cast behind;
I took a day, and found the world
Was fashioned to my mind.
     CHARLES G. D. ROBERTS, "The
     quest of the arbutus", 1896.

Contentment consists largely in not
wanting something that is out of your
reach.
     ROBERT C. (BOB) EDWARDS, *Cal-
     gary Eye Opener*, Feb. 11, 1913.

Fat men are good-natured because
good-natured men are usually fat.
     ROBERT C. (BOB) EDWARDS, *Cal-
     gary Eye Opener*, May 22, 1915.

The public will pay more for laughing
than for any other privilege.
     ROBERT C. (BOB) EDWARDS, *Cal-
     gary Eye Opener*, May 11, 1918.

Idle to grieve, the light is on the
   highway,
There are mountain meadows to
   achieve,
Beyond in the pass the airy heights
   are my way,
Idle to grieve, glad heart, idle to
   grieve.
     DUNCAN CAMPBELL SCOTT, "Idle to
     grieve", 1921.

If all our scientific improvements,
our intensive organization, our me-
chanical triumphs, all the devices which
make for increased production and
simplification of production — if all
these things do not help the worker
to greater happiness and to a better and
healthier life, what is the use of them?
     R. B. BENNETT, radio address, Jan
     4, 1935.

In Alberta, broadly speaking, happiness means credit.
     A. F. McGOUN, *C.J.E.P.S.*, 1936,
     513.

HATE.

As a matter of fact your neighbours
think just as disagreeable thoughts
about you as you think about them.
     ROBERT C. (BOB) EDWARDS, *Cal-
     gary Eye Opener*, Nov. 24, 1917.

From love of you such strength did
   flow,
I was a god to drink of it;
And now, by God, I hate you so
It makes me weak to think of it.
     L. A. MACKAY, "The ill-tempered
     lover", 1938.

Hate knows no firmer ground than
gratitude.
     A. M. KLEIN, *Hitleriad*, 1944.

HEART.

The road to the head lies through
the heart.
     T. C. HALIBURTON, *Sam Slick*,
     1838, 23.

The mechanism of the human heart,
when you thoroughly understand it, is,
like all the other works of nature,
very beautiful, very wonderful, but very
simple. When it does not work well,

the fault is not in the machinery, but in the management.

> T. C. HALIBURTON, *Nature and human nature*, 1855, I, 88.

Open, O heart, and let me view
The secrets of thy den;
Myself unto myself now show
With introspective ken.
Expose thyself, thou covered nest
Of passions and be seen;
Stir up thy brood, that in unrest
Are ever piping keen.
Ah! what a motley multitude,
Magnanimous and mean.

> CHARLES HEAVYSEGE, poem no. VII in, *Jephthah's daughter*, 1865.

In my heart are many chambers, through which I wander free;
Some are furnished, some are empty, some are sombre, some are light;
Some are open to all comers, and of some I keep the key,
And I enter in the stillness of the night.

> JOHN READE, "In my heart", 1870.

Do not squander heartbeats in cardiac disease — live within your income.

> SIR WILLIAM OSLER. *Oslerisms* (Bean), 1905.

God made a heart of gold. of gold,
Shining and sweet and true;
Gave it a home of fairest mold,
Blest it, and called it — You.

> ROBERT W. SERVICE, "Sunshine", 1912.

HEROES.

(See also: FAME)

It is natural for us to sigh for Washingtons and Franklins of our own and for endless anniversaries, to remind us of the deeds and the glories of our ancestors.

> JOSEPH HOWE, speech at his trial for criminal libel, Mar. 2, 1835.

No tongue can blazon forth their fame —
The cheers that stir the sacred hill
Are but mere promptings of the will
That conquered them, that conquers still;
And generations yet shall thrill
At Brock's remembered name.

> CHARLES SANGSTER, "Brock". Oct. 13, 1859.

What is the boasted bubble, reputation?
To-day it is the world's loud cry
Which may to-morrow die,
Or roll from generation unto generation
And magnify and grow to fame,
That quenchless glory round a great man's name.

> CHARLES HEAVYSEGE, "Good deeds", 1865.

None dreameth tonight in his bed
That ruin was near and the heroes
That met it and stemmed it are dead.

> ARCHIBALD LAMPMAN, "At the Long Sault", 1898.

Unscathed they stand, immutable, sublime,
Great-souled, beyond the barriers of gloom,
In solemn light, above the wrecks of time,
They rise triumphant, challenging the tomb.

> ALBERT D. WATSON, "Myth", 1917.

The story of a nation's heroes is the fountain from which it draws the wine of its later life. There is no inspiration that quickens the ambition of youth, stimulates public service and deepens love of country like the memory of great men who have gone.

> ARTHUR MEIGHEN, speech on Thomas D'Arcy McGee, Ottawa, April 13, 1925.

HISTORY.

(See also: NATIONAL HERITAGE; THE PAST)

Man is a recording animal.

> ROBERT GOURLAY, a favourite saying; appears on the title-page of his, *Chronicles of Canada*, Kingston, 1842.

History, without moral philosophy, is a mere string of facts; and moral philosophy, without history, is apt to become a dream.

> GOLDWIN SMITH, *Rational religion*, 1861, 20.

The historians of Canada (with the conspicuous exception of. Garneau) have been literary balloonists. Ascending to a high altitude, they have observed what was on the surface, whilst the character of the Canadian people and its changes in different stages of growth, from the present settlements of the eighteenth century to the confederate nation of today — all this has not yet been written. The people of Canada have been left out of Canadian histories.

> GEORGE SANDFIELD MACDONALD, in Celtic Soc., Montreal, *Trans.*, 1884, 7, 131.

I do not know. There are many facts in the history of this country, of which I am not aware, and a great many statements of facts in regard to history, I find controverted so often, that I am not able to state a positive opinion in regard to them.

> SIR JOHN THOMPSON, H. of C., *Debates*, April 25, 1890.

If it's all the same to history, it need not repeat itself any more.

> ROBERT C. (BOB) EDWARDS, *Calgary Eye Opener*, May 31, 1919.

Much Canadian history can only be read aright with one eye on the history of the United States.

> R. G. TROTTER, in *Can. hist. rev.* 1924, 213.

I did not realize that the old grave that stood among the brambles at the foot of our farm was *history*.

> STEPHEN B. LEACOCK, Can. Hist. Assoc., *Report*, 1925, 33.

The study of history is the playground of patriotism.

> G. M. WRONG, in *Can. hist. rev.*, 1927, 60.

I like history because my reading of it is accompanied by the comforting certainty that all the people I meet in its pages are dead.

> CECIL F. LLOYD, *Sunlight and shadow*, 1928.

History is capricious in its awards of fame. It fixes on dramatic incident and ignores the quiet service that may count for much more.

> G. M. WRONG, in *Can. hist. rev.*, 1932, 53.

Canada's history is as dull as ditchwater and her politics is full of it.

> MAURICE HUTTON, qu., *Can. hist. rev.*, 1935, 336.

History is the vast and complex tale of the working of the spirit of man.

> G. M. WRONG, *Can. hist. rev.*, 1936, 3.

In truth there is nothing in history like the problem of today.

> R. H. COATS, in *Can. jour. econ. pol. sci.*, 1938, 152.

The Laurentian School.

> Term used in 1940's to denote historians who stressed the theme of national unity as against sectionalism; their "symbol" the St. Lawrence River.

HOME.

(See also: HOUSES)

If you want to know how to valy home, you should go abroad for a while among strangers.

> T. C. HALIBURTON, *Sam Slick*, 1838, 126.

O near lights, and far lights,
And every light a home!
And how they gladden, sadden us,
Who late and early roam!

> ARTHUR STRINGER, "Night travel", 1907.

Laddie, little laddie, come with me over the hills,
Where blossom the white May lilies, and the dogwood and daffodils;
For the Spirit of Spring is calling to our spirits that love to roam
Over the hills of home, laddie, over the hills of home.

> LILIAN LEVERIDGE, "Over the hills of home", 1918.

HONESTY.

I believe it is in politics as in other matters, honesty is the best policy.

> T. C. HALIBURTON, *Sam Slick*, 1838, 119.

Where there is no confidence, there can be no honesty.

> T. C. HALIBURTON, *Sam Slick*, 1838, 125.

I am getting too old to form part of the school of 'chiselers', that is a bad school; I stick to the old rule, honesty is the best policy in the long run.

> SIR L. H. LAFONTAINE, letter to R. Baldwin, 1851.

I wonder, Carling, if God ever made a man as honest as you look.

> SIR JOHN A. MACDONALD to Sir John Carling ("Honest John") in Council; Carling was a minister in Macdonald's cabinet, 1882-1891.

If honesty is exiled from the farm, where will it find a home?

> GOLDWIN SMITH, Weekly sun. Oct. 3, 1906.

Men are able to trust one another, knowing the exact degree of dishonesty they are entitled to expect.

> S. B. LEACOCK, "The woman question," Maclean's mag., Oct., 1915.

Don't place too much confidence in a man who boasts of being as honest as the day is long. Wait until you meet him at night.

> ROBERT C. (BOB) EDWARDS, Calgary Eye Opener; attributed.

HOPE.

Hope is a pleasant acquaintance, but an unsafe friend.

> T. C. HALIBURTON, Sam Slick's wise saws, 1853, I, 281.

You can't live on hope, and hope deferred makes the heart sick.

> THOMAS C. HALIBURTON, Sam Slick's wise saws, 1853, ch. XII; the latter part of the quotation is from the Bible.

Hope is a slender reed for a stout man to lean on.

> THOMAS C. HALIBURTON, Sam Slick's wise saws, 1853, ch. XIII.

The houses hope builds are castles in the air.

> THOMAS C. HALIBURTON, Sam Slick's wise saws, 1853, ch. XIII.

So came the Autumn's ruddy prime, And all my hopes, which had no morrow.

Like sea-weed cast upon the beach, Like drift-wood barely out of reach Of waves that were attuned to sorrow, Lay lifeless on the strand of time.

> GEORGE MARTIN, in Can. birthday book, 1887, 302.

So to address our spirits to the heighth, And so attune them to the valiant whole,
That the great light be clearer for our light,
And the great soul the stronger for our soul.

> ACHIBALD LAMPMAN, "The largest life", Atlantic mo., Mar., 1899.

For stormy times and ruined plans Make keener the determined will, And Fate with all its gloomy bans Is but the spirit's vassal still:
And that deep force, that made aspire
Man from dull matter and the beast, Burns sleeplessly a spreading fire, By every thrust and wind increased.

> ARCHIBALD LAMPMAN, "Phokaia", 1900.

Hope is faith holding out its hands in the dark.

> GEORGE ILES, Canadian stories, 1918, 167.

HORSES.

There are only two things worth lookin' at in a horse, action and soundness; for I never saw a critter that had good action that was a bad beast.

> T. C. HALIBURTON, Sam Slick, 1836, ch. XXVII.

Oh, much I wish that I were able To build a house like Cartwright's stable,
For it doth cause me great remorse To be worse lodged than Cartwright's horse.

> DR. JAMES SAMPSON, mayor of Kingston, 1839-40, and 1844, on the stables of J. S. Cartwright.

The spur won't hurt when the hide is thick.

> THOMAS C. HALIBURTON, Sam Slick's wise saws, 1853, ch. XII.

For, be we either man or hoss, We've all some inborn sin:

And what is Christianity
But just a breakin' in?
Now, I gives all my hosses, sir,
A Christian edication;
And nor a one but has some sense
Of moral obligation.
    ALEXANDER McLACHLAN, "Old
    hoss", 1874.

The Kentucky of Canada.
    Prince Edward Island, so called
    because of its harness racing.

Lord Ronald said nothing; he flung
himself from the room, flung himself
upon his horse and rode madly off in
all directions.
    STEPHEN B. LEACOCK, "Gertrude
    the governess", in *Nonsense novels*,
    1911.

Lucky, lucky white horse, lucky,
    lucky lee!
Lucky, lucky white horse, bring luck
    to me.
    Western Ontario rhyme; qu. *J.
    Amer. folklore*, 1938, 61.

HOUSES.

The bigger the house the bigger the
fools be that's in it.
    T. C. HALIBURTON, *Sam Slick*,
    1836, chap. XXIX.

A small house well filled is better
than an empty palace.
    THOMAS C. HALIBURTON, *Sam
    Slick's wise saws*, 1853, ch. 1.

We live in a rickety house
    In a dirty dismal street,
Where the naked hide from day
    And thieves and drunkards meet.
    ALEXANDER McLACHLAN, "We live
    in a rickety house", 1861.

John Tomkins lived in a house of
    logs,
On the second concession of Deer;
The front was logs, all straight and
    sound —
The gable was logs, all tight and
    round —
The roof was logs, so firmly bound —
And the floor was logs, all down to
    the ground —
    The warmest house in Deer.
    WILLIAM W. SMITH, "The second
    concession of Deer", 1888.

HOWE, JOSEPH.

I wish to live and die a British
subject, but not a Briton only in the
name.
    JOSEPH HOWE, speech in N. S.
    Legislature, Feb. 11, 1837.

That pestilent fellow, Howe.
    SIR JOHN A. MACDONALD, letter,
    October, 1867: 'Nova Scotia... has
    declared as far as she can against
    Confederation, but she will be
    powerless for harm, although
    that pestilent fellow, Howe, may
    endeavour to give us some trouble
    in England.'

There were more seminal ideas in
that man's head than in any other
man's with whose history I am familiar.
    SIR JOHN A. MACDONALD, to George
    Johnson, 1886.

The Tribune of Nova Scotia.
    A popular reference to Howe.

HUDSON BAY.

His name is written on the deep, the
    rivers as they run
Will bear it timeward o'er the world,
    telling what he has done.
    THOMAS D'A. McGEE, "The death
    of Hudson", 1858.

Canada must control Hudson's Bay
absolutely; it is the front and central
door; and a knocker must be put on it.
    W. F. MACLEAN, speech to Cana-
    dian Club, Toronto, Feb. 24, 1904.

Hudson Bay will become the Mediterranean of the North.
    LORD GREY, Governor General, Nov.,
    1910.

On To The Bay!
    ON-TO-THE-BAY ASSOCIATION, form-
    ed in Winnipeg in 1924 to press for
    completion of the Hudson Bay
    Railway; motto.

HUDSON'S BAY COMPANY.
(See also: FUR TRADE)

The Governor and Company of
Adventurers of England trading into
Hudson's Bay.
    Charter of Incorporation, granted
    by Charles II, signed May 2, 1670.

Pro Pelle Cutem.

> The Company's motto, from the coat-of-arms — "The skin for the fur", [i.e., the beaver fur]; in more recent days, "Skin for skin".

Sleeping at the edge of a frozen sea.

> JOSEPH ROBSON, *An account of six years residence in Hudson's-Bay*, 1752.

Here Before Christ.

> Early nineteenth century; northern hunters' saying for meaning of the Company's initials.

The Company.

> Expression used in the West and North-West from early 19th. century.

There can be no question that the injurious and demoralizing sway of that company over a region of four millions of square miles, will, ere long, be brought to an end, and that the destinies of this immense country will be united with our own. It is unpardonable that civilization should be excluded from half a continent, on at best but a doubtful right of ownership, for the benefit of two hundred and thirty-two shareholders.

> TORONTO *Globe*, 1852.

What! sequester our very tap-root? Take away the fertile lands where our buffaloes feed! Let in all kinds of people to squat and settle and frighten away the fur-bearing animals they don't kill and hunt. Impossible! Destruction — extinction — of our time-honoured industry. If these gentlemen are so patriotic, why don't they buy us out?

> H. H. BERENS, governor of H. B. C., to Duke of Newcastle, 1863, qu., Watkin, *Canada and U. S.*, 1887, 120.

The Hudson's Bay Company never amounted to a damn until the North West Company joined it.

> ANON., qu., Pinkerton, *Gentlemen adventurers*, 1931, 113.

The Hudson's Bay Company is one of the most hidebound concerns in existence.

> SIR W. VAN HORNE letter to W. Whyte, 1891; qu. in Vaughan: *Van Horne*, 1920, 196.

HUMBUG.

It cannot be denied that in dealings with the public just a little touch of humbug is immensely effective, but it is not necessary.

> SIR WILLIAM OSLER, *Internal medicine as a vocation*, 1897.

The greatest men of the past were all Masters of Humbug, and so are the greatest men to-day.

> SIR W. VAN HORNE, letter, 1919, qu. in Vaughan: *Van Horne*, 1920, 357.

I assure you that there never was such humbug as this proposal.

> JAMES H. THOMAS, Secretary of State for Dominion Affairs, on trade proposals of R. B. Bennett, Gt. Brit., H. of C., *Debates*, Nov. 27, 1930, 1550.

HUNTING.

> Let us be much with nature: not as they
> That labour without seeing, that employ
> Her unloved forces, blindly without joy,
> Nor those whose hands and crude delights obey
> The old brute passion to hunt down and slay.
>
> ARCHIBALD LAMPMAN, "On the companionship with nature", 1900.

It is a strange anomaly that man, the greatest killer in the universe, and almost the only one that kills for sport when there is no need — he is the one who deplores and condemns killing by any other agency than himself. Hunting is a good thing: good for man, and not bad for the game; except for those individuals that are overtaken by the slayer.

> WILLIAM E. SAUNDERS, in *W. E. Saunders — naturalist*, 1949, 29.

I
IDEALS.

Her bright visions vanished into thin air.

> THOMAS C. HALIBURTON, *Sam Slick's wise saws*, 1853, ch. VI.

O! pathless world of seeming!
O! pathless world of mine whose deep ideal
Is more my own than ever was the real.

> PAULINE JOHNSON, "Shadow river", 1895.

To have striven, to have made an effort, to have been true to certain ideals — this alone is worth the struggle. Now and again in a generation one or two snatch something from dull oblivion.

> SIR WILLIAM OSLER, address, "Study of the fevers of the South", Atlanta, May 6, 1896.

To us the money-getting art
Is but the one thing real;
We seldom cherish in our heart
A holy, high ideal.

> ALEXANDER McLACHLAN, "Rein auld Adam in", 1900.

We want to be a nation but we cannot be a nation unless we fairly put before the people ideals which will appeal to all men whatever their religion or their race.

> SIR WILFRID LAURIER, speech in Orillia, Oct. 19, 1904.

Let our purpose be ideal and our action be practical.

> Sir WILFRID LAURIER, attributed.

It's a fine thing to have your head in the air, but it's always best to have your feet on the ground.

> JOHN OLIVER, speech at Liberal convention, Vancouver, 1927.

Somebody once told me that if I aimed at the sky I might at least hit a tree. If I wanted to hit a tree I'd shoot straight at it.

> JOHN OLIVER, Premier of B. C., 1918-27.

We must have social ideals as distinguished from what we have called the individual right.

> R. B. BENNETT, speech to Montreal Board of Trade, Jan. 26, 1935.

Our bitterest wine is always drained from crushed ideals.

> ARTHUR STRINGER, *The devastator*, 1944, 116.

IDEAS.

The poor man of one idea is always in danger of being laughed at by people who have none.

> ROBERT C. (BOB) EDWARDS, *Calgary Eye Opener*, June, 6, 1902.

One should never spoil a good theory by explaining it.

> PETER McARTHUR, *To be taken with salt*, 1903, 152.

Ideas are born; they develop; they are transformed; but they never die.

> SIR ANDREW MACPHAIL, *Dalhousie rev.*, 1925, 22.

IMAGINATION.

It is perfectly true, and a truth always to be borne in mind by statesmen, that, in politics as in other departments of life, the imagination has its claims as well as the reason, and that while the one is convinced the other requires to be impressed.

> GOLDWIN SMITH, in, *Can. monthly*, 1879, 211.

The truth is, imagination, in itself, has no place in the equipment of a permanent writer. Imagination invents, it does not create.

> SIR ANDREW MACPHAIL, R.S.C., *Proc.*, 1939, 131.

IMMIGRATION.

> (See also: EMIGRATION; SETTLERS; UNION JACK)

I am led to conceive it indispensably necessary to overwhelm and sink the [French -] Canadian population by the introduction of a greater number of English protestants, and this I believe to be practicable.

> JONATHAN SEWELL, letter to Sir James Craig, early 1810.

How great the ardor which their
souls inspired,
Who, leaving far behind their native
plain,
Have sought a home beyond the
western main;
And braved the terrors of the stormy
seas,
In search of wealth, of freedom, and
of ease.

OLIVER GOLDSMITH, (Canadian),
"The rising village", 1825.

Dear, most justly dear to every land
beneath the sun are the children born
in her bosom, and nursed upon her
breast; but when the man of another
country, wherever born, speaking whatever speech, holding whatever creed,
seeks out a country to serve and
honour and cleave to in weal or in
woe, — when he heaves up the anchor
of his heart from its old moorings, and
lays at the feet of the mistress of his
choice, his New country, all the hopes
of his ripe manhood, he establishes by
such devotion a claim to consideration,
not second even to that of the children
of the soil.

THOMAS D'ARCY MCGEE, speech
in Quebec, May, 10, 1862.

The best kind of emigration agent
is the successful settler in the new
district.

THOMAS WHITE, H. of C., *Debates*,
Mar. 4, 1884.

Sifton's pets.

Reference to European immigrants
brought to Canada through efforts
of Clifford Sifton, when Minister
of Interior, 1896 to 1905.

The scum of Europe.

Term sometimes used to describe
immigrants, 1900 to 1905.

New Canadians.

HOWARD A. KENNEDY, from his
book, *New Canada and the new
Canadians*, 1907.

When I speak of quality I have in
mind, I think, something that is quite
different from what is in the mind of
the average writer or speaker upon the
question of immigration. I think a
stalwart peasant in a sheep-skin coat,
born on the soil, whose forefathers
have been farmers for ten generations,

with a stout wife and a half-dozen
children, is good quality.

SIR CLIFFORD SIFTON, speech to
Toronto Board of Trade, March,
1922; *Maclean's mag.*, April 1,
1922, 16. Sifton made similar
statements when he was Minister
of the Interior, 1896-1905. (See
also, POLITICAL PHRASES.)

Dazzled by sun and drugged by
space they wait,
These homeless peoples, at our prairie
gate;
Dumb with the awe of those whom
fate has hurled,
Breathless, upon the threshold of a
world!

ISABEL ECCLESTONE MACKAY, "Calgary station", 1922.

IMMORTALITY.

The heavens will not unveil them-
selves,
Yet mortal eyes may see
In mortal frames the budding flowers
Of immortality.

ALEXANDER MCLACHLAN, "A
dream", 1856.

I ask is there end of it — any?
If any, when comes it anigh?
I could die not the one death but
many
To know and be sure I should die...

To know that somewhere in the
distance
When Nature shall take back my
breath,
I shall add up the sum of existence,
And find that its total is — death!

GEORGE F. CAMERON, "All heart-
sick", 1887.

Yet, patience — there shall come
Many great voices from life's outer
sea,
Hours of strange triumph, and, when
few men heed,
Murmurs and glimpses of eternity.

ARCHIBALD LAMPMAN, "Outlook",
1888.

Space, in the dim predestined hour,
Shall crumble like a ruined tower.
I only, with unfaltering eye,

Shall watch the dreams of God go
by.

CHARLES G. D. ROBERTS. "The un-
sleeping", 1896.

The immortal spirit hath no bars
To circumscribe its dwelling place;
My soul hath pastured with the stars
Upon the meadow-lands of space.

FREDERICK G. SCOTT, "Dawn", 1899.

There is a part of me that knows,
Beneath incertitude and fear,
I shall not perish when I pass
Beyond mortality's frontier.

BLISS CARMAN, "Non omnis
moriar", 1901.

Thus on, till the light of all being
is rippling around us
On paths we have trod:
Till the sun bursts aloft o'er the hills
where the morning hath found us
Entempled with God.

ALBERT D. WATSON, "Woman",
1923.

I shall say, Lord, "Is it music, is it
morning,
Song that is fresh as sunrise, light
that sings?"
When on some hill there breaks the
immortal warning
Of half-forgotten springs.

MARJORIE PICKTHALL, "Resurgam",
(1925).

And in that twilight world, whose
floodless sea
Washes the margin of a silent land,
We shall not walk alone, but hand
in hand,
And Love shall warm our immortality
With an eternal spring; since even
death
Cannot dispart our souls, nor chill
our mingled breath.

AUDREY ALEXANDRA BROWN, "Lao-
damia", 1931.

IMPERIALISM.

(See also: COLONIES AND
COLONIALISM)

I am an Imperialist because I will
not be a Colonial.

STEPHEN B. LEACOCK, Univ. mag.,
Feb., 1907, 133.

There can be no lasting Imperialism
which conflicts with Canadian nationality.

DR. MICHAEL CLARK, speech in
Calgary, Sept. 11, 1913.

They talks of England's glory and
a - 'oldin' of our trade,
Of Empire and 'igh destiny until
we're fair flim-flammed;
But if it's for the likes o' that that
bloody war is made,
Then wot I say is: Empire and 'igh
destiny be damned!

ROBERT W. SERVICE, "A song of
the sandbags", 1916.

INDEPENDENCE.

(See also: CANADIAN-BRIT-
ISH RELATIONS; FREEDOM;
LIBERTY; STATUS; SOVER-
EIGNTY)

We cannot be independent.

WILLIAM LYON MACKENZIE, speech
to Reformers, Sept., 1834.

I have no reason to believe that
anything can make them generally
desirous of separation, except some
such act of the Imperial Government
as shall deprive them of all hopes of
obtaining real administrative power.

LORD DURHAM, Report, 1839.

If in the hidden decrees of that
wisdom by which this world is ruled,
it is written that these countries are
not for ever to remain portions of the
empire, we owe it to our honour to
take good care that, when they separate
from us, they should not be the only
countries on the American continent
in which the Anglo-Saxon race shall be
found unfit to govern itself.

LORD DURHAM, Report, 1839.

I see in British North America a
region grand enough for the seat of
a great empire. I find its inhabitants
vigorous, hardy, energetic... I find
them jealous of the United States
and of Great Britain, as they ought
to be; and therefore, when I look
at their extent and resources, I
know that they can neither be conquered by the former nor permanently held by the latter. They will be

independent, as they are already self-maintaining.

> WILLIAM H. SEWARD, *Cruise to Labrador*, 1857.

> Rob me of all the joys of sense,
> Curse me with all but impotence;
> Fling me upon an ocean oar,
> Cast me upon a savage shore;
> Slay me! but own above my bier:
> "The man now gone still held yet here,
> The jewel, Independence".
>
> THOMAS D'A. McGEE, "Independence", 1858.

If independence were to take place now it would end in our drifting into the United States, but while I hold this view, I believe that the day for independence will come, and unless we were prepared for it, unless our legislation be framed with that view, we will be found then in the same position as now, and being unprepared for a separate political existence, we will have no choice with regard to our future.

> SIR ALEXANDER T. GALT, H. of C., *Debates*, Feb., 1870.

We no more advocate Independence than we advocate the Day of Judgment.

> WILLIAM A. FOSTER, Speech to Canadian National Association, 1875.

I could not argue in favour of either independence or annexation. If ever the time came that either had to be seriously discussed I would argue it only in one way, and that would be on horseback with my sword.

> GEORGE T. DENISON (Police magistrate of Toronto), remarks at National Club dinner, 1880.

I am one of those who believe that this country should have the right to negotiate its commercial treaties. I go a step further, I believe this country should have the right to negotiate every treaty... I see no reason why the people of Canada should not look forward to Canada becoming a sovereign and independent State... Sir, I was born a British colonist, but do not wish to die a tadpole British colonist. I do not wish to die without having all the rights, privileges and immunities of the citizen of a nation.

> AMOR DE COSMOS, H. of C., *Debates*, April 21, 1882, 1084.

Gentlemen, we want no independence in this country, except the independence that we have at this moment.

> SIR JOHN A. MACDONALD, in *Report in honour of Macdonald*, 1885, 103.

> First feel throughout the throbbing land
> A nation's pulse, a nation's pride —
> The independent life — then stand
> Erect, unbound, at Britain's side!
>
> CHARLES MAIR, "In memory of William A. Foster", (1888).

I hold out to my fellow-countrymen the idea of independence, but, whenever the day comes, it must come by the consent of both countries, and we shall continue to keep the good feeling and the good will of the motherland.

> SIR WILFRID LAURIER, H. of C., *Debates*, 1892, 1142.

I cling to the hope that — sooner or later, and rather soon than late — there may be born into the world an independent Canadian Commonwealth; nerving itself to solve, after its own fashion, the many racial and religious, moral and political, economic and material problems which confront us; united by enduring links of kinship and sympathy, hope and admiration, with three of the leading nations of the world; advancing, more effectively than now, our own varied interests as well as the true welfare of the old land, the proud mother of free nations as well as free parliaments.

> EDWARD BLAKE, letter to Laurier, 1892.

No man can be independent beyond the trust of his fellowmen in his capacity, judgment, and probity. Bullheadedness is not independence.

> SIR WILLIAM VAN HORNE, letter to W. F. Luxton, Winnipeg; qu., Vaughan, *Van Horne*, 1920, 245.

The words — a colony, a nation — never before in the history of the world were these two words associated before; never before were they applied to the same community, implying as they do at once the independence and the power of a sovereign people.

> SIR WILFRID LAURIER, speech in Liverpool, June 12, 1897.

Independent, we could not survive a decade.

> STEPHEN B. LEACOCK, Empire Club speech, Toronto, 1907.

We are on the very verge of independence.

> W. S. FIELDING, H. of C., *Debates*, April 21, 1921.

My opinion is that Canada should assume a position of practical independence and carry on her own foreign policy without reference to anybody else and that Great Britain should have absolute control of her own policy without any interference from Canada.

> SIR CLIFFORD SIFTON, letter to John Willison, June 30, 1921.

INDIANS.

They approach like foxes, attack like lions, then fly away like birds.

> FATHER PAUL LE JEUNE, on the Iroquois, in *Jesuit relations*, 1632-39.

Let the savages enjoy their Desarts in quiet.

> THOMAS GAGE, 1772, qu., *Can. hist. rev.*, 1932, 154.

For the prairie Indians the love of rum is their first inducement to industry; they undergo every hardship and fatigue to procure a skinfull of this delicious beverage, and when a nation becomes addicted to drinking, it affords a strong presumption that they will soon become excellent hunters.

> DUNCAN McGILLIVRAY, 1794-5, *Journal*, ed., A. S. Morton, 1929, 47.

Spanish civilization crushed the Indian; English civilization scorned and neglected him; French civilization embraced and cherished him.

> FRANCIS PARKMAN, *France and England*, 1865, 44.

What I offer you is to be while the water flows and the sun rises.

> ALEXANDER MORRIS, treaty negotiations with the Indians, North-West Angle, Lake of the Woods, Oct. 1, 1873. Variations of the phrase were used by the Indian chiefs, such as POUNDMAKER. Aug, 23, 1876, "as long as the sun shines and water runs".

The memory of the Redman
How can it pass away,
While his names of music linger
On each mount and stream and bay;
While Musquodoboit's waters
Roll sparkling to the main,
While falls the laughing sunbeam
On Chegogin's fields of grain?

> RICHARD HUNTINGTON, Yarmouth, N. S., "Indian names of Acadia", about 1875.

Once all this mighty continent was ours,
And the Great Spirit made it for our use.

> CHARLES MAIR, *Tecumseh*, 1886.

Thar's good and bad in Injun,
An' thar's good and bad in White;
But, somehow, they is allus wrong,
An' we is allus right.

> JOHN E. LOGAN, "The Injun", 1915.

The Protestant Indian is an Indian while the Catholic Indian is a Catholic. Scratch any sort of Protestant Indian and below the skin lie all the aspirations of his natural religion.

> J. M. CLARKE, *L'Ile Percée*, 1923.

What we want is a really impartial history of North America written from the Indians' point of view.

> E. R. ADAIR, *Can. hist. rev.*, 1932, 341.

INDUSTRY.

> (See also: BUSINESS; FREE TRADE; MANUFACTURING; TRADE; WORK)

Your factories... go ahead on the English a long chalk.

> THOMAS C. HALIBURTON, *Sam Slick*, 1838, 26.

What think you, little river Thames, of our great Ottawa that flings its foam eight hundred miles? What does it mean when science has moved us a little further yet, and the wheels of the world's work turn with electric force? What sort of asset do you think then our melting snow and the roaring river-flood of our Canadian spring shall be to us? What say you, little puffing steam-fed industry of

England, to the industry of coming Canada?

> Stephen B. Leacock, Empire Club speech, Toronto, Mar. 19, 1907.

One captain of industry is worth a good many of the rank and file.

> Wm. Peterson, Can. Club, Ottawa, speech, Jan. 7, 1911.

Production, production, and more production!

> Sir Thomas White, 1917; misquoted by the newly-formed Canadian Press to western, anti-protection newspapers as "Protection, protection, and more protection!"

Industry exists for the sake of humanity, not humanity for the sake of industry.

> W. L. Mackenzie King, *Industry and humanity*, 1918; also, speech on accepting leadership of Liberal Party, August 1919, Ottawa.

Labor can do nothing without capital, capital nothing without labor, and neither labor or capital can do anything without the guiding genius of management; and management, however wise its genius may be, can do nothing without the privileges which the community affords.

> W. L. Mackenzie King, Can. Club speech, Montreal, Mar. 17, 1919.

Whatever comes of the phase through which we are now passing I am sure that the world will be richer in the belief that industry is not for the enrichment of a few but rather for the betterment of the many.

> W. L. Mackenzie King, speech in Edmonton, July, 1933.

Canada's vast untouched — and untouchable — resources.

> A witticism of the 1930's.

INTELLIGENCE.

> (See also: Mind; Thought; Wisdom and Unwisdom)

Of all the seventeen senses, I like common sense about as well as any on 'em, after all.

> T. C. Haliburton, *Sam Slick*, 1840, 218.

You can grow corn or potatoes, but you cannot grow brains. Brains come hard and they come high.

> Sir Wm. Osler, Can. Club, Toronto, Dec. 29, 1904.

As the pen is mightier than the sword so are brains mightier than the muscles.

> Robert L. Borden, speech in Gananoque, Jan. 17, 1906.

INTOLERANCE.

> Intolerance is want of sense;
>   Judge people by their deeds;
> For Mammon's tools make wise men fools
>   By playing on their creeds.
>
> Alexander McLachlan, "The spirits of the press", 1900.

What I inveigh against is a cursed spirit of intolerance, conceived in distrust and bred in ignorance, that makes the mental attitude perennially antagonistic even bitterly antagonistic to everything foreign, that subordinates everywhere the race to the nation, forgetting the higher claims of human brotherhood.

> Sir William Osler, "Chauvinism in medicine", *Montreal med. journal*, 1902.

IRISHMEN.

They are always in love or in liquor, or else in a row; they are the merriest shavers I ever seed.

> T. C. Haliburton, *Sam Slick*, 1836, ch. XVI.

We are here living not on the banks of the Boyne, but on the St. Lawrence. We are new men in a new country. Our affairs are with the Imperial Government and the American Republic, not with James II or William III.

> Thomas D'Arcy McGee, Montreal *New Era*, July 21, 1857.

> Where'er I turned, some emblem still
>   Roused consciousness upon my track;
> Some hill was like an Irish hill,
>   Some wild bird's whistle called me back;
> A sea-bound ship bore off my peace,

Between its white, cold wings of
woe;
Oh, if I had but wings like these,
Where my peace went I, too, would
go.
THOMAS D'A. McGEE, "Home-sick
stanzas", 1858.

We Irishmen, Protestant and Catholic, born and bred in a land of religious
controversy, should never forget that
we now live and act in a land of the
fullest religious and civil liberty. All
we have to do is each for himself to
keep down dissension which can only
weaken, impoverish and keep back the
country.
THOMAS D'A. McGEE, speech
in Quebec, 1862.

Far from their own beloved isle
Those Irish exiles sleep;
And dream not of historic past,
Nor o'er its memories weep;
Down where the blue St. Lawrence
tide
Sweeps onward, wave on wave,
They lie — old Ireland's exiled dead,
In cross-crowned lonely grave.
THOMAS O'HAGAN, "Days of sorrow
— Grosse Isle", Aug. 15, 1909.

ISOLATION.

Never did the "Empress Island" appear so magnificently grand, — she
stood by herself, and there was a peculiar splendour in the loneliness of her
glory.
ROBERT COONEY, Compendious hist.
N. B., 1832, Intro.

In these troublesome days when the
great Mother Empire stands splendidly
isolated in Europe.
SIR GEORGE E. FOSTER, H. of C.,
Debates, Jan. 16, 1896; London
Times reported a speech of Joseph
Chamberlain, Jan. 22, under head-
ing, "Splendid isolation".

Whether splendidly isolated or dan-
gerously isolated, I will not now debate;
but for my part, I think splendidly
isolated, because this isolation of England comes from her superiority.
SIR WILFRID LAURIER, H. of C.,
Debates, Feb. 5, 1896.

Canada cannot be a hermit nation
LORD JELLICOE, remark made 1910,
and afterwards.

If ever there were a time when
Canada should turn a deaf ear to the
siren song of European diplomats, it
is now. Canada ought to sail by,
lashed like Ulysses to the nationalist
mast, with her ears stuffed with taxes.
JOHN S. EWART, in Toronto Star,
Mar. 22, 1923.

May I be permitted to add that
in this Association of Mutual Insurance
against fire, the risks assumed by the
different States are not equal? We
live in a fire-proof house, far from in-
flammable materials. A vast ocean
separates us from Europe.
RAOUL DANDURAND, speech, L. of N.
Assembly, Oct. 2, 1924.

We do not believe that isolation from
interest in world affairs is possible for
Canada. No happening of any magni-
tude abroad is without its repercussions
on our fortunes and our future.
W. L. MACKENZIE KING, H. of C.,
Debates, June 18, 1936, 3868, on
Italo-Ethiopian conflict.

The Province of Canada bred many
views, and the least of these was
isolation.
G. DE T. GLAZEBROOK, in Can. Hist.
Assoc., Rept. 1938, 104.

Canada makes isolation impossible
for the United States.
JOHN MACCORMAC, Canada, America's problem, 1940, 1.

J

JESUS CHRIST.

What a Friend we have in Jesus,
All our sins and griefs to bear!
What a privilege to carry
Everything to God in prayer!
JOSEPH SCRIVEN, "What a Friend
we have in Jesus", 1884.

This Man of April walks again —
Such marvel does the time allow —
With laughter in His blessed bones,
And lilies on His brow.
LEO KENNEDY, "Words for a resur-
rection", 1936.

Not in these the source —
But in the sound of invisible trumpets blowing

Around two slabs of board, right-
angled, hammered
By Roman nails and hung on a
Jewish hill.

> E. J. PRATT, "Brebeuf and his
> brethren", 1940.

JEWS.

And down these nineteen centuries
anew
Comes the hoarse-throated, brut-
alized refrain,
"Give us Barabbas, crucify the Jew!"
Once more a man must bear a
nation's stain.

> E. PAULINE JOHNSON, "Give us
> Barabbas", written after Captain
> Alfred Dreyfus was exiled to
> Devil's Island, 1894.

There is no mania quite so self-
revealing as that of Jew-baiting.

> JOHN W. DAFOE, *Winnipeg Free
> Press*, April 1, 1933.

JOURNALISM.

It is perfectly true that the works
of a journalist are ephemeral: they
go into the nether world of old files
and are forgotten. But does not the
same fate befall a good many books?
Look at the back stacks of any great
library. What a necropolis of the
immortals is there.

> GOLDWIN SMITH, speech to the
> Canadian Press Assoc., June 3,
> 1881.

The journalist may be a powerful
and effective reformer; he is seldom a
sober and prudent statesman. A wise
journalist will not go to parliament.
A wise statesman will keep out of
journalism.

> SIR JOHN WILLISON, in, *Federation
> of Canada*, 1917, 53.

JUDGES.

It is not sufficient that the Bench
should be pure, but it must also be
above suspicion.

> SIR WILFRID LAURIER, H. of C.,
> *Debates*, Feb. 6, 1884, 135.

True enough, I am, I believe, fully
competent to discharge my judicial
duties, but the time will surely come

and cannot be far distant when I shall
no longer be competent and may not
have the discernment to be aware of my
incapacity. I might then be tempted
to continue in office when I could no
longer perform its duties with satisfaction to the public.

> J. W. RITCHIE, Equity Judge, N. S.,
> on his retirement, qu., *Can. law jr.*,
> 1912, 600.

I have myself heard a very able
judge, afterwards chief justice of
Ontario, on a prisoner being acquitted
of the charge of stealing a cap, tell
him to go and not steal any more caps.

> W. R. RIDDELL, *Can. hist. rev.*,
> 1924, 373.

Some of the Sections of this Bill
go further than we have ever gone.
They make a judge out of a man who
is not a lawyer.

> R. B. BENNETT, H. of C., *Debates*,
> 1937, 2426, on Combines Invest-
> igation Act.

JUSTICE.

> (See also: LAW AND LAW-
> YERS)

The great secret is speedy justice.
> T. C. HALIBURTON, *Sam Slick*,
> 1838, 108.

To protest against the injustice would
be idle; philanthropy likes injustice.
> GOLDWIN SMITH, *The Bystander*,
> April, 1883, 96.

Justice is the same everywhere. Justice is the same, whether it be on the
banks of the Saskatchewan or on the
banks of the Red River; justice demands
that the same treatment which has
been extended to the half-breeds on
the banks of the Red River shall also
be extended to the half-breeds on the
banks of the Saskatchewan.

> EDWARD BLAKE, H. of C., *Debates*,
> July 6, 1885.

I am not here to dispense justice, I
am here to dispose of this case according to law. Whether this is or is not
justice is a question for the legislature
to determine.

> SIR THOMAS W. TAYLOR, Chief
> Justice of Manitoba, 1887-99, a
> retort to a lawyer.

If I really thought you were guilty, I would give you ten years.

JUDGE CHARLES B. ROULEAU (d. 1910), Edmonton, on sentencing a Chinese to two years for an offence.

Be ours a nation evermore
That no oppression blights,
Where justice rules from shore to shore,
From Lakes to Northern Lights.

ALBERT D. WATSON, "Hymn for Canada", 1913.

Chivalry is a poor substitute for justice, if one cannot have both. Chivalry is something like the icing on cake, sweet but not nourishing.

NELLIE MCCLUNG, In times like these, 1915, 54.

'Tis easy enough to be merciful,
But to be just is an excellence
Beyond all flight of sentiment!

TOM MACINNES, "Justice", 1918.

K

THE KING.

(See also: THE CROWN)

No one can look into futurity and say what will be the destiny of this country. Changes come over nations and peoples in the course of ages. But, so far as we can legislate, we provide that, for all time to come, the Sovereign of Great Britain shall be the Sovereign of British North America.

SIR JOHN A. MACDONALD, Confederation debates, Feb. 6, 1865, 33.

Most of us are conscious by this time that in England the Sovereign's name is William Ewart, and that in Canada it is John.

GOLDWIN SMITH, The Bystander, Oct., 1883, 260, referring to Gladstone, and Macdonald.

The compact which the King makes with his people when he ascends the Throne is a compact which he makes with us as well as with the people of the Mother Country.

SIR ROBERT L. BORDEN, H. of C., Debates, Mar. 1, 1901.

The perpetuation of monarchical forms, even though the life has long since gone out of them, doubtless tends to act as a curb to the fullest expression of democracy.

A. R. M. LOWER, in Can. Hist. Assoc. Rept., 1930, 70.

Surpassed was mystic One in Three and Three in One: God in three persons was outnumbered by the British King in seven persons, the Septennity.

A. R. M. LOWER, Colony to nation, 1946, 486.

KING, W. L. MACKENZIE.

Mackenzie King is doing excellent work and I believe that he has quite a political future before him.

SIR WILFRID LAURIER, letter to Lord Minto, April 13, 1909.

I can tell you in my heart I am pretty radical.

W. L. MACKENZIE KING, speech in Vancouver, Sept. 28, 1935.

Mr. King is a great man by almost any definition. You may not like him, and many do not, wasting their entire lives in hatred of him. But you cannot deny him.

BRUCE HUTCHISON, The unknown country, 1942, 96.

I am proud to believe there is no separation between those who are nearest to us, and I believe in the survival of the human personality. Thus I know that if I have had any success in life it has been due to my father and mother.

W. L. MACKENZIE KING, speech 25th anniversary, leadership of the Liberal Party, Ottawa, Aug. 7, 1944.

He is said to be a man whose mind is strictly empiric, untroubled by feelings of inconsistency, representing the quintessence of the popular view of the moment, a judgment surely borne out by his political conduct. He is the ordinary man writ large.

A. R. M. LOWER, in Can. hist. rev., 1946, 238.

KINGSTON, ONT.

Indeed, it may be said of Kingston, that one half of it appears to be burnt down, and the other half not to be built up.

> CHARLES DICKENS, *American notes,* 1842.

Ah, it looks very well from the water.

> EDWARD VII, remark to Sir Richard Cartwright. In 1860 he toured Canada (as Prince of Wales), and was kept aboard ship in Kingston harbour as a result of a difficulty arising out of his refusal to march under an arch erected by Orangemen.

KNOWLEDGE.

(See also: INTELLIGENCE)

If they knew more of each other, I guess they'd lay aside one half their fears and all their abuse.

> T. C. HALIBURTON, *Sam Slick,* 1st. ser., 1836, 110.

We grasp at loved shadows —
While grasping, they're gone;
The fruit of our knowledge
Is still the *unknown.*
We scale the blue summits,
For which we have longed
To sit down and sigh for
The regions beyond.

> ALEXANDER MCLACHLAN, "A dream" 1856.

A longing still haunts us,
Wherever we go,
And knowledge increases
The draft of our woe;
And all that we cling to
Is fleeting as breath,
And life is the valley
And shadow of death.

> ALEXANDER MCLACHLAN, "A dream" 1856.

Knowledge is ever fatal, for Romance Can only live in shades of ignorance.

> CHARLES HEAVYSEGE, poem no. V, in *Jephthah's daughter,* 1865.

Faith, science, doubt profound;
Searching for ampler knowledge from afar,
By turns have soared to question every star,
Have probed the earth to tell us whence we are,
And whither bound.

> DANIEL WILSON, *Can. birthday book,* 1887, 90.

Most ignorant are we of what we are most assured.

> GEORGE M. GRANT, in, *Can. mag.,* Oct. 1900, 492.

The greater the ignorance the greater the dogmatism.

> SIR WILLIAM OSLER, *Montreal med. jour.,* 1902, 684.

The knowledge of most men is just enough to make them aggressively ignorant.

> PETER MCARTHUR, *To be taken with salt,* 1903, 155.

It's awfully hard for a woman to pretend not to know the things she ought not to know.

> ROBERT C. (BOB) EDWARDS, *Calgary Eye Opener,* Sept. 7, 1912.

The quest for righteousness is Oriental, the quest for knowledge Occidental.

> SIR WILLIAM OSLER, speech, Jewish Hist. Soc., London, Apr. 27, 1914.

Knowing things that are not so is the worst kind of ignorance.

> ROBERT C. (BOB) EDWARDS, *Calgary Eye Opener,* Nov. 3, 1917.

Nearly all the knowledge in the world has been acquired at the expense of somebody's burnt fingers.

> ROBERT C. (BOB) EDWARDS, *Calgary Eye Opener,* Feb. 2, 1918.

Ignorance may find a truth on its doorstep that erudition vainly seeks in the stars.

> GEORGE ILES, *Canadian stories,* 1918, 168.

Discovery begins by finding the discoverer.

> GEORGE ILES, *Canadian stories,* 1918, 169.

L

LABOUR.

(See also: DEEDS AND DOING; INDUSTRY; WORK)

Labour is the only means of creating wealth.

> WILLIAM LYON MACKENZIE, *Constitution for the State of Upper Canada,* 1837.

United to support, not combined to injure.

TORONTO TYPOGRAPHICAL SOCIETY, motto adopted 1844.

Neither labour nor idleness has a road that leads to happiness, one has no room for the heart and the other corrupts it.

T. C. HALIBURTON, *Sam Slick's wise saws*, 1853, I, 205.

It is in obedience to foreign agitation carried on by paid agents who have nothing to lose as the result of their mischievious counsels that the printers of this city have succumbed.

TORONTO *Globe*, Mar. 26, 1872.

We may destroy our happiness by inoculating our industrial system with the maladies of a distant country [England] and an alien state of society.

TORONTO *Globe*, Mar. 26, 1872, on strikes.

I love this land of forest grand!
    The land where labour's free;
Let others roam away from home,
    Be this the land for me!
Where no one moils and strains and toils,
    That snobs may thrive the faster;
And all are free as men should be,
    And Jack's as good's his master!

ALEXANDER MCLACHLAN, "Young Canada, or, Jack's as good as his master", 1874.

Our aristocracy of toil
    Have made us what you see,
The nobles of the forge and soil,
    With ne'er a pedigree!

ALEXANDER MCLACHLAN, "Young Canada, or, Jack's as good as his master", 1874.

No English need apply.

Term used by a few western farmers in advertisements for hired help, about 1900; English-speaking help usually protested against degrading conditions of work and meagre wages.

No Orientals need apply.

A notice outside many B. C. pulp-mills and other factories, 20th. century.

Never in the history of Canada have labour unions shown so much activity; never have they been so well organized, and never has that organization made such determined, and in many cases unreasonable, efforts to secure for labour the domination of Canadian factories, and to wrest from the employer his inherent rights, to control the policy of his business and manage it as he thinks best.

CANADIAN MANUFACTURERS' ASSOCIATION, in, *Industrial Canada*, Oct., 1903, 129.

From the union's standpoint the scab may be a mean man, but sometimes he is an heroic one.

SIR W. VAN HORNE, 1912; qu., in Vaughan: *Van Horne*, 1920. 37.

I propose that any government of which I am the head will at the first session of Parliament initiate whatever action is necessary to that end [to protect the agriculturist and the worker, the manufacturer and the consumer], or perish in the attempt.

R. B. BENNETT, election speech, Winnipeg, June 9, 1930; usually quoted as "I will end unemployment or perish in the attempt".

Facing that situation he found it necessary, in order to do what he thought would satisfy the unemployed, to ask not for $20,000,000, $40,000,000, $60,000,000, $80,000,000 or $1,000,000,-000, but to ask this parliament to give a blank cheque which he might fill in for as much as he wished to draw.

W. L. MACKENZIE KING, H. of C., *Debates*, Feb. 8, 1932, 37, on the policy of R. B. Bennett; origin of the phrase "blank cheque".

The curse of labour is past.
We have thrown the packs from our shoulders, wiped the sweat from our brows, yet multiplied the work which is not of our hands.

E. J. PRATT, "A prayer-medley", 1937.

From those condemned to labour
For profit of another
We take our new endeavour.

F. R. SCOTT, "Dedication", in, *Poetry mag.*, April, 1941.

Under the dark industrial sky
we wonder why we have to die
who living, were valued at a wage

that starved our youth and murdered
age?

> JAMES WREFORD, "Kirkland Lake",
> 1942.

LAKES.

The great inland seas of Canada.

> JOHN MACTAGGART, *Three years
> in Canada*, 1829, II, 322.

Red in the mists of the morning
Angry, coloured with fire,
Beats the great lake in its beauty,
Rocks the wild lake in its ire.

> WILFRED CAMPBELL, "Down in the
> island camp", 1889.

Domed with the azure of heaven,
Floored with a pavement of pearl,
Clothed all about with a brightness
Soft as the eyes of a girl,
Girt with a magical girdle,
Rimmed with a vapour of rest —
These are the inland waters,
These are the lakes of the west.

> WILFRED CAMPBELL, "The lakes of
> the west", 1889.

Out in a world of death, far to the
northward lying,
Under the sun and the moon, under
the dusk and the day;
Under the glimmer of stars and the
purple of sunsets dying,
Wan and waste and white, stretch
the great lakes away.

> WILFRED CAMPBELL, "The winter
> lakes", 1889.

How I long for Huron's shore:
How I long for Huron's beaches.
Where the wind-swept, shining
reaches
Wind in mists and are no more.

> WILFRED CAMPBELL, "By Huron's
> shore", 1889.

It sleeps among the thousand hills
Where no man ever trod,
And only Nature's music fills
The silences of God.

> FREDERICK G. SCOTT, "The un-
> named lake", 1897.

Lake Superior is all the same stuff
as what towns pay taxes for, but it
engulfs and wrecks and drives ashore,
like a fully accredited ocean — a

hideous thing to find in the heart of
a continent.

> RUDYARD KIPLING, *Letters to the
> family*, 1908.

LAND.

(See also: POLITICAL SLO-
GANS)

Along the whole of the north shore I
did not see one cart-load of earth and
yet I landed in many places. Except at
Blanc Sablon there is nothing but
moss and short, stunted shrub. In fine
I am rather inclined to believe that this
is the land God gave to Cain.

> JACQUES CARTIER, *Voyage to Cana-
> da*, (1534), (trans.) ; descriptive
> of the St. Lawrence Gulf and
> Labrador; *cf.*, Genesis, IV, 12.

In the North American Colonies...
the function of authority most full of
good or evil consequences has been
the disposal of the public land.

> LORD DURHAM, *Report*, 1839.

Canada gardens.

> A term adopted about 1845 in
> English counties, Kent, Yorkshire,
> Gloucestershire, etc., to describe
> small unfenced allotments provided
> for the poor; usually shortened to
> "The Canada".

Our future is on the land.

> A popular French Canadian phrase.
> (trans.)

Plaintiff, you go and divide the land
into two parts and you, defendant,
then take your choice.

> SIR MATTHEW BAILLIE BEGBIE,
> decision in a trial involving division
> of property between two brothers,
> at Kamloops, B. C., about 1860.

God knows there's plenty of earth
for all of us!
Then why must we sweat for it, deny
for it,
Pray for it, cry for it,
Kill, maim and lie for it,
Struggle and suffer and die for it —
We who are gentle and sane?

> LLOYD ROBERTS, "If I must", 1916.

The landless man to the manless land.

> The policy formulated by ROBERT
> FORKE, *Minister of Immigration*,
> 1926 to 1930.

LANGUAGES.

(See also: BILINGUALISM)

Avoid awc-cent! Avoid awc-cent!

BISHOP JOHN STRACHAN'S advice to the students of Trinity College, which he founded in 1851.

His Excellency reads French, and speaks it with the pure Parisian accent. He also reads Greek, Latin and Italian, and has made considerable progress in the study of Hieroglyphics.

WILLIAM LEGGO, *Administration of Lord Dufferin*, 1878, 68.

In Europe no man's education is complete until he knows French. This is because the French language, for 300 years and more, has been the language of arts and letters. It will always remain with me the language of art and literature, but it has not the same force, the same elasticity, as English. If I were your age I would not leave school until I could speak and write French.

SIR WILFRID LAURIER, speech at McMaster University. Dec. 17, 1913.

I can see no reason why we in Canada, when we have developed a style of our own, should not describe ourselves as using an English vocabulary, but a Canadian language.

B. K. SANDWELL, Can. Club, Ottawa. Mar. 13, 1920.

I myself talk Ontario English; I don't admire it, but it's all I can do; anything is better than affectation.

STEPHEN B. LEACOCK, *How to write*, 1943, 121.

In Canada we have enough to do keeping up with two spoken languages without trying to invent slang, so we just go right ahead and use English for literature, Scotch for sermons, and American for conversations.

STEPHEN B. LEACOCK, *How to write*, 1943.

LAURIER, SIR WILFRID.

(See also: POLITICAL SLOGANS)

Silver-Tongued Laurier.

P. D. Ross, despatch to the Montreal *Star*, Mar. 17, 1886, after hearing Laurier's speech in House of Commons on Riel's execution.

Nice chap, that. If I were twenty years younger, he'd be my colleague.

SIR JOHN MACDONALD, to Sir Joseph Pope, May, 1891.

I am a democrat to the hilt.

SIR WILFRID LAURIER, statement made after being knighted at a public function, London, Eng., 1897.

As far as Sir Wilfrid Laurier is concerned, you can say that he is too English for me with his programme of Imperial federation.

SIR CHARLES TUPPER, in *La Presse*, Montreal, Aug. 20, 1900. (trans.)

That dam' dancing-master who had bitched the whole show.

DR. S. JAMESON (of "Jameson Raid" fame) to Rudyard Kipling, qu. in his, *Something of myself*, 1937, 196; about 1902.

I would rather do business with a cad who knows his own mind.

JOSEPH CHAMBERLAIN, to Lady Minto (1904), qu. by J. Buchan, *Lord Minto* 205.

Not many years now remain to me. The snows of winter have taken the place of spring; but, however I may shew the ravages of time my heart still remains young, and I feel that I have as much strength as ever for the service of my country.

SIR WILFRID LAURIER, speech in Sorel, Sept. 6, 1908. (trans.).

I do not pretend to be an Imperialist. Neither do I pretend to be an anti-Imperialist. I am a Canadian first, last and all the time. I am a British subject by birth, by tradition, by conviction; by the conviction that under British institutions my native land has found a measure of security and freedom it could not have found under any other regime.

SIR WILFRID LAURIER. H. of C., *Debates*, Feb. 3, 1910.

I am a Canadian. Canada has been the inspiration of my life. I have had before me as a pillar of fire by night and a pillar of cloud by day a policy of true Canadianism, of moderation, of conciliation.

> Sir Wilfrid Laurier, speech in St. John, Que., 1911.

The Plumed Knight.

> A popular nickname, after 1911; see, Political Slogans — "Follow my white plume!"

If you please, paint me as a ruler of men.

> Sir Wilfrid Laurier, attributed. 1916, as statement to Charles Huot who painted his portrait as one of a group in the Assembly chamber, Quebec.

I am a politician.

> Sir Wilfrid Laurier, a saying of his later years.

It has been my lot to run the whole gamut of prejudices in Canada. In 1896 I was excommunicated by the Roman priests, and in 1917 by Protestant parsons.

> Sir Wilfrid Laurier, letter, late 1917.

Do you think we can trust the b...s with the old man's body?

> Charles Murphy, remark to a Press Gallery correspondent, on the funeral arrangements made for the burial of Laurier who died Feb. 17, 1919, referring especially to the former Liberals who joined Borden's Union Government in 1917.

A man who had affinities with Machiavelli as well as with Sir Galahad.

> John W. Dafoe, Laurier, 1922.

He was, above all others, the nemesis of the Imperialists.

> A. G. Dewey, in Can. hist. rev., 1927, 284.

The farmers began whetting their axes for him on the rough edges of long-delayed hopes.

> L. E. Ellis, Reciprocity, 1911, 1939, 20.

He was never any good at figures — other than those of speech.

> Paul Bilkey, Persons, papers and things, 1940.

LAW AND LAWYERS.

Resort shall be had to the laws of Canada and not to the laws of England.

> Quebec Act, draft of Aug. 18, 1774, printed in Quebec Gazette.

That sheet anchor, that mainstay, that blessed shield, that glorious institution — the rich man's terror, the poor man's hope, the people's pride, the nation's glory — Trial by Jury.

> T. C. Haliburton, Sam Slick, 1838, 109.

Wherever there is authority, there is a natural inclination to disobedience.

> T. C. Haliburton, Sam Slick's wise saws, 1853, I, 186.

It is of the very last importance that the administration of the affairs of the country should be according to law.

> Sir John A. Macdonald, speech in St. Catharines, 1860.

The Justice, he feels very big,
And boasts what the law can secure,
But has two different laws in his wig,
Which he keeps for the rich and the poor.

> Alexander McLachlan, "The emigrant", 1861.

Prisoner: it is far from a pleasant duty for me to have to sentence you only to imprisonment for life... Your crime was unmitigated, diabolical murder. You deserve to be hanged! Had the jury performed their duty I might now have the painful satisfaction of condemning you to death, and you, gentlemen of the jury, you are a pack of Dalles horse thieves, and permit me to say, it would give me great pleasure to see you hanged, each and every one of you, for declaring a murderer guilty only of manslaughter.

> Judge Matthew B. Begbie, at trial of the gunman, Gilchrist, in B. C., Jan., 1863.

The Statute books are exceedingly muddled. I seldom look into them.

> Judge Matthew B. Begbie (d. 1894), qu., Can. portraits, 1940, 91.

Boys, I am here to keep order and to administer the law. Those who don't want law and order can 'git', but those who stay with the camp, remember on what side of the line the camp is; for, boys, if there is shooting in Kootenay there will be hanging in Kootenay.

> JUDGE PETER O'REILLY, to American miners at Wild Horse Creek, B. C., 1864.

The preservation of law and order. A phrase identified with the R.C. M.P. since its early days; about 1875.

To legislate in advance of public opinion is merely to produce anarchy instead of maintaining law and order.

> ALEXANDER MACKENZIE, speech on prohibition bill, H. of C., 1877.

The law is a hard, queer thing. I do not understand it.

> POUNDMAKER, statement to the court at his trial, 1885.

I have had some experience, both in defending criminals and in prosecuting them; I have never shrunk in my calling, as a member of the Bar, from taking any man's case, no matter how desperate it might be, for the purpose of saying for him what he might lawfully say for himself; but I have sometimes spurned the fee of a blatant scoundrel who denounced everybody else in the world, and was himself the most truculent savage of them all.

> SIR JOHN THOMPSON, H. of C., *Debates*, June 28, 1892, on Sir Richard Cartwright.

Sergeant Fones has the fear o' God in his heart, and the law of the land across his saddle, and the newest breechloading at that.

> SIR GILBERT PARKER, *Pierre and his people*, 1892, 6.

For Law immutable hath one decree,
'No deed of good, no deed of ill can die;
All must ascend unto my loom and be Woven for man in lasting tapestry, Each soul his own.'

> ISABELLA V. CRAWFORD, "The King's garments", 1905.

The law in Canada exists and is administered, not as a surprise, a joke,

a favour, a bribe, or a Wrestling Turk exhibition, but as an integral part of the national character — no more to be talked about than one's trousers

> RUDYARD KIPLING, *Letters to the family*, 1908.

Desperate conditions justify radical methods, for law is anything which is boldly asserted and stoutly maintained.

> LAURA E. McCULLY, *Maclean's mag.*, Nov., 1911.

And they dwelt in sweet co-union, while the world looked on in awe,
For they lived and wrought by the law of Love, and not by the love of Law.

> ROBERT J. C. STEAD, "Mother and son", 1917.

If your honour please, I would not for a moment mutilate the majesty of the law nor contravene the avoirdupois of the testimony, but I would ask you to focalize your five senses on the proposition I am about to propound to you. In all criminal cases there are three essential elements — the *locus in quo*, the *modus operandi* and the *corpus delicti*. In this case I think I am safe in saying the *corpus delicti* and the *modus operandi* are all right, but there is an entire absence of the *locus in quo*. I therefore ask for a dismissal of the case.

> ROBERT C. (BOB) EDWARDS, *Calgary Eye Opener*, qu., Stubbs, *Lawyers*, 186.

I think that learned cousel is abusing the privilege of being stupid.

> SIR JAMES LOUGHEED, when chairman of Senate divorce committee, about 1920.

Ignorance of the Law is no excuse, and yet some Judges continue to get by.

> ANON., *Willison's monthly*, June, 1926, 13.

I saw the gallows lifted high
And in the cruel rope
The twisted law and sin of man Strangled the Saviour's hope.

> J. E. H. MACDONALD, "Gallows and cross", 1933.

I bind the Soul that fathered me;
I am the Law, and resolute

Against the growing of the Soul,
I hang, behead, electrocute.

> J. E. H. MacDonald, "The hanging", 1933.

The more you allow the courts to clarify things the worse you make them.

> Henri Bourassa, in H. of C., 1935; *Method of amending the B. N. A. Act*, 10.

LEAGUE OF NATIONS.

I saw the brat born, and I am going to stay with it as long as it has a bit of life in its body.

> John W. Dafoe, speech, Empire Club, Toronto, Jan. 30, 1936.

You can't destroy that ideal. You can't bury it. You can't forget it. You may postpone it indefinitely or for generations but it will survive the tumult and the shouting. It will be there as long as there are stars in the Heavens, a beacon light to the generations.

> John W. Dafoe, speech, Empire Club, Toronto, Jan. 30, 1936.

These questions [Imperial relations, and defence], so politely retired to the wings, are now in the centre of the Canadian stage to which they returned the moment the League of Nations, with assurances of the most distinguished consideration, was ushered out into the darkness by Mr. Mackenzie King.

> John W. Dafoe, *Canadian-American affairs*, 1937, 225; reference to Mr. King's speech at Geneva, Sept. 29, 1936.

LETTERS.

Harry, my boy, never write a letter if you can help it, and never destroy one.

> Sir John A. Macdonald to Col. H. R. Smith, Dep. Sgt.-at-arms, H. of C., 1872-92; qu., *Correspondence*, ed. by Pope, p. xxiii.

The Prime Minister is too fond of signing letters in the name of the people of Canada.

> J. L. Ralston, H. of C., *Debates*, April 23, 1934, on R. B. Bennett.

LIBERAL PARTY.

> (See also: Clear Grits; Political Parties ; Political Phrases; Reform Party)

The Grits.

A term derived from "Clear Grits" (*q. v.*) and applied after 1855 to the Brownites and Clear Grits, predecessors of the Liberal Party, and accepted by them to signify a modified version of original Clear Grit radicalism.

We are a free and happy people, and we are so owing to the liberal institutions by which we are governed, institutions which we owe to the exertions of our forefathers and the wisdom of the mother country. The policy of the Liberal party is to protect these institutions, to defend and extend them, and, under their sway, to develop the latent resources of our country. That is the policy of the Liberal party: it has no other.

> Sir Wilfrid Laurier, speech, Club Canadien, Quebec City, June 26, 1877. (trans.)

The Party of Purity.

> Liberal Party boast, about 1878.

See the faces of the Grits.
    Grizzly Grits,
What a woe-begone expression at
    present o'er them flits.
They are thinking, thinking deeply
How to run this country cheaply
And they wonder
    How in thunder
It is going to be done.
But the people — they who vote —
    of their twaddle take no note,
For they know the dismal, dreary,
    direful dole
    Of the Grits
Of the moribund, morose and melancholy Grits, Grits, Grits, Grits.
The greedy, grubby garrulous old Grits.

> The People's Almanac, supp. to *Montreal Gazette*, 1891.

One Man, one Vote.

> Liberal Party slogan, Convention of 1893.

The fault of the Liberal party was voluble virtue.

SIR JOHN WILLISON, *Reminiscences*, 1919, 36, referring to the government of 1874 to 1878.

The Liberal party will continue to stand as its illustrious leaders stood in the past, for unity, good will, and the open mind.

W. L. MACKENZIE KING, speech to Liberal supporters, Aug. 1919.

There never was a Farmers' Party while the Liberals were in power.

LIBERAL PARTY, *Group govt. compared with responsible govt.*, 1921.

Individual members of the Liberal party may have done what they should not have done, but the whole party is not thereby disgraced. The party is not disgraced, but it is in the valley of humiliation.

W. L. MACKENZIE KING, H. of C., *Debates*, July 30, 1931, 4387, after the Beauharnois Power inquiry.

It believes that personality is more sacred than property. In all its policies it has been guided by that principle above everything else.

W. L. MACKENZIE KING, H. of C., *Debates*, Feb. 27, 1933.

If I cease to lead the party, I shall never cease to have the party's interest near to my heart.

W. L. MACKENZIE KING, speech to Liberals on his possible retirement and the calling of a national convention to select his successor, Ottawa, Jan. 20, 1948.

LIBERALISM.

Our Holy Father, the Pope, and after him the archbishop and bishops of this province, have declared that Catholic Liberalism is a thing to be regarded with the abhorrence with which one contemplates a pestilence; no Catholic is allowed to proclaim himself a moderate Liberal; consequently this moderate Liberal cannot be elected a representative by Catholics.

IGNACE BOURGET, Roman Catholic bishop of Montreal, 1876, on Dr. Fortier, Liberal candidate, Chambly by-election. (trans.)

For my part, as I have always said, I am a Liberal. I am one of those who think that everywhere, in human things, there are abuses to be reformed, new horizons to be opened up, and new forces to be developed.

SIR WILFRID LAURIER, speech, Club Canadien, Quebec City, June 26, 1877. (trans.)

He who has not the privilege of being born a Liberal can never become one; and he who, not being born a Liberal, becomes one afterwards, will fail in his Liberal principles and will become a traitor and a renegade.

SIR WILFRID LAURIER, speech, at Club National, Montreal, May, 1884. (trans.)

I am a Liberal of the old School, one of those who wish Government to mind its own business, who desire that at last man should have a chance of self-development, and who are no more inclined to submit to the tyranny of majorities calling themselves the State than to the tyranny of kings.

GOLDWIN SMITH, *Loyalty*, 1891, 4.

I am a Liberal of the English school. I believe in that school which has all along claimed that it is the privilege of all subjects, whether high or low, whether rich or poor, whether ecclesiastic or layman, to participate in the administration of public affairs, to discuss, to influence, to persuade, to convince, but which has always denied, even to the highest, the right to dictate to the lowest.

SIR WILFRID LAURIER, H. of C., *Debates*, Mar. 3, 1896.

I am a Liberal of the British school. I am a disciple of Burke, Fox, Bright, Gladstone, and of the other Little Englanders who made Great Britain and its possessions what they are.

HENRI BOURASSA, H. of C., *Debates*, Mar. 13, 1900, 1828.

It is never the purpose of Liberalism to obtain office — it is always the purpose of Liberalism to secure power. And power — to Liberalism — means only the opportunity to serve the people.

C. GORDONSMITH, in, Montreal *Daily Telegraph*, July 12, 1913.

LIBERTY.

(See also: FREEDOM)

Independent thought, the salt without which all our liberties would lose their savour.

GOLDWIN SMITH, *The Empire*, 1863, v.

The spirit of liberty is not the result of culture. It may be found in the lowest man.

SIR WILFRID LAURIER, speech in Toronto, Dec. 10, 1886.

Without fair Liberty to make
The key-stone of the world's whole plan,
The arch we heap o'erhead will break,
And some fair morrow man will wake
To find beneath the ruins — man!

GEORGE F. CAMERON, "She is not mine", 1887.

Out of a thousand years of suffering, bloodshed and contention, there has emerged in the last century the principle of common liberty. What is this liberty? It is the right of the men and women — not the men and women of the privileged classes only, but the men and women of all other classes — to live their lives, mentally, physically, morally without interference to person or property.

SIR CLIFFORD SIFTON, speech in Winnipeg, July 30, 1917.

Democracy implies liberty, something of which Canadians are so sure that they never mention it.

GEORGE M. WRONG, *Canadians*, 1938, 412.

LIES AND LIARS.

(See also: TRUTH)

To the first charge, Your Excellency I answer that it is a lie, to the second charge I say that it is a damned lie, and to the third charge that it is a damned infernal lie, and your Excellency I have no more to say.

THOMAS TREMLETT, Chief Justice of Newfoundland, letter to the Governor, 1811.

I can draw as long a bow as any Indian or author.

THOMAS C. HALIBURTON, *Sam Slick's wise saws*, 1853, ch. XIX.

Canadians as a rule are far too tolerant of fraud and falsehood.

SIR RICHARD CARTWRIGHT, speech, Seaforth, Ont., Oct. 27, 1886.

"They say" is the biggest liar in Canada or any other country.

ROBERT C. (BOB) EDWARDS, *Calgary Eye-opener*, Aug. 22, 1903.

The three biggest liars in Alberta are: Robert Edwards, Gentleman; Hon. A. L. Sifton [Premier of Alberta]; Bob Edwards, Editor of *The Eye-Opener*.

ROBERT C. (BOB) EDWARDS, *Calgary Eye Opener*; attributed.

Lo, something fair has risen like
A lily from the sod!
And the lie is now the truth of it,
Become the splendid truth of it,
Glory be to God!

TOM MACINNES, "White magic", 1918.

LIFE.

(See also: BEHAVIOUR; CONDUCT OF LIFE; TIME; VIRTUE)

When pleasure is the business of life it ceases to be pleasure.

T. C. HALIBURTON, *Sam Slick's wise saws*, 1853, I, 205.

The great secret of life is to learn to earn one's bread.

THOMAS C. HALIBURTON, *Sam Slick's wise saws*, 1853, ch. VI

Life is a chart as well as a coast, and a little care will keep you clear of rocks, reefs, and sandbars.

THOMAS C. HALIBURTON, *Sam Slick's wise saws*, 1853, ch. XVII.

This life ain't all beer and skittles.

T. C. HALIBURTON, *Nature and human nature*, 1855, I, 60.

The decencies of life, when polished, become its brightest ornaments.

T. C. HALIBURTON, *Nature and human nature*, 1855, II, 258.

To hunt and to be hunted makes existence;
For we are all or chasers or the chased;
And some weak, luckless wretches ever seem

Flying before the hounds of circumstance...
CHARLES HEAVYSEGE, *Saul*, 1857,
pt. 2.

We walk in blindness and dark night
Through half our earthly way;
Our clouds of weaknesses obscure
The glory of the day.
CHARLES SANGSTER, "My prayer",
1860.

What shadows we are, what shadows
we pursue.
JOSEPH HOWE, speech at Ottawa
Y. M. C. A., Feb. 27, 1872.

But four times twenty years gives
Fate,
Divides, controls, bids consecrate —
Twenty for growing, for laughter,
and yearning,
Twenty for loving, and mating, and
learning,
Twenty for making a name with the
best,
Twenty for wisdom, remembrance,
and — rest.
He who would have Life's full estate,
Keeps thus his years inviolate.
FREDERICK A. DIXON, "Four times
twenty", 1884.

We only know that we are here,
That life is brief and death is sure;
That it is noble to endure
And keep the eye of conscience clear.
GEORGE MARTIN, "W. H. Magee",
1887.

Cities might change and fall,
and men might die,
Secure were we, content to dream
with you
That change and pain are shadows
faint and fleet,
And dreams are real, and life is only
sweet.
ARCHIBALD LAMPMAN, "The frogs",
1888.

The play is life; and this round earth
The narrow stage whereon
We act before an audience
Of actors dead and gone.
BLISS CARMAN, "In the wings",
1892.

Pillared dust and fleeing shadow
As the roadside wind goes by,

And the fourscore years that vanish
In the twinkling of an eye.
BLISS CARMAN, "Pulvis et umbra",
1893.

Blue, blue was the heaven above me,
And the earth green at my feet;
"O Life! O Life!" I kept saying,
And the very word seemed sweet.
ARCHIBALD LAMPMAN, "Life and
nature", 1896.

There is a beauty at the goal of life,
A beauty growing since the world
began,
Through every age and race, through
lapse and strife
Till the great human soul complete
her span.
ARCHIBALD LAMPMAN, "The largest
life", *Atlantic monthly*, Mar., 1899.

Lovely humanities bloom among
vanities,
Beamings of peace 'mid our tumult
and strife;
Spiritualities close by realities,
Oh, who can read us the riddle
of life?
ALEXANDER MCLACHLAN, "Life's
contradictions", 1900.

Thy life is thine to make or mar,
To flicker feebly, or to soar, a star;
It lies with thee — the choice is
thine, is thine.
ROBERT W. SERVICE, "Quatrains",
1907.

Unto my friends I give my thoughts,
Unto my God my soul,
Unto my foe I leave my love —
These are of life the whole.
ETHELWYN WETHERALD, "Legacies",
1907.

Fate has written a tragedy; its name
is "The Human Heart",
The theatre is the House of life,
Woman the mummer's part:
The Devil enters the prompter's box
and the play is ready to start.
ROBERT W. SERVICE, "The harpy,"
1907.

Variability is the law of life.
SIR WILLIAM OSLER; attributed.

The pulse of our life is in tune with
the rhythm of forces that beat

In the surf of the farthest star's sea,
and are spent and regathered to
spend.
> FREDERICK GEORGE SCOTT, "A
> dream of the prehistoric", 1910.

A little gain, a little pain,
A laugh, lest you may moan;
A little blame, a little fame,
A star-gleam on a stone.
> ROBERT W. SERVICE, "Just think,"
> 1912.

Living itself is life's completest treasure.
> PETER MCARTHUR, *In pastures
> green*, 1915, 331.

For life is as a leaf is, and like a
flower it fails.
> MARJORIE PICKTHALL, "Song",
> 1916.

While some of us have more ups and
downs in this world than others, we'll
all be on the dead level sooner or later.
> ROBERT C. (BOB) EDWARDS, *Calgary
> Eye Opener*, Nov. 11, 1916.

The pains of Life are all too many,
And the Way is doubtful everywhere;
But I have gone as far as any,
And seen — and I do not despair!
> TOM MACINNES, "Persistence",
> 1918.

And while your body wears away,
And all your thoughts disintegrate,
You weave new vestures every day,
And dreams with dreams obliterate:
For you the outer ways await
Because of your desire to be:
But high or low, thro' every state,
You remain essentially.
> TOM MACINNES, "Ballade of the
> self concealed", 1918.

The ring of spears, the winning of
the fight,
The careless song, the cup, the love
of friends,
The earth in spring — to live, to
feel the light —
'Twas good the while it lasted: here
it ends.
> JOHN MCCRAE, "Upon Watts' picture
> *Sic transit*", 1919.

I do not care, because
I see with bitter calm,

Life made me what I was,
Life makes me what I am.
> ROBERT W. SERVICE, "The coco-
> fiend", 1921.

Brief sweet laughter and tears,
A tumult of eddying strife,
Drift and the wreckage of years —
Life.
> NORAH M. HOLLAND, "Episodes",
> 1924.

Life has given me of its best —
Laughter and weeping, labour and
rest,
Little of gold, but lots of fun;
Shall I then sigh that all is done?
No, not I; while the new road lies
All untrodden, before my eyes.
> NORAH M. HOLLAND, "Life," 1924.

Come, flaunt the brief prerogative
of life,
Dip your small civilized foot in this
cold water
And ripple, for a moment, the smooth
surface of time.
> F. R. SCOTT, "Surfaces", 1945.

LITERATURE.

> (See also: BOOKS AND READING;
> CRITICS; LITERATURE,
> CANADIAN; POETRY)

There are stranger things in reality
than can be found in romances.
> THOMAS C. HALIBURTON, *Sam
> Slick's wise saws*, 1853, ch. VI.

A national literature is an essential
element in the formation of national
character. It is not merely the record
of a country's mental progress; it is
the expression of its intellectual life,
the bond of national unity, and the
guide of national energy.
> EDWARD H. DEWART, *Selections
> from Can. poets*, 1864, ix.

The translation of Homer into verse
is the Polar Expedition of literature,
always failing, yet still desperately
renewed.
> GOLDWIN SMITH, *Cowper*, 1885, 91.

Write the truth, for that is what
makes literature.
> GEORGE M. WRONG, remark to the
> Canadian Authors Assoc., Toronto,
> Jan. 19, 1929.

Without faith there can be no satire, and without satire no secure and clarified faith.

F. R. Scott, in W. P. Percival, *Leading Can. poets*, 1948, 243.

LITERATURE, CANADIAN.

The standard literature of Canada must be looked for in her newspapers.

Susanna Moodie, *Mark Hurdlestone*, 1853, I, xx.

Our colonial position, whatever may be its political advantages, is not favourable to the growth of an indigenous literature. Not only are our mental wants supplied by the brain of the Mother Country, under circumstances that utterly preclude competition; but the majority of persons of taste and education in Canada are emigrants from the Old Country, whose tenderest affections cling around the land they have left.

Edward H. Dewart, *Selections from Can. poets*, 1864, xiv.

I believe the existence of a recognized literary class will by and by be felt as a state and social necessity.

Thomas D'A. McGee, speech to Literary Club, Montreal, 1867.

It must be admitted that Canada has not yet produced any works which show a marked originality of thought. Some humorous writings, a few good poems, one or two histories, some scientific and constitutional productions, are alone known to a small reading public outside of Canada. Striking originality can hardly be developed to any great extent in a dependency which naturally, and perhaps wisely in some cases, looks for all its traditions and habits of thought to a parent state. It is only with an older condition of society, when men have learned at last to think as well as to act for themselves, to originate rather than to reproduce, that there can be a national literature.

John G. Bourinot, *Intellectual development of the Can. people*, 1881, 116.

Canada is ambitious of having a native literature; let her wait, and if she has the gift, it will come. She will one day awake and find herself famous in the world of letters.

Goldwin Smith, *Bystander*, 1890, 291.

Canada is a political expression. This must be borne in mind when we speak of Canadian literature.

Goldwin Smith, *Canada and the Can. question*, 1891, 47.

Great deeds are greater than great sonnets, and Canada's call to her sons is a stirring one of action; for the poetry of action exists just as does the poetry of words and the great deed that is accomplished is more glorious than the great sonnet.

Sir Arthur Conan Doyle, Can. Club, Montreal, June 4, 1914.

There will never be a Canadian literature until Canadians abandon the delusion that there ever can be such a thing as "Canadian" literature.

Sir Andrew Macphail, R. S. C., *Proc.*, 1939, II, 127.

Any Canadian who turns up his nose at a Canadian book because it is a Canadian book, is a foule byrd.

Lawrence J. Burpee, qu., *Can. author*, Mar., 1943, 6.

A study of the vast untouched field of obscenity and blasphemy ranging from academic halls to the lumber and mining camps and the army would throw interesting light on the problem of realistic literature in Canada.

H. A. Innis, in *Can. hist. rev.*, 1944, 57.

LOVE.

There is a private spring to everyone's affection; if you can find that, and touch it, the door will fly open, tho' it was a miser's heart.

T. C. Haliburton, *Sam Slick's wise saws*, 1853, I, 70.

"Love is swift as hawk or hind,
Chamois-like in fleetness,
None are lost that love can find,"
Sang the maid, with sweetness.

Charles Sangster, "Lost and found", 1860.

O Love builds on the azure sea,
And Love builds on the golden sand;

And Love builds on the rose-winged
cloud,
And sometimes Love builds on the
land.

ISABELLA V. CRAWFORD, "Malcolm's
Katie", 1884.

Of love's fair ministers thou art the
chief.
To jaded souls, asleep beside their
vows,
Thou givest hopes, keen joys and
vague alarms;
Beneath thy touch the brown and
yellow leaf
Turns to pink blossom, and the spring-
bright boughs
Frame lovers running to each other's
arms.

ETHELWYN WETHERALD, "Absence,"
1907.

I have sought beauty through the
dust of strife,
I have sought meaning for the
ancient ache,
And music in the grinding wheels
of life:
Long have I sought, and little
found as yet
Beyond this truth: that Love alone
can make
Earth beautiful, and life without
regret.

ARTHUR STRINGER, "The final
lesson", 1907.

What Love anticipates may die in
flower,
What Love possesses may be mine
an hour,
But redly gleam in life's unlit
Decembers
What Love remembers.

ETHELWYN WETHERALD, "What love
remembers", 1907.

Oh, for a love like the air.
So infinite, soundless and broad
That every child of the earth may
share
The joy of the heart of God!

ALBERT D. WATSON, "The poet's
prayer", 1913.

It is easier to love in spite of faults
than because of virtues.

ROBERT C. (BOB) EDWARDS, Calgary Eye Opener, Dec. 11, 1915.

Here we came when love was young.
Now that love is old,
Shall we leave the floor unswept
And the hearth acold?

BLISS CARMAN, "The homestead",
1916.

In the stars that gem the blue
Of the night,
In the storm and the dew,
There is light;
In the clouds that split with thunder,
In the soul athrill with wonder,
Over all and through and under,
There is Love and Light.

ALBERT D. WATSON, "To worlds
more wide", 1917.

When a man is in love for the first
time he thinks he invented it.

ROBERT C. (BOB) EDWARDS, Calgary Eye Opener, Nov. 24, 1917.

Love goes where it is sent.

Proverb, Victoria Beach, N. S.

Love will ever find a way
To turn the darkest night to day:
Out of chaos and mischance,
And every wicked circumstance,
'Twill build itself a home again
Within the erring hearts of men;
But hell is made by its inhabitants.

TOM MACINNES, "Love", 1918.

Heart of my heart, O come with me
To walk the ways of Arcadie.

NORAH M. HOLLAND, "The awaken-
ing of the lily", 1924.

One-sided love lasts best.

STEPHEN B. LEACOCK, in Queen's
quart., 1935, 79.

LOYALTY.

(See also: NATIONALITY;
PATRIOTISM)

All suspicion of disloyalty we cast
aside as the product of ignorance or
cupidity; we seek for nothing more
than British subjects are entitled to;
but we will be contented with nothing
less.

JOSEPH HOWE, Letters to Lord
John Russell, 1839.

The raily loyal people, like the raily
religious people, don't talk about it
for everlastin'ly.

T. C. HALIBURTON, Sam Slick,
1840, 140.

No consideration of finance, no question of balance for or against them, upon interchange of commodities, can have any influence upon the loyalty of the inhabitants of the British Provinces, or tend in the slightest degree to alienate the affections of the people from their country, their institutions, their Government and their Queen.

> JOSEPH HOWE, speech in Detroit, July, 1865.

Loyalty to the Queen is a noble sentiment in which all true Liberals share, but loyalty to the Queen does not require a man to bow down to her manservant, her maidservant, her ox or her ass.

> ALEXANDER MACKENZIE, speech, with a bow at the last word in the direction of his political opponent, William Macdougall, at Lambton, election 1867.

True Loyalty's to Motherland
And not to Canada,
The love we bear is second-hand
To any step-mama.

> JOSEPH D. PEMBERTON, letter to *British Colonist* (Victoria, B. C.), early 1870.

Shall not our love this rough, sweet land make sure,
Her bound preserve inviolate, though we die?
O strong hearts of the North,
Let flame your loyalty forth.
And put the craven and base to an open shame,
Till earth shall know the Child of Nations by her name!

> CHARLES G. D. ROBERTS, "An ode for the Canadian confederacy", 1880.

One loyal man is as good as ten rebels.

> SIR JOHN THOMPSON, speech in Owen Sound, Ont., Nov. 15, 1886.

O triune Kingdom of the brave,
O sea-girt island of the free,
O Empire of the land and wave,
Our hearts, our hands are all with thee!
Stand, Canadians, firmly stand,
Round the flag of Fatherland!

> JOHN T. LESPERANCE, "Empire first", 1889.

I think you will accept the proposition readily, that there was a time when there was no such thing as Canadian loyalty.

> GEORGE W. ROSS, speech, Empire Club, Toronto, 1905.

Loyalty, like affection, is a thing of the heart; it is not of the mouth or the pocket.

> SIR ANDREW MACPHAIL, *Essays in politics*, 1909.

So far as I have been able to trace it this cry of loyalty appears to have taken its origin from certain hysterical women of the male sex, chiefly resident in Toronto.

> SIR RICHARD CARTWRIGHT, speech in Toronto, Aug. 29, 1911, on reciprocity issue.

Loyalty without intelligence may degrade a man to the level of a beast.

> PETER McARTHUR, qu., Deacon, *McArthur*, 66.

A Canadian's first loyalty is not to the British Commonwealth of Nations but to Canada and Canada's king, and those who contest this, in my opinion, render a disservice to the Commonwealth.

> LORD TWEEDSMUIR, speech to Can. Inst. Int'l. Affairs, Montreal, Oct. 12, 1937.

In Canada to be disloyal means to be disloyal to Great Britain. Such a crime as disloyalty to Canada scarcely exists.

> JOHN MacCORMAC, *Canada*, 1940, 127.

LUCK.

That's his misfortune and not his fault.

> THOMAS C. HALIBURTON, *Sam Slick's wise saw*, 1853, ch. I; adapted from earlier usage.

Misfortunes often put us wise to our own carelessness.

> ROBERT C. (BOB) EDWARDS, *Calgary Eye Opener*, June 18, 1910.

If your luck isn't what it should be write a "p" in front of it and try again.

> ROBERT C. (BOB) EDWARDS, *Calgary Eye Opener*, Jan. 13, 1912.

Chance, the essence of gambling, finds its complete embodiment in the lottery. The glory of a human being is reason, judgment, will power, and control over himself and his personal affairs. The lottery is the negation of all that. It is, in fact, the complete apotheosis of chance.

SIR GEORGE E. FOSTER, H. of C., *Debates*, June 17, 1931.

I am a great believer in luck, and I find the harder I work the more I have of it.

STEPHEN B. LEACOCK; attributed.

LUMBERING.

Come all ye jolly shanty-boys, if ye want to hear a song,
Come sit ye down beside me. and I'll not detain you long,
'Tis of ten of our Canadian boys who volunteered to go,
To break the jam on Geary's rocks. with their foreman, Young Monroe.

ANON., "The jam on Geary's rocks", song with *locale* on River Trent

Oh, when we get down to Quebec town,
The girls they dance for joy.
Says one unto another one.
'Here comes a shantyboy!'
One will treat us to a bottle.
And another to a dram,
While the toast goes round the table
For the jolly shanty-man.

Lumbermen's song, "O ye maidens of Ontario".

Come all ye maids of Simcoe.
give ear to what I write,
In crossing Lake Ontario
where raftsmen take delight.
In crossing Lake Ontario
as jolly raftsmen do,
While your lowland, loafing farmers can stay at home with you.

Lumbermen's song. "The maids of Simcoe".

The Main John.

Lumbermen's expression for woods bosses; originated in New Bruns-

wick, from John B. Glasier (1809-1894) N. B. lumberman and Senator.

The ravenous sawmills in the pine wilderness are not unlike the huge dragons that used in popular legend to lay waste the country; and like dragons, they die when their prey, the lordly pines, are all devoured.

WILLIAM H. WITHROW, *Our own country: Canada*, 1889.

Mc.

MACDONALD, SIR JOHN A.

John A. Macdonald is now the recognized leader, but he is anything but strong in reality.

JOHN LANGTON, letter to his brother, April 17, 1856.

Sir John A. Macdonald is about to retire to private life, a thoroughly used-up character.

TORONTO *Globe*, Aug., 1858.

I know enough of the feeling of this meeting to know that you would rather have John A. drunk than George Brown sober.

SIR JOHN A. MACDONALD, election speech, early in his career. after being attacked by the *Globe*; qu., Biggar, *Anecdotal life*, 194.

Ah, John A., John A., how I love you! How I wish I could trust you!

ANON., Liberal member of the Legislature, 1863, to Sir John A. Macdonald; qu., Cartwright, *Reminiscences*, 1912, 47.

We have fought the battle of Confederation. We have fought the battle of unity. We have had party strife, setting Province against Province. And more than all, we have had, in the greatest Province, every prejudice and sectional feeling that could be arrayed against us. I throw myself on this House; I throw myself on this country; I throw myself on posterity, and I believe that, notwithstanding the many failings of my life, I shall have the voice of this country rallying round me. And, sir, if I am mistaken in that, I can confidently appeal to a higher court — to the court of my conscience and to the court of posterity.

> SIR JOHN A. MACDONALD, speech in defence of his railway policy, H. of C., *Debates* Nov. 3, 1873.

Well! John A. beats the devil.

> LUTHER H. HOLTON, remark on Macdonald's restoration to office, election 1878.

A rum 'un to look at, but a rare 'un to go!

> SIR JOHN A. MACDONALD's frequently repeated likening of himself to an old nag. Once, when riding to Markham Township Fair with Squire Millikan, he met an Irishman who had ridden over from Yonge Street on an old horse to see him. Sir John commented on the horse and the man said, "Faith, he's like yourself, Sir, a bit worse for wear." The reply was, "Yes, he's like myself, a rum 'un to look at, but a rare 'un to go."

Old Reynard.

> Term used in reference to his artfulness and subtlety in politics.

Old Tomorrow would be just the name for Sir John.

> COL. A. G. IRVINE, commissioner N.W.M.P. late in 1881 to his adjutant, Supt. Cotton, and Ronald Prevost, in Ottawa; qu., Biggar, *Anecdotal life*, 320.

The Wizard of the North.

> A popular term.

A British subject I was born, and a British subject I hope to die.

> SIR JOHN A. MACDONALD, H. of C., *Debates*, 1882, 1078. Also, "As for myself, my course is clear. A British subject I was born — a British subject I will die," in, "To the electors of Canada", Feb. 7, 1891.

Of all the Dominion statesmen,
We ne'er expect to see,
One to compare in Canada
With Sir John A., K.C.B.

> CONSERVATIVE PARTY song, election of June 1882.

He cannot resist the solicitations of partisans, except perhaps in the case of judicial appointments, in regard to which his best sentiment is peculiarly romantic.

> GOLDWIN SMITH, letter to W. D. Le Sueur, June 2, 1882.

I will say this for that old scoundrel John A. Macdonald, that if he once gave you his word, you could rely on it.

> SIR RICHARD CARTWRIGHT, qu., Pope, *Day of Macdonald*, 1915, 118.

Sir John A. Macdonald, cabinet-maker.

> SIR JOHN A. MACDONALD, inscription in a visitor's book.

It is a happy association of ideas, and what a lamented friend of mine called the "eternal fitness of things", that a gentleman who in his life has done justice to so many John Collinses should at last find a John Collins to do justice to him.

> SIR RICHARD CARTWRIGHT, in House of Commons, on the publication of a biography of Macdonald by J. E. Collins, 1883.

When this man is gone, who will there be to take his place? What shepherd is there who knows the sheep or whose voice the sheep know? Who else could make Orangemen vote for Papists, and induce half the members for Ontario to help in levying on their own province the necessary blackmail for Quebec? Yet this is the work which will have to be done if a general break-up is to be averted.

> GOLDWIN SMITH, *The Week*, Feb. 28, 1884, 194.

You'll never die, John A.

> ANON., to Sir John A. Macdonald, when he spoke at a demonstration in his honour at Toronto, Dec. 17, 1884.

The present government will last as long as Sir John Macdonald and when Sir John disappears, after him the deluge.

> SIR WILFRID LAURIER, speech at Somerset, Que., Aug. 2, 1887. (trans.)

I had no boyhood. From the age of fifteen I began to earn my own living.

SIR JOHN A. MACDONALD to a friend, in his later years.

It is late, Bowell, good night.

SIR JOHN A. MACDONALD to Mackenzie Bowell on leaving the House chamber for the last time, May 22, 1891.

Sir John Macdonald now belongs to the ages, and it can be said with certainty that the career which has just been closed is one of the most remarkable careers of this century.

SIR WILFRID LAURIER, H. of C., *Debates*, June 8, 1891.

Before the grave of him who, above all, was the father of Confederation, let not grief be barren grief.

SIR WILFRID LAURIER, H. of C., *Debates*, June 8, 1891.

It may be said, without any exaggeration whatever, that the life of Sir John Macdonald, from the date he entered Parliament, is the history of Canada, for he was connected and associated with all the events, all the facts which brought Canada from the position it then occupied — the position of two small provinces, having nothing in common but their common allegiance, united by a bond of paper, and united by nothing else — to the present state of development which Canada has reached.

SIR WILFRID LAURIER, H. of C., *Debates*, June 8, 1891.

Death comes not with mere surcease of breath
To such as him. "The road to dusty death"
Not "all his yesterdays" have lighted. Nay,
Canada's "Old Tomorrow" lives today
In unforgetting hearts, and nothing fears
The long tomorrow of the coming years.

PUNCH, June 20, 1891.

Had he been a much worse man he would have done Canada much less harm.

SIR RICHARD CARTWRIGHT, *Reminiscences*, 1912. 198.

Only a Mohammed can come back to Mecca; only a Napoleon can return from Elba; only a Calvin can come back to Geneva; and only a Macdonald could come back to Ottawa after what occured in 1873 [the Pacific scandal].

B. H. STAUFFER, Empire Club speech, Feb. 18, 1915.

Opposition was but ever a spur to his valour.

HECTOR CHARLESWORTH, *Can. scene.* 1927. 10.

McGEE, THOMAS D'ARCY.

Yea, we like children stood
When in his lofty mood
He spoke of manly deeds which he might claim,
And made responses fit
While heavenly genius lit
His melancholy eyes with lambent flame,
And saw the distant aureoles,
And felt the Future thunder in our souls.

CHARLES MAIR, "In memory of Thomas D'Arcy McGee", 1868.

Was it a wonder that a cry of agony rang throughout the land when murder, foul and most unnatural, drank the life-blood of Thomas D'Arcy McGee?

W. A. FOSTER, *Canada first, or, our new nationality*, 1871.

D'Arcy McGee was, in truth, the Mazzini of Canadian national unity.

W. STEWART WALLACE, in *Can. hist. rev.*, 1920, 147.

MACKENZIE, ALEXANDER.
(Explorer)

I now mixed up some vermillon in melted grease, and inscribed, in large characters, on the South-East face of the rock on which we had slept last night, this brief memorial — 'Alexander Mackenzie from Canada by land, the twenty-second of July, one thousand seven hundred and ninety-three'.

ALEXANDER MACKENZIE, *Voyages*, 1801, 349, inscription made on the shore of Dean Channel, Bella Coola River, B. C., **celebrating the first crossing of the continent north of Mexico.**

MACKENZIE, ALEXANDER.

(Politician)

Consequences had to go to pieces before Alexander Mackenzie. God give us more such as he was, honest and true.

S. H. BLAKE, speech at East York, after the funeral of Mackenzie, April, 1892.

Remember Mackenzie's mistakes!

Admonition used among Liberals after 1896, referring to Mackenzie's submission to a wing of the party noted for its concern for principle and zeal.

We loved him for the enemies he had made.

SIR WILFRID LAURIER, speech in Massey Hall, Feb. 20, 1906.

If his strong point was having been a stone-mason, his weak point was being a stone-mason still.

GOLDWIN SMITH, Reminiscences, 1910, 436.

MACKENZIE, WILLIAM LYON.

He is a little red-haired man about five feet nothing and extremely like a baboon but he is the O'Connell of Canada.

JOHN LANGTON, letter to his father, April 25, 1834.

I am incapable of moderating the spirit of party — I am hot and fiery & age has not yet tempered as much as I could wish my political conduct & opinions.

W. L. MACKENZIE, letter to J. Neilson, Nov. 23, 1835; P.A.C., Neilson papers, VIII.

My creed has been — social democracy — or equality of each man before society — and political democracy, or the equality of each man before the law.

W. L. MACKENZIE, in Mackenzie's Gaz., Dec. 23, 1840.

Every evil which he discerned was in his estimation truly an evil and all evils were about of equal magnitude... He felt a longing desire to right the wrongs which he saw everywhere around him. This therefore, consti-

tuted, as he believed, his mission as a public man in Canada.

EGERTON RYERSON, Story of my life, 1884,, 186-7.

A cowardly ruffian, who curiously enough bore not an Irish but a Scottish name.

SIR JOHN W. FORTESCUE, History British army, 1923, XI, 504.

M

MAJORITY.

There's no tyranny on airth equal to the tyranny of a majority.

T. C. HALIBURTON, Sam Slick, 1838, 59.

Sandfield Macdonald didn't possess even a drinking majority; a man daren't go out to drink for fear the Ministry would be defeated before he got back.

ANON., on the session of Feb. 19 to March 21, 1864.

Given a Government with a big surplus, and a big majority and a weak Opposition, and you would debauch a committee of archangels.

SIR JOHN A. MACDONALD to Richard Cartwright, about 1869, qu. by Cartwright, Reminiscences, 1912. 305.

If anyone tells me that fidelity to party and fidelity to country are always compatible, or that the wisdom of mere numbers is the wisdom of heaven, then I tell him that he loves applause far more than he loves truth.

ARTHUR MEIGHEN, farewell tribute to R. B. Bennett, speech in Toronto, Jan. 16, 1939.

MANITOBA.

Manitoba is the key to the territories of the North West.

SIR GEORGES E. CARTIER, H. of C., Debates, May 2, 1870, on the establishment of the Province.

The Prairie Province.

J. C. HAMILTON, The prairie province, 1876; from the title of the book which gave the phrase general circulation; after 1905 it was extended to include Saskatchewan and Alberta, in "The Prairie Provinces".

From its geographical position, and its peculiar characteristics, Manitoba may be regarded as the keystone of that mighty arch of sister provinces which spans the continent from the Atlantic to the Pacific. It was here that Canada, emerging from her woods and forests, first gazed upon her rolling prairies and unexplored North-West, and learned as by an unexpected revelation, that her historical territories of the Canadas, her eastern seaboards of New Brunswick, Labrador, and Nova Scotia, her Laurentian lakes and valleys, corn lands and pastures, though themselves more extensive than half-a-dozen European kingdoms, were but the vestibules and antechambers to that till then undreamed-of Dominion whose illimitable dimensions alike confound the arithmetic of the surveyor and the verification of the explorer.

> LORD DUFFERIN, speech at City Hall, Winnipeg, Sept. 29, 1877.

The Manitoba Boom.

> A period of prosperity in the province, 1879 to 1883.

The Postage Stamp Province.

> A popular name given to the province after 1870 because of its original size and shape; speech of R. P. ROBLIN, Winnipeg, Mar. 7, 1907.

He who drinks Red River water once, must drink it again.

> Popular saying in the North-West, about 1880.

The Cinderella of Confederation.

> JOHN NORQUAY, in Manitoba budget speech, 1884.

Manitoba First!

> Motto, 1884, of MANITOBA FIRST PARTY which contended that their interest lay solely in provincial advancement.

I know that through the grace of God I am the founder of Manitoba.

> LOUIS RIEL, Queen versus Louis Riel, 1886, 147.

Softly the shadows of prairie-land wheat
Ripple and riot adown to her feet;
Murmurs all Nature with joyous acclaim,

Fragrance of summer and shimmer of flame.

> EMILY MCMANUS, "Manitoba", 1913.

MANNERS.

(See also: BEHAVIOUR)

It's our custom, and custom, you know, will reconcile one to 'most anything.

> T. C. HALIBURTON, Sam Slick, 1836, ch. XXVII.

This was my first lesson, that squeamishness and indelicacy are often found united; in short, that in manners, as in other things, extremes meet.

> T. C. HALIBURTON, Sam Slick, 1838, 175.

Civility is a cheap coin that is manufactured for nothing, and among folks in general goes further than dollars and cents.

> THOMAS C. HALIBURTON, Sam Slick's wise saws, 1853, ch. IX.

Vulgarity is always showy.

> T. C. HALIBURTON, Nature and human nature, 1855, I, 205.

Etiquette is a beneficent invention that enables a naturally disagreeable person to live with another without coming to blows.

> PETER MCARTHUR, To be taken with salt, 1903, 148.

MANUFACTURING.

(See also: INDUSTRY)

Let us beware how we allow the establishment of manufactures in Canada; she would become proud and mutinous like the English colonies. So long as France is a nursery to Canada, let not the Canadians be allowed to trade, but kept to their wandering, laborious life with the savages, and to their military exercises.

> MARQUIS DE MONTCALM, letter written before the fall of Quebec, 1759.

We are manufacturers not merely of articles of wood and stone, and iron and cotton and wool. We manufacture enthusiasms; we manufacture a feeling of pride in our country, a spirit of independence.

> CYRUS A. BIRGE, pres. of Canadian Manufacurers' Assoc., *Industrial Canada*, Oct. 1903, 103.

If we make we are rich, if we do not make we inevitably become poor.

> GEORGE E. DRUMMOND, speech to Can. Manufacturers' Assoc., Montreal, July 21, 1904.

On Thursday I will beat them and on Friday I will continue to protect their just interests.

> SIR WILFRID LAURIER, on manufacturers, speech in Montreal, Sept. 19, 1911.

Made in Canada.

> Slogan adopted by manufacturers after the Reciprocity election, 1911.

We were not prepared to admit that there was any article that could not at some point in Canada, and in time, be successfully manufactured.

> CANADIAN MANUFACTURERS' ASSOCIATION, Rept. of ann. meeting, in. *Industrial Canada*, 1912, 334.

MAPLE.

This tree — the maple — which grows in our valleys... at first young and beaten by the storm, pines away, painfully feeding itself from the earth, but it soon springs up, tall and strong, and faces the tempest and triumphs over the wind which cannot shake it any more. The maple is the king of our forest; it is the symbol of the Canadian people.

> DENIS B. VIGER, speech, June 24, 1836, St. Jean-Baptiste Soc., Montreal. (trans.)

Frosty nights and warm sun make the maple sap run.

> Saying of pioneer Ontario farmers.

Hail to the pride of the forest, hail
To the maple tall and green,
It yields a treasure which never shall fail
While leaves on its boughs are seen.
When the snows of winter are melting fast,
And the sap begins to rise,

And the biting breath of the frozen blast
Yields to the spring's soft sighs.

> SUSANNA MOODIE, *Roughing it in the bush*, 1852.

Resolved, — That all Native Canadians joining the procession, whether identified with the National Societies or not, should wear the maple leaf as an emblem of the land of their birth.

> JAMES H. RICHARDSON, resolution adopted by a meeting of national societies, Toronto, Aug. 21, 1860, called to arrange a welcome for Prince of Wales (King Edward VII); regarded as the date of the adoption of the emblem for Canada.

All hail to the broad-leaved maple,
With its fair and changeful dress!
A type of our youthful country
In its pride and loveliness.

> HENRY F. DARNELL, "The maple", 1864.

In days of yore the hero, Wolfe,
Britain's glory did maintain,
And planted firm Britannia's flag
On Canada's fair domain,
Here may it wave, our boast, our pride,
And, joined in love together,
The Thistle, Shamrock, Rose entwine,
The Maple Leaf forever!

Chorus —

The Maple Leaf, our emblem dear,
The Maple Leaf forever!
God save our Queen, and heaven bless
The Maple Leaf forever!

> ALEXANDER MUIR, "The maple leaf forever", 1867. (See also: WOLFE, JAMES)

The scarlet of the maples can shake me like a cry,
Of bugles going by.

> BLISS CARMAN, "A vagabond song", 1894.

Scarlet when the April vanguard
Bugles up the laggard Spring,
Scarlet when the bannered Autumn
Marches by unwavering.

> BLISS CARMAN, "The grave-tree", 1898.

Above them are being planted the maples of Canada, in the thought that

her sons will rest the better in the shade
of the trees they knew so well in life.

> ARTHUR MEIGHEN, at Vimy Ridge,
> July 3, 1921.

There is a story written no art can
    ever name,
And golden
The fiery heralds run.
Across the fields of Canada we trace
    their path of flame.

> A. M. STEPHEN, "Scarlet and gold
> — the maples", 1923.

THE MARITIMES.

Your destiny and ours, is as inseparable as are the waters which pour into
the Bay of Chaleur, rising though they
do, on the one hand on the Canadian,
and on the other on the New Brunswick Highlands. Geographically we
are bound up beyond the power of
extinction.

> THOMAS D'ARCY MCGEE, speech
> in St. John, N. B., August, 1863.

Herring-backs.

A popular name for Maritimers,
about 1875.

Come all you jolly lumbermen,
Whose better years have fled,
And I will sing of halcyon days
Before we had Confed;
When title to respect was writ
Upon each horny hand,
And the man who swung a broadaxe
Was a power in the land.

> HEADLEY PARKER, "The days of
> Duffey Gillis", 1899.

The age of wood, wind and water.

> ROYAL COMMISSION ON DOMIN-
> ION-PROVINCIAL RELATIONS, Re-
> port, vol. 1, 1940, 22; the phrase
> refers to the "Golden Age" of the
> Maritime Provinces, the pre-Con-
> federation era of prosperity based
> on fish and lumber exports, wooden
> shipbuilding, and the carrying
> trade.

We give you ships and tides and men
Anchors a-weigh and wind-filled sail
We give you back the sea again
In sailors' song and rousing tale;
And inland where the dark hills rise
Between you and the salt-thick foam

You hear the surf, the sea-gulls' cries
And eastward turn your hearts toward
home.

> EILEEN CAMERON HENRY, "Harmony
> harbour", June, 1947.

MARRIAGE.

(See also: MEN AND WOMEN)

What a pity it is that marryin' spoils
courtin'.

> THOMAS C. HALIBURTON, Sam
> Slick's wise saws, 1853, ch. XVII.

Matrimony likes contrasts; friendship seeks its own counterparts.

> T. C. HALIBURTON, Sam Slick's
> wise saws, 1853, II, 79.

All girls regard marriage as an envi-
able lot, or a necessary evil.

> T. C. HALIBURTON, Nature and
> human nature, 1855, I, 157.

There must have been a charming
climate in Paradise. The temperature
was perfect; and connubial bliss, I
allot, was real jam up.

> T. C. HALIBURTON, Nature and
> human nature, 1855, 273.

Women, in a general way, don't look
like the same critters when they are
spliced, that they do before; matrimony,
like sugar and water, has a natural
affinity for, and tendency to acidity.

> T. C. HALIBURTON, Nature and
> human nature, 1855, II, 260.

A marriage to-day,
    And a funeral to-morrow;
A short smile of joy,
    And a long sigh of sorrow.

> ALEXANDER MCLACHLAN, "The
> vision", 1856.

One of our maxims should be —
"Early marriages, and death to old
bachelors."

> THOMAS D'A. MCGEE, speech
> in Quebec, May 10, 1862.

Whatever facilitates marriage prevents impurity, and whatever adds to
the prosperity of the people facilitates
marriage.

> GOLDWIN SMITH, The Bystander,
> Sept., 1880, 497.

If a girl could only marry the best man at her wedding there would be fewer matrimonial smash-ups.

ROBERT C. (BOB) EDWARDS, *Calgary Eye Opener*, Aug. 4, 1906.

Adultery is the same the world over; it's only the method of approach that varies.

SIR JAMES LOUGHEED, chairman of the Senate divorce committee, about 1920.

If it is a wedding let it be a wedding.

Newfoundland outport saying; qu., Devine, *Folklore of Nfld.*, 1937.

Protestant marriage is legalized concubinage.

JAMES VINCENT CLEARY, first Roman Catholic archbishop, Kingston, 1896.

Our children climb upon her knee
And lie upon her breast,
And ah! her mission seems to me
The highest and the best;
And so I say with pride untold,
And love beyond degree,
This woman with the heart of gold
She just keeps house for me.

JEAN BLEWETT, "She just keeps house for me", 1897.

So truly as a young man married is a young man marred, is a woman unmarried, in a certain sense, a woman undone.

SIR WILLIAM OSLER, "Nurse and patient", address, 1897, in *Aequanimitas*; from Shakespeare, "A young man married is a man that's marred".

The woman with the ideal husband very likely wishes she had some other kind.

ROBERT C. (BOB) EDWARDS, *Calgary Eye Opener*, Dec. 6, 1913.

Mating is like dinner-hour: the more fashionable you are the later it occurs.

ARTHUR STRINGER, *Christina and I*, 1929.

MEDICINE HAT, ALTA.

The only commonplace thing about the spot was its name — Medicine Hat,

which struck me instantly as the only name such a town could carry.

RUDYARD KIPLING, *From tideway to tideway*, 1892.

You people in this district seem to have all Hell for a basement.

RUDYARD KIPLING, late 1907; qu. in Board of Trade, *Medicine Hat*, 1910, 39.

MEMORY.

The glow of mind, the spirit's light,
    Which time or age can never take,
Will still shine on, undimmed and bright,
    And many a holy rapture wake.

JOSEPH HOWE, "Tho' time may steal the roseate blush", 1827.

Memory is nothin' but experience.

T. C. HALIBURTON, *Sam Slick's wise saws*, 1853, I, 277.

The memory of past favours is like a rainbow, bright, vivid, and beautiful; but it soon fades away. The memory of injuries is engraved on the heart, and remains for ever.

T. C. HALIBURTON, *Sam Slick's wise saws*, 1853, I, 292.

Recollection
Will stick like smut upon one's memory.

CHARLES HEAVYSEGE, *Saul*, 1857.

Summers and summers have come, and gone with the flight of the swallow;
Sunshine and thunder have been, storm, and winter, and frost;
Many and many a sorrow has all but died from remembrance.

CHARLES G. D. ROBERTS, "The Tantramar revisited", 1887.

And lonely memory searching through,
Found no such stars in the orbèd past,
As the glad first greeting 'twixt me and you,
And the sad, mad meeting which was our last.

NICHOLAS F. DAVIN, "The Canadian year", 1889.

When you feel like doing a foolish thing remember that you have to live with your memory.

ROBERT C. (BOB) EDWARDS, *Calgary Eye Opener*, Mar. 30, 1917.

Memory is cultivated and praised, but who will teach us to forget? A thousand remembrances of our folly and failure but lead us to expect more folly and failure.

GEORGE ILES, *Canadian stories*, 1918, 172.

Memory is one of the least reliable manifestations of the mind; it is the handmaid of will and desire.

J. W. DAFOE, in *Clifford Sifton*, 1931, 140.

MEN.

(See also: MEN AND WOMEN; PEOPLE; POPULATION; WOMEN)

The human mind naturally adapts itself to the position it occupies. The most gigantic intellect may be dwarfed by being 'cabind'd, cribb'd confined'. It requires a great country and great circumstances to develop great men.

SIR CHARLES TUPPER, "The political condition of Brit. N. Amer.", a lecture in St. John, N. B., 1860.

Above all nations is humanity.

GOLDWIN SMITH, an aphorism, about 1870; carved on a bench at Cornell University, where Smith taught; also, "Over all nations is Humanity", by W. L. MACKENZIE KING, *Industry and humanity*, 1918.

Here we are, all together
Birds of a flock, but not of feather;
Lawyers, doctors, rogues and printers,
A jolly lot of evil thinkers.

ROBERT MURDOCH, "A toast", 1890.

Send me better men to deal with, and I will be a better man.

SIR JOHN A. MACDONALD, to a farmer-elector, qu. by Cartwright, *Reminiscences*, 1912, 46.

For I am of that forlorn hope
That is the only hope of man —
From corner stone to curve and cope
I am a cosmopolitan!

GEORGE F. CAMERON, "Proem", 1873.

I am disposed to judge of measures more than men.

DONALD A. SMITH (LORD STRATHCONA) election speech, 1878.

What is man, poor sinful man, or any of his race,
Without a greater power to keep him in his place?

JAMES GAY, "What is man?", [1885].

I compassed time, outstripped the starry speed,
And in my soul apprehended space,
Till, weighing laws which these but blindly heed,
At last I came before Him face to face,
And knew the Universe of no such span
As the august infinitude of man.

CHARLES G. D. ROBERTS, "In the wide awe and wisdom of the night", 1893.

Linked to all his half-accomplished fellows,
Through unfrontiered provinces to roam —
Man is but the morning dream of nature,
Roused to some wild cadence weird and strange.

BLISS CARMAN, "Beyond the gamut", 1894.

From the seer with his snow-white crown
Through every sort and condition
Of bipeds, all the way down
To the pimp and the politician.

ARCHIBALD LAMPMAN (died 1899), an epigram, qu., in E. K. Brown. *On Can. poetry*, 1943, 85.

To grant an ordinary man equality is to make him your superior.

PETER MCARTHUR, *To be taken with salt*, 1903, 146.

As a freeborn British subject I feel that to trust any man as an equal, be he a dustman or a dupe, I am paying him the highest compliment in my power.

PETER MCARTHUR, *To be taken with salt*, 1903, 149.

Teach me the lesson that Mother
    Earth
    Teacheth her children each hour,
When she keeps in her deeps the
    basic root,
    And wears on her breast the
    flower.

And as the brute to the basic root
    In the infinite cosmic plan,
So in the plan of the infinite mind
    The flower of the brute is man.
    WILFRED CAMPBELL, "The lyre
    degenerate", 1905.

Evolution is an immense discovery,
the most momentous ever made... Still,
we are what we are, not apes but men.
    GOLDWIN SMITH, In quest of light,
    1906, 14.

Men become great as Nations grow,
they are purified through suffering.
    J. W. ROBERTSON, Can. Club,
    Toronto, Jan. 24,, 1910.

The minute a man is convinced that
he is interesting, he isn't.
    STEPHEN B. LEACOCK; attributed.

Men who make the greatest sacrifices
ask nothing in return.
    SIR RICHARD CARTWRIGHT. qu.,
    Stand. dict. Can. biog., 1934, 103.

Just try to get the Cosmic touch.
The sense that "you" don't matter
    much.
A million stars are in the sky;
A million planets plunge and die.
A million million men are sped;
A million million wait ahead.
Each plays his part and has his
    day —
    What ho! the world's all right, I
    say.
    ROBERT W. SERVICE, "The world's
    all right", 1912.

The average man has more than one
kick coming — to him.
    ROBERT C. (BOB) EDWARDS, Cal-
    gary Eye Opener, Dec. 15, 1917.

Men will never disappoint us if we
observe two rules: 1. To find out what
they are; 2. To expect them to be just
that.
    GEORGE ILES, Canadian stories,
    1918, 175.

With good-will, and a touch of mirth,
    To clear and clean and plant and
    plan
The common levels of the Earth —
    What more should God then ask
    of Man?
    TOM MACINNES, "Polity", 1918.

Doctors, auctioneers and bakers.
Dentists, diplomats and fakirs.
Clergymen and undertakers.
    E. J. PRATT, "The witches' brew",
    1925.

Starving for fragance on the lilied
    hills,
    Hungry for colour in a bower of
    rose,
Grieving for beauty amid daffodils,
    Man — the enigma — goes.
    WILSON MACDONALD, "Enigma",
    1931.

Man the afraid, infirm, impure!
    Yet how he can love and how
    endure.
Endure to the end and rise again,
Victorious victim of passion and pain.
    GEORGE H. CLARKE, "Halt and
    parley", 1934.

MEN AND WOMEN.

An Iroquois arrow made many a
widow.
    ISABEL FOULCHÉ-DELBOSC (1650-
    65), in Can hist. rev., 1940, 141.

Any man that onderstands horses, has
a pretty considerable fair knowledge of
women, for they are just alike in temper,
and require the same identical treatment. Incourage the timid ones, be
gentle and steady with the fract-
ious, and lather the sulky ones like
blazes.
    T. C. HALIBURTON, Sam Slick,
    1836, ch. X.

The moment a feller has a woman's
secret he is that woman's master.
    T. C. HALIBURTON, The attaché,
    2nd. ser., 1844, 71.

There is a young lady I have set
my heart on; though whether she is a-
goin' to give me hern, or give me the
mitten, I ain't quite satisfied.
    T. C. HALIBURTON, Nature and
    human nature, 1855.

Men continually study women, and know nothing about them. Women never study men, and know all about them.
> ROBERT C. (BOB) EDWARDS, *Calgary Eye Opener*, Oct. 15, 1910.

If a man understands one woman he should let it go at that.
> ROBERT C. (BOB) EDWARDS, *Calgary Eye Opener*, Jan. 13, 1912.

Women know men better than they know themselves and better than men ever suspect.
> SIR JOHN WILLISON, *Reminiscences*, 1919, 178.

To me the trying part is being a woman at all. I've come to the ultimate conclusion that I am a misfit of the worst kind. In spite of a superficial femininity — emotion with a foreknowledge of impermanence, a daring mind with only the tongue as an outlet, a greed for experience plus a slavery to convention — what the deuce are you to make of that? — as a woman? As a man, you could go ahead and stir things up *fine*.
> MARJORIE PICKTHALL, letter, Dec. 27, 1919, qu. in Pierce, *Pickthall*, 104.

If only men could read women's thoughts they would take many more risks than they do.
> ROBERT C. (BOB) EDWARDS, *Summer annual*, 1920, 36.

Man, in carving his future, usually finds a woman the mallet behind his chisel.
> ARTHUR STRINGER, *The devastator*, 1944, 115.

MILITIA.

The Men of Gore.
> The loyal forces under the command of Sir Allan MacNab during the rebellion of 1837 in Uper Canada: Gore was a district around Hamilton.

You must not take the militia seriously, for though it is useful for suppressing internal disturbances, it will not be required for the defence of the country, as the Monroe Doctrine protects us against enemy aggression.
> SIR WILFRID LAURIER, 1902, to Lord Dundonald; *My army life*, 1926, 191.

Perhaps the most expensive and ineffective military system of any civilized community in the world.
> COL. HAMILTON MERRITT, qu., *Can. hist. rev.*, 1923, 98.

MIND.

He is quite a 'case', I do assure you.
> THOMAS C. HALIBURTON, *Sam Slick*, 1840, 112.

It is good to have an open mind, but be sure it is not open at both ends.
> A Toronto preacher, qu., *Willison's monthly*, Oct., 1925, 173.

His mind is a muskeg of mediocrity.
> JOHN MACNAUGHTON, on a Canadian professor; *Queen's quart.*, 1934, 362.

MINING.

As false as a diamond from Canada.
> A popular French saying, after 1542, when Jacques Cartier returned from Canada with quartz which he thought was precious until it was tested. (trans.)

The Argonauts.
> A name given to the first miners in the Cariboo gold fields, 1850's.

The Fifty-eighters.
> A British Columbia term for prospectors in the Cariboo district, from the year of the discovery of gold, 1858.

Wherever there's a Father of Rivers there's a mother of placers.
> B. C. coast miners, late 19th. century; the Indian name for the Fraser was, "Father of Rivers".

If the head of the rat is in Alaska and its tail in Montana, the body lies in British Columbia.
> B. C. coast miners, about 1898.

I wanted the gold, and I sought it;
I scrabbled and mucked like a slave.

Was it famine or scurvy — I fought
it;
I hurled my youth into a grave.
I wanted the gold and I got it —
Came out with a fortune last fall,—
Yet somehow life's not what I thought
it,
And somehow the gold isn't all.

> ROBERT W. SERVICE, "The spell of
> the Yukon", 1907.

For we'll sing a little song of Cobalt,
If you don't live there it's your fault.
Oh, you Cobalt, where the wintry
breezes blow,
Where all the silver comes from,
And you live a life and then some,
Oh, you Cobalt, you're the best old
town I know.

> LEONARD F. STEENMAN, "The Cobalt
> song", 1910.

Sure I've got
Warts on my fingers
Corns on my toes
Claims up in Porcupine
And a bad cold in my nose.
So, put on your snowshoes
And hit the trail with me
To P-o-r-c-u-p-i-n-e, — that's me.

> JOHN E. LECKIE, "The Porcupine
> song", 1910; for a variant, see Mac-
> Dougall, *Two thousand miles of
> gold*, 1946, 136.

MISTAKES.

There's many a mistake made on
purpose.

> THOMAS C. HALIBURTON, *Sam
> Slick's wise saws*, 1853, ch. XVII.

If you think to run a rig on me, you
have... barked up the wrong tree.

> T. C. HALIBURTON, *Human nature*,
> 1855, 124.

MODESTY.

If there is one thing I hate more
nor another it is that cussed mock
modesty some galls have, pretendin' they
don't know nothin'. It always shows
they know too much.

> T. C. HALIBURTON, *Sam Slick*,
> 1838, 106.

Modesty is brought forward and
made way for. Assumption has the
door shut in its face.

> T. C. HALIBURTON, *Sam Slick's
> wise saws*, 1853, II, 141.

I consider that modesty is the great
national vice of Canada and the cultivation of a good healthy national con-
ceit one of the highest duties of patriotism.

> JOHN LEWIS, in, *Can. mag.*, Oct.,
> 1900, 495.

Never exaggerate your faults; your
friends will attend to that.

> ROBERT C. (BOB) EDWARDS, *Cal-
> gary Eye Opener*, Feb. 5, 1921.

MONEY.

Halifax currency.
> Term used for the Spanish silver
> dollar rated at five shillings of
> about twenty cents each in Nova
> Scotia; in use 1750-1871.

There are more fortins got savin'
than by makin', I guess.

> T. C. HALIBURTON, *Sam Slick*,
> 1836, ch. XXVI.

Presents of money injure both the
giver and receiver, and destroy the
equilibrium of friendship, and diminish
independence and self-respect.

> T. C. HALIBURTON, *Sam Slick*,
> 1838, 28.

It's not worth a sou marquee.
> Phrase common in the Maritime
> provinces meaning, of trifling value;
> a reference to French Guiana sous
> which, counterstamped by other
> West Indian colonies, were some-
> times carried north to Canada.

The holey dollar.
> Prince Edward Island phrase for
> the Spanish dollar with a round
> hole cut in the centre; early 19th.
> century.

The York Shilling.
> The Spanish reale in terms of the
> New York price of 12 ½ cents used
> in Ontario, and thus distinguished
> from the Halifax shilling of about
> 20 cents; 1800-1850.

It is easier to make money than to save it; one is exertion, the other self-denial.

T. C. HALIBURTON, *Sam Slick's wise saws*, 1853, II, 145.

The Cent Belt.

A term common in British Columbia, middle 19th century, in reference to Ontario and Quebec; old residents of British Columbia prided themselves on using no sum less than a bit, or, twelve and a half cents. In 1861 newspapers were still sold for a bit, either a liberal fifteen cents, or a stingy ten cents.

No man is rich whose expenditure exceeds his means; and no man is poor, whose incomings exceeds his outgoings.

T. C. HALIBURTON, *Nature and human nature*, 1855, II, 266.

'Tis money rules the world now,
It's rank and education,
It's power and knowledge, sense and worth,
And pious reputation.
Get cash, and 'gainst all human ills,
You're armed and you're defended,
For in it even here on earth,
All heaven is comprehended.

ALEXANDER MCLACHLAN, "Young Canada", 1861.

A blanket.

Originally a Hudson's Bay Co. note used in paying wages, during late 19th. century; in the West, a term for a dollar bill.

Ledger influence.

A phrase common in Halifax, about 1867. The votes of people who were deeply in debt to Halifax merchants were easily influenced by the threat of legal proceedings, known as "ledger influence"; later came to mean much the same as "pull".

A Shinplaster.

Paper currency of 25 cents introduced by Sir Francis Hincks, 1870, to drive out American silver.

Does thy soul to greed incline?
Dost thou treasure but for time?
Bolts and bars asunder fall;

Death shall rob thee of it all.
Hither thou canst nothing take:
Something *do*, for mercy's sake.

ALEXANDER MCLACHLAN, *Can. birthday book*, 1887, 92.

A little of the needful.

A popular phrase in New Brunswick.

After all the easiest way to get money is to earn it.

PETER MCARTHUR, *To be taken with salt*, 1903, 156.

Too many men salt away money in the brine of other people's tears.

ROBERT C. (BOB) EDWARDS, *Calgary Eye Opener*, Mar. 30, 1917.

I am very conscious of what it means to have been born in Canada, and I can think of no privilege so great as to have founded any good or enduring thing in this country. I know the value of money, but I should rather have created one of the institutions of my country than to possess millions.

SIR EDMUND WALKER, speech on his 50th. anniversary with the Can. Bank of Com., 1918.

Make money and the whole nation will conspire to call you a gentleman.

ROBERT C. (BOB) EDWARDS, *Summer annual*, 1920, 69.

The size of a dollar depends entirely upon how many more you have.

ROBERT C. (BOB) EDWARDS, *Summer annual*, 1920, 85.

There is no God but money, and Canada with its unparalleled natural resources is the most God-fearing country in the world.

CARLETON W. STANLEY, *Hibbert jour.*, 1922.

As has been said, and not improperly said, I am a man of some wealth. It is true. It is absolutely true, but I got it by my own untiring efforts in this great Western land to which I owe so much; and, what is more, I look upon it as a solemn trust in my hands to enable me to serve my country without fear or regard for the future so far as that is concerned; and I thought myself most fortunate

that the good Lord had been good
enough to permit me to be in that
happy state, for no man may serve you
as he should if he has over his shoulder
always the shadow of pecuniary obligations and liabilities. Therefore, you
may meet that story by saying that
such as I have I consecrate with myself to this service in which I am.

> RICHARD B. BENNETT, speech
> accepting the leadership of Con-
> servative Party, Winnipeg, Oct. 13,
> 1927.

MONTCALM, MARQUIS DE.

I am extolled in order to foster
Canadian prejudice.

> MONTCALM, letter to his home in
> France, about 1758. (trans.)

In truth the funeral of Montcalm
was the funeral of New France.

> FRANCIS PARKMAN, Montcalm and
> Wolfe, 1884.

Montcalm and Wolfe! Wolfe and
   Montcalm!
Quebec, thy storied citadel
Attest in burning song and psalm
How here thy heroes fell!

> CHARLES G. D. ROBERT, "Canada,"
> 1887.

MONTREAL, QUE.

(See also: ART)

A little Babylon which has over-
whelmed and intoxicated all the [Indian]
nations with the wine of its prostitution.

> ABBÉ FRANÇOIS BELMONT (d.1732),
> Histoire du Canada (mss., trans.)

We are satisfied that Montreal must
make active exertions to maintain her
position as a business centre, or she
will be cut off by Toronto, which is
making vigorous and well-directed
efforts to that end.

> MONTREAL Gazette, Jan. 22, 1870.

This is the first time I was ever in a
city where you couldn't throw a brick
without breaking a church window.

> MARK TWAIN, speech in Montreal,
> Dec. 5, 1881.

Reign on, majestic Ville-Marie!
Spread wide thine ample robes of
   state;
The heralds cry that thou art great,
And proud are thy young sons of thee.
Mistress of half a continent...

> W. D. LIGHTHALL, "Montreal", 1889.

The older generation of wealthy
Montrealers live comfortable and smugly
on "The Mountain", alike in their
devotion to their duty, to their tribal
instincts, and to economic status as
'the measure of all things.

> A. R. M. LOWER, in Can. hist. rev.,
> 1945, 327.

MOON.

The moon like a paper lantern
Is lifted over the hill,
And below in the silent valley
Even the aspens are still.

> BLISS CARMAN, "The book of
> Pierrot", 1899.

June comes, and the moon comes
Out of the curving sea,
Like a frail golden bubble,
To hang in the lilac tree.

> BLISS CARMAN, "May and June",
> 1900.

MOSQUITOES.

Such an infinit abundance of bloud-
thirsty Muskitoes, that we were more
tormented with them than ever we
were with the hot weather.

> THOMAS JAMES, The strange and
> dangerous voyage; North-west
> passage, 1631.

Abundance of Musketers & at night
could not gett wood Enough for to
make a smoke to Clear ym.

> HENRY KELSEY, Journal of a voyage,
> 1691, in the Kelsey papers, 1929,
> 26.

Oh, pray, do not bother to close the
windows. I think they are all in now.

> SIR JOHN THOMPSON, to Lady
> Minto when dining at Rideau Hall,
> 1893.

MOTHERS.

Mothers, you have a right to see
that no government be permitted to
pass laws [in the Navy matter]

destining for death those children whom
you brought forth for the country.

HENRI BOURASSA, speech in Victor-
iaville, Sept. 17, 1911.

There will be a singing in your heart,
There will be a rapture in your eyes:
You will be a woman set apart,
You will be so wonderful and wise.
You will sleep, and when from
  dreams you start,
As of one that wakes in Paradise,
There will be a singing in your heart,
There will be a rapture in your eyes.

ROBERT W. SERVICE, "The mother",
1912.

The tender hands, the loving care
  That filled my childhood years;
The gentle songs at evening sung,
  That lulled away my fears;
The tolerance, her simple faith,
  Through life's impetuous reign;
Her silent watching helpfulness,
  Come back to me again.

JAMES C. SINGER, "Mother", 1929.

Our silent strength no help in this
  assault
We watched her time creep closer
  by the hour,
And every lengthened intake each
  return,
Brought back some tender moment
  of her succour.
Each one of us was hers, and none
  his own.

F. R. SCOTT, "Bedside", 1945.

MOUNTAINS.

I would not give the bleakest knoll
on the bleakest hill of Scotland, for
all these mountains in a heap!

CAPT. JOHN GORDON, commander,
Royal Navy Pacific Squadron, 1844,
on the B. C. mountains.

That inhospitable country, that sea of
mountains.

EDWARD BLAKE, speech at Aurora,
Ont., Oct. 3, 1874, referring to the
Rockies; the phrase "sea of moun-
tains" was used by the Victoria
British Colonist, 1871, and by
George M. Grant, From ocean to
ocean, 1873.

Here, with the grand memorials of
the great Creator surrounding me, I
could spend the rest of my days content.

SIR JOHN A. MACDONALD, speech
in Yale, B. C., July 22, 1886.

The common waters, the familiar
  woods,
And the great hills' inviolate solitudes.

CHARLES G. D. ROBERTS, "Ave",
1892.

Cooling rill and sparkling fountain,
Purple peak and headland bold,
Precipice and snow-cloud mountain;
Lofty summits rising grandly into
  regions clear and cold,
And innumerable rivers that majestic-
  ally rolled.

JAMES DE MILLE, "Behind the veil",
1893.

There's a land where the mountains
  are nameless,
And the rivers all run God knows
  where.

ROBERT W. SERVICE, "The spell of
the Yukon", 1907.

The lonely sunsets flare forlorn
  Down valleys dreadly desolate;
The lonely mountains soar in scorn
As still as death, as stern as fate.

ROBERT W. SERVICE, "The land
that God forgot", 1907.

They saw the stars in heaven hung.
  They heard the great Sea's birth.
They know the ancient pain that
  wrung
  The entrails of the Earth.

FREDERICK GEORGE SCOTT, "The
storm", 1910.

I am homesick for the mountains —
  My heroic mother hills —
And the longing that is on me
  No solace ever stills.

BLISS CARMAN, "The cry of the
hill-born", 1912.

There is a mountain everyone must
  climb,
Different for all yet it is the same.
We start to climb before we have a
  name,
And nick the summit in our nick
  of time.

ROBERT FINCH, "The mountain",
1948.

MUSIC.

It may be made a question whether nations, like individuals, have not their 'Ruling passion'. If so, I shall not hesitate to pronounce the ruling passion of Canada to be a passion for dancing, but English and Canadian dancing are two distinct things. The natives appear to consider it rather in the light of an exercise conducive to health, than as a sportive amusement. Probably also the severity of the climate renders some such diversion useful as contributing to relax the too great rigidity.

> ANON., *Canadian letters, 1791 and '93; qu., Can. antiq. and numismatic jour.*, 3rd, ser., IX.

The exquisite powers of musical concert are here almost unknown, and except in two or three solitary instances hardly attempted.

> W. MOORSOM, *Letters from Nova Scotia*, 1830.

Fiddling and dancing, and serving the devil.

> T. C. HALIBURTON, *Nature and human nature*, 1855, I, 215.

A squeak's heard in the orchestra.
The leader draws across
The intestines of the agile cat
The tail of the noble hoss.

> GEORGE T. LANIGAN (d.1886), "The amateur Orlando".

And youth forgot its passion
And age forgot its woe,
And life forgot that there was death
Before such music's flow.

> WILFRED. CAMPBELL, "Orpheus", *Varsity mag.*, 1886.

No logic can grasp thee!
Love can only clasp thee!
For wholly celestial thou art!
To gauge thee by reason
Seems absolute treason
All hail to thee, Queen of the heart!

> ALEXANDER MCLACHLAN, "Music", 1900.

Bubbling spontaneously from the artless heart of child or man, without egotism and full of feeling, laughter is the music of life.

> SIR WILLIAM OSLER, *Can. med. assoc. jour.*, Feb. 1912, 152.

I spread a snare electric across the ether streams
To catch the dream enchantment with which the darkness teems;
Then down the ancient silence, like zephyrs through the wheat,
The truant tones come drifting melodious and sweet,
For all the heavens are freighted with inspiration-light;
The skies are raining music out of the lyric night.

> ALBERT D. WATSON, "Lyric night", 1923.

I never hear a violin
But I remember you;
The melody of April rain
And sunlight breaking through.

> MARY F. EDWARDS, "Alone", 1942.

I have moved to music, wrapped myself in song
As with a silver cloak, how bright, how splendid!
Lovely was song: who knows but lovlier yet
May be the silence after song is ended?

> AUDREY ALEXANDRA BROWN, "The singer grows old", 1943.

The bright
Clear notes fly like sparks through the air
And trace a flickering pattern of music there.

> F. R. SCOTT, "Overture". 1945.

N

NATIONAL HERITAGE.

A wise nation preserves its records, gathers up its muniments, decorates the tombs of its illustrious dead, repairs its great public structures, and fosters national pride and love of country, by perpetual reference to the sacrifices and glories of the past.

> JOSEPH HOWE, at the Howe family reunion, South Framingham, Mass., Aug. 31, 1871.

But that rare quality, that national dream,
That lies behind this genius at its core,
Which gave it vision, utterance; evermore,

It will be with us, as those stars that
  gleam,
Eternal, hid behind the lights of
  day,
A people's best, that may not
  pass away.
  WILFRED CAMPBELL, "Our heritage",
  1905.

Of all national assets, archives are
the most precious; they are the gift
of one generation to another and the
extent of our care of them marks the
extent of our civilization.
  ARTHUR G. DOUGHTY, *The Can.
  Archives and its activities*, 1924, 5.

No self-respecting society can neglect
or wantonly destroy the records of its
own development without living to
regret it.
  CAN. HIST. REV., editorial, 1934, 247.

NATIONAL POLICY.
  (See also: POLITICAL SLO-
  GANS; PROTECTION (TARIFF))

I say what Canada wants is a
national policy — a policy that shall
be in the interest of Canada, apart
from the principles of free trade, apart
from the principles of protection.
  SIR CHARLES TUPPER, H. of C.,
  Debates, Feb. 25, 1876, 283.

That it be resolved that this house
is of opinion that the welfare of Canada
requires the adoption of a National
Policy, which, by a judicious readjustment of the Tariff, will benefit
and foster the Agricultural, the Mining,
the Manufacturing and other interests
of the Dominion; that such a policy
will retain in Canada thousands of our
fellow-countrymen now obliged to
expatriate themselves in search of the
employment denied them at home, will
restore prosperity to our struggling
industries, now so sadly depressed, will
prevent Canada from being made a
sacrifice market, will encourage and
develop an active interprovincial trade,
and moving (as it ought to do) in the
direction of a reciprocity of Tariffs with
our neighbours, so far as the varied
interests of Canada may demand, will
greatly tend to procure for this country,
eventually, a reciprocity of Trade.
  SIR JOHN A. MACDONALD, resolution
  moved in H. of C., March 12,
  1878; *Journals*, 78.

The cradle of the National Policy.
  A reference to the city of Hamilton,
  Ont., about 1878.

N. P.
  Term used, less for brevity than
  ridicule, by opponents of Sir John
  A. Macdonald's National Policy,
  after 1876; but also used by Macdonald in his correspondence.

The New National Policy.
  CANADIAN COUNCIL OF AGRICULTURE,
  new platform adopted Nov. 29,
  1918, in opposition to the National
  Policy of 1879.

NATIONALISM.

A racial nationalism involves either
isolation, or the supremacy of a dominant race in a mixed state... The
wonder-worker is thus not race but
liberty. Let us dismiss forever the
superstition that there is any magic
in race to hold people together and
effect political unity. It is partnership in common liberties which unites
people. The growth of the new nationalism in the British Empire is just
a growth of liberty.
  GEORGE WRONG, *Amer. hist. rev.*,
  1916-17, 51.

There are too many nasty little
self-centred nations in the world already; God forbid that Canada should
add one to the number!
  W. L. GRANT, in *Can. hist. rev.*,
  1923, 80.

The most substantial Canadian nationalism in times of peace has been
economic nationalism.
  J. B. BREBNER, in Can. Hist. Assoc.,
  Rept., 1904, 8.

The nation must be something greater than the sum of its parts. If it is not
so, it ceases to exist, it has lost the
will to continue. By this elusive yet
valid test, the Canadian people have
created and are creating a nation.
  GEORGE W. BROWN, in Can. Hist.
  Assoc. *Rept.*, 1944, 4.

NATIONALITY.

(See also: FUTURE; PATRIOT-
ISM; UNITY)

Provincialism and nationality are
different degrees of the same thing, and
both take their rise in the same feeling,
love of country.

T. C. HALIBURTON, *Sam Slick*,
1840, 271.

A New Nationality.

THOMAS D'ARCY MCGEE, in *The
new era,* in an article written in
the summer of 1857; the phrase
reappeared in 1865 in Parliament
in the debate on Confederation.

I see in the not remote distance
one great nationality bound, like the
shield of Achilles, by the blue rim of
ocean. I see it quartered into many
communities, each disposing of its
internal affairs, but all bound together
by free institutions, free intercourse
and free commerce. I see within the
round of that shield the peaks of the
western mountains and the crests of
the eastern waves, the winding Assiniboine; the five-fold lakes, the St.
Lawrence, the Ottawa, the Saguenay,
the St. John and the basin of Minas.

THOMAS D'A. MCGEE, speech,
Legislative Assembly, May 2, 1860.

A Canadian nationality, not French-
Canadian, nor British-Canadian, nor
Irish-Canadian — patriotism rejects
the prefix — is, in my opinion, what
we should look forward for, — that is
what we ought to labour for, that is
what we ought to be prepared to
defend to the death.

THOMAS D'A. MCGEE, speech in
Quebec, May 10, 1862.

We have a large class whose national
feelings turn toward London, whose
very heart is there; another large class
whose sympathies centre here at Quebec,
or in a sentimental way may have some
reference to Paris; another large class
whose memories are of the Emerald
Isle, and yet another whose compar-
isons are rather with Washington; but
have we any class of people who are
attached, or whose feelings are going
to be directed with any earnestness, to

the City of Ottawa, the centre of the
new nationality that is to be created?

CHRISTOPHER DUNKIN, *Confed. debates,* 1865.

I would desire to see, Gentlemen, our
new national character distinguished by
a manly modesty as much as by mental
independence; by the conscientious
exercise of the critical faculties, as
well as by the zeal of the inquirer.

THOMAS D'A. MCGEE, address,
"The mental outfit of the new
Dominion", Montreal, Nov. 4, 1867.

I congratulate you on the legislative
sanction which has been given by the
Imperial Parliament to the Act of
Union, under the provisions of which we
are now assembled and which has laid
the foundation of a new nationality that
I trust and believe will, ere long, extend its bounds from the Atlantic to
the Pacific Ocean.

LORD MONCK, speech from the
Throne, Nov. 7, 1867; presumably
drafted by Sir John A. Macdonald.

It is impossible to foster a national
spirit unless you have national interests
to attend to.

EDWARD BLAKE, speech at Aurora,
Ont., Oct. 3, 1874.

The time will come when that national spirit which has been spoken of will
be truly felt among us, when we shall
realize that we are four millions of
Britons who are not free.

EDWARD BLAKE, speech at Aurora,
Ont., Oct. 3, 1874.

The seed they sowed has sprung at
last,
And grows and blossoms through
the land.

CHARLES MAIR, "In memory of
William A. Foster", (1888); a
reference to the "Canada First"
movement.

To make a nation there must be a
common life, common sentiments, common aims, and common hopes.

GOLDWIN SMITH, *The Bystander,*
Dec. 1889, 78.

Whatever pride of country a Canadian has, its object, for the most part, is outside Canada.

> Anon., quoted in: *Canada first* (W. A. Foster) 1890.

Any attempt to call Canada a nation in the world sense, in the sense of international law or international negotiations, is simply an attempt to lift oneself by pulling at one's boot straps.

> W. S. Fielding, H. of C., *Debates*, Sept. 11, 1919, 185.

I will readily admit anything that looks like national self-assertion; anything which advances Canada along the road to nationhood appeals to me.

> Ernest Lapointe, H. of C., *Debates*, May, 1920.

Canadian national life can almost be said to take its rise in the negative will to resist absorption in the American republic.

> Delbert Clark, in *Can. and her great neighbor*, ed. H. F. Angus, 1938.

Canada is a nation of the new world.

> W. L. Mackenzie King, speech in London, Eng., Sept. 4, 1941.

In our comfortable part of the world national maturity was to be measured in terms of a formal status intended actually to maintain a position of irresponsible dependency.

> R. G. Trotter, in *Can. hist. rev.*, June, 1945.

NATURE.

(See also: Outdoors)

Natur' is natur' wherever you find it.

> T. C. Haliburton, *Sam Slick*, 1836, ch. XXI.

The class of people to whom this country is so admirably adapted are formed of the unlettered and industrious labourers and artisans. They would not spare the ancient oak from feelings of veneration, nor look upon it with regard for any 'thing but its use as timber. They have no time, even if they possessed the taste, to gaze abroad on the beauties of nature.

> Catherine P. Traill, *Backwoods of Can.*, 1836, 154.

Wherever natur' does least, man does most.

> T. C. Haliburton, *Sam Slick*, 1838, 157.

I sketch from nature and the draught is true.
Whate'er the picture, whether grave or gay,
Painful experience in a distant land
Made it my own.

> Susanna Moodie, 1852, *Roughing it in the bush*, title-page.

Not only in the cataract and the thunder
  Or in the deeps of man's uncharted soul,
But in the dew-star dwells alike the wonder,
  And in the whirling dust-mote the Control.

> Charles G. D. Roberts, "Immanence", 1896.

Have you seen God in His splendours, heard the text that nature renders?

> Robert W. Service, "Call of the wild", 1907.

Something in my inmost thinking
  Tells me I am one with you,
For a subtle bond is linking
  Nature's offspring through and through.

> Frederick George Scott, "In the winter woods", 1910.

The Praying-Mantis mounts the stair,
Her tiny arms upheld in prayer;
In chasuble and stole,
She stands to read my soul.

> Annie C. Dalton, "The praying-mantis", 1935.

I am weak before the wind; before the sun
  I faint; I lose my strength;
I am utterly vanquished by a star;
  I go to my knees, at length,
Before the song of a bird; before
  The breath of spring or fall
I am lost; before these miracles
  I am nothing at all.

> A. M. Klein, "Out of the pulver and the polished lens", 1936.

The worm has grown no teeth, no jaws, no spiked claws, no poison fang, no armoured back, no speedy feet:

nothing. Yet how it has endured!
Soft, slow, blind, brainless, defenceless,
it crawls stupidly through the earth.
through time, through life; persisting
over change and race, from the far
past to the far future.

> THOMAS B. ROBERTON, *Newspaper
> pieces*, 1936, 47.

> The grace that is a tree
> belongs to me;
> The quietness of stone
> I make my own;
> from the strong hills I borrow
> courage to face tomorrow.
> My flesh itself is kin
> to earth and all therein
> and of my brother's heart
> I am a part.
>
> JEAN WHITMAN, "Kinship", 1938.

NAVY.

Laurier's tin-pot navy.

> Term used by opponents to Lau-
> rier's navy policy, 1909 and later;
> RODMOND P. ROBLIN, premier of
> Manitoba, speech in Winnipeg, Oct.
> 26, 1909.

The people, who will be prepared
for a Canadian navy when it will be
necessary, do not wish to have a navy
which is Canadian in time of peace
and Imperial in time of war; that is
to say, a navy which will be Canadian
when it is to be paid for, in order to be
Imperial when it is required for use.

> FREDERICK D. MONK, H. of C.,
> *Debates*, 1910-11, col. 612; quoting
> from a Liberal newspaper. *Atha-
> baska gazette*, Dec. 1, 1910.

NECESSITY.

Make a merit of necessity.

> THOMAS C. HALIBURTON, *Sam
> Slick's wise saws*, 1853, ch. V.

Needs must when the Devil drives.

> THOMAS C. HALIBURTON, *Sam
> Slick's wise saws*, 1853, ch. XIII.

NEW BRUNSWICK.

The Province of the Loyalists.
A popular term.

In these uncertain times, the duty
of New Brunswick is to draw, if possible, into closer relations with the loyal
Provinces of Canada, though it may
be for her interest to connect herself
commercially with the United States.
Duty and interest lead two different
ways.

> FREDERICTON *Headquarters*, Jan.
> 27, 1864.

> Sweet maiden of Passamaquoddy,
>   Shall we seek for communion of
>   souls
> Where the deep Mississippi meanders,
>   Or the distant Saskatchewan rolls?
> Ah, no! in New Brunswick we'll find
>   it —
>   A sweetly sequestered nook —
> Where the swift gliding Skoodoowabs-
>   kooksis
>   Unites with the Skoodoowabskook.
>
> JAMES DE MILLE, "Sweet maiden
> of Quoddy", originally, "Lines to
> Florance Huntingdon, Maine", in,
> *New Dominion and true humorist*,
> Saint John, April 16, 1870, 171.

NEW YEAR.

> We stood on the bridge of the Ages —
>   The current of Time upon earth.
> The Old Year was sealing its record,
>   The New Year had come to the
>   birth.
> In silence we stood by the ebb-tide
>   And watched it melt into the sea —
> A drop in that infinite ocean
>   That has been and ever shall be.
>
> MARY JANE LAWSON, "Midnight
> between the old year and the new",
> Dec. 31, 1882.

And so the old year has beautifully
passed here in its faultlessly white
snow robes, and the new has taken its
place. What a wonderful record it
has left in science, in research, in dis-
coveries historical, and the light thrown
thereby on the origin and progress of
human development... The human unit
and the composite of races and nations
are seething with unrest, change, and
re-formations. Upheaval first: what
price results?

> SIR GEORGE E. FOSTER, entry in his
> Diary, Jan. 1, 1930.

NEWFOUNDLAND.

The Newfoundland fisheries are more valuable than all the mines of Peru.

> LORD BACON, about 1608; attributed; also: "Greater than the gold mines of Golgonda, there is none so rich".

Quærite prime regnum Dei.

> Provincial motto, on Arms granted by letters patent Jan. 1, 1637; trans.: Seek ye first the kingdom of God.

The Ancient Colony.

> Popular name for the Island.

...Some place far abroad
Where sailors gang to fish for cod.

> ROBERT BURNS, "The twa dogs", 1786.

Remember the day
When Carter and Shea
Crossed over the 'say',
To barter away
The rights of Terra Nova.

> Anti-confederation ditty, 1865; Carter and Shea were delegates to the Quebec Conference.

Men, hurrah, for our own native isle, Newfoundland,
Not a stranger shall hold one inch of her strand;
Her face turns to Britain, her back to the Gulf.
Come near at your peril, Canadian wolf!

> Newfoundland anti-confederation ballad, election 1869.

The people of Newfoundland shrink from the idea of linking their destinies with a Dominion in the future of which they can at present see nothing to inspire hope, but much to create apprehension.

> NEWFOUNDLAND, H. OF ASS., 1870, quoted. Toronto *Weekly Globe*, Feb. 25, 1870.

Fishocracy.

> P. TOCQUE, *Newfoundland, as it was*, 1878, 86. Term used to describe well-to-do merchants opposed to self-government.

The Fisherman who would sell Bait to a Frenchman would steal the pennies off his dead mother's eyes.

> A political placard, Newfoundland, at the time of the passage of the Bait Act, 1886.

Black Monday.

> Dec. 10, 1894, the first day of the panic caused when the Commercial Bank and the Union Bank closed their doors.

A home entirely surrounded by hospitality.

> Newfoundlanders' popular description of their land, often used in answer to the phrase, "A piece of rock entirely surrounded by fog."

I find that Newfoundland is said to be celebrated for its codfish, its dogs, its hogs, its fogs, and its bogs! That is a very erronious opinion, I assure you.

> SIR WILLIAM WHITEWAY, speech in London, Eng., July 5, 1897.

When sun rays crown thy pine-clad hills,
And Summer spreads her hand,
When silvern voices tune thy rills,
We love thee, smiling land...

As loved our fathers, so we love,
Where once they stood, we stand;
Their prayer we raise to Heaven above,
God guard thee, Newfoundland.

> SIR CAVENDISH BOYLE, Governor of Nfld., 1901-04, "Ode to Newfoundland".

The purity of the air of Newfoundland is without doubt due to the fact that the people of the outports never open their windows.

> J. G. MILLAIS, *Newfoundland and its untrodden ways*, 1907.

The Norway of the New World.

> Term used in government advertisements, 1915.

NEWSPAPERS AND THE PRESS.

While we do not assume too much for the Press, we are fully aware of its influence, and of the benefits which it confers. Among other things which renders an unshackled press so important in a civilized land, is its being the instrument by which legal and legislative occurrences are circulated over a vast extent of country.

PHILIP HOLLAND, in *Acadian Recorder*, Feb. 27, 1830.

We are paid for our labour in the satisfaction afforded our readers — the information diffused throughout the Province, and in the consciousness that in after times, these reports will convey to the generation that succeeds us, very valuable data from which to judge of the character and sentiment of the present age, and of the early habits and conditions of the country.

JOSEPH HOWE, *Novascotian*, Apr. 24, 1834.

We would wear the coarsest raiment; we would eat the poorest food; and crawl at night into the veriest hovel in the land to rest our weary limbs, but cheerful and undaunted hearts; and these jobbing justices should feel, that one frugal and united family could withstand their persecution, defy their power, and maintain the freedom of the press. Yes, gentlemen, come what will, while I live, Nova Scotia shall have the blessing of an open and unshackled press.

JOSEPH HOWE, speech at his trial for criminal libel, Mar. 2, 1835.

I conjure you to judge me by the principles of English law, and to leave an unshackled press as a legacy to your children. You remember the press in your hours of conviviality and mirth — Oh, do not desert it in this its day of trial.

JOSEPH HOWE, speech at his trial for criminal libel, Mar. 2, 1835.

Let not the sons of the Rebels look across the border to the sons of the Loyalists, and reproach them that their press is not free.

JOSEPH HOWE, speech at his trial for criminal libel, Mar. 2, 1835.

Our wood paying subscribers will please send us a few cords of wood at their earliest convenience.

Cornwall Observer, Dec. 18, 1835.

If I can be proscribed to-day for defending myself and my friends in the newspapers, another Nova Scotian may be rejected to-morrow because the Governor likes not the colour of his hair.

JOSEPH HOWE, speech in Cumberland County, autumn 1844.

Once a printer, always a printer.

TORONTO TYPOGRAPHICAL SOCIETY, motto, 1845.

The Editors of all the Great Liberal Organs are Roman Catholics, with an exception, and that one is an anythingarian.

HALIFAX *Morning Post*, 1847.

The Halifax Express.

A system organized by six New York City newspapers whereby European news was received at Halifax, then relayed by "pony express" to Digby, by boat to St. John, N. B., then by telegraph to New York. First used Feb. 21, 1849, this marked the inception of the Associated Press.

Suppose we take the rule about the press. Be free, but not personal; free, but decent; free, but not treasonable to each other; free, but not licentious.

T. C. HALIBURTON, *Sam Slick's wise saws*, 1853, II, 194.

The Canadian cannot get along without his newspaper any more than an American could without his tobacco.

SUSANNA MOODIE, *Mark Hurdlestone*, 1853, I, xxii.

It's a damned sharp curve, but I think we can take it.

ROBERT SMILEY, editor *Hamilton Spectator*, telegram to Sir John A. Macdonald, 1854, on being asked to stop attacks on Robert Spence, Reformer, who was about to become a coalition colleague of Macdonald's.

Party leadership and the conducting of a great journal do not harmonize.

GEORGE BROWN, letter to Luther H. Holton, May 13, 1867.

What, what, what,
What's the news from Swat?
Sad news,
Bad news,

Comes by the cable led
Through the Indian Ocean's bed.
Through the Persian Gulf, the Red
Sea and the Med-
Iterranean — he's dead;
The Akhoond is dead!

> GEORGE T. LANIGAN, "A threnody",
> ("The Akhoond of Swat") after
> seeing the news, "The Akhoond of
> Swat is dead", in London news-
> papers, Jan. 22, 1878.

Politics and vituperation, temperance and vituperation, religion and
vituperation; these three dietetic
articles, the vituperative sauce invariably
accompanying, form the exclusive jour-
nalistic pabulum of three-quarters of
the people of Ontario.

> SARA JEANETTE DUNCAN, *The
> Week*, Sept. 30, 1886, 707.

It is no part of a newspaper's function to defend a corporation: it is
always able to defend itself.

> SIR CLIFFORD SIFTON, frequently
> said to John W. Dafoe, about 1900.

The *News* may be congratulated on
having, under its new management,
shown force enough to brave the second
greatest of the three tyrannical powers
which militate against independence —
Party, Popular Passion, and Ads. Ads
probably are the greatest of the three,
but the next greatest is Popular Passion.

> GOLDWIN SMITH, letter to John
> Willison, Jan. 20, 1903.

It is well known in this country that
I am never interviewed.

> SIR WILFRID LAURIER, cable to
> Lord Strathcona, London, on Eng-
> lish press report of Dec. 22, 1909
> in which he was reported as
> expressing himself to a news-
> paperman as being favourable to
> the British Liberal cause.

Covers Prince Edward Island like
the dew.

> *Guardian of the Gulf*, Charlotte-
> town, P. E. I. newspaper, motto.

The press never killed a public man
who deserved to live.

> SIR JOHN WILLISON, *Reminiscences*,
> 1919, 66.

The Misleader.

> The Regina *Leader-Post*, so called
> by many Saskatchewan farmers
> because of its opposition to the
> Wheat Pool in 1923.

I pay no attention whatever to the
press.

> W. L. MACKENZIE KING, to Lord
> Beaverbrook, qu., Hardy, *Mackenzie
> King of Canada*, 1949, 289.

Any journal whose opinions are made
on the premises by its owners and
officers, and the making of which is
affected only by consideration of public
interest so far as they make an appeal
and by the interests of the property
itself, is an independent journal.

> J. W. DAFOE, in *Can. hist. rev.*,
> 1936, 62.

The newspaper whose support of a
party is bought and paid for, directly
or indirectly, out of party funds, is
a propagandist sheet and not a public
journal.

> J. W. DAFOE, in *Can. hist. rev.*,
> 1936, 62.

NIAGARA FALLS.

The Niagara River near this place
is only the eighth of a league wide,
but it is very deep in places, and so
rapid above the great falls that it
hurries down all the animals which
try to cross it, without a single one
being able to withstand its current.
They plunge down a height of more
than five hundred feet, and its fall is
composed of two sheets of water and
a cascade, with an island sloping down.
In the middle, these waters foam and
boil in a fearful manner. They
thunder continually, and when the wind
blows in a southerly direction, the noise
they make is heard for from more than
fifteen leagues.

> FATHER LOUIS HENNEPIN, *Descrip-
> tion de la Louisiane*, 1683, (1678).
> (trans.)

I am metamorphosed; I am trans-
lated; I am an ass's head, a clod,
a wooden spoon, a fat weed growing
on Lethe's brink, a stock, a stone, a
petrification. For have I not seen

Niagara, the wonder of wonders, and felt — no words can tell *what* disappointment.

> Anna Jameson, *Winter studies*, 1838, I, 83.

When I first saw the falls I was disappointed in the outline. Every American bride is taken there, and the sight must be one of the earliest, if not the keenest, disappointments in American married life.

> Oscar Wilde, press interview, New York, 1882.

Here all the fury since the world was young
Is chanted on one tongue.

> Wilson Macdonald, "Niagara", 1926.

NIGHT.

And when day passed and over heaven's height,
  Thin with the many stars and cool with dew,
  The fingers of the deep hours slowly drew
The wonder of the ever-healing night.

> Archibald Lampman, "The frogs", 1888.

Who are the mimes of the air
That wept on the woe of our flight,
That chanted a bitter despair
In the dark haunted heart of the night?

> Wilfred Campbell, "The last ride", 1889.

In the wide awe and wisdom of the night
  I saw the round world rolling on its way,
Beyond significance of depth or height,
  Beyond the interchange of dark and day.

> Charles G. D. Roberts, "In the wide awe and wisdom of the night, 1893.

Night, like a sacristan with silent step,
Passes to light the tapers of the stars.

> Bliss Carman, "Winter", 1921.

Have you ever noticed how much larger your troubles appear at night?

> Robert C. (Bob) Edwards, *Calgary Eye Opener*, Sept. 24, 1921.

NORTH.

(See also: Arctic)

This North whose heart of fire
Yet knows not its desire
Clearly, but dreams, and murmurs in the dream.

The hour of dreams is done. Lo, on the hills the gleam!

> Charles G. D. Roberts, "Ode for the Canadian Confederacy", 1880.

Oh, we are the men of the Northern Zone;
  Shall a bit be placed in our mouth?
If ever a Northman lost his throne
  Did the conqueror come from the South?
Nay, nay — and the answer blent
  In chorus is southward sent:
'Since when has a Southerner's conquering steel
  Hewed out in the North a throne?
Since when has a Southerner placed his heel
  On the men of the Northern zone!'

> R. K. Kernighan, "Men of the Northern Zone," 1896.

Plumb-full of hush to the brim.

> Robert W. Service, "The spell of the Yukon", 1907.

It has been said that power, that empire came from the north. Northern people have always stood for courage and unconquerability. They have the muscle, the wholesomeness of life, the strength of will.

> Donald A. Smith (Lord Strathcona), to William Garson, qu., in B. Willson, *Life of Strathcona*, 1915, 601.

If the average American or European university graduate has ten ideas about the North, nine of them are wrong.

> V. Stefansson, *The northward course of Empire*, 1922.

We should not regard the Eskimos as foreigners but as friends. They are your fellow citizens. Their future is bound up in our future. If Canada is

but a thin southern strip across which
plies a shuttle railway we shall have
no remarkable future.

VILHJALMUR STEFANSSON, in Toronto *Star*, April 14, 1933.

NORTH WEST REBELLION, 1885.

Had I been born on the banks of the
Saskatchewan, I would myself have
shouldered a musket to fight against the
neglect of governments and the shame-
less greed of speculators.

SIR WILFRID LAURIER, speech,
Champ de Mars, Montreal, Nov.
22, 1885; "the musket speech".

Before that time, when we were not
enlightened, the word of the priest was
the word of truth; but after that, when
we got to be a little more enlightened,
we saw that they could tell us lies.

GABRIEL DUMONT, at the Music Hall
Montreal, Apr. 24, 1888; *Le Pays*,
10 July, 1915.

NORTHERN LIGHTS.

The sun has scarcely set behind the
dark, wavy outline of the western hills,
ere the Aurora Borealis mimics its
setting beams, and revels with wild
delight in the heavens, which it claims
as its own, now ascending with meteor
speed to the zenith, then dissolving
into a thousand rays of variegated
light, that vie with each other which
shall first reach the horizon; now
flashing bright, brilliant and glowing,
as emanations of the sun, then slowly
retreating from view pale and silvery
white, like wandering moonbeams.

T. C. HALIBURTON, *Old judge*, 1849.

Here's to the Land of the rock and
the pine;
Here's to the Land of the raft
and the river!
Here's to the Land where the sun-
beams shine,
And the night is bright with the
North-lights' quiver!

WILLIAM W. SMITH, "Here's to the
land", 1888.

In the north behold a flushing,
Then a deep and crimson blushing,
Followed by an airy rushing
Of the purple waves that rise!

As when armèd host advances,
See a silver banner dances,
And a thousand golden lances
Shimmer in the Boreal skies!

J. K. FORAN, "Aurora Borealis",
1895.

There in the awe we crouched and
saw with our wild, uplifted eyes
Charge and retire the hosts of fire
in the battlefield of the skies.

ROBERT W. SERVICE, "Ballad of
the Northern Lights", 1909.

NOSES.

Juno, it's better never to wipe a
child's nose at all, I guess, than to
wring it off.

T. C. HALIBURTON, *Sam Slick*,
1836, ch. XI.

I gaze, and as I gaze the wonder
grows, how one small face can carry
so much nose.

ARTHUR H. GILLMOR, H. of C.,
Debates, 1879, to James Domville,
another member.

Shame! It's more than a shame.
'Snoutrage!

J. R. CAMERON, editor *Hamilton
Spectator*, on a Conservative newspaper's statement that it was a
shame to discuss Sir John A.
Macdonald's nose when his son
Hugh John's qualifications for public office were under consideration, about 1900.

NOVA SCOTIA.

(See also: MARITIMES)

The very delicate meadows, with
roses white and red, and the very good
fat earth.

SIR WILLIAM ALEXANDER, *Encouragement to colonies*, 1624.

Annapolis, Annapolis! Oh, yes,
Annapolis must be defended; to be sure,
Annapolis should be defended. Pray,
where is Annapolis?

DUKE OF NEWCASTLE, Prime Minister, 1758; Horace Walpole,
George II, 1822.

What, is Cape Breton an island?
wonderful! My dear sir, you always

bring us good news. Egad! I'll go directly and tell the King that Cape Breton is an island.

> DUKE OF NEWCASTLE, Prime Minister; attributed by Smollett, *Humphrey Clinker*, 1771.

Of all the vile countries that ever were known,
In the frigid or torrid or temperate zone,
From the accounts I have heard there is not such another;
It neither belongs to this world or the other.

> American Revolutionary song.

Good God, what sums the nursing of that ill-throven, hardvisaged and ill-favored brat, Nova Scotia, has cost to this wittol nation.

> EDMUND BURKE, speech in Gt. Brit., H. of C., Feb. 11, 1780; *wittol* means cuckolded and submissive.

Nova Scarcity.

> Term used by disaffected United Empire Loyalists, 1783, especially the literary group in Halifax.

Bluenose.

> The origin of this nickname is believed to be derived from the MacIntyre Blue potato, a long tuber with blueish eyes and "nose". As early as 1787 shipments of potatoes to Boston were invoiced as "blue noses". The Loyalist settlers in Annapolis and King's County applied the name to previous settlers. Much used by T. C. HALIBURTON, *Sam Slick*, 1836, and later books.

We profess to be *Colonial* and not merely *Nova Scotian* Patriots.

> COLONIAL PATRIOT, Pictou, N. S., July 22, 1829.

We are few in numbers; our country is but a narrow tract, surrounded by populous States; and we have no prospect of distinction — I had almost said of future safety — but from high mental and moral cultivation, infusing into every branch of industry such a degree of intellectual vigour as shall insure success, multiply population, and endow them with productive power.

> JOSEPH HOWE, speech, Halifax Mechanics Inst., 1834.

We bloom amid the snow.

> NOVA SCOTIA PHILANTHROPIC SOCIETY, motto, adopted 1834, and associated with the mayflower which was made the provincial floral emblem by statute, I Ed. VII, Cap. 10, 1936.

The graveyard of the Atlantic.

> Sable Island; popular term.

This place (that is, Nova Scotia) is as fertile as Illanoy or Ohio, as healthy as any part of the Globe, and right alongside of salt water; but the folks want three things, Industry, Enterprise, Economy.

> T. C. HALIBURTON, *Sam Slick*, 1836, ch. XXXIII.

In the Acadian land on the shores of the basin of Minas,
Distant, secluded, still, the little village of Grand Pré
Lay in the fruitful valley.

> HENRY W. LONGFELLOW, *Evangeline*, 1847.

It will be our pride to make Nova Scotia a Normal School for the rest of the colonies showing them how representative institutions may be worked so as to secure international tranquility and advancement in subordination to the paramount interests and authority of the Crown.

> JOSEPH HOWE, letter to Charles Buller, Feb. 12, 1848.

Boys, brag of your country. When I am abroad, I brag of everything that Nova Scotia is, has, or can produce; and when they beat me at everything else, I turn round on them and say, 'How high does your tide rise?'

> JOSEPH HOWE, speech in Nova Scotia, qu., Grant, *Howe*, 1906, 2.

To the Nova Scotian, the province is his native place, but North America is his country. The colony may become his home when the provinces become a nation. It will then have a name, the inhabitants will become a people, and the people have a country and a home. Until that period it would seem as if they were merely comers and goers.

> T. C. HALIBURTON, *Old judge*, 1849, II, 228.

You don't need a big field to raise a big turnip.

> JOSEPH HOWE, on Nova Scotia, qu. in G. M. Grant, *Joseph Howe*, 1906, 37.

Munit heac et altera vincit. (One defends and the other conquers.)

> Motto on the provincial coat-of-arms.

You have got us, and now you have got to keep us.

> JOSEPH HOWE, a remark made about 1869 to Cartwright and others.

And where the Acadian village stood, its roofs o'ergrown with moss,
And the simple wooden chapel with its altar and its cross,
And where the forge of Basil sent its sparks toward the sky,
The lonely thistle blossomed, and the fire-weed grew high.

> A. W. H. EATON, "The re-settlement of Acadia", 1889.

Obstinate as an Acadian.

> Qu. as a "proverb" in, *Review hist. publications*, 1900, 95.

The Mayflower Province.

> A popular term.

From the sea-light of Yarmouth to the headlands of Bras d'Or,
From the swinging tides of Fundy to the wild Southern Shore.
The Gaspereau Valley, the dikes of Grand Pré,
Farms and mines and fishing fleets, river, lake and bay,
Lunenburg and Halifax and lovely Margaree,
Is all the Land of Acadie, the Sweetheart of the Sea.

> BLISS CARMAN, "Forever and forever", 1929.

O

OLD AGE.

(See also: YOUTH)

I heard the city time-bells call
Far off in hollow towers,
And one by one with measured fall
Count out the old dead hours.

I felt the march, the silent press
Of time, and held my breath;
I saw the haggard dreadfulness
Of dim old age and death.

> ARCHIBALD LAMPMAN, "An impression", 1884.

Senility has its privileges.

> EDWARD FARRER, comment on Chief Justice Lewis Wallbridge of Manitoba, 1884, on his denouncing in court statements which appeared in the Winnipeg *Times*.

Down the long road that dips into the valley,
The love-crowned visions of our youth have fled;
While like lost mariners we keep a tally
Of the sad years in desolation sped.

> JAMES McCARROLL, "The elm tree", 1889.

Modern science has made to almost everyone of you the present of a few years.

> SIR WILLIAM OSLER, *Montreal med. jour.*, 1895, 561.

I have no desire to live to "a good old age". So long as my health continues as it is now, and that I can work, I am quite willing even as long as Methuselah, but at the first sign of weakening, let Providence, which has ever been kind to me, take me away. Nothing so sad as to survive one's self.

> SIR WILFRID LAURIER, letter to John Willison, Nov. 21, 1901.

I am suffering from the incurable disease of over eighty years.

> GOLDWIN SMITH, to friends, Niagara Falls, N. Y., 1903.

My second fixed idea is the uselessness of men over sixty years of age, and the incalculable effect it would be in commercial, political and in professional life if, as a matter of course, men stopped work at this age. In that charming novel *The fixed period*, Anthony Trollope discusses the practical advantages in modern life of a return to this ancient usage, and the plot hinges on the admirable scheme of a college into which men at sixty retired for a year of peaceful contemplation before a peaceful departure by chloroform. As it can be maintained that all the great advances have come from men under forty, so the history of the world shows that a very large proportion of the evils may be traced to the sexagenarians, nearly all the great mistakes politically and socially, all of the worst poems, most of the bad pictures, a majority of the bad novels and not a few of the bad sermons and speeches.

> SIR WILLIAM OSLER, farewell address at John Hopkins Univ., Feb. 22, 1905; gave rise to reports he advised chloroform after 60, denied in statement of Feb. 28, also in *Medical record*, Mar. 4, 1905.

Most people who are old enough to know better often wish they were young enough not to.

> ROBERT C. (BOB) EDWARDS, *Calgary Eye Opener*, Apr. 30, 1912.

One can always tell when one is getting old and serious by the way that holidays seem to interfere with one's work.

> ROBERT C. (BOB) EDWARDS, *Calgary Eye Opener*, Dec. 20, 1913.

I only wish I knew some great
Exultant vice to stimulate
What spark of life remains to spend:
But this I feel, as the hour grows late,
Sleep is the best thing in the end.

> TOM MACINNES, "Ballade of sleep", 1918.

She volunteered that she was a widow, and that forty was only her professional age.

> JOHN MURRAY GIBBON, *Pagan love*, 1922.

Old age is the "Front Line" of life, moving into No Man's Land.

> STEPHEN LEACOCK, "This business of growing old", 1940.

I feel age like an icicle down my back.

> DYSON CARTER, *Night of flame*, 1943, 154.

Here's news for you and you're the last one told:
Slow down, my dear Cecelia. You are old.

> L. A. MCKAY, "High time for Cecelia", 1946.

ONTARIO.

For the purpose of Commerce, Union, and Power, I propose that the site of the Colony should be in that great Peninsula between the Lakes Huron, Erie and Ontario, a spot destined by nature sooner or later to govern that interior world.

> JOHN GRAVES SIMCOE, letter to Sir Joseph Banks, Jan. 8, 1791.

It will be the very mockery of a province, 300 or 400 families scattered over a country some 400 miles in length, not having any towns and scarcely a village in the province.

> A. LYMBURNER, speech, Mar. 16, 1791.

The Queen's Bush.

> The area of the province between Toronto and Lake Huron, large tracts of which were colonized by the Canada Company, founded 1824; also called, "The Huron Tract".

If you lose Upper Canada, you will lose all your colonies, and if you lose them you may as well lose London.

> DUKE OF WELLINGTON, to the Colonial Office, on the rebellion of 1837.

The Western peninsula must not get control of the ship. It is occupied by Yankees and Covenanters — in fact, the most yeasty and unsafe of populations.

> SIR JOHN A. MACDONALD, letter to Brown Chamberlin, June 21, 1856, in *Chamberlin papers*, Pub. Arch.

Ut incepit fidelis sic permanet. (As loyal she began so shall she [ever] remain.)

> Motto on provincial coat-of-arms.

The premier province of Canada. (1897)

The Banner Province.

> Popular titles for the province.

Ontario is the milch cow for the other provinces.

> A popular saying. The Toronto *Globe*, Nov. 4, 1879 refers to an earlier use; also, *The Week*, May

29, 1884, 402: "Ontario suspects that she is the milch cow"; and, MITCHELL HEPBURN, speech in Toronto, Oct. 6, 1938.

Ontario is a state of mind, bounded on the east by a foreign language, on the north by wilderness, on the west by the hungry prairies, and on the south by another country.

DOROTHY DUNCAN, *Here's to Canada!*, 1941.

OPPORTUNITY.

We will never have a big country, nor big men, unless we give them individual opportunity — unless we encourage that individual enterprise that grasps opportunity. Why remove these incentives to men to grapple with large conditions and schemes? Why take them out of their control? Such a policy is designed to dwarf and stunt the individual and, as a result, we shrivel nationally and we shrivel politically.

GEORGE W. ROSS, speech in Toronto, April 19, 1906.

Opportunity comes to some men more frequently than to others but there are very few it does not visit at some time or other.

DONALD A. SMITH (Lord Strathcona), qu., Pedley, *Strathcona*, 162.

The chief immediate direction of social effort should be towards the attempt to give to every human being in childhood adequate food, clothing, education, and an opportunity in life. This will prove to be the beginning of many things.

STEPHEN B. LEACOCK, *Unsolved riddles of social justice*, 1920, 151.

ORANGEMEN.

Derry's sons alike defy
  Pope, traitor, or defender,
And peal to heaven their 'prentice cry,
  Their patriot "No surrender."

OGLE R. GOWAN, a founder (1830) of the Orange Association of British America.

Here's a needle,
  Here's a thread,
To sew a pig's tail
  To an Orangeman's head.
  Roman Catholic children's rhyme, Grey County, Ont., 19th. cent.

Teeter, totter,
Holy water,
Sprinkle the Catholics every one,
If that won't do,
We'll cut them in two,
And put them under the Protestants' drum.
  Children's rhyme, Grey and Brant counties, Ont., 19th. cent.; variant of Old Country rhyme.

Up the long ladder,
  Down the short rope,
To hell with King Billy!
  Three cheers for the Pope!
  Children's rhyme, Ontario, 19th. century; the sentiments of the last two lines were frequently reversed.

They have dined him and wined him
  in manner most royal,
Addressed and harangued him
  to prove they are loyal;
They have bored him in parks,
  and they've bored him in halls,
Danced him almost to death
  in no end of balls.
They have bored him in colleges,
  bored him in schools,
And convinced him that
  Orange fanatics are fools.
  R. J. DE CORDOVA, *The Prince's visit; tour of the Prince of Wales, 1860*, 1861.

OTTAWA, ONT.

(See also: CITIES AND TOWNS — NICKNAMES, etc.)

As Bytown is not overrun with Americans it may probably turn out a moral, well-behaved town, and afford a lesson to its neighbours.

JOHN MACTAGGART, *Three years in Can.*, 1829, II, 219.

If the Province of Canada is to remain one, it is essential that its Seat of Government should be fixed and recognized by all.

SIR EDMUND HEAD, letter to Labouchere, Mar. 28, 1857.

With the exception of Ottawa, every one of the cities proposed [as the capital site] is an object of jealousy to each of the others.

SIR EDMUND HEAD, *Confidential memo.*, Oct., 1857.

The Westminster in the Wilderness.
A derisive term used in Montreal, Toronto, and other cities, 1858, when Ottawa was chosen as capital.

The buildings were magnificent; style, extent, site, and workmanship all surprisingly fine... The buildings were just five hundred years in advance of the time; it would cost half the revenue of the province to light and heat and keep them clean. Such monstrous folly was never perpetrated before.

GEORGE BROWN, on the Parliament Buildings; letter to Sir J. A. Macdonald, Aug. 15, 1864.

A miserable little house.
GEORGE BROWN, on Rideau Hall. letter to Sir John A. Macdonald. Aug. 15, 1864.

It contains acres of plaster and miles of cornice.
JONATHAN MCCULLY, reference to the Parliament Buildings, in a speech made in Nova Scotia, 1866.

Aye, but think of the attractions of Ottawa! They may be very great, but I think I may be pardoned if I prefer an old city beside the Thames. London is large enough for me, and you will no doubt prefer London with its magnificent proportions to Ottawa with its magnificent distances.

JOSEPH HOWE, speech in Bridgetown, N. S., 1867.

I would not wish to say anything disparaging of the capital, but it is hard to say anything good of it. Ottawa is not a handsome city and does not appear destined to become one either.

SIR WILFRID LAURIER, speech in Montreal, May 19, 1884. (trans.)

A sub-arctic lumber-village converted by royal mandate into a political cockpit.

GOLDWIN SMITH; attributed.

I keep a green spot in my heart for the city of Ottawa, and when the day comes, as it will come by and by, it shall be my pleasure and that of my colleagues, I am sure to make the city of Ottawa as attractive as possibly could be; to make it the centre of the intellectual development of this country and above all the Washington of the North.

SIR WILFRID LAURIER, address to the Reform Assoc. of Ottawa, June 19, 1893.

Above her river, above her hill,
Above her streets of brief renown,
In majesty austere and still
Ottawa's gloried towers look down.
WILFRED CAMPBELL, in Campbell and Martin, *Canada*, 1907, 95.

Grandeur is written on thy throne,
Beauty encompasseth thy mien;
The glory of the North alone,
Is thine, O Ottawa, my Queen.
Here as the years of promise roll
Shall gather all a nation's pride.
JAMES E. CALDWELL, "Ottawa", 1907.

Fair, in the South, fair as a shrine that makes
The wonder of a dream, imperious towers
Pierce and possess the sky, guarding the halls
Where our young strength is welded strenuously.
DUNCAN CAMPBELL SCOTT, "Ottawa before dawn", 1926.

OUTDOORS.

I fear no power a woman wields,
While I can have the woods and fields.
ERNEST MCGAFFEY (b.1861). "Song".

A white tent pitched by a glassy lake,
Well under a shady tree.
Or by rippling rills from the grand old hills,
Is the summer home for me.
I fear no blaze of the noontide rays,
For the woodland glades are mine.
The fragrant air, and that perfume rare —
The odour of forest pine,
JAMES D. EDGAR, "Canadian camping song", 1893.

The mighty voice of Canada will ever
call to me.
I shall hear the roar of rivers where
the rapids foam and tear,
I shall smell the virgin upland with
its balsam-laden air,
And shall dream that I am riding
down the winding woody vale
With the packer and the packhorse
on the Athabaska Trail.

> SIR ARTHUR CONAN DOYLE, "The
> Athabaska Trail", 1919.

There is virtue in the open; there is
healing out of doors;
The great Physician makes his rounds
along the forest floors.

> BLISS CARMAN, "An open letter,
> Christmas, 1920", written while a
> patient at Lake Placid, N. Y.

P

PACIFIC SCANDAL.

These hands are clean!

> SIR JOHN A. MACDONALD attribu-
> ted by J. W. Bengough, in a
> cartoon in *Grip*, Aug. 16, 1873.

The Pacific Slander.

> SIR CHARLES TUPPER's phrase in
> reply to "The Pacific Scandal",
> 1873.

The Pacific Scandal shattered at one
blow the fabric which Sir John Macdonald kept together by his skill in
manipulation of individual interests,
and the cohesive power of public
plunder.

> TORONTO *Globe*, Jan. 22, 1874.

PARLIAMENT.

> (See also: CABINET MINIS-
> TERS; GOVERNOR-GENERAL;
> MAJORITY; PARLIAMENT,
> MEMBERS OF; ROYAL COM-
> MISSIONS; SENATE)

Here I sincerely hope will be an
end of Parliament in this Province.

> LORD DALHOUSIE, letter, Nov. 22,
> 1827; qu., *Can. hist. rev.*, XII, 134.

The Bow-Wow Parliament.

> The Newfoundland parliament, es-
> pecially the first, 1833; from a
> caricature by JOHN DOYLE ("H.D.")

in his, *Political sketches* — sketch
no. 187, March 30, 1832, in which
a Newfoundland dog as Speaker
puts the motion, "As many as
are of that opinion say... Bow!
Of the contrary... Wow! I think
the Bows! have it".

The Bread-and-Butter Parliament.

> The Upper Canada Assembly of
> 1836; Sir Francis Bond Head
> campaigned against the Reformers
> and warned the electors that their
> bread and butter depended on the
> way they voted.

Parliament is a grand inquest which
has the right to inquire into anything
and everything.

> SIR JOHN A. MACDONALD, speech,
> 1861; qu., Biggar, *Anecdotal life*,
> 182.

As a Parliament they could do as
they liked with their own.

> SIR JOHN A. MACDONALD, in House
> of Commons, 1869, on increase of
> Nova Scotia subsidy without Impe-
> rial Act; from a statement of the
> Duke of Newcastle, that his par-
> ty had a right "to do what they
> liked with their own".

I could not have treated Parliament
as a pregnant woman, and prolonged its
existence for the sake of the lesser
life attached to it.

> LORD DUFFERIN, despatch to the
> Colonial Office, summer, 1873, on
> the question of proroguing after
> revelations made regarding the
> "Pacific Scandal".

The privileges of Parliament are the
privileges of the People, and the rights
of Parliament are the rights of the
People.

> EDWARD BLAKE, speech in London,
> Aug. 28, 1873.

The Legislature [of the Province]
within its jurisdiction can do everything
that is not naturally impossible, and
is restrained by no rule human or
divine. If it be that the plaintiffs
acquired any rights, which I am far
from finding, the Legislature had the
power to take them away. The prohibition "Thou shalt not steal" has no
legal force upon the sovereign body.

> JUDGE W. F. RIDDELL, 18 *Ont. law
> reports*, 1909, 279.

The public interest demands a dissolution of this House of Commons... His Excellency having declined to accept my advice to grant a dissolution, to which I believe under British practice I was entitled, I immediately tendered my resignation.

W. L. MACKENZIE KING, H. of C., *Debates*, 1926, 5059.

Parliament will decide.

W. L. MACKENZIE KING; attributed to him as a declaration of policy. See, WAR, statements of September 1936, and March 30, 1939.

PARLIAMENT, MEMBERS OF.

The law! the law! never mind the law — turn him oot; turn him oot!

JOHN STRACHAN, 1821, in Legislative Council, Toronto, on being informed that the law did not permit the Assembly to expel the reformer Barnabas Bidwell.

You are representatives of the people, and I put it to you, as you are greatly honoured, should you not greatly dare? You are sent to do your duty to your constituents, whether your acts always give satisfaction or not.

JOSEPH HOWE, speech in N. S. Legislature, Mar. 22, 1841.

Brown promised, in terms that could not be withstood,
If we gave him a seat, it should be for our good,
Nor can we complain that he's altered his tone:
He sits for our good, but — he lies for his own.

ALEXANDER McDOUGALL (of Nova Scotia), "On a member of the House of Assembly not remarkable for his veracity", *Bentley's misc.*, Feb. 1843, 160.

How many Canadian M. P. P.'s could obtain third class certificates from the most lenient of our educational examination boards?

R. J. MACGEORGE, in: *Streetsville weekly review*, May 26, 1855.

A new member requires the experience of his first session in the house to teach him how to hang up his overcoat

and hat and take his seat in a manner béfitting a gentleman.

SIR JOHN A. MACDONALD; attributed as a frequent statement.

Call in de membr'.

SIR GEORGE E. CARTIER, in the Assembly, especially about 1860, in terminating debates on Rep. by Pop.; "The really solid argument was Cartier's contemptuous conclusion to all debate: "Call in de membr'" — O. D. Skelton, *Sir A. T. Galt*, 212.

Free and independent men in the Legislature, as in the country, are the best counterpoise to faction and the main-spring of a nation's progress and greatness.

EGERTON RYERSON, *New Can. Dominion*, 1867, 25.

Yes, 'tis pleasant to think as I sit in the gallery,
They agree upon one thing, and that is their salary.

Grip (Toronto), Feb. 15, 1879.

A man goes to Ottawa burning with zeal to inaugurate political liberation. Six months or a year produces sleeping-sickness.

AUGUSTUS BRIDLE ("Domino"), *Masques of Ottawa*, 1921.

PARLIAMENTARY DEBATES.

It happens, unfortunately, to be true, that there is no kind of intelligence about which the public are so indifferent as that which is usually contained in the speeches delivered on the floor of Parliament.

TORONTO *Daily Leader*, May, 19, 1855.

That vast repository of talk.

J. W. DAFOE, *Clifford Sifton*, 1931, 166; ref. to *Hansard*.

PARLIAMENTARY REPRESENTATION.

(See also: POLITICAL PHRASES)

Representation by population. Justice for Upper Canada! While Upper Canada has a larger population by one hundred and fifty thousand than Lower Canada, and contributes more than double the amount of taxation to the general revenue, Lower Canada has an equal number of representatives in parliament.

> TORONTO *Globe*, Oct. 1, 1853, statement of policy.

The Upper Canadians boast of their rapidly increasing population, but wealth ought to be taken into account as well as population, and the codfish of Gaspé Bay ought to be represented as well as the 250,000 Grits of Western Canada.

> SIR GEORGE E. CARTIER, H. of Assembly, April 5, 1861. "Codfish" was a word much used thereafter by Upper Canada advocates of Rep. by Pop.

We say we have representation by population, but we have not representation by population unless the population has a representation in the legislature equivalent to its strength at the polls.

> EDWARD BLAKE, speech at Aurora, Oct. 3, 1874.

I do not think a system under which a majority in one constituency elects a member, the minority being hopeless, helpless, without any representation of its own at all, is a good system.

> EDWARD BLAKE, speech at Aurora, Oct. 3, 1874.

It is all very well to tell contemporaries that posterity must reap the benefit of the enormous public works undertaken at the consolidation of the Dominion. But posterity has no representative in Parliament.

> *Canadian Monthly*, vol. 1, 1878, 239.

PASSION.

In a moment it will borrow,
  Flashing in a gusty train,
Laughter and desire and sorrow
  Anger and delight and pain.

> ARCHIBALD LAMPMAN, "Passion", 1888.

Give me a meeting or assembly of men, whether it be small or large, and in that meeting I will find passions and prejudices, noble in themselves, but which can be easily excited into dangerous passions and prejudices.

> SIR WILFRID LAURIER, H. of C., *Debates*, Feb. 17, 1890.

The natural man has only two primal passions, to get and to beget.

> SIR WILLIAM OSLER, *Science and immortality*, 1904, ch. 2.

There is little passion in Canadian life. Suspicion and jealousy of the United States and admiration for England are not passions.

> A. L. PHELPS, in *Univ. Tor. quart.*, 1939, 87.

THE PAST.

> (See also: DESTINY; FUTURE; HISTORY; NATIONAL HERITAGE)

It is the most unpoetical of all lands there is no scope for imagination; here all is new — the very soil seems newly formed; there is no hoary ancient grandeur in these woods; no recollections of former deeds connected with the country.

> ANON., in Catherine P. Traill, *Backwoods of Can.*, 1836, 154.

Ghosts! There are no ghosts in Canada. The country is too new for ghosts. No Canadian is afearded of ghosts.

> SUSANNA MOODIE, *Roughing it in the bush*, 1852, ch. 12.

To mourn today over the wreck of yesterday only increases the loss, and diminishes the value of what little is left to us.

> T. C. HALIBURTON, *Sam Slick's wise saws*, 1853, I, 277.

But yet, do not withhold the grateful tear
For those, and for their works, who are not here.
Not here? O yes! our hearts their presence feel,
Viewless, not voiceless; from the deepest shells
On memory's shore harmonious echoes steal,

And names which in the days gone
  by were spells
Are blent with that soft music.
JOSEPH HOWE, "Our fathers", ode
written for the first Provincial
Industrial Exhibition of Nova
Scotia, Oct., 1854.

Now is the burden of it all "No more".
No more shall, wandering, we go
  gather flowers,
Nor tune our voices by the river's
  brink,
Nor in the grotto-fountain cool our
  limbs,
Nor walking in the winter woo the
  sun.
CHARLES HEAVYSEGE, Jephthah's
daughter, 1865.

Tho' boasting no baronial halls,
Nor ivy-crested towers,
What past can match thy glorious
  youth,
Fair Canada of ours?
Fair Canada,
Dear Canada,
This Canada of ours!
JAMES D. EDGAR, "This Canada of
ours," 1870.

Still we hear the tones regretful for
  the goodly times no more;
Still that sentimental slobbering for
  the brave old days of yore,
And sometimes we can't help thinking,
  while folks of the by-gone dream,
Of the comforts we're enjoying in
  these sneered-at days of steam.
H. K. COCKIN, in, Can. birthday
book, 1887.

The dead hand has too long hampered
the freedom of the living.
JAMES ROBERTSON, D. D., Report
to Presbyterian Assembly, 1895.

May every joy that perished
  Be mirrored in our gaze,
And in our speech the beauty
  Of all our vanished days.
ETHELWYN WETHERALD, "A wish",
1907.

Behold, behold the invulnerable
  ghosts
Of all past greatnesses about thee
  stand.
MARJORIE PICKTHALL, "Canada to
ngland", 1914.

A European can find nothing to
satisfy the hunger of his heart. The
air is too thin to breathe. He requires
haunted woods, and the friendly presence of ghosts... For it is possible,
at a pinch to do without gods. But
one misses the dead.
RUPERT BROOKE, Letters from
America, 1916, 154-6.

Whatever a man has been he continues to be.
GEORGE ILES, Canadian stories,
1918, 178.

We have become so accustomed to
saying, and hearing others say, that
we have no past, that we forget that
what may have been true of a hundred
years ago has had time in which to
change. It has changed. We have
made history. We have acquired customs, legendary lore, relics. Above all,
relics.
HELEN E. WILLIAMS, Spinning-
wheels and homespun, 1923, 173.

While other animals have memory,
man alone builds up a formal story of
his life in the past and is governed by
its traditions.
G. M. WRONG, in Can. hist. rev.,
1933, 4.

As a matter of truth, health and
happiness have been better in adversity
and no man need feel he has failed
unless, in looking back, the retrospect
is blank, or unless time and events
have proved that he was wrong. Whether now judged right or wrong, whatever
I have said, whatever I have done, is
going to remain unrevised and un-
repented.
ARTHUR MEIGHEN, speech in Winnipeg Conservative Convention, Dec.
9, 1942.

PATRIOTISM.

(See also: LOYALTY; NATION-
ALITY)

A patriot is none of your raving,
railing, ranting, accusing radicals —
nor is he one of your idle, stall-fed,
greasy, good for nothing sinecurists or
pluralists; he is in deed and in truth
a friend to his country.
WILLIAM LYON MACKENZIE, Colonial Advocate, May 4, 1826.

Mori, the more you get, *pro patria, dulce est,* the sweeter it is.

> THOMAS C. HALIBURTON, *Sam Slick,* attributed.

Patriotism is the trump card of a scoundrel.

> T. C. HALIBURTON, *Sam Slick,* 1840, 28.

I hope to see the day... when there will be no other term to our patriotism, but the common name of Canadian, without the prefix of either French or British.

> THOMAS D'A. McGEE, letter to constituents, 1859.

Love for Canada has to be acquired by the prosperity of the country, and from our children.

> JOHN S. HELMCKEN, B. C., *Debates on Confederation,* 1870, 13.

Love your country, believe in her, honor her, work for her, live for her, die for her. Never has any people been endowed with a nobler birthright, or blessed with prospects of a brighter future.

> LORD DUFFERIN, speech in Toronto, Sept. 24, 1878.

There can be no patriotism without nationality.

> GOLDWIN SMITH, *Political destiny of Can.,* 1878.

When we heard that they [the Gordon Highlanders] had justified fully the confidence placed in them, that they had charged like veterans, that their conduct was heroic and had won for them the encomiums of the Commander-in-Chief and the unstinted admiration of their comrades, who had faced death upon a hundred battlefields in all parts of the world, is there a man whose bosom did not swell with pride, that noblest of all pride, that pride of pure patriotism, the pride of the consciousness of our rising strength, the pride of the consciousness that on that day it had been revealed to the world that a new power had arisen in the West?

> SIR WILFRID LAURIER, H. of C., *Debates,* Mar. 13, 1900, 1847.

Some men, and all cattle, lack patriotism.

> GEORGE M. GRANT, qu., *Principal Grant,* 1904, 396.

Patriotism is not based upon prejudice.

> SIR WILFRID LAURIER, speech in Sorel, Sept. 28, 1904.

There is Ontario patriotism, Quebec patriotism, or Western patriotism, each based on the hope that it may swallow up the others, but there is no Canadian patriotism, and we can have no Canadian nation when we have no Canadian patriotism.

> HENRI BOURASSA, Can. Club, Toronto, Jan. 22, 1907.

Patriotic sentiments have never in the history of the world stood long against the pocket-book. This is an unhappy truth which cannot be escaped.

> SIR W. VAN HORNE, letter, 1914?; qu. in Vaughan: *Van Horne,* 1920, 345.

True patriotism is as quiet and cheerful as sunlight, as modest as a maid used to be, as faithful under difficulties as a dog or a good wife, as solicitous for the national honour as for the individual's interest and as ready to die in a fair and honest quarrel as a man to go to bed after a hard day's work.

> CECIL F. LLOYD, *Sunlight and shadow,* 1928.

Mr. Lower has long been a patriot in search of a *patria.*

> P. E. CORBETT, in *Can. hist. rev.,* 1941, 117.

PATRONAGE.

Patronage is power; our men won the victory, and they are entitled to the prize money.

> J. H. PRICE, letter to Robert Baldwin, Feb. 6, 1843.

If you have any axes to grind, send them down to Toronto by Mr. O'Reilly.

> JOHN SANDFIELD MACDONALD, speech in Hamilton, 1867; a reference to O'Reilly, the government candidate in an election; known as the "Axe-grinding speech".

Friends (?) expect to be benefited by offices they are unfit for, by contracts they are not entitled to, by advances not earned. Enemies ally themselves with friends and push the friends to the front. Some dig trenches at a distance and approach in regular siege form. A weak minister here would ruin the party in a month and the country very soon.

ALEXANDER MACKENZIE, letter to Thomas Hodgins, April 27, 1875.

To think that after naming my only son William Lyon Mackenzie, I am still denied any post by a government that calls itself Liberal!

ANON., letter to Sir Wilfrid Laurier, 1896; qu. Skelton, *Laurier*, II, 273.

He has sent me bishops and archbishops, priests and laymen, until I am absolutely familiar with all his merits, and his one demerit of being over zealous in his own behalf.

SIR WILFRID LAURIER, letter to John Willison, Oct. 12, 1903.

The patronage system is one of Canada's social evils — a canker, a disease more blighting, more demoralizing than any other social disease that infects the body politic today.

WILLIAM IRVINE, in, *Nutcracker*, Feb. 3, 1917, 6.

The distribution of patronage was the most important single function of the government.

O. D. SKELTON, in *Life of Laurier*, 1921, II, 270.

We farmers work on the principle that the hog that gets fat first will be the one to be killed off first.

JOHN OLIVER, Premier of British Columbia, about 1920, to his friends, on patronage.

Patronage spells the death of efficiency in its largest and broadest sense; it invariably places the emphasis not only on the wrong factors but on the irrelevant ones... Party patronage in the civil service is now a sign of political immaturity, a relic of barbaric days, a sure symptom of pettifogging politics.

R. MACGREGOR DAWSON, in *Can. jour. econ. and pol. sci.*, 1936, 291.

PEACE.

I knew by the smoke that so peacefully curled
Above the green elms, that a cottage was near;
And I said, if there's peace to be found in the world,
A heart that is humble might hope for it here.

THOMAS MOORE, lines inspired by a scene on Burlington Bay, Ontario, 1804.

And still I preached, and wrought, and still I bore my message,
For well I knew that on and upward without cease
The spirit works for ever, and by Faith and Presage
That somehow yet the end of human life is Peace.

ARCHIBAD LAMPMAN, "The land of Pallas", 1899.

When the strength of man is shattered.
And the powers of earth are scattered,
From beneath the ghastly ruin Peace shall rise!

ARCHIBALD LAMPMAN, "War", 1899.

I do not believe that universal peace is either possible or desirable. If it were possible and could be brought about, I feel sure it would result in universal rottenness.

SIR W. VAN HORNE, letter to S. S. McClure, 1910.

Peace comes by power rather than by preaching.

SIR JOHN S. WILLISON, speech, International Polity Club, Toronto, Feb. 12, 1914.

When our children's children shall talk of War as a madness that may not be;
When we thank our God for our grief today, and blazen from sea to sea
In the name of the dead the banner of Peace... *that will be Victory.*

ROBERT W. SERVICE, "The song of the Pacifist", 1916.

The making of peace is in fact more difficult than has been the winning of the war.

> JOHN W. DAFOE, speech, Canadian Club, Winnipeg, April 8, 1919.

THE PEOPLE.

(See also: CLASSES; MEN; SOCIETY)

Sarve the public nine hundred and ninety-nine times, and the thousandth, if they don't agree with you, they desart and abuse you.

> T. C. HALIBURTON, *Sam Slick*, 1836, ch. XV.

Some people are too good to be interesting.

> ROBERT C. (BOB) EDWARDS, *Calgary Eye Opener*, Oct. 28, 1911.

All men are essentially noble. Constitutionally, there are no common people.

> ALBERT D. WATSON, "The immortals", 1913.

Somehow the people who do as they please seem to get along just about as well as those who are always trying to please others.

> ROBERT C. (BOB) EDWARDS, *Calgary Eye Opener*, Mar. 9, 1918.

It rather occurs to me that it's the commonplace people who *do* things.

> STEPHEN B. LEACOCK, "The soul call", 1920.

The people... may make mistakes but they will be their own mistakes and will be the better for them than if someone tried to think for them too much, and probably be just as apt to be mistaken.

> ALEX. J. MCPHAIL, *Diary*, 1940, 93.

I've always found that you can control people better if you don't see too much of them.

> W. L. MACKENZIE KING, qu., Hardy, *Mackenzie King of Canada*, 1949, 94.

PERSONALITIES.

(See also: HEROES; PERSONALITIES (NICKNAMES); and names of individuals)

And they accuse us, gentlemen, of disloyalty! And to whom, do you think? To Sir Charles Metcalfe! Is Sir Charles Metcalfe the embodiment of the British Constitution? Is the British Constitution liable to be carried off by a cancer?

> LEWIS T. DRUMMOND, Montreal politician, speech to his constituents, about 1844. Metcalfe was Governor-General, 1843-1845, and died of cancer, 1846.

The Lord of the Bed-chamber sat in his shirt
(And D — dy the pliant was there),
And his feelings appeared to be very much hurt,
And his brow overclouded with care.

> JOSEPH HOWE, "Lord of the Bedchamber", (first verse), in *Nova Scotian*, May 20, 1845, on Lord Falkland, Governor.

The Other MacNab.

> SIR ALLAN MACNAB, inscription on the reverse of the card of a visitor, and returned to him — Archibald, Chief of MacNab, known as "The MacNab".

I consider him of more importance to the connexion than three regiments.

> LORD ELGIN on Robert Baldwin's loyalty to Britain, letter to Lord Grey, Jan. 28, 1850. In a letter June 28, 1851, Elgin refers to him as "The most Conservative public man in U. Canada."

Nicknames stick to people, and the most ridiculous are the most adhesive.

> T. C. HALIBURTON, *Sam Slick's wise saws*, 1853, II, 51.

He will not set the St. Lawrence on fire but he is a shrewd common sense man, and understands human nature, as his unlimited influence in the District of Quebec shows.

> SIR JOHN A. MACDONALD on Francis X. Lemieux, letter to J. Langton, Feb. 6, 1855.

True Wizard of the Wild! whose art,
An eye of power, a knightly heart,
A patient purpose silence-nurst,
A high, enduring, saintly trust —
Are mighty spells — we honor these,
Columbus of the inland seas!

THOMAS D'A. MCGEE, "The launch of the *Griffin*", 1858; a reference to LaSalle.

You damned pup, I'll slap your chops for you!

SIR JOHN A. MACDONALD to Sir Oliver Mowat, H. of Assembly, April 19, 1861.

He contained in his own complex and painful nature the chief springs of his triumphs, his failures, and his death.

FRANCIS PARKMAN, *Discovery of the great West*, 1869, 430, on La-Salle.

He is the worst negotiator I ever saw in my life.

SIR JOHN A. MACDONALD, letter to Sir John Rose, Feb. 13, 1873, on Sir Hugh Allen.

I could lick that man Smith quicker than hell could frizzle a feather.

SIR JOHN A. MACDONALD, Nov. 5, 1873, in lobby, H. of C., after Donald A. Smith (Lord Strathcona) stated he could no longer "conscientiously" support the government on the Pacific Railway scandal.

Mr. Cauchon's offense smells rank to heaven.

TORONTO *Globe* 1873, on Joseph Cauchon's action in speculating at the expense of inmates of the Quebec Asylum; in 1875 Cauchon was taken into the Liberal cabinet.

Many surpassed him in cruelty, none equalled him in capacity and vigor.

FRANCIS PARKMAN, *Count Frontenac and New France*, 1877, 458, ref. to Frontenac.

That fellow Smith is the biggest liar I ever met.

SIR JOHN A. MACDONALD, H. of C., *Debates*, May 10, 1878, 2564; a reference to Donald A. Smith (Lord Strathcona).

Mowat, that little tyrant.

SIR JOHN A. MACDONALD, speech at Yorkville June 1, 1882, on Sir Oliver Mowat, Premier of Ontario.

I, as a member of the Liberal-Conservative party owe him such a debt of gratitude that if it shall be necessary to retain his services in the party which he does not lead, and which would not have him for a leader, and which barely tolerates him as a supporter — if it be necessary in order to retain him in that capacity, I, for one, will propose a subsidy to Parliament to keep him there.

SIR JOHN THOMPSON, on Sir Richard Cartwright, H. of C., *Debates*, June 28, 1892.

He above all others made in the same mould, which, thank God, nature broke when she cast him.

SIR JOHN THOMPSON, on Sir Richard Cartwright, H. of C., *Debates*, June 28, 1892.

I think you are the damndest —. I was going to say the damndest fool I have ever known, but I can't say that because I have known two or three others who completed their record by dying in their foolishness, while your record is still incomplete and there is a faint chance that you may yet make a turn and end under suspicion of having had some sense.

SIR W. VAN HORNE, letter to W. F. Luxton, founder of the Man. *Free Press*, 1895; qu., Vaughan, *Van Horne*, 1920, 245.

The Earl [of Aberdeen] himself was a sensible and inoffensive man, but his wife was the most aggressive busybody who ever presided over Rideau Hall.

Saturday Night, Toronto, Oct. 4, 1898.

He has but one principle, that of self-interest. He has only one desire, the desire to insult. He belongs to the school of lying, hypocrisy and cowardice.

E. E. CINQ-MARS, in, *La Presse*, May 26, 1906 (trans.); H. of C., *Debates*, May 29, 1906, 4032; a reference to Sir George E. Foster.

Goldwin Smith was... a Little Englander of Little Englanders. He saw nothing in the Empire... but a burden on England.

> *Times Weekly*, London, June 10, 1910, 420.

The cult of commercialized Christianity, in Ontario at least, has been placed on the basis of an exact science. The three great exponents of that cult are John Wesley Allison, Joseph Wesley Flavelle, and Newton Wesley Rowell. *Ego* is their god, *autos* their creed and *moi-même* their practice.

> CHARLES MURPHY, H. of C., *Debates*, Mar. 19, 1918, 39.

A dynamo run by dynamite.

> D. B. HANNA, *Trains of recollection*, 1924, 40, on Sir William Van Horne.

He is an American wolf in the Canadian sheep-fold in the skin of a Missouri mule.

> *Can. Milling and Grain Jour.* May 15, 1926, 5, on Henry Wise Wood.

I have nothing to say against Mr. Bennett, but I must say I don't like his friends.

> L. A. TASCHEREAU, speech in Ste. Anne de Beaupré, July 20, 1930, on R. B. Bennett.

It is rather hard on the Court of St. James but it is a great relief to the Province of Ontario.

> AGNES MCPHAIL, H. of C., *Debates*, Mar. 26, 1931, on the appointment of Howard Ferguson as High Commissioner to London.

Mr. Bennett does not impress me as having much imperial sentiment. To him these imperial problems were simply matters of business — an opportunity for seeing how much he could get out of others and how little he could give himself.

> VISCOUNT SNOWDEN, *Autobiography*, 1934, on R. B. Bennett.

Tradition made Carleton divine; research makes him human. The portrait of this Irishman, as touched up by his English biographer, was almost an idol to Canadians. The picture was beautiful — that of a soldier, a political sage, and one might almost add, a saint all combined. It ·was made for

worship, not for understanding. No such perfect man was ever born, not even in Ireland.

> A. L. BURT, in Can. Hist. Assoc., *Rept.*, 1935, 76.

PERSONALITIES (NICKNAMES)

The Abe Lincoln of Canada.

> *Andrew Broder*, M. P. for Dundas, Ont., 1896 to 1917.

The Apostle of the Prairies.

> *Dr. James Robertson*, superintendent of Presbyterian missions in the West, 1881-1902.

The Axe-Grinder.

> *John Sandfield Macdonald*, Premier of Ontario; opposition's sobriquet, 1868; because of his political attitude of *quid pro quo.*

The Bald Eagle of the Plains.

> *Nicholas Flood Davin*, M. P. for Assiniboia, 1887-1900.

The Bear.

> Usually, "Bear" Ellice, a reference to *Edward Ellice* (d.1863) English merchant and M. P., long connected with the fur-trading companies in Canada; his son, also named Edward Ellice, was sometimes called "Young Bear".

The Beaver.

> *Lord Beaverbrook* (William Maxwell Aitken), born Maple, Ont. 1879.

The Belted Knight.

> *Slr Allan MacNab*, knighted in 1838 for his services in leading the loyal forces in the Niagara peninsula during the rebellion of 1837.

Big Thunder.

> *E. B. Wood, M. P.,* so called by T. D'A. MCGEE because of his loud voice; also, *William Paterson*, so called by his Indian constituents in South Brant.

The Black Tarte and the Yellow Martin.

> *J. Israel Tarte*, and *Joseph Martin*, Liberal leaders, so called by SIR JOHN THOMPSON, speech in Pictou, N. S., 1894.

Blue Ruin Dick.

> *Sir Richard Cartwright,* Member of Parliament and Senator from 1863 to 1912.

The Coon.

> *Malcolm C. Cameron,* member of the House of Commons, 1867 to 1898.

The Demosthenes of Canada.

> *Louis Joseph Papineau;* later applied to *Sir George Foster.*

L'enfant terrible.

> *J. B. E. Dorion,* (1826-1866) politician and journalist.

The Father of British Columbia.

> *Sir James Douglas,* founder of Fort Victoria, 1843, later governor of Vancouver Island, and of British Columbia.

The Father of British Preference.

> *Sir Louis Davies,* who introduced the preferential policy in 1892.

The Father of Canadian Geology.

> *Abraham Gesner* of Nova Scotia after publication of his book, *Remarks on the geology of Nova Scotia,* 1836.

The Father of Standard Time.

> *Sir Sandford Fleming,* who first advocated a universal method of reckoning time, 1879.

The Father of the Ottawa.

> *Philemon Wright,* 1760-1839, first settler in the Hull, Quebec, district, 1800.

Father of the Railway.

> *Sir Allan MacNab,* a term popular in Hamilton where he was instrumental in bringing the Great Western Railway to the city in 1854.

The Father of the Saguenay.

> *William Price,* English lumber operator, 1789-1867.

Fighting Frank Carvell.

> *Frank B. Carvell,* Minister of Public Works in the Union Government, 1917-19.

Fighting Joe.

> *Joseph Martin,* member of Manitoba Legislature, 1883-92; led the attack on separate schools; Premier of British Columbia, 1900.

The First Great Canadian.

> *Pierre Le Moyne, Sieur d'Iberville,* from title of a biography by Charles B. Reed, 1910.

The Good Samaritan of Labrador.

> *Sir Wilfred Grenfell,* early 20th. century.

The gramophone of Mackenzie and Mann.

> *Arthur Meighen,* so called by R. B. BENNETT, H. of C., *Debates,* May 13, 1914; Mackenzie and Mann were railway promoters.

The Grand Old Man of Canada.

> *Sir Charles Tupper* in his later years; he died Oct. 30, 1915, age 94; also, *Sir William Mulock,* died 1944, age 100.

The Great Mother.

> *Queen Victoria,* so called by western Indians, middle Nineteenth Century.

The Hanging Judge.

> *Sir Matthew Baillie Begbie,* appointed a judge in British Columbia, 1858, and Chief Justice, 1870.

The Hero of Kars.

> *Sir Wm. Fenwick Williams,* of Nova Scotia, from his defeat of the Russians, Sept. 29, 1855, during his defence of the Fortress of Kars, later surrendered.

Honest John.

> Popular term applied to *John Carling, John Costigan, John Oliver,* and others.

Hug-the-machine Preston.

> *W. T. R. Preston,* civil servant, who sent a telegram on Jan. 12, 1899, to Donald McNish, Liberal Party victor in a West Elgin by-election, worded: "Hug the machine for me". The telegram was obtained by the Conservatives and published.

The Hungry Adventurer.
W. R. Meredith, Ontario Conservative leader, from a manifesto by Archbishop JAMES V. CLEARY read in Kingston churches May 28, 1894, during an election.

The Hyena.
Sir Francis Hincks, used about 1850 by GEORGE BROWN and his supporters; a reference to his ruthlessness in debate.

King of the Fur-Traders.
Sir George Simpson (1792-1860), governor of the Hudson's Bay Company.

The King of the Gatineau.
Alonzo Wright, member of the Assembly and House of Commons, 1862-91.

The Knight of the Rueful Countenance.
Sir Richard Cartwright, Member of Parliament and Senator from 1863 to 1912.

The Laird of Dundurn.
Sir Allan MacNab, who built Dundurn Castle, Hamilton.

The little corporal of Lower Canadian politics.
Sir Georges E. Cartier (1814-1873).

The Little Rebel.
William Lyon Mackenzie; a favorite term of GEORGE BROWN's.

Little Thunder.
Arthur Sturgis Hardy, Premier of Ontario, 1896-99, in his early political days, because of his oratory.

The man of one idea.
Robert Baldwin, a scornful taunt used by opponents, about 1840.

The Master of the Administration.
J. Israel Tarte, member of Laurier's cabinet, so called by Conservatives, 1902.

The Minister of Elections.
Robert Rogers, Conservative government minister under Borden, so termed by the Liberals, about 1917.

The Nation-maker.
Amor de Cosmos, so called by his opponents of Victoria, B. C., after his speech of April 21, 1882; see, INDEPENDENCE.

The Nestor of Canadian Politics.
Sir Richard Cartwright (d.1912), a popular nickname ; TORONTO *Globe*, Dec. 11, 1902.

The Old Man Eloquent.
Joseph Howe in his later years; TORONTO *Globe*, Mar. 2, 1872.

Old Tomorrow.
See: MACDONALD, SIR JOHN A.

Peter the Great and Ivan the Terrible.
Peter J. Veniot, Liberal Premier, and *Ivan T. Rand*, Attorney General, so called by JOHN B. M. BAXTER, N. B. election, 1925.

The Pope of Methodism.
Egerton Ryerson, so called by JOHN LANGTON; see: RYERSON, EGERTON; later applied to *Dr. Albert Carman*, general supt., Methodist Church, 1883-1915; in 1925 applied to *Rev. S. D. Chown*, at time of forming of the United Church of Canada.

Radical Jack.
Lord Durham, an English nickname used in Canada after 1837.

Red Michael.
Dr. Michael Clark, Progressive, later Liberal, member of the House of Commons, about 1920.

The Rupert of debate.
Sir Richard Cartwright, so called because of his skill as a debater; SIR WILFRID LAURIER also called *Sir Louis Davies*, "A Rupert of debate."

The Sage of Bothwell.
David Mills, Member of Parliament and Senator from 1867 to 1902.

The Sage of The Grange.
Goldwin Smith, from the name of his home in Toronto.

Smooth William.
Sir William Whyte, superintendent, western lines, C.P.R., d.1914.

Sweet William.

William Pugsley, also called "Slippery Bill" by his opponents because of his soft voice; also, *William H. Draper,* because of his oratorical powers.

The Tiger.

Or, "Tiger" Dunlop, a reference to *William Dunlop,* surgeon in the war of 1812, adventurer in India, and later a settler in the Huron district and member of the Legislative Assembly.

The Tribune of the People.

Joseph Howe, a popular nickname.

The Uncrowned King of Alberta.

Henry Wise Wood, a name popular in the mid-1920's.

Wandering Willie.

William McDougall (1822-1905), a founder of the Clear Grit Party, later joined the Conservatives at Confederation.

The Watch-dog of the Treasury.

J. Lorn McDougall, Auditor-General of Canada who resigned June 21, 1904.

The wild man of the cloister.

Goldwin Smith, so called by DISRAELI; see, Haultain. *Smith,* 205, 231.

PERSONS.

[A person is] a male person, including an Indian and excluding a person of Mongolian of Chinese race.

CANADA FRANCHISE ACT, 1885.

Their Lordships have come to the conclusion that the word persons includes members of the male and female sex, and that therefore the question propounded by the Governor-General must be answered in the affirmative; and that women are eligible to be summoned and become members of the Senate of Canada.

PRIVY COUNCIL (London, Eng.) decision, as reported in Montreal *Gazette,* Oct. 19, 1929.

PIONEERS.

(See also: IMMIGRATION; SETTLERS)

I hear the tread of pioneers
Of nations yet to be,
The first low wash of waves where soon
Shall roll a human sea.

JOHN G. WHITTIER, "The seer", written 1846 on receiving an eagle's feather from Lake Superior.

There is a history which, if it were only recorded or capable of being recorded, would be interesting indeed, and would furnish us with a religion of gratitude. It is the history of the pioneer in all his lines. The monument of that history is the fair land in which we live.

GOLDWIN SMITH, *The Bystander,* Oct. 1883, 329.

No one who has made a study of the pioneers of Ontario can doubt for a moment the inspiration of their toil. They wanted homes.

PETER MCARTHUR, *In pastures green,* 1915, 43.

POETRY.

I would rather have written that poem, gentlemen, than take Quebec tomorrow.

MAJOR-GENERAL JAMES WOLFE, referring to Grey's "Elegy written in a country church-yard", the night before he was killed on the Plains of Abraham, Sept. 13, 1759; see Hume, *History of England,* ch. 30.

Will nobody write a few songs for Canada?

THOMAS MACQUEEN, in *Huron Signal,* qu., Morgan, *Bibliotheca canadensis,* 1867, 273.

There is probably no country in the world, making equal pretensions to intelligence and progress, where the claims of native literature are so little felt, and where every effort in poetry has been met with so much coldness and indifference, as in Canada.

EDWARD H. DEWART, *Selections from Can. poets,* 1864, x.

He was a half-cut schoolmaster and a quarter-cut poet.

> Robertson Davies' great-grandmother on J. R. (Andrew John) Ramsay, versifier who died 1907.

Dear Sir: Now Longfellow is gone there are only two of us left. There ought to be no rivalry between us two.

> JAMES GAY, Poet Laureate of Canada and Master of All Poets, letter to Lord Tennyson, 1883, in, *Poems*.

I do not know whether a Baron or a Poet Laureate gets any wages in England. In Canada there is no pay.

> JAMES GAY, letter to Lord Tennyson, 1883, in *Poems*.

A gift more perilous than the painter's: he
In his divine moments only sees
The inhumanities of color, we
Feel each and all the inhumanities.

> GEORGE F. CAMERON, 1885, foreword to "Lyrics, in pleasant places".

You've piped at home, where none could pay,
Till now, I trust your wits are riper;
Make no delay, but come this way,
And pipe for them that pay the piper!

> CHARLES G. D. ROBERTS, "The poet bidden to Manhattan Island", 1887.

The breasts of some of our Canadian birds of song throb with patriotism, but on opening an American magazine you will find them, at least as soon as they are feathered, warbling on a foreign bough.

> GOLDWIN SMITH, *The Week*, Aug. 31, 1894, 950.

The poets of 1861.

> A reference to poets born in or near that year: C. G. D. Roberts, Bliss Carman, Archibald Lampman, Duncan Campbell Scott, and Wilfred Campbell.

Reform ye scribblers, leave your mists and frogs,
Lakes, loons, and *Injuns* and Acadian bogs —
And hang the eternal paddle up to dry;
Canoes, good sooth; when Pegasus can fly,

To read our bards the world might well mistake
Our wide Dominion for an endless lake,
Dotted with isles where birch expressly grows
The raw material for bark canoes.

> ALEXANDER C. STEWART, *The poetical review*, 1896, 24.

The Maple Leaf School.

> A term sometimes applied to writers of patriotic verse.

The vision of the better and the higher things come to the people not so often through the preacher as through the poet.

> SIR WM. OSLER, Can. Club, Toronto, Dec. 29, 1904.

Nothing will sustain you more potently than the power to recognize in your humdrum routine, as perhaps it may be thought, the true Poetry of life — the poetry of the commonplace, of the ordinary man, of the plain, toil-worn woman, with their loves and joys, their sorrows and their griefs.

> SIR WILLIAM OSLER, "The student life", address, 1905, in, *Aequanimitas*.

The only poet in Canada was very nice to me in Ottawa. Canada's a bloody place for a sensitive real poet like this to live all his life in.

> RUPERT BROOKE, letter to Wilfred Gibson, from Toronto, 1913, on D. C. Scott.

We require more rage in our poets.

> D. C. SCOTT, "Poetry and progress", 1922.

A piece of writing is not poetry just because it rhymes. Nor is it poetry just because it doesn't rhyme. Nor again does a thing become poetical because it makes no sense as prose, and is quite unintelligible to ordinary common sense. Nor will any amount of disturbance of the ordinary rules of grammar, the freedom called 'poetic license', in and of itself make poetry, any more than a liquor license can make liquor. In other words both the old idea of rhymed verse turned out to measure, and the new idea of free verse turned out to grass, are equally erroneous.

> STEPHEN B. LEACOCK, *How to write*, 1943.

In what Canadian poets have tried to do there is an interest for Canadian readers much deeper than what the achievement in itself justifies.

> NORTHROP FRYE, *Can. forum*, Dec., 1943, 207.

Go, find your house and inse—t the key and put down the night-lock.
Undress with the blinds down and touch the pillows, and dream
Of Pickthall walking hand in hand with her fairies
And Lampman turning his back on Ottawa.

> RAYMOND SOUSTER, "To the Canadian poets", 1944.

His lines run wherever his pen goes,
Mine grope the miles from heart to head;
His will tire before he does;
Mine will move when I am dead.

> ROBERT FINCH, "Poet on poet", 1946.

"But, but...", you say, "But, but..."
But me no buts.
The one thing that our poets need is guts.

> L. A. MACKAY, "And spoil the child", 1948.

POKER (GAME).

Poker is not a game but an education.
> SIR WILLIAM VAN HORNE, qu., W. Vaughan, *Van Horne*, 1920.

I hold only two pairs of deuces.
> CHARLES J. DOHERTY (d.1931), in his first poker game.

POLITICAL PARTIES.

Party is merely a struggle for power.
> Attributed incorrectly to SIR JOHN A. MACDONALD. At London, Ont., 1860, he said, "There were, unfortunately, no great principles on which parties were divided... politics became a mere struggle for office".

We must support our supporters.
> JOHN SANDFIELD MACDONALD, Premier of Ontario, 1867-71.

But in this country what is there for Conservatives to conserve or for Reformers to reform?
> GOLDWIN SMITH, in *Can. monthly* April, 1872.

When a matter of great importance is brought home to the minds of the people the withes of party become as tow. This is our encouragement and the source of our hope.
> W. A. FOSTER, speech before Canadian National Association, Feb. 1875.

The idolatry of the heathen is not greater than the idolatry of party politics today.
> GEORGE M. GRANT, 1884: qu., Can. Hist. Assoc., *Report*, 1942, 6.

The ins and outs cannot be segregated under the old names of Reformer and Conservative. Tory and Grit are merely synonymous with cat and dog and convey no notion save that of difference in momentum.
> W. A. FOSTER, *Canada first; memorial*, 1890, 55.

The Liberals are the continental, their opponents the anti-continental party.
> GOLDWIN SMITH, in *Bystander*, May, 1890.

It is not enough to have good principles; we must have organization also. Principles without organization may lose, but organization without principles may often win.
> SIR WILFRID LAURIER, speech at opening of Reform Club. Ottawa, June 19, 1893.

Parties are not made to order. They are born out of great issues. They degenerate into factions.
> JOHN WILLISON, speech, Can. Club, Toronto, Feb. 15, 1904.

The Liberals and Conservatives differ very little really in their opinions upon crucial questions, and their views as to administration are almost identical... They have come to regard each other without alarm: they know each other too well and resemble each other too closely.

ANDRÉ SIEGFRIED, *Race question*, 1907, 143.

[Politicians] exert themselves to prevent the formation of homogeneous parties divided according to creed or race or class. The purity of political life suffers from this, but perhaps the very existence of the Federation is the price. The existing parties are thus entirely harmless.

A. SIEGFRIED, *Race question*, 1907, 143.

The first loyalty of a public man is to consider the welfare of the people he represents. If he is a party man his next duty will be to work faithfully in the interests of his party, and in so doing he will be working both in the interests of his party and of the country. But he must never forget that the permanent strength of any party must rest on the firm basis that its policy and administration is superior to that of any other party offering its services.

JOHN OLIVER, Premier of B. C., 1918-27.

In Canada ideas are not needed to make parties, for these can live by heredity and, like the Guelfs and Ghibellines of mediæval Italy, by memories of past combats.

JAMES BRYCE (Viscount), *Canada, an actual democracy*, 1921, 19.

The day is passing when political parties can get into office and run the country merely because they are political parties.

BROOKE CLAXTON, in *Can. hist. rev.*, 1934, 68.

The political party is apparently no longer able to provide necessary compromise without the sacrifice of principles. The absence of consistency in the attitude of any English Canadian party or public leader points to the fundamental corruption of Canadian political life.

H. A. INNIS, *Pol. econ. in mod. state*, 1946, xii.

POLITICAL PHRASES.

(See also: PERSONALITIES (NICKNAMES); POLITICAL SLOGANS)

Baldwin Reformers.

Dissatisfied Reformers who joined with Sir Allan MacNab, 1854; Baldwin, in retirement, gave approval to the combination which came to represent Liberal-Conservatism under Sir John A. Macdonald; also, "Baldwin Liberals".

Ballots Before Bullets.

Phrase originating in the policy advocated by Arthur Meighen in his speech in Hamilton, Nov. 16, 1925; see also: WAR.

The Baneful Domination letter. See: ENGLAND — letter by Joseph Hume, 1834.

The Battle of the Maps.

The negotiations which led to the fixing of the boundary between Canada and Maine by the Webster-Ashburton Treaty of Aug. 9, 1842, during which both parties concealed maps favourable to the other.

Better Terms.

The readjustment of financial relations between the Dominion and Nova Scotia, sanctioned by order-in-council Jan. 25, 1869, and which led Joseph Howe, who had been demanding better terms. to enter Sir John A. Macdonald's cabinet five days later.

The Big Push letter. See: ELECTION FUNDS — letter by George Brown to John Simpson, 1872.

The Big Seven.

Phrase sometimes applied to the leaders of Confederation: Macdonald, Galt, Brown. Cartier, McGee, Tupper, and Tilley.

The Blank Cheque. See: LABOUR.

The Blockers' Brigade.

E. Macdonald, Frank B. Carvell, and *A. K. MacLean,* followers of Laurier, noted for their ability to prolong debate in the House of Commons.

The Brawling Brood of Bribers.

C. F. FRASER, Commissioner of public works, Ontario, in debate on a bribery case, Mar. 17, 1884. Originally, "This prowling brood of bribers, hatched under the eaves of the *Mail* building" — a stenographic error resulted in the alliterative phrase.

The Bread and Butter Assembly.

Popular name for Upper Canada Assembly session of 1836-37; see: PARLIAMENT.

The British Party.

Term used in Lower Canada before 1837; the small but powerful minority among the English-speaking people who exploited English and French alike; see Durham's *Report*, 1839.

The Brownites.

Also, "The Brownies"; followers of Georges Brown in Ontario, especially those who opposed Macdonald in the first general election, 1867.

The Bureaucrats.

The English-speaking minority in Lower Canada who held monopoly of administration, before 1841; also called the "Château Clique".

The Cabinet of All the Talents.

The members of Laurier's government formed July 13, 1896, including Fielding Mowat, Mulock, Sifton, Cartwright. Blair, and others; also. "The Ministry of All the Talents". from the phrase used to describe Pitt's cabinet of 1806.

The Cabinet of Antiques.

NICHOLAS FLOOD DAVIN, M. P. for West-Assiniboia, on the Bowell Administration, 1894-96.

The Campaign of Picnics.

The election of 1878. won by the Conservatives, returning Sir John Macdonald to power, after the Pacific Scandal.

Canada First.

The motto, based on a suggestion by J. D. EDGAR, of the Toronto nationalist group called after this

phrase, sometimes known as The Twelve Apostles; the movement was active 1868-75; also the title of a pamphlet by a leader, W. A. FOSTER, pub. in 1871, which served as a guide; used as a slogan by Conservatives, general election 1930.

Carnarvon Terms of Separation.

British Columbia's union with Canada was dependent on construction of the Canadian Pacific Railway, the completion of which was delayed after 1873; Lord Carnarvon, colonial secretary, in 1874 arranged an adjustment of the terms, including completion by December 31, 1890.

The Castor Party.

Phrase originated in 1885 to designate the Ultramontane element in Quebec.

The Champion of Provincial Rights.

A reference to Sir Oliver Mowat, Liberal Premier of Ontario, 1872-96.

Charter-sellers.

Liberals' term for those who continued to support Sir John A. Macdonald after the Pacific Scandal, 1873.

The Château Clique.

The English-speaking minority in Lower Canada who held monopoly of administration, before 1841; also called "The Bureaucrats".

Clear Grits. See: CLEAR GRITS.

The Clergy Reserves.

The land set apart by the Constitutional Act of 1791 "for the support and maintenance of a Protestant Clergy" in Upper Canada; in Lower Canada reserves were established in 1796. In Upper Canada the Clergy Reserves were first considered an obstruction to settlement, later, a grievance on religious grounds.

Commercial Union.

L. S. HUNTINGTON, H. of C., *Debates*, Mar. 21, 1870 in a speech advocating a customs union with the United States. The scheme was first proposed by IRA GOULD in a speech to the Montreal Board of Trade (Montreal *Gazette*, Feb. 18, 1852). The term "unrestricted reciprocity" was later adopted as less repugnant to Canadians.

The Country above Party.

The watchword of the CANADA FIRST group, 1868-75.

Cross Benchers.

Term used in 1920 to describe dissident Liberals, including T. A. Crerar and Michael Clark, who moved to seats between the right and left of the Speaker in the semi-circular theatre in Victoria Museum where the House of Commons convened after the Parliament Building fire, 1916; the Independent Party.

The Dark Lantern Brigade.

Conservative press term for the Liberal government members of H. of C. Public accounts committee, 1908, investigating sales of timber limits in the North West.

The Devil's Dozen. See: "The Noble Thirteen".

The Double C. B.

In 1867, when Sir John Macdonald received the K.C.B., Sir Alexander Galt declined the lesser honour of Commander of the Bath. out of pique; the same year Galt, who had an interest in the Commercial Bank (Ontario), quarreled with Macdonald over its winding-up, and resigned from the cabinet.

Double Majority.

Political support of English from Upper Canada and French from Lower Canada in Legislature which sustained administrations in power during 1850's, until 1858, when it was condemned. See letter, René Caron to William Draper, Sept. 17, 1845, qu., W. Weir, *Sixty years in Canada*, 1903, 23.

The Double Shuffle.

On August 6, 1858, the Macdonald-Cartier government changed the portfolios of all ministers to avoid by-elections ("the shuffle"), and the next day each returned to his original department ("the double shuffle").

The Family Compact.

MARSHALL S. BIDWELL, letter to William W. Baldwin, 1828: "I shall be happy to consult with your-self and Mr. Rolph on the measures to be adopted to relieve this pro-vince from the evils which a family compact have brought upon it."

The Family-Company-Compact.

AMOR DE COSMOS, in Victoria, B. C., *British Colonist*, 1859, vol. 1, no. 10; a reference to the policies of the governor, Sir James Douglas.

The Farmers' Platform.

Demands on tariff reform presented by delegates from the West and Ontario to the Laurier government, December, 1910, during "Siege of Ottawa".

The Fathers of Confederation. See: CONFEDERATION, FATHERS OF.

The Fathers of Responsible Government.

Term applied to Robert Baldwin and Louis Lafontaine, about 1851.

The five-cent speech, See: FINANCE — speech by W. L. M. King, 1930.

The Fourteenth Colony.

American Revolutionary term for Canada.

The Gagging Bill.

A nickname for "An Act to prevent certain meetings within this Pro-vince", passed by the Legislative Assembly, Upper Canada, 1817 (58 Geo. III, ch. 11); ROBERT GOURLAY in the *Niagara Spec-tator*, Dec. 3, 1817 wrote some doggerel verses titled, "Gagg'd, — by Jingo", in protest.

Gentlemen, I am within the lines of Torres Vedras. I will get out of them when it suits me, and not before.

SIR WILFRID LAURIER, speech in Morrisburg, Oct. 8, 1895, on Mani-toba schools remedial legislation. Laurier told the story of Welling-ton's campaign in Portugal where he spent a safe summer within the lines of Torres Vedras, watch-ing the enemy to the frustration of Marshall Massena, commander of the French, who could not assail Wellington 'within the lines'.

The Ginger Group.

The six, later ten, members of the Progressive Party in the House of Commons who seceded in June, 1924. The phrase was earlier used to denote a group of Conservative members, including W. F. Nickle, during the term of Union Government, 1917-21

The Great Coalition.

On June 30, 1864, Sir John A. Macdonald formed a ministry which included Reform Liberals George Brown, Oliver Mowat. and William McDougall.

The Great Ministry.

The second Lafontaine-Baldwin government, March, 1848 - October, 1851; a popular term; also called, "The Ministry of all the Talents". and, "The Great Administration".

The Halifax Award.

In 1877 Canada received $4,420,882 from U. S. as compensation for value of her inshore fisheries.

Hepburn's Hussars.

Popular name for police body organized by Premier Mitchell Hepburn at the time of the Ontario Automobile Workers' strike, Oshawa, 1937.

Hiving the Grits.

Sir John A. Macdonald. phrase used April, 1882, to describe redistribution of Ontario seats and an alteration of boundaries to the disadvantage of the Liberals.

Hunting in couples.

A reference to the political campaigning of Sir John A. Macdonald and John Sandfield Macdonald, first premier of Ontario, in 1867.

The Khaki Election.

A popular name for the election of 1917.

The landswap scandal.

Quebec phrase for an affair which forced the resignation of Gédéon Ouimet, Prime Minister, in 1874.

Liberals in a hurry.

A popular phrase for the twelve Liberal-Progressives and Progressives who, under the leadership of Robert Forke, joined the Liberals in H. of C., 1926.

Maritime Rights.

Phrase given publicity by H. J. Congdon, of Dartmouth, N. S., in a series of newspaper articles, late 1924; used in political campaigns 1925 in demands for economic readjustments considered necessary to balance losses since Confederation.

Men in sheepskin coats. See: Immigration.

The Ministry of All the Talents.

Also, "The Great Ministry", applied to the second Baldwin-Lafontaine ministry, 1848-51. See also: "Cabinet of All the Talents".

Mr. Speaker, there ain't nothing to it!

John Henry Pope, Minister of Railways, about 1885; attributed to him by Peter Mitchell (*Debates*, 1888. II, 1689). Some authorities say this was Pope's curt answer to charges made by Edward Blake.

The National Policy. See: National Policy; Political Slogans.

A Nest of Traitors. See: "The seven Bolters".

A New Deal.

Popular term, from U. S., given to policies proposed by R. B. Bennett in a series of broadcasts, January, 1935.

The new National Policy.

Term used for the platform of the National Progressive Party, at Winnipeg convention, Jan. 6, 1920. See also: National Policy.

The New Nationality. See: Nationality.

The Nine Martyrs.

The Liberals who supported the Coalition in Ontario's first government, 1867, among them McGill, Lauder, Cockburn, Boyd, and Beatty.

No Yankee Dictation!

A cry raised, 1872, by opponents of American control of the Canadian Pacific Railway Company.

The Noble Thirteen.

The Conservatives who voted against Sir John A. Macdonald on the Jesuit Estates Act, 1889; so-called by their Ontario supporters; nick-named the "Devil's Dozen" by Macdonald.

Not party, but the people.

GOLDWIN SMITH, slogan adopted for his publication, *The Bystander*, Feb. 1880.

The Old Guard.

The 45 Conservative followers of Macdonald in the House of Commons, 1874 to 1878, after the "Pacific Scandal".

On to Ottawa!

Slogan of the B. C. relief-camp strikers on their march to Ottawa, ended at Regina, July 1, 1935; organized by Communists.

The Pacific Scandal.

On April 2, 1873, Lucius S. Huntington charged in the House of Commons that Sir Hugh Allan and associates of the Canadian Pacific Railway had advanced money to Sir John A. Macdonald and his supporters to aid them in elections; these charges were proved correct and the result led to the election of the Liberals to power. See also: PACIFIC SCANDAL.

Le Parti rouge.

The party organized in Lower Canada under the auspices of Louis-Joseph Papineau about 1850; other leading members were A. A. Dorion, J. B. E. Dorion, L. H. Holton, and C. J. Laberge.

The Patent Combination.

Originated by FRANCIS HINCKS to describe J. Sandfield Macdonald's alliance with the Tories in his, Ontario's first, provincial government, 1867; also used by Macdonald to describe his cabinet.

The Patriots.

From the French "patriotes", the name assumed by Papineau's followers in Lower Canada who were associated in the rebellion of 1837.

Peasants in sheepskin coats.

Phrase used by Conservative Party speakers, election November, 1900; a reference to the type of immigrants preferred by Clifford Sifton. See also: IMMIGRATION.

Put me among the yeas.

SIR FRANCIS HINCKS, in House of Assembly, Sept. 5, 1854, on changing his vote for Speaker in favour of an opponent from Lower Canada, Louis V. Sicotte.

Ready, aye ready! See: CANADIAN-BRITISH RELATIONS.

The Rebellion Losses Bill.

The popular name for the Act of Indemnification, 1849, which provided for a commission to inquire into losses incurred during the rebellion of 1837.

The Red Parlour.

Liberal Party phrase, 1878, used in denunciation of consultation between the government and the manufacturers in determining amount of protection for various industries as part of the "National Policy".

Responsible Government.

A phrase first used by the Upper Canada Reformers in 1829, meaning complete departmental responsibility of the Executive. See also: RESPONSIBLE GOVERNMENT.

Responsible Government and the Voluntary Principle.

Motto of the *Examiner* established by Francis Hincks, Toronto, July 3, 1838; also of the Baldwin Reform party.

Revolt of the Eighteen.

Repudiation of Reciprocity in election of 1911 by group of Toronto Liberals, organized by Clifford Sifton and Zebulon Lash.

The Ross Bible.

Readings, omitting parts of the Old Testament, adopted by Sir George W. Ross for Ontario schools; term used in provincial election of 1886.

Rule or ruin.

Phrase used by the Reformers in criticising Sir Francis Hincks when he joined with Sir John Macdonald in the first coalition government, 1854, known as the McNab-Morin government.

The Sandfield Macdonald surplus.

The surplus of three million dollars gathered from the small revenues of the province of Ontario during the four years of government under John Sandfield Macdonald, 1867-71.

The Scandal Session.

House of Commons session, 1891-2. Conservatives, especially Sir Hector Langevin, were charged with political corruption; in Quebec similar charges were brought against the Liberals, especially Honoré Mercier.

The Seven Bolters.

The ministers, George E. Foster, Sir Charles H. Tupper, A. R. Dickey, W. H. Montague, J. G. Haggart, W. B. Ives, J. F. Wood, who resigned Jan. 4, 1896 from the cabinet of Sir Mackenzie Bowell, who called them "A Nest of Traitors".

The Shadow Government.

Also called "The Shadow Cabinet"; the ministry of seven members without portfolio who were unable to sit in the House until re-elected after accepting office under the Crown; formed by Arthur Meighen at noon, June 29, it lasted to the morning of July 2, 1926.

The Short Administration.

The Brown-Dorion administration. August 2 to 6, 1858.

The Siege of Ottawa.

Representations made to the Laurier government against the tariff by 811 farmers from the West and Ontario, December, 1910.

Siftonism.

CONSERVATIVE PARTY Opposition phrase of 1906, on the extending of the discretionary powers of departmental officials.

The Smuggling Inquiry.

Popular name for the investigation of the Customs and Excise Department by a special committee of the House of Commons beginning Feb. 8, 1926.

The Solid Eighteen.

The Liberals who won all seats in Nova Scotia in the election of 1904.

The thin red line.

CONSERVATIVE PARTY term, Manitoba, February 1905, when court investigations revealed that R. E. A. Leach, Liberal party organizer crossed off names of Conservatives from voters' lists with red ink.

The Twelve Apostles. See "Canada First".

The Unholy Alliance.

Term used by SIR WILFRID LAURIER, speech in St. John, N. B., Aug. 28. 1911, in Reciprocity election, to describe link between Borden and the Quebec Nationalists.

The United Farmers of Alberta, Our Motto Equity.

The official title of the United Farmers, after joining with the Canadian Society of Equity, 1909.

Unrestricted Reciprocity.

Free trade with the U. S., advocated by the Liberals, especially Cartwright, in 1887, and a chief plank in their platform of 1891. See also: "Commercial union"; RECIPROCITY.

POLITICAL SLOGANS.

A British subject I was born, a British subject I will die!

CONSERVATIVE PARTY, election 1891, from a statement by Sir John A. Macdonald. See MACDONALD, SIR JOHN A.

Build Up Ontario.

GEORGE W. ROSS, slogan announced by him for Ontario Liberal party of 1902, at Toronto, Nov. 11, 1901.

By a Party, With a Party, but for the Country.

CONSERVATIVE PARTY, 1875; used by SIR JOHN A. MACDONALD, speech, in Montreal, Nov. 24, 1875. See also: "With the Party, By the Party, For the Country".

Canada First; Always Canada!

SIR WILFRID LAURIER'S motto, election of 1904: also, "Canada first, Canada last and Canada always".

Canada First, then the Empire.

R. B. BENNETT, tariff policy as described in election of 1930.

Canada for the Canadians.

Used by opponents of Sir John Macdonald's government in 1872 when advocating that the charter for a transcontinental railway be refused Sir Hugh Allen's Canada Pacific company which was claimed to be dominated by Americans. SIR JOHN A. MACDONALD used the phrase as an election slogan, 1878. Associated with the Canadian Manufacturers' Association, about 1910. Used as election slogan by ARTHUR MEIGHEN in 1920's; by R. B. BENNETT in 1930's.

Canada for Us, not for U. S.

CONSERVATIVE PARTY slogan, election 1911.

Don't be Robbed of the Robb Budget.

LIBERAL PARTY slogan, election of 1926.

Don't Turn the Liberty Loan over to Quebec to Spend.

CONSERVATIVE PARTY slogan, election of 1917.

Empire or Continent, Which?

CONSERVATIVE PARTY, election of 1911.

Follow my white plume!

LIBERAL PARTY election of 1911. SIR WILFRID LAURIER, on returning from England, spoke in Montreal, July 11, 1911, — "Henry of Navarre at the battle of Ivry said, 'Follow my white plume, and you will find it always in the forefront of honour'. Like Henry IV, I say to you young men, 'Follow my white plume' —

the white hairs of sixty-nine years — and you will, I believe I can say it without boasting, find it always in the forefront of honour".

French Canadians First!

PARTI ROUGE plank, withdrawn in 1850.

Hands off Manitoba — No coercion.

The motto of the EQUAL RIGHTS LEAGUE, on the Manitoba School question; in an address issued by the League, of which D'Alton McCarthy was president, in 1896; used by Liberals in general election of that year.

Has the N. P. made you rich?

WILLIAM PETERSON, Liberal campaigner, a favorite phrase during 1896 election; a reference to National Policy.

Howe and Better Terms.

CONSERVATIVE PARTY slogan in Hants, N.S., by-election, 1868, which Joseph Howe contested successfully after he entered the cabinet of Sir John A. Macdonald.

Hurrah for Sir Francis Head and British Connection.

The rallying-cry of the Family Compact in Toronto, election of 1836.

It's King or Chaos!

LIBERAL PARTY, campaign of 1935.

It's Time for a Change.

CONSERVATIVE PARTY slogan, Ontario, directed against the Mowat and Hardy governments, 1894 and after; also, Conservative Party slogan, Nova Scotia, June, 1925.

The land for the people!

CONSERVATIVE PARTY rallying cry, 1904, referring to western lands described by Sifton as suitable only for grazing.

The land for the settler and not for the speculator.

LIBERAL PARTY slogan in the West, election of 1896.

The land for the settler, the price for the public.

> EDWARD BLAKE, address to electors of West Durham, May 23, 1882; Liberal party slogan in general election of that year; a reference to railway land-grant policy.

Laurier and the Larger Canada.

> LIBERAL PARTY slogan, election of 1904.

Laurier Prosperity.

> LIBERAL PARTY phrase, election of 1911.

Let Laurier finish his work.

> LIBERAL PARTY election slogan 1904, and 1908.

Let Robb bring in the Next Budget.

> LIBERAL PARTY slogan, election of 1926.

Let the farmer have his chance!

> LIBERAL PARTY, Quebec, election of 1911.

Let the People Decide.

> CONSERVATIVE PARTY slogan in attack on Reciprocity, election of 1911.

Let Uncle Sam go his own Way; our Way is with John Bull.

> LIBERAL PARTY tariff slogan, election of 1930.

Let Well Enough Alone!

> CONSERVATIVE PARTY cry, election of 1911, on Reciprocity, from a letter by SIR WILLIAM VAN HORNE, March 8, 1912, pub. in the press.

Meighen Will Lead Us Through.

> CONSERVATIVE PARTY, general election, 1921.

Millions for Corruption, but not a Cent for Nova Scotia.

> LIBERAL PARTY, Nova Scotia, anti-Confederation slogan in repeal election, 1886.

Mowat and the Queen, or Morrison and the Pope.

> LIBERAL PARTY of Ontario, provincial by-election, South Ontario, December, 1857; ref. to Oliver Mowat and J. C. Morrison.

Mowat must go.

> CONSERVATIVE PARTY of Ontario, provincial election 1890.

The National Policy.

> A phrase originated by SIR CHARLES TUPPER in House of Commons, February, 1870 to describe a policy of economic nationalism and protection. Adopted by Macdonald and used in election of 1878, the National policy was introduced by Tilley in his budget speech of Mar. 14, 1879. See also: NATIONAL POLICY.

No Looking to Washington!

> CONSERVATIVE PARTY slogan, election of July, 1861.

No Pay to Rebels!

> Tory denunciation of the Rebellion Losses Bill, 1849.

No Popery!

> Slogan used by opponents of Sir John A. Macdonald, election of 1857.

No Truck nor Trade with the Yankees!

> CONSERVATIVE PARTY anti-reciprocity slogan, 1911; attributed to SIR GEORGE FOSTER.

Non-sectarian Schools!

> GEORGE BROWN, general election, 1857.

The Old Man, the Old Flag, and the Old Policy.

> CONSERVATIVE PARTY campaign motto, election, 1891, coined by L. P. KRIBBS, news editor, Toronto *Empire;* also varied, as, "The Old Man, the Old Flag, the Old Party", and, "The Old Flag, the Old Policy, the Old Leader"; a reference to Sir John A. Macdonald.

Ourselves Alone.

> LIBERAL PARTY slogan local to Nova Scotia and New Brunswick, election, 1926.

Put King Back and Keep Prosperity.

> LIBERAL PARTY, election of 1926.

Reciprocity of trade, or reciprocity of tariffs.

> CONSERVATIVE PARTY, 1876-78, especially during election of 1878.

Reform the Senate!

LIBERAL PARTY slogan, 1893.

Rep. by Pop.

An abbreviation of "Representation by Population", a Tory Party plank, about 1849 to 1853, later supported by the Clear Grits and the Brown Reformers, in Upper Canada. (See also: PARLIAMENTARY REPRESENTATION)

Shall Tarte rule?

CONSERVATIVE PARTY war-cry, Ontario, general election, 1900.

Support the Governor.

CONSERVATIVE PARTY cry, New Brunswick election, July, 1856; refers to Lieutenant-Governor H. T. Manners-Sutton, who had dissolved the Assembly against advice of his council on the question of prohibition of liquor.

Thicken population!

HERBERT GREENFIELD, Premier of Alberta, slogan originated in 1925.

The traitor's hand is at thy throat, Ontario! Ontario!
Then kill the tyrant with thy vote, Ontario! Ontario!

First lines of a Liberal Party song written by JOHN W. BENGOUGH for the June, 1882 election, sung to the tune of 'Maryland, my Maryland'; Edward Blake, leader, said the song would cost him Quebec as it referred to French Canadians.

Union and Progress.

CONSERVATIVE PARTY slogan in 1867.

Vote against National Suicide.

CONSERVATIVE PARTY, election of 1911; an anti-Reciprocity slogan.

A Vote for Borden is a Vote for Bourassa.

LIBERAL PARTY slogan in Ontario, election of 1911; in Quebec, the Party slogan was "A Vote for Bourassa is a Vote for Borden", used first by SIR WILFRID LAURIER, speech in St. Eustache, Aug. 22.

A Vote for Borden is a Vote for King and Flag and Country.

CONSERVATIVE PARTY, election of 1911.

A Vote for Laurier is a Vote for the Kaiser.

CONSERVATIVE AND UNIONIST PARTY, election of 1917.

Vote the Boys Home.

CONSERVATIVE PARTY of Nova Scotia, election, June, 1925.

With the Party, by the Party, for the Country.

CONSERVATIVE PARTY, Ontario provincial election, 1883; see also, "By a Party, With a Party, but for the Country".

Work Work! Work! Work!
Let Laurier finish his work.
Talk! Talk! Talk! Talk!
Let Borden keep on with his talk.

LIBERAL PARTY campaign song, chorus, 1908.

POLITICS.

(See also: CLASSES; CORRUPTION; GOVERNMENT; PATRONAGE)

It is in politics as in horses: when a man has a beast that's near about up to the notch, he'd better not swap him; if he does, he's een amost sure to get one not so good as his own. My rule is, I'd rather keep a critter whose faults I do know, than change him for a beast whose faults I don't know.

T. C. HALIBURTON, *Sam Slick*, 1836, ch. XIV.

Now with us the country is divided into two parties, of the mammoth breed, — the *ins* and the *outs*, the administration and the opposition.

T. C. HALIBURTON, *Sam Slick*, 1836, ch. XVIII.

It's in politics as in racin', everything depends upon a fair start.

T. C. HALIBURTON, *Sam Slick*, 1836, ch. XXX.

You hear nothin' but politics, politics, politics, one everlastin' give, give, give.

T. C. HALIBURTON, *Sam Slick*, 1836, ch. XXXI.

Let patriots flourish, other deeds
displace,
Let adverse men new politics embrace;
Yet come it will when wisdom may
control,
And one sound policy conduct the
whole.

STANDISH O'GRADY, "The emigrant",
1841.

You may rest assured... those who
support me, I will support.

SIR CHARLES METCALFE, to Sir
Alexander Galt; qu. in letter, Galt
to G. R. Robinson, Dec. 7, 1843.

Our objects are open and avowed.
We seek no concealment, for we have
nothing to conceal.

ROBERT BALDWIN, speech, Mar. 25,
1844, to Reform Association.

Here lies the man who denounced
party government, that he might form
one; and professing justice to all
parties, gave every office to his own.

JOSEPH HOWE, N. S. Assembly, Feb.
24, 1845, a suggested epitaph for
James W. Johnston, Premier.

If we don't make a disturbance
about this, we shall never get in.

SIR ALLAN MACNAB, remark to John
Wilson, on the demonstrations made
during the trial of the leaders of
the rioters who burner down the
legislative building, April 1849, in
Montreal.

If I am supported by their voice, I
shall feel that I am right; if condemned,
I am ready to retire into private life,
and, perhaps, I am now fitted for little
else.

SIR ALLAN MACNAB, speech, House
of Assembly, May 23, 1856, on his
resignation from the prime minis-
tership.

I don't like agitation, even for a
good object.

T. C. HALIBURTON, speech in
Glasgow, 1857.

I may say generally, that, if elected,
my desire is to perform my duty in
Parliament in the spirit and with the
views which become a Christian politician,

SIR OLIVER MOWAT, letter, *To the
Free and Independent Electors of
South Ontario, Dec. 15, 1857;* the
phrase "Christian politician" was
frequently used by Mowat's opponents.

No go.

JOHN SANDFIELD MACDONALD, early in 1858, telegram to Sir John A.
Macdonald on being offered a
place, with two other Reformers,
in the cabinet.

If public life is the noblest of all
callings, it is the vilest of all trades.

GOLDWIN SMITH, *Lectures on
modern history,* 1861, 19; also:
"Politics, the noblest of all callings,
but the meanest of all trades", in,
Essays on questions of the day,
1893, 100.

Politically we were a pack of fools,
but we were honest in our folly, and
no man need blush at forty for the
follies of one-and- twenty, unless indeed,
he still perseveres in them.

THOMAS D'ARCY MCGEE, speech
in Wexford, Ireland, May, 1865. on
the Young Ireland movement.

We are all mere petty provincial
politicians at present; perhaps by and
by some of us will rise to the level
of national statesmen.

SIR JOHN A. MACDONALD, statement
to the Governor-general at time
of Confederation.

Anybody may support me when I am
right. What I want is a man that
will support me when I am wrong.

SIR JOHN A. MACDONALD, to Senator Dickey, of Nova Scotia, at
Confederation, qu., Biggar, *Anecdotal life,* 1891, 117; also applied
to Toronto *Mail* when it became
independent. L. J. Burpee, *Oxford
ency. Can. hist.,* 1926, 248, states
Macdonald said it to George M.
Grant, of Nova Scotia, later Principal of Queen's University.

What the hell has Strathroy ever
done for me?

JOHN SANDFIELD MACDONALD, Premier of Ontario to deputation from
town of Strathroy asking that it be
made a separate county seat, 1868.

He is finally dead as a Canadian
politician. The correspondence between
Cartier and himself, in which he comes

squarely out for independence, has rung his death-knell, and I shall take precious good care to keep him where he is. He has seduced Cartwright away, and I have found out how it was managed. Cartwright and he formed at the Club last session a sort of mutual admiration society, and they agreed that they were the two men fit to govern Canada.

> SIR JOHN A. MACDONALD, letter to Sir John Rose, Feb. 23, 1870, on Sir Alexander T. Galt.

Poetry was the maiden I loved, but politics was the harridan I married.

> JOSEPH HOWE, in his later years.

The question would be decided at once and forever if decided in a sense of leniency, but not if decided in a harsh sense, in a sense of mistaken justice; for there is no more certain fact, as proved by the most unerring testimony of historical events, than that political offences must sooner or later be forgiven.

> SIR WILFRID LAURIER, H. of C., Debates, Feb. 12, 1875, 117; Riel debate.

For us, sons of France, political sentiment is a passion; while, for the Englishmen, politics are a question of business.

> SIR WILFRID LAURIER, speech in Montreal, May 19, 1884. (trans.)

A public man should have no resentments.

> SIR JOHN A. MACDONALD, to his secretary, Joseph Pope; qu. in Pope, Sir John A. Macdonald vindicated, 1912.

[The politics of British Columbia are] government appropriations.

> ANON., to Goldwin Smith, qu. in Canada and Can. question, 1891, 220.

I hate politics, and what are considered their appropriate methods. I hate notoriety, public meetings, public speeches, caucuses, and everything that I know of that is apparently the necessary incident of politics — except doing public work to the best of my ability. Why should I go where the doing of honest work will only make me hated

and my ministry unpopular, and where I can only gain reputation and credit by practising arts which I detest, to acquire popularity?

> SIR JOHN J. C. ABBOTT, letter to a friend in Ottawa, June 4, 1891.

Father, you have no idea how I enjoy and cherish my animosities.

> SIR CHARLES HIBBERT TUPPER, to his father on being chided for holding resentments against political opponents.

I believe that with a strong following the Ross government will carry out their policy of developing New Ontario. I am chiefly interested in that; for my own constituency must get a big share of the benefit and, in this respect, Manitoulin is my politics.

> ROBERT R. GAMEY, Ontario Legis. member for Manitoulin Island. interview in Toronto Globe, Jan. 30, 1903.

This thing they call irresolution is often the very pith and marrow of statesmanship.

> SIR JOHN WILLISON, Laurier, 1903, II, 218.

No one knows better than I do that the simple course in politics is not to comprise anything, but unfortunately it is not the road to practical progress.

> SIR CLIFFORD SIFTON, letter to a resident of Brandon, Man., 1905; qu. in Dafoe, Clifford Sifton, 290.

Our politics, our public life and thought, rise not to the level of our opportunity. The mud-bespattered politicians of the trade, the party men and party managers, give us in place of patriotic statecraft the sordid traffic of a tolerated jobbery. For bread, a stone. Harsh is the cackle of the little turkey-cocks of Ottawa, fighting the while as they feather their mean nest of sticks and mud, high on their river bluff.

> S. B. LEACOCK, Empire Club speech, Mar. 19, 1907.

Let Socialism tell us plainly what it means to do and how it means to do it. If inequalities of condition could be levelled today, the inequalities of capacity, by which they were originally created, would apparently renew them tomorrow.

> GOLDWIN SMITH, letter to Provincial Labour candidate, Toronto, Oct. 12, 1908.

I am being reluctantly forced to the conclusion that the worst foes of political independence are independents. They will not accept any opinion as honest unless it agrees with their own.

> SIR JOHN WILLISON, letter to H. I. Strang, about 1908.

Well, Sir, at this moment, I have only to say that history teaches us that defeats there are which are more honourable than victories. The gentlemen on the other side of this House are welcome to all the comfort they can get out of the Drummond-Arthabaska election.

> SIR WILFRID LAURIER, H. of C., *Debates*, Nov., 1910.

The chief fault of Canadians, politically, is their diffidence and their timidity. Imperialism has taught them insufficiency, and big, robust and strong as they are, they reflect their education. Our mean colonialism is part of our fibre.

> JOHN S. EWART, *Kingdom papers*, 1911, I, 54.

Contracting!

The laconic answer of a financier, who had contributed to both Liberal and Conservative parties in the election of 1911, on being asked what his politics really were; qu. by Peter McArthur in *The Forum*, Nov., 1911, 539.

Women have cleaned up things since time began, and if women get into politics there will be a cleaning up of pigeon-holes and forgotten corners in which the dust of years have fallen.

> NELLIE L. MCCLUNG, speech in Minneapolis, May 7, 1916.

Politics, after all, is the science of compromise.

> ROBERT C. (BOB) EDWARDS, *Calgary Eye Opener*, Feb. 5, 1921.

I know what a statesman is. He is a dead politician. We need more statesmen.

> ROBERT C. (BOB) EDWARDS, *Calgary Eye Opener*; attributed.

It is never a sound policy to harbour a grudge nor even to resent an injury, except when inspired by sheer malice.

> SIR WILFRID LAURIER, letter to a western supporter, qu., Skelton, *Laurier*, 1921.

Politics is working patriotism.

> CHARLES J. DOHERTY; attributed.

For it must be remembered that in politics, as in moral character, there is no static condition; and there is just the danger that we may mistake movements for progress, and confuse activity with advance.

> W. P. M. KENNEDY, *Can. hist. rev.*, 1921, 7.

The only person sure of himself is the man who wishes to leave things as they are, and he dreams of an impossibilitiy.

> GEORGE M. WRONG, *Can. hist. rev.*, 1921, 315.

The art of politics, which is the art of free human beings living together, is therefore the most interesting of all arts. It can only seem dull and dry to us if we don't see what it is and how it concerns us.

> HOWARD A. KENNEDY, *The book of the West*, 1925.

Anybody can start a movement by beginning with himself.

> S. B. LEACOCK, "Great national problems", in *Winnowed wisdom*, 1926.

I am not one of those who believe in divorcing federal and provincial politics in their entirety. It cannot be done. One cannot be a political chameleon.

> GORDON S. HARRINGTON, N. S. Minister of Mines, provincial election, Sept., 1928.

The political instinct of the race is practical rather than logical, and one observes an invariable tendency to avoid change until it is manifest.

> SIR ROBERT BORDEN, *Canada and the Commonwealth*, 1929, 86.

The political system, as it exists in all British countries, arose from rivalries which were fought out on battlefields before they were transferred to the civil arena; and in its ethics and its philosophies it reveals its origin. Politics in its more primitive and vigorous manifestations is not a game nor a sport, but a form of civil war, with only lethal weapons barred.

> J. W. DAFOE, in *Clifford Sifton*, 1931, 172.

Canadians can be radical, but they must be radical in their own peculiar way, and that way must be in harmony with our national traditions and ideals.

> AGNES MACPHAIL, speech, Can. Club, Toronto, Mar. 4, 1935.

There is something about party politics which causes leaders of the same party frequently to regard each other with a much more hearty dislike and distrust than they feel towards most members of the opposition.

> F. H. UNDERHILL, in *Can. hist. rev.*, 1939, 392.

I have never known an important issue in Canadian politics which has not been deeply influenced and sometimes determined in its result by factors of the most purely personal kind.

> JOHN W. DAFOE, to George V. Ferguson, paraphrased in his *Dafoe*, 1948, 46.

To compromise, no doubt, is to corrupt — to corrupt the simplicity of principle, the clarity of policy — but if so, then all politics corrupt and federal politics, the politics of the vast sectional and communal aggregations, especially so. To this conclusion all purists, all doctrinaires, and all Progressives, must ultimately come or abstain from power.

> W. L. MORTON, *The Progressive party*, 1950, 292.

POOR.

Well may I love the poor, greatly may I esteem the humble and the lowly, for poverty and adversity were my nurses, and in youth and want and misery my familiar friends; even now it yields a sweet satisfaction to my soul, that I can claim kindred with the obscure cottar, and the humble labourer, of my native, ever honoured, ever loved Scotland.

> WILLIAM LYON MACKENZIE, *Colonial Advocate*, June 10, 1824.

Poverty is keen enough, without sharpening its edge by poking fun at it.

> T. C. HALIBURTON, *Sam Slick*, 1836, ch. XXI.

The poor are everywhere more liberal, more obligin' and more hospitable, according to their means, than the rich are.

> THOMAS C. HALIBURTON, *Sam Slick*, 1838, 41.

Thank God for poverty
That makes and keeps us free,
And lets us go our unobtrusive way,
Glad of the sun and rain,
Upright, serene, humane,
Contented with the fortune of a day.

> BLISS CARMAN, "The word at St. Kavin's", 1901.

This country is full of people who are starving up to their positions.

> PETER MCARTHUR, *To be taken with salt*, 1903, 158.

Pauperism exists only because of charity and would soon pass away if almsgiving ceased.

> J. J. KELSO, *Poorhouses and charity*, 1905, 11.

Hum a hymn of sixpence,
A tableful of cards
Fingers slowly shuffling
Ambiguous rewards.
When the deck is opened
The pauper once more gave
His foes the kings and aces
And took himself the knave.

> ABRAHAM KLEIN, "Soirée of Velvel Kleinberger", 1936.

The sheep graze on a thousand hills,
The cattle roam upon the plains,
The cotton waits upon the mills,
The stores are bursting with their grains,
And yet these ragged ones that kneel
To take thy grace before their meal
Are said to be thy chosen ones,
Lord of the planets and the suns!

> E. J. PRATT, "The depression ends", 1937.

POPULATION.

(See also: MEN)

Get population, and all else shall be added unto you.

> JOSEPH CHAMBERLAIN, speech, London, Eng., Nov. 11, 1895, applied by others to Canada. Chamberlain said at Toronto Dec. 30, 1887, "The first object is to get population on the land".

Your first and last need is men — men of your own stock and ideals to develop and to fill your land that it may stand erect above the shadow of any fear from without or within.

> RUDYARD KIPLING, Can. Club Ottawa speech, Oct., 21, 1907.

Aye, such a little people, but growing, growing, growing, with a march that shall make us ten millions tomorrow, twenty millions in our children's time and a hundred millions yet ere the century runs out.

> STEPHEN LEACOCK, Empire Club speech, Toronto, 1907.

We can never be really prosperous until we are populous.

> A. C. FLUMERFELT, Can. Club Montreal, Jan. 22, 1917.

Canada is one of the very few big free spaces which are still left on our planet. Who will take possession of it? The question seems to be senseless at first sight. For Canada is already in somebody's possession. But we have to become accustomed to the idea that there is nothing stationary, unshakable now; neither the inherited habits and forms of government, nor the existing rights and possessions. It is very doubtful whether those nations who suffer from a tremendous surplus population will allow a few million people to call a whole continent their own, just because they happened to be the first to arrive there.

> COLIN ROSS, Canadian Nazi, Hamburg, Germany, 1934.

POWER.

Power has a natural tendency to corpulency.

> T. C. HALIBURTON, Sam Slick, 1836, ch. XVIII.

Anything that gives power to the masses will please the masses.

> T. C. HALIBURTON, Sam Slick, 1838, 34.

A power imprudently given to the executive, or to the people, is seldom or never got back.

> T. C. HALIBURTON, Sam Slick, 1838, 63.

No man and no party can be safely entrusted with uncontrolled power.

> SIR RICHARD CARTWRIGHT, Reminiscences, 1912.

He loved power. He must rule; he could not reign.

> F. W. HOWAY, British Columbia (Scholefield), 1913, II, 175, on Sir James Douglas.

Till power is brought to pooling
And masses share in ruling
There will not be an ending
Nor any peace for spending.

> F. R. SCOTT, "Dedication," in, Poetry mag., April, 1941.

THE PRAIRIES.

(See also: THE WEST)

This plain affords nothing but Beast and grass.

> HENRY KELSEY, Journal of a voyage, 1691, in the Kelsey papers, 1929, 3.

The Red River is an oasis in the midst of a desert, a vast treeless prairie on which scarcely a shrub is to be seen. The climate is unfavourable to the growth of grain; the summer though warm enough is too short in duration, so that even the few fertile spots could with difficulty mature a potato or a cabbage.

> MONTREAL Transcript, 1856.

Palliser's Triangle.

> CAPT. JOHN PALLISER, Report, 1863. 7: "This central desert extends, however, but a short way into the British territory, forming a triangle having for its base the 49th parallel from longitude 100° [Boissevain, Man.] to 114° W [Waterton Lakes, Alta.] with its apex reaching to the 52nd parallel of latitude [lat.

of Saskatoon, Sask.]". Probably first used in discussion regarding best route for the C.P.R., late 1870's.

The opening of the prairie lands would drain away our youth and strength. I am perfectly willing personally to leave the whole country a wilderness for the next half century, but I fear if the English do not go in, the Yankees will, and with that apprehension, I would gladly see a crown colony established there.

SIR JOHN A. MACDONALD, Mar. 26, 1865, letter to E. W. Watkin, *Macdonald papers*, Pub. Arch.

The most magnificent expanse of virgin soil that remains unsubdued on the face of the earth.

A. SUTHERLAND, *Summer in prairie land*, 1881.

The Prairie Bubble.
A term used to describe the inflation of western land values, followed by collapse in 1882.

Great prairies swept beyond our aching sight
Into the measureless West; uncharted realm,
Voiceless and calm, save when tempestuous wind
Rolled the rank herbage into billows vast,
And rushing tides which never found a shore.

CHARLES MAIR, *Tecumseh*, 1886.

That great prairie ocean, that sea of green and gold in this month of May.

GEORGE M. GRANT, address to Canadian Club, N. Y., 1887.

The country should have been left the same side up as God A'mighty made it.

Popular local statement regarding the land of south-east Alberta, about 1900.

With the help of the waters of the Bow we will make these prairies stink with flowers.

LORD SHAUGHNESSY, to a friend, 1903, on irrigation.

The Prairie which is the High Veldt, plus Hope, Activity, and Reward.

RUDYARD KIPLING, *Letters to the family*, 1908.

I'll dream again of fields of grain that stretch from sky to sky
And the little prairie hamlets where the cars go roaring by,
Wooden hamlets as I saw them — noble cities still to be.
To girdle stately Canada with gems from sea to sea.

SIR ARTHUR CONAN DOYLE, "The Athabaska Trail", 1919.

Wind-swept and fire-swept and swept with bitter rain,
This was the world I came to when I came across the sea —
Sun-drenched and panting, a pregnant, waiting plain
Calling out to humankind, calling out to me!

ISABEL ECCLESTONE MACKAY, "The homesteader", 1922.

No one is born in the Prairies who can help it, and no one dies there who can get out in time.

ANON., qu. by Ramsay Traquair, *Atlantic mo.*, June, 1923.

The Dust Bowl.
The area centered in Southern Saskatchewan, from an American phrase, early 1930's.

PRAISE.

Praise to the face is open disgrace.
THOMAS C. HALIBURTON, *Sam Slick's wise saws*, 1853, ch. XXVI.

Praise is pleasant, but I never seem able to apply it to myself.
MAJORIE PICKTHALL, letter to Sir Andrew Macphail, 1921.

PRECAMBRIAN SHIELD.

The manner in which natural obstacles have isolated the country from all other British possessions in the East is a matter of considerable weight; indeed it is *the* obstacle of the country, and one, I fear, almost beyond the remedies of art.

CAPT. J. PALLISER, Gt. Brit., *Parl. papers*, 1860, cd.2732, 5.

This region of swamps and sterile pinelands has opposed an effectual barrier to communication towards the Canadas, and has forced the traffic of these remote settlements to find an outlet through Minnesota.

> CAPT. W. J. TWINING, *Reports upon the boundary*, 1878, 48.

The Canadian Shield.

> EDUARD SUESS, *Autlitz der erde*, 1888, 42. (trans.)

The Precambrian shield dominates the history as it dominates the landscape of Canada.

> MARY Q. INNIS, *Econ. hist. of Can.*, 1935.

PRESENT.

Things can't and won't remain long as they are.

> THOMAS C. HALIBURTON, *Nature and human nature*, 1855, ch. XIX.

So all desire and all regret,
   And fear and memory, were naught;
One to remember or forget
   The keen desire our hands had caught;
Morrow and yesterday were naught.

> BLISS CARMAN, "Low tide on Grand Pré", 1889.

When we are young our time is all present. When we are old there is no present, but our time becomes the aggregate days and years.

> R. D. CUMMING, *Skookum Chuck fables*, 1915, 158.

Modernity is not a fad, it is the feeling for actuality.

> D. C. SCOTT, "Poetry and progress", 1922.

The Is is the same as the Will Be And both the same as before.

> A. J. M. SMITH, "For ever and ever, Amen", 1926.

And far from pagan thought is this
That out of travail, I can say
I need no future world of bliss —
I have it here today.

> CHARLES F. BOYLE, "Vita Anabilis", 1942.

I have always found the present sufficiently interesting to occupy most of my thought.

> W. L. MACKENZIE KING, qu., Hardy, *Mackenzie King of Canada*, 1949, 367.

PRICES.

A cheap article ain't always the best; if you want a real right down first chop, genu*wine* thing, you must pay for it.

> T. C. HALIBURTON, *Sam Slick*, 1838, 123.

We hear little at this moment throughout Canada save the talk of prices rising, real estate and rents going up, mechanics and labourers striking for more wages, provisions growing dearer day by day.

> TORONTO *Globe* June, 1854.

What do you want, gentlemen? Name your price and you shall have it.

> JOHN SANDFIELD MACDONALD, Premier of Ontario 1867-1871 to a delegation; attributed.

Our regular way in arriving at our prices is to find out the cost of material and labour, and then double, to make sure of the overhead. We then add the telephone number and multiply by two. But in this case we discovered that no one but ourselves has any supply, so the price has rocketed.

> A Toronto manufacturer to a buyer, qu., *Dalhousie rev.*, 1929, 376.

PRIDE.

When reason fails to convince, there's nothin left but ridicule. If they have no ambition, apply to their feelings, clap a blister on their pride and it will do the business. It's like puttin ginger under a horse's tail; it makes him carry up real hand*sum*, I tell you.

> T. C. HALIBURTON, *Clockmaker*, 1st. ser., 1836, 69.

Pride and temper is almost always at the bottom of schism, you will find.

> T. C. HALIBURTON, *Sam Slick*, 1840, 45.

I knew humility was the dress coat of pride.

T. C. HALIBURTON, *Sam Slick*, 1840, 46.

Wounded pride should be touched lightly. The skin is thin and plagy sensative.

T. C. HALIBURTON, *Sam Slick's wise saws*, 1853, I, 294.

I have no fear of present wrong;
I cannot dream of future ill,
Against the demon of regret
My pride must prove an amulet.

GEORGE F. CAMERON, "Ysolte", 1887.

PRIME MINISTER.

The life of a statesman is always an arduous one, and very often it is an ungrateful one.

SIR WILFRID LAURIER, H. of C., *Debates*, June 8, 1891.

It is the province of Ontario which has defeated us... It is becoming more and more manifest to me that it was not reciprocity that was turned down, but a Catholic premier.

SIR WILFRID LAURIER, letter, Oct. 5, 1911, qu., Skelton, *Laurier*, II, 382.

A prime minister under the party system as we have had it in Canada is of necessity an egotist and autocrat. If he comes to office without these characteristics his environment equips him with them as surely as a diet of royal jelly transforms a worker into a queen bee.

JOHN W. DAFOE, *Laurier*, 1922, 99.

In our Dominion where sections abound, a Dominion of races, of classes and of creeds, of many languages and many origins, there are times when no Prime Minister can be true to his trust to the nation he has sworn to serve, save at the temporary sacrifice of the party he is appointed to lead.

ARTHUR MEIGHEN, tribute to R. B. Bennett, Toronto, Jan. 16, 1939.

PRINCE EDWARD ISLAND.

From Glasgow the sensible Scots are pouring out amain. Those that are poor, and cannot pay their passage, or can rake together only a trifle, are going to a rascally heap of sand, rock and swamp, called Prince Edward Island, in the horrible Gulf of Saint Lawrence; but when the American vessels come with Indian corn and flour and pork and beef and poultry and eggs and butter and cabbages and green pease, and asparagus for the soldier, and other tax-eaters that we support upon that lump of worthlessness, — for the lump itself bears nothing but potatoes, — when these vessels return, the sensible Scots will go back in them for a dollar a head, and not a man of them will be left but bedridden persons.

WILLIAM COBBETT, about 1830; qu., Campbell, *Prince Edward Island*, 77.

Pay Ay.
"P. E.", or "Prince Edward Islander", an epithet used by Maine lumberjacks about 1840. Maritime lumberjacks accepted lower wages than the Americans.

Parva sub ingenti. (The small under [the protection of] the weak.)
Motto on provincial coat-of-arms.

There is a band within this land
who live in pomp and pride,
To fill their store they rob the poor;
in pleasure will they ride.
With dishes fine their tables shine;
they move in princely style.
Those are the knaves that made us slaves and sold Prince Edward Isle.

LARRY GORMAN, song, "The history of Prince Edward Island", 1873.

Long courted; won at last.
Words on arch of welcome to Lord Dufferin, in Charlottetown, July, 1873; a reference to the entry of the Province into Confederation nine years after the Charlottetown conference.

I found the Island in a high state of jubilation and quite under the impression that it is the Dominion that has been annexed to Prince Edward.

LORD DUFFERIN, letter to Sir J. A. Macdonald, 1873, qu. in *Can. hist. rev.*, 1933, 160.

The Garden of the Gulf.
Popular term for the province.

The Million Acre Farm.

A popular term.

PROGRESS.

Then [in 1868] blood pulsed in our veins, new hopes fired our hearts, new horizons lifted and widened, new visions came to us in the night watches. We faced geography and distance and fought them to a stand-still. We shamed the croaker and the pessimist and the coward into silence, and then re-created him, as a good citizen, at the glowing fires of optimism and hope. The plains were shod with steel, the mountains tamed and tunnelled, our national arteries were filled with a rich blood of commerce, our industries grew, our workmen multiplied, our villages became towns and our towns became cities, with astonishing rapidity. Across the seas we clasped hands with our sister-nations within the Empire and surrounded as with a cordon of defence the old Empire that gave us birth.

GEORGE E. FOSTER, H. of C., *Debates*, Feb. 14, 1911.

True progress can come only as the result of thoughful, continuous, co-operative effort. This progress will necessarily be slow, but it must be continuous. Nothing can hinder it more than the mistakes of thoughtless impatience.

HENRY WISE WOOD, *Grain growers' guide*, Jan. 29, 1919, 28.

It is not within the power of the properly constructed mind to be satisfied. Progress would cease if this were the case. The greatest joy of life is to accomplish. It is the getting. not the having. It is the giving, not the keeping. I am a firm believer in the theory that you can do or be anything that you wish in this world, within reason, if you are prepared to make the sacrifices, think and work hard enough and long enough.

SIR FREDERICK BANTING, qu., *Univ. of Toronto quarterly*, 1940-41, 252.

PROTECTION (TARIFF).

(See also: NATIONAL POLICY)

Protection.

SIR ALEXANDER GALT introduced the protection principle in the Tariff Act of 1858.

The word 'protection' itself must be taboo, but we can ring the changes on National Policy, paying the U. S. in their own coin.

SIR JOHN A. MACDONALD, letter to D. L. MacPherson, Feb. 20, 1872.

Protection is a monster when you come to look at it. It is the essence of injustice. It is the acme of human selfishness. It is one of the relics of barbarism.

ALEXANDER MACKENZIE, Prime Minister, letter of 1876.

Those who cared to be protected at all, wanted all the protection they could get. They were like the squaw who said of whisky, that 'a little too much was just enough'.

SIR JOHN A. MACDONALD, in debate on introduction of National Policy, 1878; qu., Biggar, *Anecdotal life*, 137.

Yes, Protection has done so much for me I must do something for Protection!

SIR JOHN A. MACDONALD to Goldwin Smith on the eve of 1878 election; qu. by Smith in letter to Toronto *Globe*, Sept. 23, 1895.

I denounce the policy of protection as bondage — yea, bondage; and I refer to bondage in the same manner in which American slavery was bondage.

SIR WILFRID LAURIER, speech in Winnipeg, 1894.

When the workers of Canada wake up they will find that Protection is only one among the several economic fangs fastened in their "corpus vile" by the little group of railroad men, bankers, lumbermen and manufacturing monopolists who own their country.

J. A. HOBSON, *Can. today*, 1906, 47.

I have no politics other than Protection, and I hope none of you have. If you have them, I think you should sink them for the good of the Association, for Protection is the only politics the Association should recognize.

W. H. ROWLEY, 1910, address to Can. Manufacturers Assoc., in *Industrial Canada*, Oct., 1910, 322.

PROTESTANTS.

A bad man is bad enough, but a bad minister beats the devil, that's as plain as preachin'.

> T. C. HALIBURTON, *Sam Slick*, 1840, 205.

Had I but consented to take the popular side in Upper Canada, I could have ridden the Protestant horse much better than George Brown, and could have had an overwhelming majority. But I willingly sacrificed my own popularity for the good of the country, and did equal justice to all men.

> SIR JOHN A. MACDONALD, letter to a friend, Ottawa, April 20, 1869.

Our equipage for the battle field was a port-manteau and valise; in them we stored our wearing apparel, Bible and what other books we were able to get, and but a few dollars in our pockets. Our outward dress and appearance when mounted gave us the name of the Methodist cavalry.

> J. CARROLL, *Case and cotemporaries,* 1869, II, 319; reference to preachers.

He has raised the Protestant flag and sounded the Protestant war cry — Down with the French, if not with the ballot in this generation then with the bayonet in the next.

> *Manitoba Free Press,* July 26, 1889, on Dalton McCarthy.

It was the so-called genius of Protestantism to invent a form of Christianity without sacrifice.

> REV. BERNARD VAUGHAN, S. J., speech in St. Patrick's church, Montreal, Sept. 7, 1910.

PROVINCES.

It seems that the smaller the province the more trouble it will be. Columbia, Manitoba, and Prince Edward Island give me more trouble than Ontario and Quebec.

> ALEXANDER MACKENZIE, letter to Lord Dufferin, July 27, 1874.

Confederation, so far, has done nothing to fuse the races, and very little even to unite the provinces...

From the composition of a cabinet to the composition of a rifle team, sectionalism is the rule.

> GOLDWIN SMITH, *Political destiny of Canada,* 1878, 16.

Each Province has attractions for its children.

> GEORGE M. GRANT, address to Canadian Club, N. Y., 1887.

Canadian Provinces they lay
Divided by river and by bay,
Many a separate division
Among them there was not cohesion.

> JAMES MCINTYRE, "Canada before the Confederation of the Provinces", 1889.

The shreds and patches of Confederation.

> SIR RICHARD CARTWRIGHT, referring to the Maritimes and B. C. after the election of March 1891 as the source of Sir John A. Macdonald's small majority; from Shakespeare, "A king of shreds and patches."

I am now simply what I have always been — a Province man.

> LEMUEL J. TWEEDIE, speech in N. B. Legis., Mar. 1, 1901.

Provincial rights.

> A term derived from the pro-provincial decisions of the Privy Council.

Each province should be an independent country with power to do whatever it pleases. And I would have a wall between the provinces and the Dominion, and I would have no appeal, no veto, and no remedial appeal, none of all that misery we have had here since Confederation; and each province would have its own courts.

> ARTHUR BEAUCHESNE, 1935, in H. of C., *Method of amending B.N.A. Act,* 134.

The Provincial conception of nationhood.

> R. B. BENNETT, a phrase used in a speech in Winnipeg, July 5, 1937.

No Province has the right to reduce in that Province the political rights of its citizens as compared with those enjoyed by the citizens of other Provinces of Canada.

> LAWRENCE A. D. CANNON, Supreme Court decision, Mar. 4, 1938, on Alberta newspaper muzzling act.

PUBLIC OPINION.

The inhabitants of Upper Canada have apparently no unity of interest or opinion.

> LORD DURHAM, Report, 1839.

Is there no public opinion in that country?

> SIR JOSEPH CHAMBERLAIN to Sir Oliver Mowat, Premier of Ontario 1872-1896, when he said he had been in office many years.

There is no public opinion in Canada.

> PETER MCARTHUR, qu. a friend, in *New era in Canada*. ed. by Miller, 1917, 333.

Quebec does not have opinions, but only sentiments.

> SIR WILFRID LAURIER, attributed.

Government, in the last analysis, is organized opinion. Where there is little or no public opinion, there is likely to be bad government, which sooner or later becomes autocratic government.

> W. L. MACKENZIE KING, *Message of the carillon*, 1927, 139.

PURPOSE.

A purpose, a determined will,
Can soar above earth's highest hill,
And bid the troubled waves be still.

> ALEXANDER MCLACHLAN, *Can. birthday book*, 1887, 18.

Many people regard an earnest selfishness as the only earnest purpose.

> PETER MCARTHUR, *To be taken with salt*, 1903, 153.

Set the strong shaft of purpose to the cord
And send it singing to the mark.

> ROBERT NORWOOD, *Witch of Endor*, 1916.

If we be true to our just cause, the upward way will not deter us; the giants cannot overcome us.

> HENRY WISE WOOD, address at U. F. A. convention, in *U.F.A.*, Feb. 1, 1923, 17.

Q

QUEBEC CITY.

(See also: CITIES AND TOWNS — NICKNAMES)

Nothing struck me as so beautiful and grand as the location of the town of Quebec, which could not be better situated even were it to become, in some future time, the Capital of a great Empire.

> FRONTENAC, in a letter, 1672; see, *Can. hist. rev.*, II, 365.

Push on, brave boys! Quebec is ours!

> GENERAL RICHARD MONTGOMERY, to his American troops, on leading the charge at Pres-de-Ville, Quebec City, Dec. 31, 1775, just before his death.

Such works do not consist with the development of the intellect. Huge stone structures of all kinds, both in their erection and by their influence when erected, rather oppress than liberate the mind.

> HENRY THOREAU, *Excursion to Can.*, 1850.

The French thought building a fortress was colonization, and the English that blowing it up was the right way to settle the country.

> T. C. HALIBURTON, *Nature and human nature*, 1855, II, 388.

Quebec, the gray old city on the hill,
Lies with a golden glory on her head,
Dreaming throughout this hour so fair, so still,
Of other days and her beloved dead.

> JEAN BLEWETT, "At Quebec", 1897.

Like some grey warder who, with mien sedate
And smile of welcome, greets the throngs who pour
Between the portals of a wide-thrown door,
Quebec stands guardian at our water gate,
And watches from her battlemented state
The great ships passing with their living store

Of human myriads coming to our shore,
Expectant, joyous, resolute, elate.

FREDERICK GEORGE SCOTT, "Quebec", 1928.

QUEBEC PROVINCE.

Quebec, at least for an American, is certainly a very peculiar place.

BENJAMIN SILLIMAN, *Tour of Que., 1819,* 1822, 110.

Was it just that the prosperity of this great majority, and of this vast tract of country, should be for ever, or for even a while, impeded by the artificial bar which the backward laws and civilization of a part, and a part only, of Lower Canada, would place between them and the ocean? Was it to be supposed that such an English population would ever submit to such a sacrifice of its interests?

LORD DURHAM, *Report,* 1839.

My warmest aspiration for this Province has always been to see its French inhabitants executing for Canada the functions which France herself performs for Europe.

LORD DUFFERIN, reply to an address presented by Legis. Assembly of Quebec, June, 1878.

Je me souviens.

EUGÈNE TACHÉ, architect. motto added to the arms of Quebec, Feb. 9, 1883.

Quebec is the most interesting thing by much that I have seen on this continent.

MATTHEW ARNOLD, *Letters,* 1895, II, 308.

That this House is of opinion that the Province of Quebec would be disposed to accept the breaking of the Confederation Pact of 1867 if, in the other provinces, it is believed that she is an obstacle to the union, progress and development of Canada.

J. N. FRANCOEUR, motion proposed in Legislative Assembly of Quebec, Jan. 17, 1918. (trans.)

Quebec remained British because it was French.

GEORGE M. WRONG, *Canada and Amer. revolution,* 1935, 260.

QUOTATIONS.

Maxims are deductions ready drawn.

T. C. HALIBURTON, *Nature and human nature,* 1855, I, 120.

Proverbs are distilled facts steamed down to an essence.

THOMAS C. HALIBURTON, *Sam Slick;* attributed.

A wise saw is more valuable than a whole book, and a plain truth is better than an argument.

T. C. HALIBURTON, *Nature and human nature,* 1855, I, 349.

And speaking of quotation, what is its use? The use is like that of an illustration, to make a point or situation more vivid, more emphatic, by a new light, by a suggestion which may be ridiculous, elevating, degrading, which enables you sometimes to put in the hearer's mind what you hardly dare, and could not, put into your own words.

NICHOLAS F. DAVIN, in, *Can. monthly,* 1881, 285.

Nothing can stand against a really resolute quoter.

GOLDWIN SMITH, qu., *Empire Club Speeches,* April 11, 1911.

Inaccurate quotation is a sin against truth.

ROBERT W. SHANNON, *Can. mag.,* 1898, 474.

The phrase is the motive-power of the world. Corporeal man, armed with battle-ax or maxim, is but the vehicle of the phrase; the armature, the dynamo through which that subtle electric fluid we call Thought is collected, directed, and flies through space, working wonders.

ARNOLD HAULTAIN, *Univ. mag.,* Feb., 1908, 111.

The phrase, beating its rhythm, preening its crest
against a critical oar, draws at the secret
till the day the oar rests as the wave sunders
and the fastidious implication emerges
a bloom to pelt, an excalibur to wield.

ROBERT FINCH, "The reticent phrase", 1946.

R

RAILWAYS.

(See also: CANADIAN PACIFIC
RAILWAY; PACIFIC SCANDAL;
RAILWAYS (NICKNAMES);
TRANSPORTATION)

I am neither a prophet, nor the son
of a prophet, yet I will venture to
predict that in five years we shall
make the journey hence to Quebec and
Montreal and home through Portland
and St. John by rail; and I believe
that many in this room will live to
hear the whistle of the steam-engine
in the passes of the Rocky Mountains
and to make the journey from Halifax
to the Pacific in five or six days.

JOSEPH HOWE, speech in Mason's
Hall, Halifax, May 15, 1851.

To the advocates of legislative union
I say, your scheme is impracticable
without the railroads.

JOSEPH HOWE, speech in Quebec,
July 4, 1851.

Railways are my politics.

SIR ALLAN MACNAB, in Legislative
Assembly, speech made as leader
of the Opposition on granting of a
charter to the Grand Trunk Railway, 1853. (See: *Can. hist. rev.*,
vol. 28, 171, for quotation by R. J.
Macgeorge from *Streetsville weekly
rev.*, Nov. 25, 1854; also, speech by
Thomas White, H. of C., *Debates*,
Feb. 8, 1884.)

The Grand Trunk Railway governs
Canada at the present moment. Its
power is paramount. The Ministry are
mere puppets in its hands and dance
whatever tune the Company pipes.

TORONTO *Globe* Apr. 22, 1857.

I hope to see, or at least that my
children will see, a railway wholly on
British territory from the Atlantic to
the Pacific Oceans.

WILLIAM DRAPER, special commissioner to Gt. Brit., H. of C.
committee on Hudson's Bay Co.,
1857.

No Intercolonial, no Transit.

DUKE OF NEWCASTLE, letter to
E. W. Watkin, May 6, 1863: "I
added words [to the despatches to

British Columbia and Canada]
which (without dictation) will be
understood as implying 'No Intercolonial, no Transit'."

Mr. Tilley, will you stop your puffing
and blowing
And tell us which way the railway
is going?

FREDERICTON *Headquarters*, Feb. 1,
1865; on the Intercolonial Railway.

What would Montreal be without the
Grand Trunk? It has assured for us
the commerce of the West.

SIR GEORGES E. CARTIER, speech at a
banquet given in his honour, Montreal, 1866.

Great railway corporations are the
most dangerous enemies popular government ever had.

DAVID MILLS, in *Can. monthly*,
Nov., 1872; see also, H. of C.,
Debates, 1880-81, 274.

I swing to the sunset land —
The world of prairie, the world of
plain,
The world of promise and hope and
gain,
The world of gold, and the world of
grain,
And the world of the willing hand.

E. PAULINE JOHNSON, "Prairie greyhounds — C. P. R. 'No. 1' West-
bound", 1903.

I swing to the land of morn;
The grey old east with its grey old
seas,
The land of leisure, the land of ease,
The land of flowers and fruits and
trees,
And the place where we were born.

E. PAULINE JOHNSON, "Prairie
greyhounds — C. P. R. 'No. 2'
Eastbound", 1903.

We cannot wait, because time does
not wait; we cannot wait because, in
these days of wonderful development,
time lost is doubly lost; we cannot
wait, because at this moment there
is a transformation going on in the
conditions of our national life which
it would be folly to ignore and a crime
to overlook.

SIR WILFRID LAURIER, H. of C.,
Debates, July 30, 1903, 7659, on
the building of the Grand Trunk
Pacific Railway.

[The Grand Trunk Pacific will] roll back the map of Canada and add depth to the country.

SIR W. LAURIER, 1904; attributed.

That mad route, unknown, unsurveyed and uninhabited, through the North country, over granite ranges, from Winnipeg to Quebec.

MONTREAL *Star*, Jan. 23, 1904, on the Grand Trunk Pacific project.

For our own benefit, usefulness and dignity Canadians should be masters of their own country, and should have their all-Canadian route.

SIR WILFRID LAURIER, speech in Quebec, Oct. 5, 1904, on the Grand Trunk Pacific project.

Purgatory for me will be five hundred years of catching trains and two thousand years of remembering names.

FREDERICK GEORGE SCOTT, *Can. mag.*, March, 1909, 460.

Works, Clerks and Shirks.

A nickname given to three suburban local trains that ran into Saint John, N. B., about 1915.

If there is one thing that has bedevilled the public life of this country it has been the influence of railway corporations.

NEWTON W. ROWELL, H. of C., *Debates*, Oct. 21, 1919, 1259.

The efficiency of the System emphatically demands the maintenance of it in its integrity. The policy of the Conservative party toward this great undertaking will be, reduced to briefest words, "amalgamation, never; competition, ever!"

RICHARD B. BENNETT, speech in Montreal, June 26, 1930, on the Canadian National Railway.

Railways in Canada are far from being merely an economic problem. They were born of, nourished in, are, and will continue to be, part of Canadian politics.

R. McQUEEN, in *Can. hist. rev.*, 1936, 334.

RAILWAYS (NICKNAMES)

Alberta Great Eastern (Athabasca Railway) — Always Giving Employment.

Alberta Great Waterways — Almighty God Wonders — And God Willing.

Algoma Central and Hudson Bay — All Curves, Hills and Bridges.

Atlantic, Quebec and Western — The All Queer and Wobbly.

Brockville, Westport and Sault Ste. Marie — Bad Wages and Seldom See Money.

Canadian National Railways — Certainly No Rush — Collects No Revenue.

C.N.R. (Component lines and sections) — *Brandon to Portage la Prairie* — Brandon Short Line. *Campbellford subdivision* — The Submarine Division. *Charlottetown to Murray Harbour* — The Gaelic Express. *Edmonton to Blue River* — The Duck and Dodge. *Irondale, Bancroft and Ottawa* — In and Back Out. Italian Bums and Orphans. The Mary Ann. *London to Clinton* — The Butter and Egg. *Jasper to Prince Rupert* — The Burma Road. (1939-45) The Trap Line. The Turkey Trail. *Point Tupper to Inverness* — The Juridique Flyer. *Saskatoon to Calgary* — The Goose Lake Line. *Winnipegosis to Rorketon* — Coast to Coast. *Vancouver Island section.* — Route of the Christmas Tree. Two Streaks of Rust.

Canadian Northern Railway — Canadian Now and Then. The Wooden Axle.

Canadian Pacific Railway — Can't Pay Rent. Can't Promise Returns. Chinese Pacific. (Local to Vancouver, because of Oriental labour used on construction.) The Great Octopus. The Sleepy R.

C.P.R. (Component lines and sections). *Arrow Lake subdivision* — The Bow and Arrow. *Lyndonville subdiv., Maine* — Snake Alley. *Montreal to Mattawamkeag sections* — The M. & M. (From Moosehead, and Mattawamkeag sections.) The Short Line. *Montreal to Boston* — The Air Line. *Osoyoos subdiv.* — The Cantaloupe Trail. *Temiscaming subdiv.* — The Moccasin Line.

Cumberland Railway and Coal Co. — Can't Run and Can't Crawl.

Dominion Atlantic Railway — The Blueberry Special. The Dust and Rust. The Land of Evangeline Route. The Midland. (Windsor to Truro.)

Duluth, Winnipeg and Pacific — Derailments, Wrecks, and Profanity.

Edmonton, Dunvegan and British Columbia. (*Northern Alberta Railways.*) — Eat, Drink and be Cheerful. Endless Ditches and Big Curves. Enormously Dangerous and Badly Constructed. Eternally Damned and Badly Constructed. Evilly Designed and Badly Constructed.

Esquimalt and Nanaimo Railway — The Easy and Noisy. The Easy and Nice.

Flin Flon — The Flim Flam.

Grand Trunk Pacific — Get There Perhaps.

Grand Trunk Railway — The Big Suitcase. The Big Valise. The Leaky Roof. (From stencilling on many box cars.)

Great Northern — Grand Nord. Great Now and Then.

Halifax and South Western — Hellish Slow and Weary. The Fish Line (Lunenburg branch.)

Hudson Bay — The Highball Railway. The Muskeg Special. The Muskeg Unlimited.

Intercolonial — The Antigogaelicer. (Truro to Mulgrave.) The Pawns. (Branches from Halifax to Windsor, and to Pictou.)

Kettle Valley — Tea Kettle Valley.

Kingston and Pembroke — Kick and Push.

Lake Erie and Northern — Late Every Night.

London and Port Stanley — Late and Poor Service. Least Possible Service. Liver and Pork Sausage.

Minneapolis, St. Paul and Sault Ste. Marie — The Soo Line.

Minnesota and Manitoba — Murder all Manitobans.

Napanee, Tamworth and Quinte — None too Quick.

Newfoundland Railway — The Reid Railway. (1898)

Niagara, St. Catharines and Toronto — Naturally Slow and Tiresome. Never Starts on Time.

North-Western Coal and Navigation Co. — The Turkey Trail. (Narrow guage, between Lethbridge and Dunmore Jct.; 1885)

Ontario Northland (Formerly, *Temiskaming and Northern Ontario.*) — The Clay Belt Air-line. (North Bay to Cochrane.) Hepburn's Folly. (Cochrane to Moosonee.)

Ottawa Arnprior and Parry Sound — Only Abuse and Poor Salary.

Oxford and New Glasgow — The Short Line.

Pacific Great Eastern — Pat Gets Everything. Pat's Greatest Effort. Please Go Easy. Prince George Eventually. Proctor's Great Effort. The Province's Greatest Expense.

Pontiac, Pacific Junction — Push, Pull and Jerk. Push, Pull, Jump and Run.

Port Arthur, Duluth and Western — The P. and D. Poverty, Agony, Distress and Want. Poverty, Desperation and Want.

Quebec, Montreal and Southern — Quel Maudit Service.

Quebec, Montreal, Ottawa and Occidental (*C.P.R.*) — The North Shore.

St. John and Quebec — The Valley Line.

Sidney and Louisburg — Slow and Lazy.

Temiscaming and Northern Ontario (Now, *Ontario Northern.*) — Time No Object.

Temiscouata Railway — The Sportsmen's Route.

Toronto, Hamilton and Buffalo — To Hell and Back. Tramp, Hobo and Bum. Tried Hard and Busted.

White Pass and Yukon — Wait Patiently and You'll Ride.

Yarmouth and Annapolis — The Missing Link. (Digby to Annapolis.)

RAIN.

All signs of rain fail in a dry spell.
> Saying of pioneer Ontario farmers.

When the pigs run and play expect a rainy day.
> Saying of pioneer Ontario farmers.

It was a little bit arter daylight down, rainin' cats and dogs.
> T. C. HALIBURTON, *Sam Slick*, 1836, ch. XXVIII.

There is a rapture in tempestuous weather,
A sympathy with suffering, which thrills
When midnight mists around the mountains gather,
And hoarse winds howl among the moaning hills.
> ANDREW J. RAMSAY, "Win-on-ah", 1869.

The rain it falls, and the wind it blows,
And the restless ocean ebbs and flows
But the why and the wherefore no one knows.
> ALEXANDER McLACHLAN, "The rain it falls", 1874.

Washboard sky,
Not three days dry.
> Weather proverb, Western Ontario.

And ghosts of buried summers
Walk with the lonely rain.
> BLISS CARMAN, *Songs of the sea children*: XXVI, 1894.

These comforts only have I for my pain —
The frantic laws of statesmen bowed with cares
To feed me, and the slow, pathetic prayers
Of godly men that somehow it shall rain.
> FREDERICK E. LAIGHT, "Soliloquy", 1937, on prairie drought.

Sometimes, upon a crowded street
I feel the endless rain come down,
And in the old magnetic sound
I hear the opening of a gate
That loosens all the seven seas.
> F. R. SCOTT, "Lakeshore", 1950.

REBELLION, 1837.

> (See also: MACKENZIE, WILLIAM LYON)

The time has come to melt our spoons into bullets.
> WOLFRED NELSON, in the summer of of 1837, attributed.

Four rebels captured; shot accordingly.
> COL. JOHN PRINCE in his account of the Battle of Windsor, Dec. 1838; attributed.

When I was a rebel.
> SIR GEORGES E. CARTIER, a favourite expression of his later years.

I carried my musket in '37.
> SIR JOHN A. MACDONALD, in his later years.

The enterprise of a few vain, vicious, feather-brained men: it had neither spirit nor substance, deriving what poor strength it had from enemies of England... in America.
> J. W. FORTESCUE, *Hist. British army*, vol. XI, 1923.

What Canada lost was a small army of so-called renegades, among whom were some thugs, criminals, and a sprinkling of the harebrained, but the great majority were men with character, ability, and ideals of good citizenship. Canada has been vastly the poorer for their exile.
> LOUIS B. DUFF, in *Can. hist. rev.*, 1938, 215.

RECIPROCITY, 1854.

It was floated through on champagne.
> A taunt made by those opposed to the treaty which was signed in Washington; qu. by Laurence Oliphant, Lord Elgin's private secretary, *Episodes in a life of adventure*, 1887, 47.

RECIPROCITY, 1911.

(See also: TRADE)

Now is the accepted time. Canada is at the parting of the ways. Shall she be an isolated country, as much separated from us as if she were across the ocean, or shall her people and our people profit by the proximity that our geography furnishes and stimulate the trade across the border that nothing but a useless, illogical and unnecessary tariff wall created?

> WILLIAM H. TAFT, U. S. pres., address to Illinois State Legis., Springfield, Feb. 11, 1911.

There are six and one-half per cent of fools in Canada, of which one per cent are for Reciprocity.

> SIR WILLIAM VAN HORNE, a favorite saying, 1911.

I am out to do all I can to bust the damned thing.

> SIR WILLIAM VAN HORNE, a remark on the Reciprocity movement of 1911.

I am absolutely opposed to Reciprocity and if the West were prepared to make me Prime Minister to-morrow, if I would support that policy, I would not do it.

> SIR ROBERT L. BORDEN, speech in Brandon, June 20, 1911.

Our trade is about $97.00 per capita, and theirs $33.00 per capita. In other words the water in our millpond stands at 97 and theirs at 33 — and they want us to take away our dam. Shall we not say: — "Not by a 'dam' site!"

> SIR WILLIAM VAN HORNE, speech at St. Andrews', N. B., Sep. 2, 1911; similar to a press statement made in Montreal, Feb. 22, 1911.

On September 21, 1911, the Canadian people put behind them the temptation to break the economic bonds by which they had been welded as a nation, affirming their determination to remain loyal subjects of St. James and King Streets.

> FRANK H. UNDERHILL, in *Can. hist. rev.*, 1935, 387.

REFORM.

Changing one thing for another is not always reform.

> T. C. HALIBURTON, *Sam Slick*, 1840, 159.

Reforms are not applicable to reformers, for those who liberate others must themselves be free.

> T. C. HALIBURTON, *The old judge*, 1849.

You can't reform 'em, the only way is to cloriform them.

> T. C. HALIBURTON, *Sam Slick's wise saws*, 1853, II, 282.

In my judgment there is no more urgent reform than educating public and private opinion to unselfishness, & until that reform is achieved all other reforms are impossible.

> SIR WILFRID LAURIER, letter to Blake, Dec. 20, 1882.

Make me over in the morning
From the rag-bag of the world!

> BLISS CARMAN, "Spring song", 1894.

No great reform can be achieved except at the sacrifice of some opinion, even by those who are the most ardently in favour of it. The true reformer is not he who always adheres stubbornly to his own ideas, but the true reformer is he who, after having earnestly combatted for his opinions, then yields in order to attain some greater end, and to facilitate the change from the old to the new order of things.

> SIR WILFRID LAURIER, H. of C., *Debates*, Mar. 25, 1907, 5294.

Changes for the better are often resented. Old boots were once new — and hated.

> GEORGE ILES, *Canadian stories*, 1918, 172.

I have recovered the radicalism of my youth.

> SIR CLIFFORD SIFTON, to his friends 1919.

Disaster precedes reform.

> PETER MCARTHUR, a favorite expression.

Do not forget that in the history of social reform it is difficult to name a time when reactionary interests have not sought to block progressive measures by the specious argument that, by them, personal liberty was endangered.

R. B. BENNETT, radio address, Jan. 7, 1935.

REFORM PARTY.

Up, Brother Reformers! organize committees; appoint canvassers; call meetings; put forth your strength in a good cause, and manifest at the hustings that to you the peace and prosperity of Upper Canada are dear. Be diligent, untiring, faithful and watchful — bring up your brethren who are unable to walk to the polls — cheer the hearts of the downcast — confirm the wavering — and let the frowns of honest men abash every mercenary hireling.

WILLIAM LYON MACKENZIE, address to the Reformers of Upper Canada, Toronto, Sept., 1834.

It has always been the boast of the Reform party that it was greatly made up of the sturdy yeomanry of the land and by far the most intelligent and incorruptible of that.

TORONTO *Globe*, Aug, 1, 1867.

REGINA, SASK.

(See also: CITIES AND TOWNS — NICKNAMES, etc.)

Success to Regina, queen city of the plains!

JUDGE F. G. JOHNSON, toast proposed at official christening of the townsite, Aug. 23, 1882.

If you had a lit-tle more wood, and a lit-tle more water, and here and there a hill, I think the prospect would be improved.

SIR JOHN A. MACDONALD, on transcontinental trip via C.P.R., 1886, to a Regina citizen who asked what he thought of the "prospect".

Golden-girdled by the harvest, Youth triumphant in her eyes, Starry splendours crown Regina When the sunset's crimson dies.

A. M. STEPHEN, "Wascana", 1928.

RELIGION.

(See also: BELIEF; THE CHURCH; GOD; JESUS CHRIST)

It must give uneasiness to any person who has any regard for religion to witness the general inattention to even the external duties of the Sabbath, both in the United States and Canada. Instead of preserving a tolerably decent behaviour on that day, it is commonly spent in drinking, shooting, fishing, or some such amusement, and that even by many who consider themselves to have good moral character.

J. GOLDIE, *Diary, journey through U. C.,* 1819. 55.

Every man's religion is his own, and nobody else's business.

T. C HALIBURTON, *Sam Slick*, 1836, ch. XXIV.

The misfortun' is, we are all apt to think Scriptur' intended for our neighbors, and not for ourselves.

T. C. HALIBURTON, *Sam Slick*, 1836, ch. XXIV.

If I had my religion to choose, and warn't able to judge for myself, I'll tell you what I'd do: I'd just ask myself, Who leads the best lives?

T. C. HALIBURTON, *Sam Slick*, 1836, ch. XXIV.

I don't like preachin' to the narves instead of the judgment.

T. C. HALIBURTON, *Sam Slick*, 1838, 52.

The mackerel run as freely into a Catholic's or Baptist's net as into any other, and I naturally enough ask myself why as a legislator I should make distinctions which God in His own good providence has not made?

JOSEPH HOWE, letter to his constituents, Oct. 22, 1840.

By means of Church Endowments, church has been set against church, family against family, sectarian hatred has been fostered, religion has been brought into contempt by the scramble for public plunder, and infidelity has been in no small degree promoted by the sight of men preaching one day the worthlessness of lucre, and battling on the next to clutch a little of that same commodity, though gained by the grossest partiality and injustice — and all this to serve the cause of religion.

GEORGE BROWN, 1851; qu., Buckingham, *Life of Mackenzie*, 12.

They have the ten commandments at their fingers' ends.

THOMAS C. HALIBURTON, *Sam Slick's wise saws*, 1853, ch. XV.

It is easier to make an infidel than a convert.

T. C. HALIBURTON, *Nature and human nature*, 1855, II, 145.

I am satisfied that the best civilizers are missionaries.

SIR JOHN A. MACDONALD, speech, 1861; qu., Biggar, *Anecdotal life*, 182.

I am an outside pillar of the Church.

JOHN SANDFIELD MACDONALD, first Premier of Ontario, about 1870.

Let me know only this — *I was lost and undone,*
But am saved by the blood of the Crucified One;
And I'm *wise* although knowing no more!

PAMELIA V. YULE, "Littlewit and Loftus", 1881.

Whether they come from the Catholics of Quebec or from the Protestants of Ontario, appeals to prejudice are deplorable. For my part, I have as much aversion for the man who appeals to Catholic prejudices in the province of Quebec, as for the man who appeals to Protestant prejudices in the province of Ontario.

SIR WILFRID LAURIER, speech at Somerset, Que., Aug. 2, 1887. (trans.)

The repeated attacks of a liberal population upon this body are unworthy of Quebec City;... it is necessary that the processions of the Salvation Army, ridiculous as they may appear to some, must have full liberty of progress; and if need be I am prepared to march at their head to protect them.

SIR WILFRID LAURIER, 1887; in, Pacaud, ed., *Laurier letters*, 1935, 28.

So long as I have a seat in this House, so long as I occupy the position I do now, whenever it shall become my duty to take a stand upon any question whatever, that stand I will take, not from the point of view of Roman Catholicism, not from the point of view of Protestantism, but from a point of view which can appeal to the consciences of all men, irrespective of their particular faith, upon grounds which can be occupied by all men who love justice, freedom, and toleration.

SIR WILFRID LAURIER, H. of C., *Debates*, Mar. 3, 1896.

About the only people who don't quarrel over religion are the people who haven't any.

ROBERT C. (BOB) EDWARDS, *Calgary Eye Opener*, Oct, 15, 1910.

There are dangers: all may become secular; there are wonderful possibilities: all may become sacred. For good or for evil we are out into the new world. Exclusive religion must more and more give way to an all-inclusive religion. Religion in the future will no longer be identified with the Church and Sundays and prayers and priests, it will become the every day life of the common man — that or nothing.

JAMES S. WOODSWORTH, "Sermons for the unsatisfied", in, *Grain growers' guide*, July 7, 1915, 8.

I have no temple and no creed,
I celebrate no mystic rite;
The human heart is all I need
Wherein I worship day and night.

ROBERT NORWOOD, "After the order of Melchisedec", 1917.

If I, a mere automaton
In a brief and paltry play,
Am but a group of atoms drawn
Powerless upon my way
To mud again, as savants say —
Why then at the heart of me
What is this that needs must pray?
There is no end to mystery.

TOM MACINNES, "The ballade of the mystic and the mud", 1918.

When we in touch with heathen come,
We send them first a case of rum,

Next, to rebuke their native sin,
We send a missionary in.

> STEPHEN B. LEACOCK, *College days*,
> 1923, 90.

You were never meant to sit in a
corner hatching the addled egg of your
personal salvation.

> JOHN MACNAUGHTON, sermon in a
> Kingston, Ont., Presbyterian
> church; *Queen's quart.*, 1933, 363.

The religion of tomorrow will be less
concerned with the dogmas of theology
and more concerned with the social
welfare of humanity.

> T. C. DOUGLAS, *Research rev.*,
> Regina, 1934, 2.

Sometimes you saw what others could
not see.
Sometimes you heard what no one
else could hear: —
A light beyond the unfathomable
dark,
A voice that sounded only to your
ear.

> CHARLES G. D. ROBERTS, "To a
> certain mystic", 1934.

My religion and my philosophy of
life are founded upon a belief in the
scientific development of man, up to an
ultimate knowledge of the Truth as
taught by Christ; and the development
of a social system in perfect harmony
with Nature's laws, which are the laws
of God.

> HENRY WISE WOOD, "My religion",
> qu., Rolph, *Wood*, 1950. 63.

REVOLUTION.

The world no longer believes in the
divine right of either kings or presidents
to govern wrong; but those who seek
to change an established government
by force of arms assume a fearful
responsibility — a responsibility which
nothing but the clearest and most
intolerable injustice will acquit them
for assuming.

> GEORGE BROWN, speech in Toronto,
> 1863.

Revolt is essential to progress.

> DUNCAN CAMPBELL SCOTT. "Poetry
> and progress", 1922.

In Canada we have no revolutionary
tradition; and our historians, political
scientists, and philosophers have assidu-
ously tried to educate us to be proud
of this fact. How can such a people
expect their democracy to be dynamic
as the democracies of Britain and
France and the United States have
been?

> F. H. UNDERHILL, in Can. Hist.
> Assoc.,*Rept.*, 1946, 12.

RICH.

What a country! Here all the knaves
grow rich, and the honest men are
ruined.

> MONTCALM, 1758 (trans.); qu.,
> Parkman, *Montcalm and Wolfe.* II,
> ch. 23.

We can do without any article of
luxury we have never had; but when
once obtained, it is not human natur'
to surrender it voluntarily.

> T. C. HALIBURTON, *Sam Slick*,
> 1836, chap. II.

The *family compact* of Upper Canada
is composed of those members of its
society who, either by their abilities
and character, have been honoured by
the confidence of the executive government, or who by their industry and
intelligence have amassed wealth.

> SIR FRANCIS B. HEAD, *Narrative*,
> 1839, 464.

Much is required of them to whom
much is given.

> THOMAS C. HALIBURTON, *Sam
> Slick's wise saws*, 1853, ch. III.

When all are poor, it don't take much
to make a rich man.

> THOMAS C. HALIBURTON, *Sam
> Slick's wise saws*, 1853, ch. XIV.

The rights of the minority must be
protected, and the rich are always fewer
in number than the poor.

> SIR JOHN A. MACDONALD, 1865; qu.,
> Pope, *Confederation*, 1895, 58; a
> reference to the proposed Senate.

'Rich by nature, poor by policy',
might be written over Canada's door.

> GOLDWIN SMITH, *Canada and Can.
> question*, 1891, 24.

He made himself a great name in
  his day,
A glittering fellow on the world's
  hard way;
He tilled and seeded and reaped
  plentifully
From the black soil of human misery.
He won great riches, and they buried
  him
With splendour that the people's
  wants make grim;
But some day he shall not be called
  to mind
Save as the curse and pestilence of
  his kind.
  ARCHIBALD LAMPMAN, "Epitaph on
  a rich man", Dec. 18, 1893.

Because the fellow thinks me rich
  These days he bows to me:
The beggar bows to dollars;
  He does not bow to me.
  TOM MACINNES, "Just so", 1923.

Borne in charioted ease,
Human bodies grow effete;
Sunk in soft prosperities
Fervent spirits lose their heat.
Happier he who tries in vain
Heights no travail can attain.
  WATSON KIRKCONNELL, "Labor sal-
  vator", 1930.

RIEL, LOUIS.

The Little Napoleon of Red River.
  A nickname.

Politics will save me.
  LOUIS RIEL, after the Battle of
  Batoche, May 12, 1885; attributed.

Strangle Riel with the French flag!
That is the only use that rag can have
in this country.
  TORONTO News, May 18, 1885.

He shall hang though every dog in
Quebec bark in his favour.
  SIR JOHN A. MACDONALD, 1885, to
  a friend who urged that Riel be
  shown mercy.

Riel was fairly tried, honestly con-
victed, laudably condemned, and justly
executed.
  Winnipeg Free Press, Dec. 17, 1885.

It cannot be said that Riel was
hanged on account of his opinions. It

is equally true that he was not executed
for anything connected with the late
rebellion. He was hanged for Scott's
murder; that is the simple truth of it.
  SIR WILFRID LAURIER, letter to
  Blake, Dec. 31, 1885.

Had there been no neglect there
would have been no rebellion. If no
rebellion, then no arrest. If no arrest,
then no trial. If no trial, then no
condemnation. If no condemnation,
then no execution. They therefore who
are responsible for the first are responsible for every link in that fatal chain.
  EDWARD BLAKE, on the execution of
  Riel, 1885.

I do not propose to construct a
political platform out of the Regina
scaffold, or to create or cement party
ties with the blood of the condemned.
  EDWARD BLAKE, speech in London,
  Jan. 14, 1886.

RIGHTS.

What peoples hope for, they think at
last they have a right to, and when they
are disappointed, they actilly think
they are ill-used.
  T. C. HALIBURTON, Sam Slick's
  wise saws, 1853, I, 239.

We have no absolute rights among
us. The rights of each man, in our
state of society, end precisely at the
point where they encroach upon the
rights of others.
  SIR WILFRID LAURIER, speech
  on political liberalism, Quebec,
  June 26, 1877.

RIVERS.

So long indeed as the St. Lawrence
flows into the sea, so long will the tide
of commerce fall into and follow its
natural declivity.
  WILLIAM F. COFFIN, Canal and the
  rail, 1848, 3.

Out and in the river is winding
  The links of its long red chain,
Through belts of dusky pine-land
  And gusty leagues of plain.
  JOHN G. WHITTIER, "Red River
  voyageur", 1854.

Oh, rivers rolling to the sea
From lands that bear the maple tree.
> CHARLES G. D. ROBERTS, "Canadian streams", 1893.

O slave, whom many a cunning master drills
To lift, or carry, bind, or crush, or churn,
Whose dammed and parcelled waters drive or turn
The saws and hammers of a hundred mills.
> ARCHIBALD LAMPMAN, "To the Ottawa river", 1900.

Peace and Athabasca and Coppermine and Slave,
And Yukon and Mackenzie — the highroads of the brave.

Saskatchewan, Assiniboine, the Bow and the Qu'Appelle,
And many a prairie river whose name is like a spell.
> BLISS CARMAN, "Rivers of Canada", April 27, 1922.

The first of all our greater North American streams whose waters parted under the keel of the white man's craft... and of all the world what river can display such panoramas pregnant with history as have paraded its waters?
> J. M. CLARKE, *L'Ile Percée*, 1923; a reference to the St. Lawrence River.

ROADS.

The King's Highway.
> From early French Canadian usage. (trans.)

We find it easy enough to direct others to the right road, but we can't always find it ourselves when we're on the ground.
> T. C. HALIBURTON, *Sam Slick's wise saws*, 1853, I, 44.

From plains that reel to southward, dim,
The road runs by me white and bare;
Up the steep hill it seems to swim
Beyond, and melt into the glare.
> ARCHIBALD LAMPMAN, "Heat", 1888.

De corduroy road go bompety bomp,
De corduroy road go jompety jomp,
An' he's takin' beeg chance upset hees load

De horse dat'll trot on de corduroy road.
> WILLIAM H. DRUMMOND, "The corduroy road", 1902.

Half a log, half a log,
Half a log onward,
Shaken and out of breath.
Rode we and wondered.
Ours not to reason why
Ours but to clutch and cry
While onward we thundered.
> CARRIE M. HOOPLE, "The corduroy road", 1909.

ROMAN CATHOLICS.

(See also: FRENCH CANA-DIANS)

The free exercise of the Catholic, Apostolic, and Roman religion, shall subsist entire, in such manner that all the states and the people of the towns and countries, places and distant posts, shall continue to assemble in the churches and to frequent the sacrements as heretofore, without being molested in any manner, directly or indirectly.
> CAPITULATION OF MONTREAL, Art. XXVII, 1760; a demand made by Vaudreuil. (trans.)

In Canada, not a cape was turned, nor a mission founded, nor a river entered, nor a settlement begun, but a Jesuit led the way.
> GEORGE BANCROFT, *Hist. of the U.S.*, 1834; elaborated in later eds., 1890, II, 138.

Not only is the Church independent of the Commonwealth — she stands above it... It is not the Church that is comprised in the State; it is the State that is comprised in the Church.
> QUEBEC EPISCOPATE, Collective letter, Sept. 22, 1875.

I am not here to parade my religious sentiments, but I declare I have too much respect for the faith in which I was born to ever use it as the basis of a political organization.
> SIR WILFRID LAURIER, speech in Quebec, June 26, 1877.

I know enough of English literature, to be aware that when Shakespeare put into the mouth of King John the proud

words which he made him address to
the Pope's legate:

> No Italian priest
> Shall tithe or toll in our dominion.

he touched the British heart in its
most responsive chord.

> SIR WILFRID LAURIER, speech in
> Toronto, Sept. 30, 1889.

This violent section, you know it —
comprises the Pharisee end of Canadian
Catholicism; those who have constituted themselves the defenders of a
religion which no one attacked; those
who handle the holy water sprinkler as
though it were a club; those who have
arrogated to themselves the monopoly
of orthodoxy; those who excommunicate
right and left all whose stature is a little
greater than theirs; those who seem
to have only hatred and envy for
motive and instinct; those who insulted
Cardinal Taschereau when he was
alive and who, now that he is dead,
attack his memory; those who made
Chapleau's life bitter; those, originally,
whom the people with their picturesque
language have designated under the
name of Castors.

> SIR WILFRID LAURIER, speech in
> Montreal, Oct. 10, 1910. (trans.)

The French Canadians are more
Catholic than the Pope.

> HUGH MARTIN, *Dalhousie rev.*,
> 1925, 425.

ROYAL CANADIAN MOUNTED POLICE.

Who are the soldiers at Red River
wearing dark clothes? Our old brothers
who formerly lived there [the 6th. Regiment at Fort Garry] wore red coats.
We know that the soldiers of our great
mother wear red coats and are our
friends.

> Prairie Indians, 1872, quoted by
> Col. P. Robertson-Ross, *Sess. pa-
> pers,,* 1873, no. 9, p. cxi; a reference
> to army scarlet, and the reason for
> its adoption by the Police.

They are to be purely a civil, not a
military body, with as little gold lace,
fuss, and fine feathers as possible, not
a crack cavalry regiment, but an efficient
police force for the rough and ready

—particularly ready — enforcement of
law and justice.

> SIR JOHN A. MACDONALD, May 3,
> 1873, in the House of Commons, on
> introducing the bill establishing
> the North West Mounted Police;
> attributed.

Maintiens le droit.

> Motto of the force; advocated in
> 1873, in use 1875.

If the Police had not come to the
country, where would we be all now?
Bad men and whiskey were killing us
so fast that very few indeed of us
would have been left today. The Police
have protected us as the feathers of the
bird protect it from the frosts of
winter. I wish them all good, and trust
that all our hearts will increase in
goodness from this time forward.

> CROWFOOT, Blackfoot chief, on
> signing Treaty no. 7, at Black-
> foot Crossing, Alta., Oct. 20, 1877.

> We muster but three hundred
> In all this great lone land,
> Which stretches o'er the continent
> To where the Rockies stand;
> But not one heart doth falter,
> No coward voice complains,
> That few, too few, in numbers are
> The Riders of the Plains.

> Our mission is to plant the rule
> Of Britain's freedom here,
> Restrain the lawless savage, and
> Protect the pioneer;
> And 'tis a proud and daring trust
> To hold these vast domains,
> With but three hundred men,
> The Riders of the Plains.

> "The Riders of the Plains"; author-
> ship doubtful; the poem appears
> in *Saskatchewan Herald,* Sept. 23,
> 1878, signed "W. S. N.W.M.P."
> and dated "Coburg, 1878": *Scarlet
> and gold,* 1919, 87, assigns the
> authorship to one Boyce, together
> with J. Carroll.

Why, these fellows would ride all
day for the Government, then all night
for a bottle of whisky, and spent the
whole of their leisure devising devil-
ments, yet by the trickery of an oath and
a uniform, Romance has created the
frailest of them into perfect constables
of the peace.

> ROGER POCOCK, *A frontiersman,*
> 1903.

These are the men who battle the
blizzards, the suns, the rains,
These are the famed that the North
has named the "Riders of the
Plains,"
And theirs is the might and the
meaning and the strength of the
bulldog's jaw,
While they keep the peace of the
people and the honour of British
law.

> E. PAULINE JOHNSON, "The riders
> of the plains", 1903.

On the 17th instant, I, Corporal Hogg,
was called to the hotel to quiet a disturbance. I found the room full of
cowboys, and one Monaghan, or Cowboy
Jack, was carrying a gun, and pointed it
at me, against sections 105 and 109
of the Criminal Code. We struggled.
Finally I got him handcuffed.

> CORPORAL HOGG, report on an
> arrest at North Portal, Sask., 1906.

In the little Crimson Manual it's
written plain and clear
Those who wear the scarlet coat shall
say good-bye to fear.

> ROBERT W. SERVICE, "Clancy of
> the Mounted Police", 1909.

Yellowlegs.

> From the yellow trouser-stripes of
> the Police uniform; used by
> malcontents.

Sergeant Blue of the Mounted Police
was a so-so kind of guy;
He swore a bit, and he lied a bit, and
he boozed a bit on the sly;
But he held the post at Snake Creek
Bend in the good old British way,
And a grateful country paid him
about sixty cents a day.

> ROBERT J. C. STEAD, "A squad of
> one", 1917.

The Silent Force.

> A popular name from the title of
> a book by T. MORRIS LONGSTRETH,
> 1927.

ROYAL COMMISSIONS.

The politics of Billy King
Make honest blood to boil.
His omissions are staggering,
His Commissions are Royal.

> "CYNIC", Can. forum, June, 1938.

The English creed [is]: "As it was in
the beginning, is now, and ever shall
be, world without end, Amen"; the
American: "As it was in the beginning,
is now, and by gosh it's got to stop";
the Canadian: "As it was in the
beginning, is now, and ladies and
gentlemen, if we are going to make
any changes we will appoint a Royal
Commission to tell us how it is to
be done."

> H. M. TORY, qu., Can. hist. assoc.,
> Rept. 1940, 14.

RYERSON, EGERTON.

The Americans had their Arnold
and the Canadians have their Ryerson...
I was the dupe of a Jesuit in the garb
of a Methodist Preacher, and believed
Egerton that I had been in error in
opposing the Union... but he and his
new allies, the church and state gentry,
shall now have me on their rear.

> W. L. MACKENZIE, in Colonial
> advocate, Oct., 1833.

He is the Pope of Methodism in this
country, but he mistook his profession.
Nature intended him for a Jesuit.

> JOHN LANGTON, letter to W.
> Langton, Dec. 30, 1855.

S

SAILORS.

The blood that flowed from Nelson's
death-wound in the cockpit of the
Victory mingled with that of a Nova
Scotian stripling beside him, struck
down in the same glorious fight.

> JOSEPH HOWE, letter to Lord John
> Russell, Sept. 18, 1839.

Who, in frail barques, the ocean
surge defied,
And trained the race that live upon
the wave?
What shore so distant where they
have not died?
In every sea they found a watery
grave.

> JOSEPH HOWE, "Our fathers", Oct.
> 5, 1854.

, I was born for deep-sea faring;
I was bred to put to sea;
Stories of my father's daring
Filled me at my mother's knee.

> BLISS CARMAN, "A son of the sea",
> 1895.

SAINT BONIFACE, MAN.

The voyageur smiles as he listens
To the sound that grows apace;
Well he knows the vesper ringing
Of the bells of St. Boniface.

The bells of the Roman mission,
That call from their turrets twain,
To the boatman on the river.
To the hunter on the plain.

> JOHN G. WHITTIER, "Red River
> voyageur", written after reading
> Bond: *Minnesota, or, a trip to
> Selkirk Settlement*, 1854, 292.

SAINT JOHN, N. B.

Loyalists, my fathers, builded
This gray port by the gray sea,
When the duty to ideals
Could not let well-being be.

> BLISS CARMAN, "The ships of St.
> John", in, *Canadian mag.*, Dec.,
> 1893, 149.

SATISFACTION.

Any man who doesn't want what he
hasn't got has all he wants.

> ROBERT C. (BOB) EDWARDS. *Cal-
> gary Eye Opener*, Mar. 9, 1918.

SCIENCE.

A romantic age stands in need of
science, a scientific and utilitarian age
stands in need of the humanities.

> GOLDWIN SMITH, *The week*, April
> 28, 1893.

The golden rule of science is: Make
sure of your facts and then lie strenuously about your modesty.

> PETER MCARTHUR, *To be taken
> with salt*, 1903, 150.

In my youth, geology was nervously
striving to accomodate itself to Genesis.
Now it is Genesis that is striving to
accomodate itself to geology.

> GOLDWIN SMITH, *Lines of religious
> inquiry*, address, Toronto, 1904, 5.

The future belongs to science. More
and more she will control the destinies
of the nations. Already she has them in
her crucible and on her balances.

> SIR WILLIAM OSLER, introduction,
> *Life of Pasteur*, by Vallery-Radot,
> 1911.

Revolutions are more rapidly effected
in the arts than in the mind. A new
process, a new discovery in practical
science progresses more in a decade
than does a new thought in ten.

> SIR WILLIAM OSLER, address to
> Bibliographical Soc., London, Eng.,
> Jan. 1914.

In science the credit goes to the man
who convinces the world, not to the
man to whom the idea first occurs.

> SIR WILLIAM OSLER, "The first
> printed documents relating to
> modern surgical anesthesia", paper
> read May 15, 1918, to Hist. Sec.,
> Roy. Soc. of Med., England.

It is almost with a sense of shock
that we realize that the essence of
physics and chemistry alike lies in
the arrangements within the atom.

> R. C. WALLACE, in *Can. hist. rev.*,
> 1933, 374.

The scientist is in harmony with a
religion of man's humanity to man, but
not with man's inhumanity to man. He
has no use for organized religious bodies
that have enforced their dogmas at the
point of the sword and have sold salvation to their followers for profit, or who
have kept their people in ignorance.

> SIR FREDERICK BANTING, in, Toronto
> *Star*, July 6, 1935.

SCOTSMEN.

From the lone shieling of the misty
island
Mountains divide us and the waste
of seas —
Yet still the blood is strong, the
heart is Highland,
And we in dreams behold the
Hebrides:
Fair these broad meads — the
hoary woods are grand;

But we are exiles from our fathers'
land.

DAVID MACBETH MOIR, "Canadian
boat-song", ("The lone shieling")
in, *Blackwood's Edinburgh mag.*,
Sept., 1829, 400. A shieling is a
hut.

If I were not French I would choose
to be — Scotch.

SIR WILFRID LAURIER, speech,
Toronto Board of Trade, Jan. 5,
1893.

He builds their commerce, he sings
their songs,
He weaves their creeds with an
iron twist,
And making of laws or righting of
wrongs,
He grinds them all as the Scotchman's
grist.

WILFRED CAMPBELL, "The world-
mother", 1899.

They are the backbone of Canada.
They are all right in their three vital
parts — heads, hearts and haggis.

SIR WILLIAM OSLER, favorite remark, about 1911; qu., Cushing,
Osler, 969.

Scotsmen more than others seem to
cultivate versatility.

H. H. LANGTON, *Sir Daniel Wilson*,
1929.

SEA.

(See also: DOMINION)

If the sea was always calm, it would
poison the universe.

T. C. HALIBURTON, *Sam Slick*,
1836.

We have in Canada, it is true, the two
principal elements of nationality —
population and territory — but we
also know what we lack. Great as is
our population and our territory, there
is wanting that other element absolutely
necessary to make a powerful nation,
the maritime element. What nation has
ever been powerful without the maritime
element?

SIR GEORGES E. CARTIER, speech in
Halifax, Aug. 15, 1864.

I rejoice, moreover, that we men of
insular origin are about to recover one

of our lost senses — the sense that
comprehends the sea — that we are not
now about to subside into a character
so foreign to all our antecedents, that
of a mere inland people.

THOMAS D'ARCY MCGEE, speech
at Cookshire, Que., Dec. 22, 1864,
on confederation with the maritime
provinces.

The Union of the Provinces restores
us to the ocean, takes us back to the
Atlantic, and launches us once more on
the modern Mediterranean, the true
central sea of the western world.

THOMAS D'ARCY MCGEE, speech
at Cookshire, Que., Dec. 22, 1864.

The night has fallen and the tide
Now and again comes drifting home,
Across these aching barrens wide,
A sigh like driven wind or foam:
In grief the flood is bursting home.

BLISS CARMAN, "Low tide on
Grande Pré", 1889.

Oh, the shambling sea is a sexton old,
And well his work is done,
With an equal grave for lord and
knave,
He buries them every one.

BLISS CARMAN, "The gravedigger",
1893.

No sound nor echo of the sea
But hath tradition of your voice.

BLISS CARMAN, "The end of the
trail", 1893.

The glad indomitable sea.

BLISS CARMAN, "A sea child", 1893.

There was in Arll a little cove
Where the salt wind came cool and
free:
A foamy beach that one would love
If he were longing for the sea.

DUNCAN CAMPBELL SCOTT, "The
piper of Arll", in *Truth*, N. Y.,
Dec. 14, 1895.

Take me out, sink me deep in the
green profound,
To sway with the long weed, swing
with the drowned,
Where the change of the soft tide
makes no sound,
Far below the keels of the outward
bound.

CHARLES G. D. ROBERTS, "The
stranded ship", 1902.

Canadian history is full of sea-power; but Canadian histories are not.

WILLIAM WOOD, *All afloat*, 1914.

The shore has perils unknown to the deep.

GEORGE ILES, *Canadian stories*, 1918, 169.

And O, Her skies are bright and blue,
    Her waters bright and pure;
There's balm within Her forest shades
    All world-worn men to cure;
The wholesome Sea is at her gates
    Her gates both East and West,
Then is it strange that we should love
    This land, our Land, the best?

J. A. RITCHIE, "There is a land", 1920; origin of the lines, "The wholesome Sea is at her gates. Her gates both East and West", inscribed in stone over the entrance, House of Parliament, Ottawa.

It took the sea an hour one night,
An hour of storm to place
The sculpture of these granite seams
Upon a woman's face.

E. J. PRATT, "One hour", 1932.

There is no silence upon the earth or under the earth like the silence under the sea.

E. J. PRATT, "Silences", 1937.

There is no mountain-top but must come home
to taste the salt against her heaving side,
no crag but is an exiled reef whose foam
flashes a far white longing for her tide.
And with our happy tears and tears of woe.
we too shall swell her song with what we know.

KENNETH LESLIE, "The misty mother", 1938.

SECORD, LAURA.

Ah! faithful to death were our women of yore.
Have they fled with the past, to be heard of no more?
No, no! Though this laurelled one sleeps in the grave,

We have maidens as true. we have matrons as brave;
And should Canada ever be forced to the test —
To spend for our country the blood of her best —
When her sons lift the linstock and brandish the sword
Her daughters will think of brave Laura Secord.

CHARLES MAIR, "Ballad for brave women", 1885.

Braver deeds are not recorded
In historic treasures hoarded
Than this march of Laura Secord through the forest long ago.

CHARLES E. JAKEWAY, "Laura Secord", 1897.

One, two, three a-Laura,
Four, five six, a-Laura,
Seven, eight, nine, a-Laura,
Ten, a-Laura Secord.

ANON., qu. in B. Hume, *Laura Secord*, 1928, 32. (Ball-bouncing ryhme.)

SENATE.

(See also: PERSONS; POLITICAL SLOGANS; THE RICH)

In the Upper House, the controlling and regulating, but not initiating, branch, we have the sober second thought in legislation.

SIR JOHN A. MACDONALD, speech, Feb. 6, 1865.

For every vacancy there is a claimant who has done something, or expended something, for the party, and whose claims cannot be set aside. The Minister may feel as strongly as his critics how much the Senate would be strengthened, and his own reputation enhanced, by the introduction of some of the merit, ability and experience which do not take the stump. But party demands its pound of flesh.

GOLDWIN SMITH, *Can. monthly*, July, 1872, 67.

I do not believe it is consistent with the true notion of popular Government that we should have a Senate selected by the Administration of the day, and holding their seats for life.

EDWARD BLAKE, speech at Aurora, Ont., Oct. 3, 1874.

An absurdly effete body.

> LORD DUFFERIN, letter to Carnarvon, Oct. 10, 1874.

The Senate of Sir John Macdonald is nothing but a political infirmary and a bribery fund, nor is it possible to conceive any case in which a body so destitute of moral weight could render real service to the nation.

> *The Week,* May 1, 1884, 338.

It is not by any manner of means a trifling thing to say when I say that the value of a Senate is not only in what the Senate does but in what the Senate prevents other people from doing.

> SIR RICHARD CARTWRIGHT, Senate. *Debates,* May 17, 1906, 469.

The Senate is a bulwark against the clamour and caprice of the mob.

> SIR JAMES LOUGHEED, Conservative leader in the Senate, 1906-21; attributed.

As to myself, I have today signed my warrant of political death... How colourless the Senate — the entering gate to coming extinction. Would it have been better to have gone in the midst of conflict?

> SIR GEORGE E. FOSTER, entry in his diary, Aug. 28, 1920; actually appointed to the Senate, Sept. 23, 1921.

SETTLERS.

(See also: IMMIGRATION; PIONEERS)

Americans from the States set themselves down with very little ceremony upon the various townships bordering on their country, and begin to clear the woods, and cultivate the land, often without the knowledge or consent of its proprietors... They are certainly enterprising settlers, and improve the country more in two or three years, than the French Canadians do in a century.

> JOHN LAMBERT, *Travels through Lower Canada,* 1810, I, 142.

I canna ca' this forest hame
It is nae hame to me:

Ilk tree is suthern to my heart,
And unco' to my e'e.

> ANON., "My hame", in *Cobourg Star,* Dec. 27, 1831.

The settler is of infinitely more importance to the country than the land.

> CANADA. COMM. OF CROWN LANDS, *Report,* 1865, xx.

Fairly fit for settlement.

> CANADA, *Statutes, 44 Victoria. Cap. 1,* 1881; from a clause in the Canadian Pacific Syndicate contract which provided for a land subsidy policy.

My axe and I, we do immortal tasks;
We build up nations — this my axe and I.

> ISABELLA V. CRAWFORD, "Malcolm's Katie", 1884.

Abraham trekked out of Ur of the Chaldees under Divine guidance. Thousands of settlers in the Canadian West were moved by the same influence, though they didn't recognize it in the lantern lectures of the Dominion Government's agents, or the restrained advertisements of steamship and railway companies.

> D. B. HANNA, speech, Empire Club, Toronto, Nov. 28, 1907.

Greater than the measure of the heroes of renown,
He is building for the future, and no hand can hold him down;
Though they count him but a common man, he holds the Outer Gate.
And posterity will own him as the father of the State.

> R. J. C. STEAD, "The homesteader", 1908.

We came to build, and building, a mighty structure grew,
And ever as we builded, builded better than we knew;
And through the darkening wilderness, lo! we were led in might,
Our log-heaps made a smoke by day, a pillared flame by night.
Now, when across the continent we've seen our task expand,
To our children's children and their children's children we do bequeath this land.

> ROBERT K. KERNIGHAN, "Pioneer's anthem", 1925.

Leave them alone and pretty soon the Ukrainians will think they won the battle of Trafalgar.

STEPHEN B. LEACOCK, *My discovery of the West*, 1937, 159.

We broke new trails, wild roses at our feet,
And by the banks of the Saskatchewan
We found the thorny brakes as scented sweet
As any incense Eden gave to Man.

ANDREW GRAHAM, "To a Prairie wife", 1945.

SHIPS.

Nova Scotian ships, bearing the British flag into every quarter of the globe, are some proofs of enterprise.

JOSEPH HOWE, letter to Lord John Russell, Sept. 18, 1839.

To handle a ship you must know all the ropes.

THOMAS C. HALIBURTON, *Sam Slick's wise saws*, 1853, ch. III.

O ship incoming from the sea
With all your cloudy tower of sail
Dashing the water to the lea,
And leaning grandly to the gale.

DUNCAN CAMPBELL SCOTT, "Off Riviere du Loup", 1893.

The fog still hangs on the long tide-rips,
The gulls go wavering to and fro,
But where are all the beautiful ships
I knew so long ago?

BLISS CARMAN, "The ships of Saint John", 1921.

SIN.

(See also: GOOD AND EVIL; VIRTUE)

The greater the sinner the greater the saint.

THOMAS C. HALIBURTON, *Sam Slick's wise saws*, 1853, ch. VIII.

There is an hypocrisy in vice as well as religion.

T. C. HALIBURTON, *Sam Slick's wise saws*, 1853, II, 283.

If we begin to do wrong in fun, we are apt to end by doin' wrong in airnist.

T. C. HALIBURTON, *Sam Slick's wise saws*, 1853, II, 314.

You can win sinners, but you can't force them.

T. C. HALIBURTON, *Nature and human nature*, 1855, I, 187.

Puritans, whether in or out of church make more sinners than they save by a long chalk. They ain't content with real sin.

THOMAS C. HALIBURTON, *Nature and human nature*, 1855.

Always sinning and repenting,
Promising to sin no more:
Now resisting, now consenting,
Human to the very core.

ALEXANDER McLACHLAN, "David, king of Israel", 1874.

We are all miserable sinners.

SIR JOHN A. MACDONALD, summer, 1878; a remark at a political meeting when the Liberal Prime Minister, Alexander Mackenzie paused in a scathing attack on the "Pacific Scandal". Macdonald emphasized his interjection by drinking the remainder of the water in a glass that Mackenzie had just half-emptied.

Right hath the sweeter grace,
But Wrong the prettier face.

FREDERICK G. SCOTT, "Wrong and Right", 1894.

The sinner gets many pleasant pickings that never fall in the way of the righteous.

PETER McARTHUR, *To be taken with salt*, 1903, 154.

The way of the transgressor is very popular.

ROBERT C. (BOB) EDWARDS, *Calgary Eye Opener*, May 8, 1915.

SLEEP.

Sleep on it.

T. C. HALIBURTON, *Sam Slick's wise saws*, 1853, II, 55.

There was a time when sleep
Was wont to approach me with her soundless feet,
And take me by surprise. I called her not,
And yet she'd come; but now I even woo her,

And court her by the cunning use
   of drugs,
But still she will not turn to me her
   steps;
Not even to approach, and, looking
   down,
Drop on these temples one oblivious
   tear.
    CHARLES HEAVYSEGE, *Saul*, 1857.

When the Sleepy Man comes with the
   dust on his eyes
   (Oh, weary, my Dearie, so weary!)
He shuts up the earth, and he opens
   the skies.
   (So hush-a-by, weary, my Dearie!)
    CHARLES G. D. ROBERTS, "Sleepy
    man", 1896.

Infinite compassion is in thee un-
   sealed;
In thee, all griefs are lost, all wounds
   are healed,
And death is silent dreamless ecstasy.
    WILLIAM E. MARSHALL "To sleep",
    1907.

After all, why should I go to bed
every night? Sleep is only a habit.
    SIR WILLIAM VAN HORNE, qu.,
    Canadian mag., Sept., 1913.

SMOKING.

The moment a man takes to a pipe
he becomes a philosopher; it's the
poor man's friend; it calms the mind,
soothes the temper, and makes a man
patient under trouble.
    T. C. HALIBURTON, *Sam Slick*,
    1838, 39.

There isn't a woman living so bad
in arithmetic that she cannot calculate
how much her husband would save if
he didn't smoke.
    ROBERT C. (BOB) EDWARDS, *Cal-
    gary Eye Opener*, July 20, 1918, 2.

SNOW.

If, Pilgrim, chance thy steps should
   lead
Where, emblem of our holy creed,
   Canadian crosses glow —
There you may hear what here you
   read,

And seek in witness of the deed
   Our Ladye of the Snow!
    THOMAS D'A. McGEE, "Our Ladye
    of the Snow", 1858; a reference
    to the original church, Notre Dame
    des Neiges, which stood on "the
    Priests' Farm", Montreal.

Snow — snow — fast-falling snow!
Snow on the house-tops — snow in
   the street —
Snow overhead, and under feet —
Snow in the country — snow in the
   town,
   Silently sinking down;
Everywhere, everywhere fast-falling
   snow,
Dazzling the eyes with its crystalline
   glow!
    JENNIE E. HAIGHT, "Snow", in,
    Dewart, *Selections*, 1864, 132.

March is slain; the keen winds fly;
Nothing more is thine to do;
April kisses thee good-bye;
Thou must haste and follow too.
    ARCHIBALD LAMPMAN, "Godspeed to
    the snow", 1893.

A few bronzed cedars in their fading
   dress,
Almost asleep for happy weariness,
Lean their blue shadows on the
   puckered snow.
    ARCHIBALD LAMPMAN, "Before the
    robin", 1900.

Now soon, ah, soon, I know,
The trumpets of the north will blow,
And the great winds will come to
   bring
The pale wild riders of the snow.
    BLISS CARMAN, "Before the snow",
    1916.

Exquisite things have been said about
   snow,
Snow said them first, those exquisite
   things.
    ROBERT FINCH, "The tribute", 1949.

SOCIALISM.

There is no virtue in public ownership
outside the wisdom, capacity and integrity of those who direct such enterprises.
    SIR JOHN WILLISON, *Willison's
    monthly*, June, 1925.

True cooperation has its final goal in socialism, which is the continual observance of the Golden Rule.

> E. A. PARTRIDGE, at convention, United Farmers of Canada (Sask.), Feb. 1930.

Until Christians understand and apply the lessons of Marxism they cannot enter the Kingdom of Heaven.

> EUGENE FORSEY, in, *Towards the Christian revolution*, 1937.

If property, profit, the reward of toil, the fundamental instinct of the human race to gain, to acquire, to have, to reach somewhere, is taken away, then I for one do not feel that we have anything worth fighting for.

> ARTHUR MEIGHEN, speech in Toronto, Jan. 22, 1941.

SOCIETY.

(See also: CLASSES)

To put the multitude at the top and the few at the bottom is a radical reversion of society which every reflecting man must foresee can end only by its downfall.

> SIR FRANCIS BOND HEAD, *Narrative*, 1839, 464.

The religion of privilege has lost its power to awe or to control; and if society wishes to rest on a safe foundation, it must show that it is at least trying to be just.

> GOLDWIN SMITH, "The labour movement", speech to Mechanics Inst., Montreal, 1872.

Society is a half-blind mass, living on its traditions, not knowing whither it is going, requiring leadership that will tell it the truth.

> G. M. WRONG, in *Can. hist. rev.*, 1933, 7.

SOCIETY, POLITE.

It was none of your skim-milk parties, but superfine uppercrust.

> THOMAS C. HALIBURTON, *Sam Slick*, 1836, ch. XXVIII.

I want you to see Peel, Stanley, Graham, Shiel, Russell, Macaulay, Old Joe, and so on. They are all uppercrust here.

> T. C. HALIBURTON, *Sam Slick in England*, 1843, ch. XXIV.

Quite as much "grit" and a much harder climb are needed to reach distinction from the top as from the bottom of the social scale.

> SIR WILLIAM OSLER. *Philadelphia med. jour.*, 1899, 607.

The average society woman looks younger than she is and acts younger than she looks.

> PETER McARTHUR. *To be taken with salt*, 1903, 146.

SOLDIERS.

(See also: CONSCRIPTION, MILITARY; ENEMIES; WAR DEAD)

Cold on Canadian hills, or Minden's plain,
Perhaps that parent mourn'd her soldier slain;
Bent o'er her babe, her eyes dissolved in dew,
The big drops mingled with the milk he drew,
Gave the sad presage of his future years,
The child of misery, baptized in tears.

> JOHN LANGHORNE, "The country justice", 1774.

Tramp, tramp, tramp, the boys are marching.

> LACHLAN McGOUN, from the poem, later a song, written while the author was serving in the artillery against the Fenians, 1866.

'Twas only as a volunteer that I left my abode,
I never thought of coming here to work upon the road.
We'll keep our spirits up, my boys, and not look sad or sober.
Nor grumble at our hardships on our way to Manitoba.

> ANON., "Expedition song", Red River Expedition, 1870.

Why, what would ye have? There is not a lad that treads in the gallant ranks

Who does not already bear on his breast the Rose of a Nation's Thanks!

> ISABELLA V. CRAWFORD, "The rose of a nation's thanks", 1884.

Your bulwark hills, your valleys broad
Streams where de Salaberry trod,
Where Wolfe achieved, where Brock was slain —
Their voices are the voice of God!

> CHARLES G. D. ROBERTS, "Canadian streams", 1893.

The Old Eighteen.

> Popular term, about 1900, for the first students at Royal Military College, Kingston, opened June 1, 1876.

The man who can fight to Heaven's own height
Is the man who can fight when he's losing.

> ROBERT W. SERVICE, "Carry on," 1916.

So give me a strong right arm for a wrong's swift righting;
Stave of a song on my lips as my sword is smiting;
Death in my boots, maybe, but fighting, fighting!

> ROBERT W. SERVICE, "Song of the soldier-born", 1916.

If there is in Canada today one portion of its citizenry which more than any other is entitled to consideration, it is the men who risked their lives in battle and those who shared with them the dangers and privations of war.

> W. L. MACKENZIE KING, speech to Liberal supporters, August, 1919.

From the camp behind the hill
He could hear the bugle shrill,
"We are here! We are here!
Soldiers all!
Good cheer! We are near!
Ontario! Ontario!
Toronto! Montreal!"

> SIR ARTHUR CONAN DOYLE, "Bugles of Canada", 1922.

Zombies.

> Term used in 1944 for home-defence troops conscripted for European service.

SORROW.
(See also: DESPAIR)

Ah, sorrow, how close you tread on the heels of enjoyment!

> THOMAS C. HALIBURTON, *Sam Slick's wise saws*, 1853, ch. XXVI.

All is a mystery,
All is a wonder —
The blue vault above,
' And the green world under.
Amid our heaped knowledge
The silent soul hears
But the rattling of chains
And the pattering of tears.

> ALEXANDER MCLACHLAN, "A dream", 1856.

O foolish ones, put by your cares!
Where wants are many, joys are few;
And at the wilding springs of peace,
God keeps an open house for you.

> BLISS CARMAN, "The mendicants", 1894.

Now he has gone
Take out your sorrow,
Shake it, and iron it,
And put it on tomorrow.

> DOROTHY LIVESAY, "A song for Ophelia", 1932.

SOVEREIGNTY.

I claim for Canada this, that in future Canada shall be at liberty to act or not act, to interfere or not interfere, to do just as she pleases, and that she shall reserve to herself the right to judge whether or not there is cause for her to act.

> SIR WILFRID LAURIER, H. of C., *Debates*, Feb. 5, 1900, 72.

In Canada there is no sovereignty in the people. So far as we are concerned it is in the Parliament at Westminster, and our powers to legislate are such, and only such, as that Parliament has given us.

> A. E. RICHARDS, *Manitoba law repts.*, 1916, 13.

SPEECHES.
(See also: FREE SPEECH; TALK)

It is easier to forge iron any time than a speech, especially if you ain't broughten up to the business.

> T. C. HALIBURTON, *Sam Slick*, 1840, ch. II.

All his speeches would read both ways, so that he could interpret them as he liked: so, which ever way things eventuated, he was always right.

T. C. HALIBURTON, *Sam Slick*, 1840, 192.

Speak the truth and feel it.

JOSEPH HOWE, address to Halifax Mechanics' Institute, Sept. 11, 1845.

It's all bunkum, you know.

THOMAS C. HALIBURTON, *Sam Slick's wise saws*, 1853, ch. II.

We, in Canada, have got into the habit of delivering lectures and essays in parliament. Well, these essays we can all find in books, and it is merely lecture and water that we get, as a rule, in long speeches.

SIR JOHN A. MACDONALD, speech, 1861; qu., Biggar, *Anecdotal life*, 184.

Elegant flummery.

GOLDWIN SMITH, on speeches made by Marquis of Dufferin while Governor-General, 1872-8.

Smith is a far better speaker than I gave him credit for. He has coolness and resource and plausibility, and just that amount of venom when attacked which a good statesman ought to have.

SIR JOHN A. MACDONALD, attributed; about 1872, after hearing Donald A. Smith (Lord Strathcona) speak in the House of Commons.

Oratory is the fusion of reason and passion.

GOLDWIN SMITH; attributed.

One of those war, famine, and pestilence speeches which have so often carried the country for the Government.

SIR JOHN THOMPSON (Premier), H. of C., *Debates*, June 28, 1892, on a preceding speech made by Sir Richard Cartwright, of the Opposition.

There comes to mind the juggler who, with great dexterity, keeps several balls in the air. The balls are Isolationism, North Americanism, Imperialism and Collectivism. One sees them going up and coming down with rhythmic regular-

ity, and suddenly they are lost in polished phrases of a platitudinous peroration — the magician's handkerchief. And yet it is statesmanship honestly striving for national unity.

E. J. TARR, in, *International affairs*, 1937, 685.

I wish my tongue were a quiver the size of a cask
Packed and crammed with long venomous rankling darts.
I'd fling you more full of them, and joy in the task,
Than ever Sebastian was, or Caesar, with thirty-three swords in his heart.

L. A. MACKAY, "The ill-tempered lover", 1938.

SPORTS.

Then soop, soop, soop! soop, soop, soop!
And draw the creepin stane a wee;
The ice may thaw, the day may snaw,
But aye we're merry round the tee.

ANON., Ontario Curling Club, *Annual*, 1876, 109.

Oh! cheerful frost, we'd welcome thee,
Each curler's voice shouts loud with glee.
We'd gladly gather round the tee
And ne'er gang hame;
We'd play as long as we could see,
Grand roarin' game!

"W. TORONTO", in Ont. Curling Club, *Annual*, 1877, 106.

O wild kaleidoscopic panorama of jaculatory arms and legs.
The twisting, twining, turning, tussling, throwing, thrusting, throttling, tugging, thumping, the tightening thews.
The tearing of tangled trousers, the jut of giant calves protuberant.
The wriggleness, the wormlike, snaky movement and life of it.

ANON., "The football match", in Lighthall, *Songs of the great Dominion*, 1889, 209.

My glad feet shod with the glittering steel
I was the god of the winged heel.

CHARLES G. D. ROBERTS, "The skater", 1896.

For on the rink distinctions sink,
    An' caste aside is laid;
Whate'er ye be, the stane and tee
    Will test what stuff ye're made.
    ALEXANDER McLACHLAN, "Curling
    song", 1900.

Golf may be played on Sunday, not
being a game within the view of the
law, but being a form of moral effort.
    STEPHEN B. LEACOCK, "Why I refuse
    to play golf", in, *Other fancies*, 1923.

The iron hills surround us, solemn in
    their sleep,
The susurrus of swishing skis fills
    the atmosphere,
As rhythmically gliding, swift where
    slopes are steep
We rush the narrow speedway, drop-
    ping sudden, sheer.
    ARTHUR S. BOURINOT, "Canadian
    ski song", 1923.

SPRING.

Will the spring ever come?
    ANNA JAMESON, March 1837, in
    Toronto.

As memory of pain, all past, is
    peace,
And joy, dream-tasted, hath the
    deepest cheer,
So art thou sweetest of all months
    that lease
The twelve short spaces of the flying
    year.
    ARCHIBALD LAMPMAN, "April",
    1884.

I, the invincible,
    March, the earth-shaker;
March, the sea-lifter;
    March, the sky-render.
    ISABELLA V. CRAWFORD, "March",
    1884.

The sap flies upward. Death is over
    and done.
The glad earth wakes; the glad light
    breaks; the days
Grow round, grow radiant. Praise
    for the new life!
Praise
For bliss of breath and blood
    beneath the sun!
    CHARLES G. D. ROBERTS, "The
    waking earth", 1893.

Make me over, Mother April,
When the sap begins to stir!
Make me man or make me woman,
Make me oaf or ape or human,
Cup of flower or cone of fir;
Make me anything but neuter
When the sap begins to stir!
    BLISS CARMAN, "Spring song",
    1894.

Winter's done, and April's in the
    skies.
Earth, look up with laughter in your
    eyes!
    CHARLES G. D. ROBERTS, "An April
    adoration", 1896.

Lo, now comes the April pageant
And the Easter of the year.
Now the tulip lifts her chalice,
And the hyacinth his spear.
    BLISS CARMAN, "On Ponus Ridge",
    1909; ("Resurgam").

She comes with gusts of laughter,
    The music as of rills;
With tenderness and sweetness,
    The wisdom of the hills.
    BLISS CARMAN, "Over the wintry
    threshold", *Smart Set*, April 1913.

Now hath a wonder lit the saddened
    eyes
Long misted by a grievous winter
    clime;
And now the dull heart leaps with
    love's surprise
And sings its joy. For 'tis the happy
    time,
And all the brooding earth is full
    of chime,
And all the hosts of sleepers under-
    ground
Have burst out suddenly in glorious
    prime;
And all the airy spirits now have
    found
Their wonted shrines with life and
    love entwinèd 'round.
    WILLIAM E. MARSHALL, *Brookfield*,
    1914.

Once more in misted April
    The world is growing green.
Along the winding river
    The plumey willows lean.
    BLISS CARMAN, "An April morning",
    1916.

April is no month for burials.
Bloodroot and trilium break out
    of cover,
And crocuses stir blindly in their
    cells,
Hawthorns bloom whitely, laburnums
    shudder
Profusion from dim boughs — slight
    daffodils
Defy the pale predominance of
    colour.
April is rather a month for subtle
    spells.

LEO COX, "Rite of spring", 1933.

STARS.

Alive all heaven seems! with won-
    drous glow
Tenfold refulgent every star appears,
As if some wide, celestial gale did
    blow,
And thrice illume the ever-kindled
    spheres.

CHARLES HEAVYSEGE, poem no.
XIV, in *Jephthah's daughter*, 1865.

Beneath the spandrels of the Way
Worlds rolled to night — from night
    to day;
In Space's ocean suns were spray.

ISABELLA V. CRAWFORD, "Gisli the
Chieftain", 1905.

Now fades the glowing vesper bars
    That gird the pillars of the west,
And all the lustres of the stars
    Burn in their rooms of rest.

ALBERT D. WATSON, "Evening
peace", 1923.

I glance from humble toil and see
The star-gods go in heavenly pride;
Bright Sirius glittering through a
    tree
Orion with eternal stride.

J. E. H. MACDONALD, "Kitchen
window", 1933.

STATISTICS.

Figures are the representatives of
numbers, and not things.

T. C. HALIBURTON, *Sam Slick*,
1838, 208.

When I am Premier, you will not
have to look up figures to find out

whether you are prosperous: you will
know by feeling in your pockets.

SIR WILFRID LAURIER, speeches in
early 1890's, on dubious statistics.

If there are politicians, financiers,
economists, whose work the Dominion
Statistician has not succeeded in enriching, the fault is likely to be theirs.

G. E. JACKSON, *Can. hist. rev.*,
1922, 256.

The statistician with his plotted graph
showing where we will arrive ten years
hence is not as convincing as he was
of yore. I have seen too many fine
ascending projections dip into the cellar
these past few years.

J. W. DAFOE, in *C.J.E.P.S.*, 1938,
287.

STATUS.

(See also: CANADIAN-BRIT-
ISH RELATIONS)

A colony, yet a nation — words never
before in the history of the world
associated together.

SIR WILFRID LAURIER, speech in
London at the Queen's Jubilee,
1897; a reference to Canada.

We are reaching the day when our
Canadian Parliament will claim co-equal
rights with the British Parliament and
when the only ties binding us together
will be a common throne and a common
crown.

SIR WILFRID LAURIER, speech
at Tercentenary Celebration, Quebec, 1908.

This policy is in the best traditions
of the Liberal party. This policy is
the latest link in the long chain of
events which, following the principles
laid down by the Reformers of old
times, Baldwin and Lafontaine, step
by step, stage by stage, have brought
Canada to the position it now occupies,
that is to say, the rank, dignity and
status of a nation within the British
Empire.

SIR WILFRID LAURIER, H. of C.,
Debates, Feb. 3, 1910, 2953; on
the Naval Service Bill.

The highest future for this Dominion lies within this Empire upon conditions of equal status..

> Sir Robert Borden, *Lib.-Conservative handbook*, 1913; "Equal status", or, "Equality of nationhood" for Canada within the Empire are also associated with Borden's efforts at Paris Peace Conference. See his *Memorandum*, Mar. 12, 1919.

The same indomitable spirit which made [Canada] capable of that effort and sacrifice made her equally incapable of accepting at the Peace Conference, in the League of Nations, or elsewhere, a status inferior to that accorded to nations less advanced in their development, less amply endowed in wealth, resources, and population, no more complete in their sovereignty, and far less conspicuous in their sacrifices.

> Sir Robert Borden, H. of C., *Debates*, Sept. 2, 1919.

The status of any country is limited by the average status of its inhabitants.

> John Oliver, speech to students, Vancouver, when Premier, 1918-27.

Equal status!

> W. L. Mackenzie King, remark made on throwing a Canadian cent and an English halfpenny into the running metal, at Croydon, of the bells being made for the Peace Tower Carillon; a Canadian Press despatch, Imperial conference, 1926.

STORMS.

(See also: The Wind)

When swallows fly low a storm will soon blow.

> Saying of pioneer Ontario farmers.

Storms make oaks take deeper root.

> T. C. Haliburton, *Sam Slick's wise saws*, 1853, II, 300.

The abated blue is blotted from the sky
From calm comes chaos, and loud grows in rage
The rattling thunder, while the lightning leaps
And plays before us 'midst the firmament.

> Charles Heavysege, "Jezebel", 1867.

STRENGTH.

It may be well to have the strength of a giant, but it should not be used like a giant.

> Robert Baldwin, letter to Sir Francis Hincks, Jan. 27, 1848.

Where there is much strength, there ain't apt to be much gumption.

> Thomas C. Haliburton, *Sam Slick's wise saws*, 1853, ch. XV.

STUDENTS.

The value of a really great student to the country is equal to half a dozen grain elevators or a new transcontinental railway.

> Sir William Osler, "The student life", 1905.

Except it be a lover, no one is more interesting as an object of study than a student.

> Sir William Osler, "The student life", 1905.

What is the student but a lover courting a fickle mistress who ever eludes his grasp?

> Sir William Osler, "The student life", 1905.

The true student is a citizen of the world, the allegiance of whose soul, at any rate, is too precious to be restricted to a single country. The great minds, the great works, transcend all limitations of time, of language and of race, and the scholar can never feel initiated into the problems of the elect until he can approach all of life's problems from the cosmopolitan standpoint.

> Sir William Osler, "The student life", 1905.

Whoever ceases to be a student has never been a student.

> George Iles, *Canadian stories*, 1918, 169.

SUCCESS.

(See also: Conduct of Life; Failure)

It is done by a knowledge of soft sawder and human natur'.

> T. C. Haliburton, *Sam Slick*, 1836, ch. II.

There's nothin' like leavin' all's well alone.

> T. C. HALIBURTON, *Sam Slick*, 1838, 136.

It's the early bird that gets the worm.

> T. C. HALIBURTON, *Sam Slick's wise saws*, 1853, I, 146.

A feller with one idea grows rich, while he who calls him a fool dies poor.

> T. C. HALIBURTON, *Sam Slick's wise saws*, 1853, I, 314.

The great secret of success is intense faith in oneself.

> TORONTO *Globe*, May 23, 1865.

The laws of creation insist on respect;
Believe in the virtues of cause and effect;
Trust only to truth, and you'll ne'er be misled,
If you would be master and sit at the head.

> ALEXANDER McLACHLAN, "If you would be master", 1874.

We know that success depends not upon absolute perfection, but with individuals as with Governments, to make the fewest mistakes is the criterion of success.

> DONALD A. SMITH (Lord Strathcona), election speech, 1878.

Prosperity never spoils a man that adversity cannot crush.

> ROBERT C. (BOB) EDWARDS, *Calgary Eye Opener*, Nov. 24, 1917.

There is no better training for uncommon opportunities than diligence in common affairs.

> GEORGE ILES, *Canadian stories*, 1918, 173.

To conquer finely, or to sink
Debonair against defeat,
This is the rarest grace I think —
This is the fate that I would meet.

> TOM MacINNES, "Ballade of action", 1918.

The path to success is paved with good intentions that were carried out.

> ROBERT C. (BOB) EDWARDS, *Calgary Eye Opener*, Nov. 22, 1919.

Had the men who undertook any great enterprise since time began realized half the obstacles and discouragements they would meet, they would never have started, but fortunately they didn't — and don't.

> SIR WILLIAM VAN HORNE, a favorite maxim; qu., in Skelton, *Sir A. T. Galt*, 1920, 560.

Save half of what you earn; look ahead; and hang on — never let go!

> DONALD A. SMITH (Lord Strathcona), qu., Macdonald, *Can. portraits*, 1925, 146.

Keep in mind, though, this eternal truth: Difficulties do not crush men, they make them.

> ARTHUR MEIGHEN, speech at St. Mary's, Ont., Sept. 13, 1942.

SUMMER.

I do wish I could jist slip off my flesh and sit in my bones for a space, to cool myself.

> T. C. HALIBURTON, *Sam Slick*, 1838, 86.

This dreamy Indian-summer day
Attunes the soul to tender sadness;
We love — but joy not in the ray:
It is not summer's fervid gladness,
But a melancholy glory
Hovering softly round decay,
Like swan that sings her own sad story
Ere she floats in death away.

> SUSANNA MOODIE, "Indian summer", 1864.

With throb of throstle and with throat of wren,
Full of soft cheepings comes the longed-for May;
With myriad murmuring life throughout each day,
It grows and greens in grove and field and glen.

> J. ALMON RITCHIE, "May time". 1885.

In the sloped shadow of my hat
I lean at rest, and drain the heat;
Nay more, I think some blessèd power
Hath brought me wandering idly here:
In the full furnace of this hour
My thoughts grow keen and clear.

> ARCHIBALD LAMPMAN, "Heat", 1888.

In intervals of dreams I hear
    The cricket from the droughty
      ground;
The grasshoppers spin into mine ear
    A small innumerable sound.
    ARCHIBALD LAMPMAN, "Heat", 1888.

Here's to the day when it is May
    And care as light as a feather,
When your little shoes and my big
    boots
    Go tramping over the heather.
    BLISS CARMAN, "A toast", 1892.

Fair the land lies, full of August,
    Meadow island, shingly bar,
Open barns and breezy twilight,
    Peace, and the mild evening star.
    BLISS CARMAN, "The ships of St.
    John", in, *Canadian mag.* Dec. 1893.
    148.

Now the goldenrod invades
Every clearing in the hills:
The dry glow of August fades,
And the lonely cricket shrills.
    BLISS CARMAN, "At the yellow of
    the leaf", 1903.

This short Canadian summer,
    Whose every lonesome breath
Holds hint of autumn and winter,
    As life holds hints of death.
    WILFRED CAMPBELL, in, Campbell
    and Martin, *Canada*, 1907, 134.

Behold, now, where the pageant of
    high June
Halts in the glowing noon!
The trailing shadows rest on plain
    and hill;
The bannered hosts are still,
While over forest crown and mountain
    head
The azure tent is spread.
    BLISS CARMAN, "The tent of noon",
    1915.

This is July of the bountiful heat,
Month of wild roses, and berries, and
    wheat.
    ALBERT D. WATSON, "July", 1917.

While we welter
In the swelter
Of the Pestilential Heat
Drinking Sodas
In Pagodas
At the Corner of the Street
It seems to me

That it would be
My highest aspiration
To Sail away
On a Holiday
Of Arctic Exploration.
    STEPHEN B. LEACOCK, College days,
    1923, 108. .

SUN.

And all the swarthy afternoon
    We watched the great deliberate
    sun
Walk through the crimsoned hazy
    world
    Counting his hilltops one by one.
    BLISS CARMAN, "The eavesdropper",
    1893.

The sun, down the long mountain
    valley rolled,
A sudden swinging avalanche of gold.
    ARCHIBALD LAMPMAN, "A dawn on
    the Lievre", 1900

The sun can find no darkness any-
    where,
Where'er his bright eye turns is
    daylight fair.
    ALBERT D. WATSON, "Lux ubique".
    1908.

The harvest sun lay hot and strong
    On waving grain and grain in
    sheaf,
On dusty highway stretched along,
    On hill and vale, on stalk and
    leaf.
    JEAN BLEWETT, "The firstborn",
    1922.

The Sun would gain nothing in beauty
by appearing but once a year.
    TOM MACINNES, *Complete poems*,
    1923.

T

TALK.

        (See also: ARGUMENT;
        SPEECHES)

Whenever you make an impression
on a man, stop; your reasonin' and
details may ruin you.
    T. C. HALIBURTON, *Sam Slick*,
    1836.

I was plaguy apt to talk turkey.
    THOMAS C. HALIBURTON, *Traits of
    American humor*, 1852, I, 79.

Conversation is more than half the time a refuge from thought or a blind to conceal it.

> T. C. HALIBURTON, *Sam Slick's wise saws*, 1853, I, 161.

I have learnt a good deal from my own talk.

> T. C. HALIBURTON, *Sam Slick's wise saws*, 1853, II, 168.

I shouldn't mind your rippin' out an oath or two now and then, for thunder will burst and it clears the air.

> THOMAS C. HALIBURTON, *Sam Slick's wise saws*, 1853, ch. VI.

Fellows who have no tongues are often all eyes and ears.

> T. C. HALIBURTON, *Sam Slick's wise saws*, 1853, II, 281.

You have to cant a little with the world, if you want even common civil usage.

> THOMAS C. HALIBURTON, *Sam Slick's wise saws*, 1853, ch. X

Write the word down, for partitions have ears.

> THOMAS C. HALIBURTON, *Sam Slick's wise saws*, 1853, ch. XI.

Look wise, say nothing, and grunt. Speech was given to conceal thought.

> SIR WILLIAM OSLER, *Oslerisms* (Bean), 1905.

Consider the virtues of taciturnity. Speak only when you have something to say.

> SIR WILLIAM OSLER, *Johns Hopkins Hosp. bull.*, 1919, 198.

Silence is a powerful weapon.

> SIR WILLIAM OSLER, *Johns Hopkins Hosp. bull.*, 1919, 198.

TARIFF.

(See also: PROTECTION (TARIFF): RECIPROCITY; TRADE)

Tariff for revenue only.

> LIBERAL PARTY platform plank, adopted at Ottawa Convention, 1893.

The tariff of abominations.

> LIBERAL PARTY phrase for the protective tariff of Sir John A. Macdonald and his successors, modified by W. S. Fielding, 1897.

Adequate protection is that which would at all times secure the Canadian market to Canadians in respect to all Canadian enterprises.

> SIR ROBERT BORDEN, speech in Montreal, Oct. 15, 1904.

The ramparts of gold.

> ARTHUR MEIGHEN, phrase used to denounce the protectionist tariff favoured by some Liberals, in, H. of C., *Debates*, 1910, 1917.

The only way to settle a Tariff is to cut its head off just in front of its tail.

> MICHAEL CLARK, H. of C., *Debates*, May 25, 1920.

Protection on apples in British Columbia, Free Trade in the Prairie Provinces and rural parts of Ontario, Protection in industrial centres in Ontario, Conscription in Quebec and Humbug in the Maritimes.

> ARTHUR MEIGHEN, speech in Montreal, Nov. 14, 1921, on W. L. Mackenzie King's interpretation of the Liberal platform of 1919, in the election campaign of 1921.

TAXATION.

They pay no taxes for perhaps nearly the same reason that you can't talk the breeks off a Hielandman.

> LORD DALHOUSIE, letter, [1824?] quoted, *Can. hist. rev.*, XII, 122.

Do, Canadians, clean your firelocks and fight like game cocks to get yourselves taxed to uphold the tax gatherer at 30 per cent.

> W. L. MACKENZIE, in *The Constitution*, June, 7, 1837.

The Government of Canada acting for its Legislature and people cannot, through those feelings of deference which they owe to the Imperial authorities, in any manner waive or diminish the right of the people of Canada to decide for themselves both as to the mode and extent to which taxation shall be imposed.

> SIR ALEXANDER T. GALT, Executive minutes, Nov. 12, 1859, in Series E, State Book U, in Public Archives.

The smuggler is a check upon the extravagance of governments and the increase of taxation. Any government that raises its tariffs too high, or increases its taxation too far, will be kept in check by smugglers.

JOSEPH HOWE, speech in Detroit, Aug. 14, 1865.

However much the Canadian taxpayer may favour a policy of strict economy in the abstract, he likes nothing so little as its application.

SIR JOSEPH POPE, *Memoirs of Macdonald*, 1894, II, 141.

It is a sound principle of finance, and a still sounder principle of government, that those who have the duty of expending the revenue of a country should also be saddled with the responsibility of levying and providing it.

SIR WILFRID LAURIER, H. of C., *Debates*, Feb. 21, 1905, 1434.

The promises of yesterday are the taxes of today.

W. L. MACKENZIE KING, H. of C., *Debates*, June 16, 1931.

A tax upon international good will.

W. L. MACKENZIE KING, H. of C., *Debates*, July 17, 1931; on taxation of magazines entering Canada.

TEACHERS.
(See also: EDUCATION)

The great secret of life is to hear lessons, and not to teach them.

THOMAS C. HALIBURTON, *Sam Slick's wise saws*, 1853, ch. XX.

The teacher is the key. To what purpose do you build brick schoolhouses, elect trustees, and send your children to school unless you have an efficient teacher to instruct them? And you cannot get good teachers at the present rate of pay.

EDWARD BLAKE, speech at Aurora, Ont., Oct. 3, 1874.

The teacher's life should have three periods, study until twenty-five, investigation until forty, professional until sixty, at which age I would have him retired on a double allowance.

SIR WILLIAM OSLER, "The fixed period", address, Johns Hopkins Univ., Feb. 22, 1905.

It is well for young men to remember that no bubble is so iridescent or floats longer than that blown by the successful teacher.

SIR WILLIAM OSLER, address, Royal Infirmary, Glasgow, Oct. 4, 1911.

I owe a lot to my teachers and mean to pay them back some day.

STEPHEN B. LEACOCK, *College days*, 1923, 118.

A dull teacher, with no enthusiasm in his own subject, commits the unpardonable sin.

R. C. WALLACE, *A liberal education*, 1932.

To be allowed to teach children should be the sign of the final approval of society.

G. BROCK CHISHOLM, speech in Washington, D. C., Oct. 23, 1945.

He had the educator's peculiar genius for imparting knowledge without himself assimilating it.

P. G. HIEBERT, *Sarah Binks*, 1947.

TELEPHONE.

Mr. Watson, come here, I want you.

ALEXANDER G. BELL, to his assistant, March 10, 1876, the first intelligible words transmitted by telephone.

It was I who invented the telephone and it was invented wherever I happened to be at the time. Of this you may be sure, the telephone was invented in Canada. It was made in the United States. The first transmission of a human voice over a telephone wire, where the speaker and the listener were miles apart, was in Canada. The first transmissions by wire in which the conversation was carried on reciprocally over the same line was in the United States.

ALEXANDER G. BELL, speech, Can. Club, Ottawa, Mar. 27, 1909.

THEATRE.

Actors in Canada are little too much of the Fly by Night order to hold a high social status.

HORTON RHYS, *A theatrical trip*, 1861.

I find writing about the Canadian theatre or drama depressingly like discussing the art of sailing among the bedouins. There is so little to be said on the subject save to point out why there is none.

> MERRILL DENISON, *Year book of the arts in Canada*, 1929.

THOMPSON, DAVID.

Thus I have fully completed the survey of this part of North America from sea to sea; and by almost innumerable astronomical observations have determined the position of the Mountains, Lakes and Rivers, and other remarkable places on this continent; the maps of all of which have been drawn, and laid down in geographical position, being now the work of twenty-seven years.

> DAVID THOMPSON, on reaching the Pacific, July, 1811.

He was the greatest land geographer the British race has produced.

> J. B. TYRRELL, in *Geog. jour.*, Jan., 1911; also, "He was the greatest practical land geographer the world has produced", in, Can. Hist. Assoc., *Rept.*, 1927, 14.

From Churchill to the Assiniboine
And up the Saskatchewan,
Back and forth, through all the North
His purpose drove him on,
Making a white man's trail for those
Who should come when he was gone.

> BLISS CARMAN, "David Thompson, explorer"; recited by the author, Lake Windermere, B. C., Aug. 30, 1922 at Thompson centenary celebration.

Intrepid, strenuous, indomitable, he overcame every obstacle with a concentrated, prudent, and persistent enthusiasm. Confronting all the perils of the Unknown, taking his life in his hand, forcing his way through mountains by untrodden paths, running furious rapids in improvised canoes, deserted by followers and guides, threatened by hostile and suspicious tribesmen, by cold and starvation, his energy and courage never failed or faltered.

> SIR FREDERICK WILLIAMS-TAYLOR, in Can. Hist. Assoc., *Rept.*, 1927, 9.

THOMPSON, SIR JOHN.

Thompson has just two faults. He is a little too fond of satire, and a little too much of a Nova Scotian.

> SIR JOHN A. MACDONALD, on Sir John Thompson, about 1885-91; Macdonald also said, "The great discovery of my life was my discovery of Thompson".

Thompson will never make a politician. He won't even consider whether a thing is good for the party until he is quite sure that it is good for the country.

> An anonymous Conservative, to C.R.W. Biggar, about 1892.

THOUGHT.

> (See also: IDEAS; INTELLIGENCE)

Concealment is guilt. Hidin' thoughts, like hidin' things, shows there's a secret.

> T. C. HALIBURTON, *Sam Slick's wise saws*, 1853, II, 46.

The thoughts despised, as new or strange,
May yet in regal triumph reign;
The form and garb of truth may change,
And yet the inner life remain.

> EDWARD H. DEWART, "A plea for liberty", 1869.

In the mighty field of thought
There are battles to be fought,
Revolutions to be wrought;
Up, and be a hero!

> ALEXANDER McLACHLAN, "Up, and be a hero", 1874.

The heterodoxy of one age is the orthodoxy of the next.

> GOLDWIN SMITH in *Can. monthly*, 1879, 241.

His faculty of picking the brains of other people was but an imperfect substitute [for the lack of reading and thought].

> GOLDWIN SMITH, *Bystander*, 1883, 149.

Thank God, the lowliest man can be
An uncrowned monarch in the world
of thought.

> THOMAS B. P. STEWART, "Lines to my mother", 1887.

Friend, though thy soul should burn
    thee, yet be still.
Thoughts were not made for strife, nor
    tongues for swords.
He that sees clear is gentlest of his
    words,
And that's not truth that has the
    heart to kill.
The whole world's thought shall not
    one truth fulfil.
Dull in our age, and passionate in
    youth,
No mind of man hath found the
    perfect truth,
Nor shalt thou find it; therefore,
    friend, be still.
    ARCHIBALD LAMPMAN, "The truth",
    1888.

Wisest is he, who, never quite secure,
    Changes his thoughts for better
    day by day:
Tomorrow some new light will shine,
    be sure,
    And thou shalt see thy thought
    another way.
    ARCHIBALD LAMPMAN, "The truth",
    1888.

In the heart of a man
    Is a thought upfurled,
Reached its full span
    It shakes the world,
And to one high thought
Is a whole race wrought.
    CHARLES G. D. ROBERTS, "A song
    of growth", 1893.

When we think we are simply trying
our wings in that new state into which
we shall yet be born.
    PETER MCARTHUR, *To be taken
    with salt*, 1903, 151,

Men will bear almost any evil rather
than go through the awful pain of
thinking, of really thinking, and thinking for themselves, and then of
following to the end the results of their
thought.
    G. M. WRONG, speech, Canadian
    Club, Ottawa, Dec. 8, 1916.

By conscientious smoking and drink-
    ing
They had kept themselves from the
    horror of thinking.
    STEPHEN B. LEACOCK, *College days*,
    1923, 95.

You say it's this or that,
    That nothing lies between:
Here is all black and foul;
    There is all white and clean.
    WILSON MACDONALD, "The fun-
    damentalist", 1937.

In Canada the theorist is still an
object not only of suspicion but of fear.
    P. E. CORBETT, in *Can hist. rev.*,
    1941, 118.

The compassed mind must quiver
    north
    though every chart defective:
there is no fog but in the will,
    the iceberg is elective.
    EARLE BIRNEY, "World conference",
    1945.

No nation can achieve its true destiny
that adopts without profound and cou-
rageous reasoning and selection the
thoughts and styles of another.
    LORNE PIERCE, *A Canadian people*,
    1945.

TIME.
              (See also: THE PRESENT)

We reckon hours and minutes to be
dollars and cents.
    T. C. HALIBURTON, *Sam Slick*,
    1836, ch. II.

Folks that have nothin' to do like
to see how the time goes.
    T. C. HALIBURTON, *Sam Slick*,
    1838, 177.

Adown the deep where the angels
    sleep
Came drawn the golden chime
Of those great spheres that sound
    the years
For the horologue of time.
Milleniums numberless they told
Milleniums a millionfold
From the ancient hour of prime.
    CHARLES HEAVYSEGE, "Twilight",
    1865.

And what is Time, with all her cares,
Her wrinkles, furrows, and grey hairs,
The hag that swallows all she bears;

The mystic where, the when and how,
The awful, everlasting now,
The funeral wreath upon my brow?
    ALEXANDER MCLACHLAN, "Man",
    1874.

Time enough to bid the Devil good morning when you meet him.

> EDWARD BLAKE, article in London, Eng., *Daily news*, Aug. 5, 1892, 3.

The mount, the star, the germ, the deep,
They all shall wake, they all shall sleep.
Time, like a flurry of wild rain,
Shall drift across the darkened pane.

> CHARLES G. D. ROBERTS, "The unsleeping", 1896.

I saw Time in his workshop carving faces;
Scattered around his tools lay, blunting griefs
Sharp cares that cut out deeply in reliefs
Of light and shade; sorrows that smooth the traces
Of what were smiles.

> FREDERICK GEORGE SCOTT, "Time", 1899.

Time like a Titan bright and strong
Spreads one enchanted gleam:
Each hour is but a fluted song,
And life a lofty dream.

> ARCHIBALD LAMPMAN, "Amor vitæ", 1899.

No nation, however advanced in its industrialism or powerful in its accumulated wealth, can long survive the shock of time except through the strength derived from the character of its people. That strength must assuredly be based upon faith and upon ideals.

> SIR ROBERT L. BORDEN, speech by telephone to Associated Press, New York, April 25, 1912.

Singing or sad, intent they go;
They do not see the shadows grow;
"There yet is time," they lightly say,
"Before our work aside we lay,"
Their task is but half-done, and lo,
Cometh the night.

> JOHN MCCRAE, "The night cometh", 1913.

The passing of time so quickly would not be so regrettable were life not so short.

> R. D. CUMMING, *Skookum Chuck fables*, 1915, 160.

Ah! the clock is always slow;
It is later than you think;
Sadly later than you think;
Far, far later than you think.

> ROBERT W. SERVICE, "It is later than you think", 1921.

The greatest solvent of political problems, if they are to be solved at all adequately, is time. The greatest danger lies in hastening the harvest of the years and in attempting to reap in advance of general political development.

> W. P. M. KENNEDY, *Constitution of Canada*, 1922, 458.

TITLES OF HONOUR.

Half a yard of blue ribbon is a plaguy cheap way of rewardin' merit, as the English do; and, although we larf at 'em (for folks always will larf at what they ain't got, and never can get), yet titles ain't bad things as objects of ambition, are they?

> T. C. HALIBURTON, *Sam Slick*, 1836, ch. XXIX.

I hope the practice of conferring honours will not degenerate into a matter of course and a number of honours be bestowed upon each change of Ministers.

> SIR JOHN A. MACDONALD, memorandum to Gov. Gen., Mar. 6, 1879.

The fountain of honour is merely one of the taps in the party bar.

> GOLDWIN SMITH, *Bystander*, May, 1890, 255.

Sir John is a K. C. M. G., and you are Casey, N. G.

> NICHOLAS FLOOD DAVIN, 1898, to George Casey, M. P.; answer to the conundrum as to the difference between him and Sir John Bourinot.

It would simplify matters if the king would hit the Canadian census returns with the flat of his sword and make all the adult males knights.

> ROBERT C. (BOB) EDWARDS, *Calgary Eye Opener*, July 29, 1911.

I am quite prepared, if we can do it without any disrespect to the Crown of

England, to bring our titles to the market-place and make a bonfire of them.

> SIR WILFRID LAURIER, H. of C., *Debates*, April 8, 1918, 500.

How could I accept a knighthood? Good heavens! I shovel off my own sidewalk and stoke my own furnace.

> JOHN W. DAFOE, qu. in *Can. hist. rev.*, 1929, 240; Dafoe was offered a title by Sir Robert Borden, Prime Minister, 1911-20.

We, Your Majesty's most dutiful and loyal subjects, the House of Commons of Canada in Parliament assembled, humbly approach Your Majesty, praying that Your Majesty hereafter may be graciously pleased:— to refrain hereafter from conferring any title of honour or titular distinction upon any of your subjects domiciled or ordinarily resident in Canada, save such appelations as are of a professional or vocational character or which appertain to an office.

> W. F. NICKLE, proposed address to the King, May 14, 1919; adopted May 22, 1919; H. of C., *Debates*, 2395.

If we are to have no titles, titular distinctions or honours in Canada, let us hold to the principle and have none. Let us abolish them altogether. But if the sovereigns or heads of other countries are to be permitted to bestow honours on Canadians, for my part, I think we owe it to our own sovereign to give him that prerogative before all others.

> W. L. MACKENZIE KING. H. of C., *Debates*, 1929, 86.

TORONTO, ONT.

> (See also: CITIES AND TOWNS — NICKNAMES, etc.)

I dreamt not then that, ere the rolling year
Had filled its circle, I should wander here
In musing awe; should tread this wondrous world,
See all its store of inland waters hurled
In one vast volume down Niagara's steep;

Or calm behold them, in transparent sleep,
Where the blue hills of old Toronto shed
Their evening shadows o'er Ontario's bed.

> THOMAS MOORE, lines written to Lady Charlotte Rawdon, 1804.

The streets of York are regularly laid out, intersecting each other at right angles. Only one of them, however, is yet completely built; and in wet weather the unfinished streets are, if possible, muddier and dirtier than those of Kingston. The situation of the town is very unhealthy, for it stands on a piece of low marshy land, which is better calculated for a frog-pond or beaver-meadow than for the residence of human beings.

> EDWARD A. TALBOT, *Five years residence in the Canadas*, 1824, I, 102.

Dover is one of the vilest blue-devil haunts upon the face of the earth, except Little York in Upper Canada, when one has been there one day.

> JOHN GALT, *Autobiography*, 1833, I. 334; frequently misquoted as, "York is one of the vilest blue-devil haunts on the face of the earth"; *blue-devil*: very low spirits.

Toronto is like a fourth or fifth-rate provincial town, with the pretensions of a capital city. We have here a petty colonial oligarchy, a self-constituted aristocracy, based upon nothing real nor upon anything imaginary.

> ANNA B. JAMESON, *Winter studies and summer rambles*, 1838, I, 98.

I had been accustomed to see hundreds of Indians about my native village, then Little York, muddy and dirty, just struggling into existence; now the City of Toronto, bursting forth in all its energy and commercial strength.

> PAUL KANE, *Wanderings of an artist*, 1859.

In a few years Toronto is bound to outstrip in enterprise, and solid commercial progress, every other city in Canada as a trading centre.

> FRANK SMITH, in Montreal *Gazette*, Jan. 26, 1870.

[Toronto] is all right. The only depressing thing is that it will always be what it is, only larger, and that no Canadian city can ever be anything better or different. If they are good they may become Toronto.

RUPERT BROOKE, *Letters from America*, 1916, 84.

Indeed I have always found that the only thing in regard to Toronto which far-away people know for certain is that McGill University is in it.

STEPHEN B. LEACOCK, *My discovery of the West*, 1937, 38.

TRADE.

(See also: ADVERTISING; INDUSTRY; TARIFF)

Situated in a cold climate, she produces no commodity, except furs and skins, which she could exchange for the commodities of Europe; and consequently she could have little returns to make the English merchant.

ANON., *A letter to a great minister, on the prospect of a peace, wherein the importance of Canada is fully refuted*, 1761.

I do not like to see our hatters importing hats, and shoemakers selling foreign shoes, and tanners offering foreign leather as superior articles. The profits on the manufacture of the goods used by us accumulate in Birmingham, Sheffield, Manchester, Glasgow, Boston, and Pittsburg; to all these places we bear the same relation as the Negroes at the Bight of Benin.

ROBERT B. SULLIVAN, *Lecture*, Mechanics' Institute, Hamilton, Nov. 17, 1847.

Unless reciprocity of trade with the United States be established these colonies must be lost to England.

LORD ELGIN, letter to Grey, May 28, 1849, in Pub. Archives, *Letters of Lord Elgin*, III.

Don't trade with a man that is over sanctimonious, or you will be taken in.

T. C. HALIBURTON, *Sam Slick's wise saws*, 1853, II, 159.

There is roguery in all trades but our own.

T. C. HALIBURTON, *Nature and human nature*, 1855, II, 12.

God and nature never destined that Nova Scotia and Ontario should trade together. We trade with Ontario, to be sure. Their drummers permeate our country and sell $10,000,000 of goods annually. Where do we get the money? We get it from the people of the United States.

J. W. LONGLEY, speech at Merchants' Club, Boston, Mass., Dec. 30, 1886.

With my utmost effort, with my latest breath I will oppose the "veiled treason" which attempts by sordid means and mercenary proffers to lure our people from their allegiance.

SIR JOHN A. MACDONALD, speech, "To the electors of Canada", Feb. 7, 1891, on commercial union with U. S.; the phrase "veiled treason" is from Disraeli.

I prefer the Yankee dollar to the British shilling, especially when the Yankee dollar is near at hand and the British shilling so far away.

SIR WILFRID LAURIER, speech in Boston, Nov. 17, 1891.

British preference.

Canadian preference in tariff to British imports, instituted by W. S. Fielding, Finance Minister under Laurier, in budget speech, April 22, 1897.

If we were to follow the laws of nature and geography between Canada and the United States, the whole trade would flow from south to north and from north to south. We have done everything possible by building canals and subsidizing railways, to bring the trade from west to east and from east to west, so as to bring trade into British channels.

SIR WILFRID LAURIER, at Imperial Conference, 1907.

Their habits are the same as ours, and therefore we are induced to trade [with Americans], and cannot help it, by the force of nature.

SIR WILFRID LAURIER, qu., *Contemp. rev.*, 1911, 481.

I am a reasonable, sane and rational free-trader, but I am not such a free-trader as to strike down any legitimate industry, and I have told the manufacturers that if they are fair and reasonable they can count on my support.

W. S. FIELDING, speech in Digby, N. S., Aug. 29, 1911.

From every point of view, trade is and always will be the vital question upon which patriotism, common defence, and everything else will depend; therefore, I trust that you will pardon my inclination to devote my substance and my efforts to the upbuilding of King Trade.

SIR WILLIAM VAN HORNE, letter, 1914?, qu., Vaughan, *Van Horne*, 1920, 345.

It is part of the irony of fate that it should have fallen to the lot of the first Western Minister of Finance to drop the cut flowers of British preference on the mangled corpse of free trade.

WILLIAM IRVINE, H. of C., *Debates*, May 6, 1930.

You say our tariffs are only for the manufacturers. I will make them fight for you [farmers] as well. I will use them to blast a way into the markets that have been closed to you.

R. B. BENNETT, election speech, Winnipeg, June 9, 1930.

To bargain and barter and blast with our own kith and kin is unthinkable.

W. L. MACKENZIE KING, speech in Prince Albert, Sask., July 12, 1930, in response to a statement made by R. B. Bennett, June 9, at Winnipeg.

Unless we can trade with the outside world our condition must be one of stagnation, with the standards of living falling to ever lower levels, and with increasing strains upon the bonds that keep our federation together.

J. W. DAFOE, *Canada, an American nation*, 1935.

TRANSPORTATION.

(See also: RAILWAYS)

No country under heaven is so completely adapted for internal navigation.

[WILLIAM DUNLOP], *Statistical sketches of Upper Can.*, 1832, 58.

Within Cayuga's forest shade
The stocks were set — the keel was laid —
Wet with the nightly forest dew,
The frame of that first vessel grew.

THOMAS D'A. MCGEE, "The launch of the *Griffin*", 1858. The *Griffin* was built by La Salle and launched on Lake Erie in 1679.

Red River Carts.

Carts made entirely of wood, used by the Hudson's Bay Co. for freightage in the West, middle and late 19th. century.

You have been blessed with an abundant harvest, and soon I trust will a railway come to carry to those who need it the surplus of your produce, now — as my own eyes have witnessed — imprisoned in your storehouses for want of the means of transport.

LORD DUFFERIN, speech at City Hall, Winnipeg, Sept. 29, 1877.

It would never be a paying investment till it was filled in, and a railway run on top of it.

SIR JOHN A. MACDONALD. qu., Biggar, *Anecdotal life*, 226; on the Rideau Canal.

Canada is doing business on a back street. We must put her on a thoroughfare.

SIR WILLIAM VAN HORNE, 1886, a reference to the Canadian Pacific Railway.

Canada has been adding sides to her hopper for a long time, but has neglected to enlarge the spout.

SIR WILLIAM VAN HORNE, about 1902, when describing the shortage of freight cars to ship prairie wheat; usually quoted as, "The hopper is too big for the spout".

The All-Red Route.

SIR WILFRID LAURIER'S scheme, proposed at the Imperial conference, 1907, for a British line of transport connecting Britain with Australia, via Canada.

Anderson Chariots.

A two-wheel, horse-drawn vehicle made from a dismantled automobile by farmers of the Prairies during the depression of the early 1930's; Dr. J. T. M. Anderson was premier of Saskatchewan, 1929-34.

Bennett Buggies.

Term used during the premiership of R. B. Bennett, 1930-35, to describe motorless horse-drawn automobiles in use in Prairie provinces during drought years.

Canada in the first half of the century was the child of her waterways, and in the second the child of her railways.

A. R. M. LOWER, and History Dept., Univ. of Manitoba, qu. in Chafe and Lower, *Canada*, 1948, 287.

TRAVEL.

(See also: WANDERLUST)

An airly start makes easy stages.
T. C. HALIBURTON, *Sam Slick*, 1836, ch. XII.

I am a bird of passage — here today and gone tomorrow.
THOMAS C. HALIBURTON, *Sam Slick's wise saws*, 1853, ch. XIV.

You feel the joy of coming home,
After long leagues to France or Spain,
You feel the clear Canadian foam,
And the gulf water heave again.
DUNCAN CAMPBELL SCOTT, "Off Riviere du Loup", 1893.

There was a young woman named Bright
Whose speed was faster than light.
She set out one day
In a relative way,
And returned the previous night.
ARTHUR H. BULLER, Univ. of Manitoba botanist, about 1910.

Madam, the most extraordinary thing in this town
Is the shape of your legs.
O communication!
O rapid transit!
F. R. SCOTT, "Tourist time", 1945.

TREES.

(See also: FORESTS; MAPLES: NATURE)

You Canadians have a prejudice against trees.
SIR EDMUND HEAD, letter, qu., in *Can. hist. rev.*, V, 143.

Thou hast a secret, old elm, worth the keeping,
We children knew it not in early days;
But they who far beyond thy shade are sleeping
Revealed it to us ere they went their ways.
JAMES MCCARROLL, "The elm tree", 1889.

Outside, a yellow maple tree,
Shifting upon the silvery blue
With tiny multitudinous sound
Rustled to let the sunlight through.
BLISS CARMAN, "The eavesdropper", 1893.

A keen, sweet fragrance lies, along the air,
The odour of the tall Canadian pine:
How soft the sunbeams on his needles shine,
And where the snow has left the forests bare,
He spreads his russet carpet everywhere.
WILLIAM T. ALLISON, "The Canadian pine", 1909.

The elm is aspiration, and death is in the yew,
And beauty dwells in every tree from Lapland to Peru;
But there's magic in the poplars when the wind goes through.
BERNARD F. TROTTER, "The poplars," 1916.

I heard the cedars speak as friend to friend,
Bending easily to hear one another,
Brother with brother, who have lived long together;
Only to life have the cedars learned to attend.
ROY DANIELLS, "Epithalamion in time of peace", 1949.

TRUTH.

(See also: LIES AND LIARS; THOUGHT; WORDS)

There is no standard for truth. We cannot even agree on the meaning of words.

> GEORGE BROWN, speech in St. Lawrence Hall, Toronto, July. 1851.

There's many a true word said in jest.

> THOMAS C. HALIBURTON, *Sam Slick's wise saws*, 1853, ch. XXIV.

Standing on tiptoe ever since my youth
Striving to grasp the future just above,
I hold at length the only future —
Truth,
And Truth is Love.

> GEORGE F. CAMERON, "Standing on tiptoe", 1885.

In seeking absolute truth we aim at the unattainable, and must be content with broken portions.

> SIR WILLIAM OSLER, "Aequanimitas", May 1, 1889.

To define a truth is to limit its scope.

> PETER MCARTHUR, *To be taken with salt*, 1903, 155.

Every clear statement of truth is a blasphemy against error.

> PETER MCARTHUR, *To be taken with salt*, 1903, 156.

The truth is the best you can get with your best endeavour, the best that the best men accept — with this you must learn to be satisfied, retaining at the same time with due humility an earnest desire for an ever larger portion.

> SIR WILLIAM OSLER, "The student life", address, 1905.

Save in symbols can the truth be found?

> PETER MCARTHUR, "Courage", in, *The prodigal*, 1907, 26.

It is a hierarchy of laws liberally illustrated by facts, which so ingeniously rule and are subject to one another, stay and uphold one another, that admiration is compelled for the sagacity of the great organizer, who, with unparalleled power of systemization, constructed so imposing an edifice of fallacy.

> SIR WILLIAM OSLER, *Evolution of medicine*, 1913, on Ibn Sina's (Avicenna's) *Canon* of medical knowledge.

Error held in truth has much the effect of truth. In politics and religion this fact upsets many confident predictions.

> GEORGE ILES, *Canadian stories*, 1918, 177.

Candor may be devilish,
And truth untimely open hell;
Better pretend the thing you wish;
Anon you may, if you wish and wish,
Achieve a miracle.

> TOM MACINNES, "White magic", 1923.

I have always found that the only kind of statement worth making is an overstatement. A half-truth, like half a brick, is always more forcible as an argument than a whole one. It carries further.

> STEPHEN B. LEACOCK, *The garden of folly*, 1924

Pro and con have single stem
Half a truth dividing them.

> F. R. SCOTT, "Conflict", in, *Poetry mag.*, April, 1941.

We need fear no sacredness. Truth has nothing to fear from the earnest and sincere research for the truth.

> G. BROCK CHISHOLM, speech in New York, Oct. 29, 1945.

TUPPER, SIR CHARLES.

The Cumberland War-horse.

> A popular name for Tupper from the name of the Nova Scotia constituency which he represented in the Legislature and Parliament from 1855 to 1884.

I have been defeated by the future leader of the Conservative party.

> JOSEPH HOWE, 1855, a comment on his defeat by Tupper for election to the N. S. Assembly as member for Cumberland.

I will not play second fiddle to that damned Tupper.

> JOSEPH HOWE, 1864, on his refusal to go to the Confederation Conferences at Charlottetown and Quebec.

Pacific in trouble; you should be here.

> SIR JOHN A. MACDONALD, cablegram to Sir Charles Tupper in London, Dec. 1, 1883; a reference to the Canadian Pacific Railway.

Your presence during election contest in Maritime Provinces essential to encourage our friends. Please come. Answer.

> SIR JOHN A. MACDONALD, cablegram to Sir Charles Tupper in London, Jan. 21, 1891.

In my judgment, the chief characteristic of Tupper was courage; courage which no obstacle could down, which rushed to the assault, and which, if repulsed, came back to the combat again and again; courage which battered and hammered, perhaps not always judiciously, but always effectively; courage which never admitted defeat, and which in the midst of overwhelming disaster ever maintained the proud carriage of unconquerable defiance.

> SIR WILFRID LAURIER, H. of C., *Debates*, Feb. 17, 1916.

TWENTIETH CENTURY.

The twentieth century belongs to Canada.

> JOSEPH T. CLARK, editorial, *Saturday Night*, late 1890's. Clark, who left *Saturday Night* in 1899 to join the Toronto *Star* always claimed to be the originator of this phrase. (See: Toronto *Star*, Dec. 30, 1949, Questions and Answers.) The Rev. Dr. James Robertson has been credited with using the phrase many times during the late 1890's in the West. (See also: *Can. annual review*, 1907, 444.)

In the next century Canada may be expected to assume a somewhat similar position to that occupied by the United States in the last.

> J. B. TYRRELL, in Dawson (Yukon) *Daily Times*, Jan. 1, 1901.

Last century was the United States' century. The present is Canada's century.

> GEORGE JOHNSON, in, *Commonwealth* (Ottawa) Jan. 1901, 4.

The nineteenth century was the century of the United States. The twentieth century is Canada's century.

> JAMES W. LONGLEY, Attorney-general of Nova Scotia, speech in Boston, April 8, 1902; qu., Toronto *Globe*, April 12, 1902.

As the nineteenth century was that of the United States, so I think the twentieth century shall be filled by Canada.

> SIR WILFRID LAURIER, speech, Canadian Club, Ottawa, Jan. 18, 1904.

The twentieth century shall be the century of Canada and of Canadian development.

> SIR WILFRID LAURIER, speech in Toronto, Oct. 14, 1904.

It has been observed on the floor of this House, as well as outside of this House, that as the nineteenth century had been the century of the United States, so the twentieth century would be the century of Canada.

> SIR WILFRID LAURIER, H. of C., *Debates*, Feb. 21, 1905, 1422.

Last century made the world a neighborhood; this century must make it a brotherhood.

> J. S. WOODSWORTH, *University magazine*, Feb. 1917.

The twentieth century was once supposed to belong to Canada, but it seems more and more likely that only the first quarter of the century was really ours.

> F. W. BURTON, in *C.J.E.P.S.*, 1936, 598.

U

UNION ACT, 1841.

I was, and still am, an advocate of the union of the provinces, but an advocate not of a union of parchment, but a union of hearts and of free born men.

> ROBERT BALDWIN, speech in Legis. Assembly, Kingston; qu., Kingston

Chronicle and gazette, Sept. 17, 1842. Daniel O'Connell, the Irish agitator, first used the phrase, "A union on parchment".

A man and his wife might agree to separate, but what were they to do with the children?

> MALCOLM CAMERON, speech at Reform Convention, Toronto, Nov. 9, 1859.

Dissolution might be all very well for those living west of Toronto, but touch a man's pocket and you touch his principles.

> ALEXANDER L. McBAIN, delegate from Glengarry, speech at Reform Convention, Toronto, Nov. 10, 1859.

Whatever you do adhere to the Union — we are a great country, and shall become one of the greatest in the universe if we preserve it; we shall sink into insignificance and adversity if we suffer it to be broken.

> SIR JOHN A. MACDONALD, speech, 1861; qu., Biggar, *Anecdotal life,* 182.

UNION JACK.

All hail to the day when the Britons came over,
And planted their standard, with sea-foam still wet,
Around and above us their spirits will hover,
Rejoicing to mark how we honour it yet.
Beneath it the emblems they cherished are waving,
The Rose of Old England the road side perfumes;
The Shamrock and Thistle the north winds are braving,
Securely the Mayflower blushes and blooms.

> JOSEPH HOWE, "The flag of old England", ("Song for the centenary") June 8, 1849. Written for the one hundredth anniversary of the landing of Lord Cornwallis at Halifax. Howe also wrote "Song for the 8th. June", with a first verse as follows:

Hail to the day when the Briton came o'er
And planted his flag where the Mayflower blows,

And gathered the blossoms, unheeded before,
To entwine with the Shamrock, the Thistle, the Rose.

A union of hearts, a union of hands,
A union no man can sever,
A union of tongues, a union of lands,
And the flag — British union forever.

> LINDSAY (ONT.) *Warder,* motto on masthead; Sam Hughes was the owner and publisher from 1885.

We were taunted with waving the old flag; and a lot of traitors, a lot of cowards who have not the courage to be traitors, although they have the will, would sneer at the old flag: sneer at the loyalty we inherited from our fathers: sneer at the institutions which our fathers were so proud to leave us.

> SIR JOHN THOMPSON, speech in Toronto Auditorium, Jan. 14, 1893.

It's only a small piece of bunting,
It's only an old coloured rag;
Yet thousands have died for its honour,
And shed their best blood for the flag.

> JAMES C. MORGAN "The Union Jack" ("For Queen and Country") in, Borthwick, ed., *Poems, South African War,* 1901, 1. Morgan was inspector of schools, Barrie and North Simcoe; died 1922.

Men of Canada: keep both hands on the Union Jack!

> LORD DUNDONALD, speech on leaving Ottawa, July 26, 1904, after his dismissal from office as General Officer Commanding, Canadian Forces, by Laurier. Fred Cook, in Ottawa *Evening Citizen,* Aug. 23, 1934, p. 15, gives the credit to Sam Hughes as the originator of the phrase.

Then may it wave o'er land and sea,
Through time's eternal space:
Equality and liberty
Beneath it find their place.
No change of Flag, no change of State
Do I e'er want to see:
For the flag that's waved a thousand years
Is good enough for me.

> JOHN A. PHILLIPS, "The flag for me", about 1905; written during membership in the Press Gallery, Ottawa.

UNITED EMPIRE LOYALISTS.

Late Loyalists.

A term, sometimes scornful, applied to immigrants from the United States after 1785.

O Ye, who with your blood and sweat
Watered the furrows of this land, —
See where upon a nation's brow
In honour's front, ye proudly stand!

SARAH A. CURZON, "Loyal", 1887.

Not drooping like fugitives, they came
In exodus to our Canadian wilds,
But full of heart and hope, with heads erect
And fearless eyes victorious in defeat.
With thousand toils they forced their devious way
Through the great wilderness of silent woods
That gloomed o'er lake and stream, till higher rose
The northern star above the broad domain
Of half a continent, still theirs to hold,
Defend, and keep forever as their own,
Their own and England's, to the end of time.

WILLIAM KIRBY, "The Hungry Year", 1888.

They passed down the silent rivers which flow to the mighty lake;
They left what they'd made for England (but those who have made can make),
And founded a new dominion for God and their country's sake.

CLIVE PHILLIPPS-WOLLEY, "The U.E. Loyalists", 1917.

In the loyalist migrations at the close of the revolution, the United States had sown the neighbouring provinces with dragon's teeth, and every reformer from Gourlay to Baldwin reaped an ineradicable harvest of prejudice and suspicion.

CHESTER MARTIN, in Can. hist. rev., 1937, 3.

UNITED STATES.

(See also: BOUNDARIES; CANADIAN-AMERICAN RELATIONS)

In going from the States into Canada an Englishman is struck by the feeling that he is going from a richer country into one that is poorer, and from a greater country into one that is less.

ANTHONY TROLLOPE, North America, I, 1862.

The Monarchical government of England is a truer application of real Republican principles than that of the United States, and I have no hesitation in saying that the government of Canada is far in advance, in the application of real Republican principles, of the Government of either England or the United States.

EDWARD BLAKE, speech at Aurora, Ont., Oct. 3, 1874.

Little Canada.

New England, so called during the nineteenth century because of the influx of French Canadians.

We are living beside a great neighbour who, I believe I can say without being deemed unfriendly to them, are very grasping in their national acts, and who are determined upon every occasion to get the best in any agreement which they make.

SIR WILFRID LAURIER, H. of C., Debates, Oct. 23, 1903, 14814.

We have one neighbour and one only, and that one an industrial colossus. It lies for four thousand miles along our border, producing what we produce and doing constant but legitimate battle to forestall us in the world's markets and in our own. There is the dominating fact that meets Canadians every morning.

ARTHUR MEIGHEN, address at the Guildhall, London, on receiving the Freedom of the City, July 15, 1921.

Nothing is more conspicuously lacking in Canada than a generous recognition of the greatness of the American people, in the sense in which they are one of the great peoples of the world.

> H. F. ANGUS, *Canada and her great neighbor*, 1938.

What Ottawa thinks today Washington will say tomorrow.

> WILLIAM W. WADE, *International jour.*, 1951, 41.

UNITY.

I expected to find a contest between a government and a people: I found two nations warring in the bosom of a single state: I found a struggle not of principles but of races: and I perceived that it would be idle to attempt any amelioration of laws or institutions, until we could first succeed in terminating the deadly animosity that now separates the inhabitants of Lower Canada into hostile divisions of French and English.

> LORD DURHAM, *Report*, 1839.

Union, Peace, Friendship, and Fraternity.

> LOUIS H. LAFONTAINE, words addressed to Reformers of Upper Canada, 1841; motto also used over platform on which Laurier spoke at Toronto, Oct. 16. 1900.

The blood of no brother, in civil strife poured,
In this hour of rejoicing encumbers our souls!
The frontier's the field for the patriot's sword,
And cursed is the weapon that faction controls!

> JOSEPH HOWE, "The flag of old England", 1848.

One voice, one people, one in heart
And soul, and feeling, and desire.

> CHARLES SANGSTER, "Brock", in *Hesperus*, 1864.

I view the diversity of races in British North America in this way: we are of different races, not for the purpose of warring against each other, but in order to compete and emulate for the general good.

> SIR GEORGE CARTIER, *Confederation debates*, Feb. 7, 1865, 60.

We don't know each other. We have no trade with each other. We have no facilities, or resources, or incentives, to mingle with each other. We are shut off from each other by a wilderness, geographically, commercially, politically and socially. We always cross the United States to shake hands. Our interests are not identical, but the very opposite — they are antagonistic and clashing.

> HALIFAX *Acadian Recorder*, July 27, 1866, on Confederation.

If ever, in time to come, we should have the misfortune to become divided — as foreigners have sought before — that will be the signal for all disasters which we have until now so happily avoided. But let us hope that the lessons of the past will guide us in the future!

> LOUIS RIEL, to the Nation of the Northwest, April, 1870.

Let but our statesmen do their duty, with the consciousness that all the elements which constitute greatness are now awaiting a closer combination; that all the requirements of a national higher life are here available for use; that nations do not spring Minerva-like into existence; that strength and weakness are relative terms, a few not being necessarily weak because they are few, nor a multitude necessarily strong because they are many; that hesitating, doubting, fearing, whining over supposed or even actual weakness, and conjuring up possible dangers, is not the true way to strengthen the foundations of our Dominion, to give confidence to its continuance.

> WILLIAM A. FOSTER, *Canada first*, 1871.

Is there a man amongst us who forgets that when Papineau was struggling for the rights of his race and for the constitutional liberty which we to-day enjoy, his principal coadjutors were John Nelson, the Scotchman, and O'Callaghan, the Irishman?

> SIR WILFRID LAURIER, speech in Quebec, 1877.

Shall we not be one race, shaping and wielding the nation?
Is not our country too broad for the schisms which shake petty lands?

Yea, we shall join in our might, and
keep sacred our firm federation,
Shoulder to shoulder arrayed, hearts
open to hearts, hands to hands!
BARRY STRATON, "85", 1884.

Father of Unity, make this people
one.
CHARLES G. D. ROBERTS, "A collect
for Dominion Day", 1885.

Below the island of Montreal
the water that comes from the north
from Ottawa unites with the waters
that come from the western lakes,
but uniting they do not mix. There
they run parallel, separate, distin-
guishable, and yet are one stream,
flowing within the same banks, the
mighty St. Lawrence, and rolling on
toward the sea bearing the commerce
of a nation upon its bosom — a
perfect image of our nation.
SIR WILFRID LAURIER, speech
in Toronto, Dec. 10, 1886.

Were those not brave old races? —
Well, here they still abide;
And yours is one or other,
And the second's at your side.
W. D. LIGHTHALL, "The battle of
La Prairie", 1889.

There is no use in attempting mani-
fest impossibilities, and no impossibility
apparently can be more manifest than
that of fusing or even harmonizing a
French and Papal and a British and
Protestant community.
GOLDWIN SMITH, The Bystander,
Dec. 1889, 78.

We have come to a period in the
history of this young country where
premature dissolution seems to be at
hand. What will be the outcome? How
long can the present fabric last? Can
it last at all?
SIR WILFRID LAURIER, letter to
Edward Blake, 1891.

The one calamity above all others
which stands before this country is
that political divisions should follow
the division of race or the division of
religion. The one danger which
menaces the future of this country
and the union of this country, now so
happily being accomplished, is that
men should stand arrayed against each
other on the question of government,
because they differ with regard to
religion, because they differ with regard
to race.
SIR JOHN THOMPSON, H. of C.,
Debates, Sept. 7, 1892.

Any policy which appeals to a class,
to a creed, to a race, or which does not
appeal to the better instincts to be
found in all classes, in all creeds, and
in all races, is stamped with the stamp
of inferiority. The French-Canadian
who appeals to his fellow-countrymen
to stand by themselves, aloof from the
rest of the continent; the English-Cana-
dian who appeals to his fellow-countrymen on grounds affecting them alone,
may, perhaps, win the applause of
those whom they may be addressing,
but impartial history will pronounce
their work as vicious in conception as
it is mischievous and wicked in its
tendency.
SIR WILFRID LAURIER, qu., Ross,
Patriotic recitations, 1893, 181.

If there is anything to which I have
given my political life, it is to try to
promote unity, harmony and amity
between the diverse elements of this
country. My friends can desert me,
they can remove their confidence from
me, they can withdraw the trust they
have placed in my hands; but never shall
I deviate from that line of policy.
Whatever may be the consequences,
whether loss of prestige, loss of
popularity, or loss of power, I feel
that I am in the right, and I know
that a time will come when every man...
will render me full justice on that score.
SIR WILFRID LAURIER, H. of C.,
Debates, Mar. 13, 1900, 1842.

There is no bond of union so strong
as the bond created by common dangers
faced in common.
SIR WILFRID LAURIER, H. of C.,
Debates, Mar. 13, 1900.

Fraternity without absorption, union
without fusion.
SIR WILFRID LAURIER, a phrase used
in speech to St. Jean Baptiste
Society, Montreal, June 25, 1901.
(trans.)

How are we to unify Canada? There
is but one possible way: Make her a
nation in name as well as in fact. Let
her throw off her mean colonial

wrappings and let her assume her
rightful place among the nations of
the world. Give us a common pride.

JOHN S. EWART, *Kingdom papers*,
1911, I, 55.

For all were pledged, with teeth and
claws
To racial brood and comradeship,
Devoted to the national cause
And loyal to the boundary strip.

EDWIN J. PRATT, "The witches'
brew", 1925.

Today we are a united people, seeking
first and foremost an enduring unity;
not a unity which aims at uniformity,
but a unity which delights in diversity.

W. L. MACKENZIE KING, *Message
of the carillon*, 1927, 103.

Deep down in the Anglo-Saxon nature
the world over is enshrined the belief
that the toleration of differences is the
measure of civilization.

VINCENT MASSEY, speech in New
York, Dec. 10, 1928.

Ours is a strange fraternity,
Forged by a common calumny,
And unified by slander.

VINCENT MASSEY, "The angler and
the diplomat", Jan. 15, 1929.

I believe that Canada's first duty to
the League [of Nations] and to the
British Empire, with respect to all
the great issues that come up, is, if
possible, to keep this country united.

W. L. MACKENZIE KING, H. of C.,
Debates, Mar. 23, 1936, 1333.

Our Canada, from sea to sea,
Four signs of valour knows;
The thistle and the fleur-de-lys,
The shamrock and the rose.

ARTHUR STRINGER, "When maple
leaves turn red", 1938.

A strong and dominant national
feeling is not a luxury in Canada, it
is a necessity. Without it this country
could not exist. A divided Canada can
be of little help to any country, and
least of all to itself.

W. L. MACKENZIE KING, H. of C.,
Debates, Mar. 30, 1939.

V

VANCOUVER, B. C.

(See also: CITIES AND TOWNS
— NICKNAMES, etc.)

With a hand on my hip and the cup
at my lip,
And a love in my life for you.
For you are a jolly good fellow, with
a great, big heart, I know:
So I drink this toast
To the "Queen of the Coast".
Vancouver, here's a Ho!

E. PAULINE JOHNSON, "A toast",
1903.

VANITY.

What a slovenly old world this would
be if all the vanity were eliminated.

ROBERT C. (BOB) EDWARDS, *Calgary Eye Opener*, Aug. 28. 1920.

VIRTUE.

Vice makes virtue look well to its
anchors.

THOMAS C. HALIBURTON, *Sam
Slick's wise saws*, 1853, ch. XVII.

There is no station in this life
That is from ills exempted;
Virtue would be an easy thing
If we were never tempted.

ALEXANDER McLACHLAN, "Poverty's
compensations", 1856.

All the virtue he could boast
Was not found in any creed.

BLISS CARMAN, "Saint Kavin",
1894.

No special virtues are needed, but the
circumstances demand the exercise of
them in a special way. They are seven,
the mystic seven, your lamps to lighten
at...tact, tidiness, taciturnity, sympathy,
gentleness, cheerfulness, all linked
together by charity.

SIR WILLIAM OSLER, Commencement
address to Johns Hopkins Univ.
nurses, May 7, 1913.

We grist our grain with bloody hands
We turn our mill with sweat and
breath:
We are the men that Virtue brands;
In youth we build the house of
Death.

NEIL TRACY, "Penitentes", 1938.

VOTING.

(See also: ELECTIONS; MAJORITY)

Vote for no man whose conduct in private and public life is not above suspicion, and inquire with due diligence before you give your suffrages.

WILLIAM LYON MACKENZIE, *Address to the Reformers of Upper Canada*, Toronto, Sept. 1834.

There is no inalienable right in any man to exercise the franchise.

SIR JOHN A. MACDONALD, *Debates on Confederation*, 1865.

I would be most willing to vote confidence in the Government [loud cheers from the Government side], if I could do so conscientiously [loud cheers from the Opposition].

DONALD A. SMITH (Lord Strathcona) H. of C., *Debates*, Nov. 5, 1873, on the "Pacific Scandal".

Religion and race are, of course, observable forces within our body politic; but as far as I have remarked the divisions of party are perpendicular rather than horizontal, and in a country or borough election, as often as not, Catholic will be found voting against Catholic, Orangeman against Orangeman, Frenchman against Frenchman, and, what will perhaps cause less surprise, Irishman against Irishman.

LORD DUFFERIN, speech in London, England, July 8, 1875.

There he lies, the noble son of Ontario, perchance in some foreign land where instead of the butternut of his native homestead, the gloomy cypress guards his lonely grave, but though the dread trumpet remain unblown, yet one blast of the old familiar party horn summons him to the same old polling booth.

WILLIAM H. DRUMMOND, speech, Can. Club, Toronto, Nov. 21, 1905.

This is a matter of evolution and evolution is only a working out of God's laws. For this reason we must not attempt to hurry it on.

JAMES P. WHITNEY, on woman suffrage; qu., *Mail and Empire*, Mar. 21, 1911.

A vote for the Government means that another man will take your place. A vote for the Opposition means that you stay here for the rest of your life.

Wording of placards displayed at Vimy Ridge, 1917, at time of soldiers' voting, general election.

There is no real power in money, power is in the vote.

HENRY WISE WOOD, *Grain growers' guide*, Aug. 4, 1920, 10.

The citizens go on voting Liberal because they are conservative.

RAMSAY TRAQUAIR, *Atlantic monthly*, June 1923, 822.

VOYAGEURS.

The French and Canadians have always been remarkable for roving in the Desarts and seating themselves amongst the Indians.

GEN. THOMAS GAGE, 1770, in C. E. Carter, *Correspondence of Gage*, 1931, 212.

The Greeks, with all their wood and river Gods, were not so qualified to name the natural features of a country as the ancestors of these French Canadians; and if any people had a right to substitute their own for the Indian names, it was they.

HENRY THOREAU, *Excursion to Canada*, 1850.

We shun the noise of the busy world,
For there's crime and misery there,
    And the happiest life
    In this world of strife
Is that of the Voyageur.

JOHN F. McDONNELL, "The voyageur's song", 1864.

The Canadian voyageurs will become a forgotten race, or remembered, like their associates, the Indians, among the poetical images of past times, and as themes for local and romantic associations.

WASHINGTON IRVING, *Astoria*, 1886, 25.

W

WANDERLUST.

There's a race of men that don't fit in,
    A race that can't stay still;
So they break the hearts of kith and
    kin,
        And they roam the world at will.
    ROBERT W. SERVICE, "The men that
    don't fit in", 1907.

Let us probe the silent places, let us
    seek what luck betide us;
Let us journey to a lonely land I
    know.
    ROBERT W. SERVICE, "Call of the
    wild", 1907.

Change was his mistress, Chance his
    councillor:
Love could not keep him; Duty forged
    no chain.
The wide seas and the mountains
    called to him,
And grey dawns saw his campfires in
    the rain.
    THEODORE G. ROBERTS, "Epitaph
    for a voyageur", 1913.

WAR.

(See also: DEFENCE; FOR-
EIGN RELATIONS)

The Aristook War.
    The dispute over the boundary
    between New Brunswick and Maine
    which led to a settlement in the
    Ashburton Treaty of 1842; also
    called, "The Lumbermen's War".

In some development of socialism,
something that will widen patriotism
beyond the bounds of nationalism, may
rest the desire of the race in this
matter; but the evil is rooted and
grounded in the abyss of human passion,
and war with all its horrors is likely
long to burden the earth.
    SIR WILLIAM OSLER, address,
    "Study of the fevers of the South",
    May 6, 1896.

Whilst I cannot admit that Canada
should take part in all the wars of
Great Britain, neither am I prepared
to say that she should not take part in
any war at all.
    SIR WILFRID LAURIER, H. of C.,
    Debates, Feb. 5, 1900, 68.

War everywhere. When Britain is
at war, Canada is at war; there is no
distinction. If Great Britain, to which
we are subject, is at war with any
nation Canada becomes liable to invasion, and so Canada is at war.
    SIR WILFRID LAURIER, H. of C.,
    Debates, Jan. 12, 1910, 1735;
    also, speech in Montreal, Dec. 12,
    1914.

If England is at war we are at war
and liable to attack. I do not say
that we shall always be attacked,
neither do I say that we would take
part in all the wars of England. That
is a matter that must be guided by
circumstances, upon which the Canadian
Parliament will have to pronounce, and
will have to decide in its own best
judgment.
    SIR WILFRID LAURIER, H. of C.,
    Debates, Feb. 3, 1910, 2965.

All the manliness of the civilized
world is due to wars or to the need of
being prepared for wars. All the highest qualities of mankind have been
developed by wars or the dangers of
wars. Our whole civilization is the
outgrowth of wars. Without wars,
religion would disappear. All the enterprise of the world has grown out
of the aggressive, adventurous, and
warlike spirit engendered by centuries
of wars.
    SIR WILLIAM VAN HORNE, letter
    to S. S. McClure, 1910.

We have taken the position in
Canada that we do not think we are
bound to take part in every war, and
that our fleet may not be bound in
all cases, and, therefore, for my part
I think it is better under such circumstances to leave the negotiations of these
regulations as to the way in which the
war is to be carried on to the chief
partner of the family, the one who has
to bear the burden in part on some
occasions, and the whole burden perhaps
on other occasions.
    SIR WILFRID LAURIER, speech,
    Imperial Conference, 1911, Proc.,
    117.

When England is at war we are at
war.
    SIR WILFRID LAURIER, H. of C.,
    Debates, Jan. 12, 1912, 1064.

Most of the wars and afflictions that have come on the world are due to attempts made by incompetent people to be their brothers' keepers.

PETER McARTHUR, qu., Deacon, McArthur, 105.

The final Court of Appeal is military power.

JAMES MAVOR, speech, Canadian Military Inst., Jan. 27, 1914.

We have long said that when Great Britain is at war, we are at war; to-day we realize that Great Britain is at war and that Canada is at war also.

SIR WILFRID LAURIER, H. of C., Debates, Aug. 9, 1914, 9.

When the call comes our answer goes at once and it goes in the classical language of the British answer to the call of duty: 'Ready, aye, ready'.

SIR WILFRID LAURIER, H. of C., Debates, Aug. 19, 1914.

It's easy to fight when everything's right,
And you're mad with the thrill and
~~the glory;~~

It's easy to cheer when victory's near,
And wallow in fields that are gory.
It's a different song when every-thing's wrong,
When you're feeling infernally mortal;
When it's ten against one, and hope there is none,
Buck up, little soldiers, and chortle!

ROBERT W. SERVICE, "Carry on", 1916.

Now war is a funny thing, ain't it?
It's the rummiest sort of a go,
For when it's most real,
It's then that you feel
You're a-watchin' a cinema show.

ROBERT W. SERVICE, "The odyssey of 'Erbert 'Iggins", 1916.

The root of strife is not that final force
That bends the bow to breaking;
Give but one unkind thought free course
And war is in the making.

ALBERT D. WATSON, "Making war", 1917.

When we, the Workers, all demand:
"What are we fighting for?"...

Then, then we'll end that stupid crime, that devil's madness — War.

ROBERT W. SERVICE, "Michael", 1921.

If ever the time should come when the spectre of 1914 should again appear I believe it would be best, not only that Parliament should be called, but that the decision of the Government, which, of course, would have to be given promptly, should be submitted to the judgment of the people at a general election before troops should leave our shores. This would contribute to the unity of our country in the months to come and would enable us best to do our duty.

ARTHUR MEIGHEN, speech in Hamilton, Nov. 16, 1925.

In the sweet by-and-by imperialistic ambitions and international fears may possibly give place to the reign of the golden rule; but until that time arrives clashing interests will yield their natural fruits — dislike, fear, hostility, hatred, preparation for war, and war.

JOHN S. EWART, Roots and causes of wars, 1925.

Man must know, if he has any capacity for reason, that modern war doesn't come to an end, that you can't bring it to an end in an honourable peace and make a new start. It sets going a process of destruction that goes on year after year in widening circles of damage and violence.

J. W. DAFOE, Empire Club speech, Jan. 30, 1936.

The Canadian parliament reserves to itself the right to declare, in the light of the circumstances existing at the time, to what extent, if at all, Canada will participate in conflicts in which other members of the Commonwealth may be engaged.

W. L. MACKENZIE KING, League of Nations Assembly, Sept., 1936; H. of C., Debates, 1938, 3183.

If Canada is faced by the necessity of making a decision on the most serious and momentous issue that can face a nation, whether or not to take part in war, the principle of responsible government which has been our guide and our goal for a century past, demands that that decision be made by the parliament of Canada.

W. L. MACKENZIE KING, H. of C., *Debates*, Mar. 30, 1939.

The idea that every twenty years this country should automatically and as a matter of course take part in a war overseas for democracy or self-determination of other small nations, that a country which has all it can do to run itself should feel called upon to save, periodically, a continent that cannot save itself, and to these ends risk the lives of its people, risk bankruptcy and political disunion, seems to many a nightmare and sheer madness.

W. L. MACKENZIE KING, H. of C., *Debates*, Mar. 30, 1939, 2419.

More roads are opened than are closed by bombs
And truth stands naked under the flashing charge.

F. R. SCOTT, "Recovery", 1945.

WAR DEAD.

Growing to full manhood now,
With the care-lines on our brow,
We, the youngest of the nations,
With no childish lamentations,
Weep as only strong men weep,
For the noble hearts that sleep,
Pillowed where they fought and bled,
The loved and lost, our glorious dead!

FREDERICK G. SCOTT, "In Memoriam: Those killed in the Canadian North West, 1885."

In Flanders Fields the poppies grow
Between the crosses, row on row,
That mark our place, and in the sky
The larks, still bravely singing, fly,
Scarce heard amidst the guns below.
We are the dead. Short days ago
We lived, felt dawn, saw sunset glow,
Loved and were loved; and now we lie
In Flanders Fields.

JOHN MCCRAE, "In Flanders Fields", *Punch*, Dec. 8, 1915.

Not since her birth has our earth seen such worth loosed upon her.

RUDYARD KIPLING, "The children, 1914-18", verse three; inscription in Memorial Chamber, Peace Tower, Ottawa.

Nor was their agony brief, or once only imposed on them.
The wounded, the war-spent, the sick received no exemptic :
Being cured they returned and endured and achieved our redemption.

RUDYARD KIPLING, "The children, 1914-18", verse four; inscription in Memorial Chamber, Peace Tower, Ottawa.

That flesh we had nursed from the first in all cleanness was given
To corruption unveiled and assailed by the malice of Heaven —

RUDYARD KIPLING, "The children, 1914-18", verse five; inscription in Memorial Chamber, Peace Tower, Ottawa.

Not we the conquered. Not to us the blame
Of them that flee, of them that basely yield;
Nor ours the shout of victory, the fame
Of them that vanquish in a stricken field.

JOHN MCCRAE, "The unconquered dead", 1919.

Fifty thousand Canadian soldiers under the sod in Europe is the price Canada has paid for the European statesmanship which drenched the continent in blood.

NEWTON W. ROWELL, speech, League of Nations, Geneva, Dec. 8, 1920.

Here in the heart of Europe we meet to unveil a memorial to our country's dead. In earth which has resounded to the drums and tramplings of many conquests, they rest in the quiet of God's acre with the brave of all the world. At death they sheathed in their hearts the sword of devotion, and now from the oft-stricken fields they hold aloft its cross of sacrifice, mutely beckoning those who would share their immortality. No words can add to their fame, nor so long as gratitude holds a place in men's hearts can our forgetfulness be suffered to detract from their renown. For as the war dwarfed by its magnitude all contests of the past, so the wonder of human resource, the splendour of human heroism, reached a height never witnessed before.

> ARTHUR MEIGHEN, Address at Thelus Military Cemetary, Vimy Ridge, at unveiling of Cross of Sacrifice, July 3, 1921.

Down the old road, alone he reappears
His promised word he keeps;
All's well, for over there among his peers
A happy warrior sleeps.

> JOHN CEREDICION JONES, "The returning soldier"; the last two lines are inscribed in the Memorial Chamber, Peace Tower, Ottawa. Jones was born in Wales, 1883 and died in Chapleau, Aug. 19, 1947. See: John Hughes, Ottawa *Journal*, Nov. 11, 1948.

Take these men for your ensamples
Like them remember that prosperity can be only for the free
That freedom is the sure possession of those alone
Who have the courage to defend it.

> Inscription on Soldiers' Tower, University of Toronto campus, erected 1924.

From little towns in a far land we came,
To save our honour and a world aflame;
By little towns, in a far land, we sleep,
And trust those things we won to you to keep.

> RUDYARD KIPLING, inscription on war memorial, Sault Ste. Marie, Ont., unveiled Sept. 2, 1924.

They braced their belts about them
And crossed, in ships, the sea.
They fought, and found six feet of ground
And died for you and me.

> Inscription supplied by Dr. R. H. Arthur for Sudbury War Memorial, 1928. Taken from A. E. HOUSMAN's poem XXXII, *Last poems*:
> "They braced their belts about them,
> They crossed in ships the sea,
> They sought and found six feet of ground
> And there they died for me."

The following lines, written by RUDYARD KIPLING in response to a local request, were not used:
"We, giving all, gained all;
Neither lament us nor praise;
Only, in all things recall,
It is fear, not death, that slays."

We ask but this: that in your brave tomorrows
You keep our faith, who, rich in youth and pride,
Gave up our lives to quell old fears and sorrows —
Till you forget, we shall not twice have died.

> JOHN E. NIXON, "The unreturning", March, 1946.

WAR, EUROPEAN, 1914-18.

But today, while the clouds are heavy and we hear the booming of the distant thunder, and see the lightning flashes above the horizon, we cannot, and we will not, wait and deliberate until the impending storm shall have burst upon us in fury and disaster.

> SIR ROBERT L. BORDEN, H. of C., *Debates*, Dec. 5, 1912.

Because it is the world's fight for freedom, Britain, reluctantly but resolutely, speaks the word, and Canada also answers Ay!

> TORONTO *Globe*, Aug. 4, 1914.

The time of trial is upon this country and Empire. It will do us good in the end. God and the right will finally triumph.

> SIR GEORGE E. FOSTER, H. of C., *Debates*, Aug. 22, 1914, 98.

We may be in it for months and we may be in it for years. It is a time for toil and bloody sweat, for courage and good cheer.

> ARTHUR MEIGHEN, Empire Club speech, Dec. 17, 1914.

Canada, not forced by any law or rule has voluntarily taken part in this war, placing herself in opposition to great powers. Canada has stepped into nationhood. No longer can we play the part of minors, who cannot transact our own business. Hereafter we shall not be allowed by the great nations of the world to put ourselves in that position. They will say that if we can make war we can do our own business and give our answers to their questions.

SIR CLIFFORD SIFTON, speech in Montreal, Jan. 25, 1915.

Have you seen the badge of courage on the soldiers who march by?
The deathless name of Canada — the name for which they die?
Does it wake no martial ardour — is your soul put on a shelf?
Can you still go back to nothing — to nothing but yourself?

W. A. FRASER, in Toronto *News* Nov. 6, 1915.

I am not afraid to become a German subject. I ask myself if the German régime might be favourably compared with that of the Boches of Ontario.

ARMAND LAVERGNE, speech in Legislature, Quebec, Jan. 13, 1916.

For the first contingent, our recruiting plans were, I think, different from anything that had ever occurred before. There was really a call to arms, like the fiery cross passing through the Highlands of Scotland or the mountains of Ireland in former days.

SIR SAM HUGHES, H. of C., *Debates*, Jan. 26, 1916, 292.

In conjunction with the Third Army, the Canadian Corps will take Vimy Ridge.

Army operation order, April 1917.

Remember the *Llandovery Castle!*
CANADIAN CORPS cry on going into action Aug. 8, 1918, east of Amiens; a reference to the hospital ship sunk by Germans with Canadian doctors and nurses aboard.

Canada's Hundred Days.
The victorious drive of the Canadian Corps, Aug. 4 to Nov. 11, 1918.

At this time the proper occupation of the living, is first, to honour our heroic dead; next, to repair the havoc, human and material, that surrounds us; and, lastly, to learn aright and apply with courage the lessons of the war.

ARTHUR MEIGHEN, speech at Vimy Ridge, July 3, 1921.

WAR OF 1812.

Mr. Madison's War.
A popular reference; James Madison was President of the U. S. 1809-17.

We are engaged in an awful and eventful contest. By unanimity and despatch in our councils and by vigour in our operations, we will teach the enemy this lesson: that a country defended by free men, enthusiastically devoted to the cause of their King and constitution, can never be conquered.

GENERAL ISAAC BROCK, speech to Upper Canada Legislature, July 27, 1812.

The war might be called Madison's Patent-Nostrum. For to our House of Assembly it has been a timely emetic, to our Country, a gently sweating cathartic — one threw up two traitors, the other threw off some, and by the way of appendix, hung up some. A sedative will be prescribed should further symptoms require it.

UPPER CANADA ALMANACK, FOR THE YEAR 1815, printed by John Cameron.

The War of 1812 was not a war engaged in by Canadians for Canada, it was a war to maintain British connection.

GEORGE W. ROSS, Empire Club speech, 1905.

WAR, WORLD, 1939-45.

Let us remember that if the democracies fail, Canada is the richest prize among the nations of the world.

R. J. MANION, speech in Ottawa, 1939.

Germany and Japan don't want swamps and jungles. They want you — great, rich, sprawling Canada, rich with her endless wheat-bearing acres where a *Herrenvolk* could lord it over a slave population.

ERIC KNIGHT, C.B.C. broadcast, Mar. 1, 1942.

The Canadian Army overseas is a dagger pointed at the heart of Berlin.

GEN. A. G. L. MCNAUGHTON, speeches in England, 1942.

We didn't cross the Channel to fight
for England, but felt rather that we
were going forth to fight, along with
England, for Canada.

> ABBÉ SABOURIN, on the Dieppe
> Raid, in *Le Jour*, Dec., 1942.
> (trans.)

WEATHER.

(See also: CLIMATE; STORMS)

When muskrats build their houses
high look for a hard winter.

> Saying of pioneer Ontario farmers.

Here winter's breath is rude,
  His fingers cold and wan;
But what's his wildest mood
  To the tyranny of man?

> ALEXANDER MCLACHLAN, *The
> emigrant*, 1861.

Canada has a climate nine months'
winter and three months late in the
fall.

> Popular American saying, late 19th.
> century; also applied by residents
> of Ontario and Quebec to Nova
> Scotia.

Man wants but little here below zero.

> ROBERT C. (BOB) EDWARDS, *Cal-
> gary Eye Opener*, Feb. 4, 1905.

There is no such thing as bad
weather; only our lack of appreciation
of it.

> WILLIAM E. SAUNDERS, remark to
> P. A. Taverner, May. 1905.

I know of nothing so absolutely
pitiless as weather.

> JOHN MCCRAE, letter from the
> trenches, Jan. 25, 1917.

If a cock crows as he goes to bed,
He will wake up with a wet head.

> Simcoe, Ont., rhyme; qu., *Jour.
> Amer. folklore*, 1918, 7.

Evening red and morning grey
Is the sure sign of a fair day.
Evening grey and morning red
Sends the shepherd wet to bed.

> Brantford, Ont. rhyme; qu., *Jour.
> Amer. folklore*, 1918, 6.

A fine Christmas, a fat Churchyard.
Winter thunder means Summer's
hunger.

A year of snow, a year of plenty.
A warm Christmas, a cold Easter.
A red sun got water in his eye.

Evening red and morning grey,
Double signs of one fine day.

> Newfoundland weather lore prov-
> erbs; qu., Devine, *Folk lore of Nfld.*,
> 1937.

Anyone who foretells Alberta weather
is either a newcomer or a fool.

> FRANK OLIVER, qu., *Can. hist. rev.*,
> 1946, 143.

THE WEST.

(See also: ANNEXATION;
NORTH-WEST REBELLION;
THE PRAIRIES; SETTLERS)

Civilization will no doubt extend over
these low hills.

> DAVID THOMPSON, *Narrative*,
> 1784-1812.

The temptation to go West where the
climate is milder and the land unen-
cumbered with timber — is much
greater than is generally supposed.
It has existed to such an extent as to
be familiarly known as the 'Prairie
Fever'.

> A. G. HAWKE, 1840, *Report, chief
> emigration agent*; Public Archives,
> *Upper Canada sundries*.

Out and in the river is winding
  The links of its long red chain,
Through belts of dusky pine land
  And gusty leagues of plain.

> J. G. WHITTIER, "Red River voya-
> geur", 1860.

One thing is very important: unless
the English government shall promptly
respond to the manifest destiny of the
great interior of British America —
the basin of Lake Winnipeg — the
speedy Americanization of that fertile
belt is inevitable.

> J. W. TAYLOR, American Consul
> at Winnipeg, letter to Hon. S. P.
> Chase, July 17, 1861, in *U. S.
> Treasury, Relations between U. S.
> and British North America*, p. 26.
> (37 Congress, 2nd Session. House
> of Representatives, Executive docu-
> ment, no. 146.)

The Fertile Belt.

> JOHN PALLISER, *Report*, 1863, 18; used in immigration literature, 1880-90; now known as the Park Belt.

If Canada is to remain a country separate from the United States it is of great importance to her that they (the United States) should not get behind us by right or by force, and intercept the route to the Pacific... But in any other point of view, it seems to me that the country is of no present value to Canada. We have unoccupied land enough to absorb immigration for many years, and the opening up of the Saskatchewan would do to Canada what the Prairie lands of Illinois are doing now — drain away our youth and our strength.

> SIR JOHN A. MACDONALD, letter to Sir Edward W. Watkin, Mar. 27, 1865.

Canada is bound to the North-West by the ties of discovery, possession, and interest. The country is ours by right of inheritance.

> ALEXANDER MORRIS, speech in House of Commons, 1867.

We hope to see a new Upper Canada in the North-West Territory — in its well-regulated society and government, in its education, morality and religion.

> TORONTO *Globe*, June 2, 1869.

Say to England that she does not want these sour grapes which hang so far beyond her reach... a country whose destinies God has indissolubly wedded to ours by geographical affinities which no human power can sunder, as He has divorced it from Canada by physical barriers which no human power can overcome.

> ST. PAUL [MINN.] *Daily Press*, Dec. 23, 1869.

I have always feared the entrance of the North-West into Confederation, because I have always believed that the French-Canadian element would be sacrificed; but I tell you frankly it had never occurred to me that our rights would be so quickly and so completely forgotten.

> ARCHBISHOP ALEXANDRE TACHÉ, letter to Cartier, 1869, qu., in Benoît, *Taché*, II, 7. (trans.)

This was the time of day for quiet in nature, but in fancy we caught the rumble of wagons on well-travelled roads, the shriek of the locomotive, the hum of machinery, the lowing and bleating of herds and flocks, the tinkle of the cow-bell, the ringing of the church and school bells — I could hear all these in anticipation, for verily the land before me was worthy, and in good time it would come to its inheritance.

> JOHN McDOUGALL, *Life in the far west, 1868-72*, 1903, 99.

The Great Lone Land.

> WILLIAM BUTLER, *The great lone land*, 1872.

All aboard for the West!

> SIR GEORGES E. CARTIER, H. of C., *Debates*, June 1, 1872, 938, on the passing of the Pacific Railway Act.

My terms I am going to lay down before you; the decision of our Chiefs; ever since we came to a decision you push it back. The sound of the rustling of the gold is under my feet where I stand; we have a rich country; it is the Great Spirit who gave us this; where we stand upon is the Indians' property, and belongs to them.

> MAWEDOPENAIS, Salteaux chief, at treaty parley, North-West Angle, Lake of the Woods, Oct. 3, 1873.

God's Country.

> The Half-Breeds' term for the valley of the Saskatchewan in their trek from Manitoba during 1870's.

It has left us with a small population, a scanty immigration and a North-west empty still.

> EDWARD BLAKE, *To the members of the West Durham Reform Convention, Feb. 6, 1891*; a reference to the Conservative party; sometimes misquoted: "An empty west, empty still".

One of the principal ideas western men have is that it is right to take anything in sight provided nobody else is ahead of them. As a rule it is sound policy for the government to fall in with this idea and encourage the people to go ahead.

> SIR CLIFFORD SIFTON, letter to a western Liberal M.P., August, 1897.

We're a hundred dollars from any-where.

Popular saying, Winnipeg, early 20th. Century.

The American Invasion.

The movement of settlers from Kansas and other States into the West after 1900.

The Banana Belt.

Derisive term used by newspapers, especially in Winnipeg, in reference to northwest Saskatchewan, which was depicted in immigration litera-ture as having a mild climate. F. M. Sclanders of Saskatoon Board of Trade, 1908-16, was the owner of a carefully nurtured banana tree. Also, the name of a school district in north-western Saskatchewan.

The Last Best West.

CANADA, DEPT. OF THE INTERIOR, from a title of a pamphlet puplished about 1905 and distributed in Europe and the U. S. to attract settlers. (Defined by Sandilands, *Western Canadian dictionary*, 1912: "A favourite term for describing a new district beyond which one must not dream of anything better.")

I shall be content, when the history of this country shall be written, to have the history of the last eight or nine years, so far as Western administration is concerned, entered in my name.

SIR CLIFFORD SIFTON, H. of C., *Debates*, May 31, 1906.

What care I here for all Earth's creeds outworn,
The dreams outlived, the hopes to ashes turned,
In that old East so dark with rain and doubt?
Here life swings glad and free and rude, and I
Shall drink it to the full, and go content.

ARTHUR STRINGER, "Morning in the Northwest", 1907.

The North-West will be American.

GOLDWIN SMITH, *Reminiscences*, 1910, 417.

Had it not been for the mysterious potency of the West, awaiting the day when it should be incorporated in the Union, it is doubtful whether any Dominion would have been called into being.

SIR ROBERT FALCONER, speech, "The quality of Canadian life", 1917.

Our West never went through a riotous youth; it has few memories to be forgotten.

SIR ROBERT FALCONER, speech, "The quality of Canadian life", 1917.

Western Canada has paid for the development of Canadian nationality, and it would appear that it must continue to pay. The acquisitiveness of eastern Canada shows little sign of abatement.

H. A. INNIS, *History of the C.P.R.*, 1923, 294.

The story of the frontier like a saga
Sang through the cells and cloisters of the nation.

E. J. PRATT, *Brébeuf and his brethren*, 1940.

To the native of the prairies Alberta is the far West; British Columbia the near East.

EDWARD A. MCCOURT, *Can. West in fiction*, 1949, preface.

WHEAT.

(See also: TRANSPORTATION)

It almost now seems all in vain
For to expect high price for grain.

JAMES MCINTYRE, "Lines read at a dairy-men's supper", 1889.

Raise less hell and more wheat.

SIR WILLIAM VAN HORNE, attri-buted, as advice given to Manitoba farmers; qu., Nichols, *Can. Press*, 17.

Give us a good harvest and a bloody war in Europe.

A prayer attributed to the Canadian pioneer in the West.

The Granary of the Empire.

From the legend on an arch at the Diamond Jubilee, London, 1897: "The Granary of the Empire, Free Homes for Millions, God bless the Royal Family"; in 1902, at Coronation ceremonies in London, an arch of wheat in the Strand carried the motto, "Canada, the Granary of the Empire".

The world's bread basket is western Canada.

> CANADA. DEPT. OF THE INTERIOR, *Western Canada*, 1899. (Pamphlet issued under the authority of Clifford Sifton).

Number One, Manitoba Hard.

> Graded Canadian wheat, famous from 1899, rated the best in the world, and much in demand during 1920's and early 1930's.

The Granary of the World.

> CANADA. DEPT. OF THE INTERIOR, *Canada, the granary of the world*, a pamphlet issued in December 1903.

All the speculation in the world never raised a bushel of wheat.

> ROBERT C. (BOB) EDWARDS, *Calgary Eye Opener*, Feb. 10, 1912.

What's our ambition? Why, we aim to be
The Empire's, nay, the whole world's granary.
A lofty mark, i' faith, to find our place
Just in the belly of the human race.

> L. A. McKAY, "Fidelia vulnera amici", 1931.

The Wheat Pool was as much a religious institution as the church.

> HENRY WISE WOOD, (d. 1941) in his later years.

WIND.

Cease, Wind, to blow
And drive the peopled snow,
And move the haunted arras to and fro,
And moan of things I fear to know
Yet would rend from thee, Wind, before I go
On the blind pilgrimage.
Cease, Wind, to blow.

> BLISS CARMAN, "The red wolf", 1892.

Tonight the wind roars in from sea;
The crow clings to the straining tree;
Curlew and crane and bittern flee
The dykes of Tantramar.

> CHARLES G. D. ROBERTS, "The tide on Tantramar", 1893.

The wind changed every way and fled
Across the meadows and the wheat;
It whirled the swallows overhead,
And swung the daisies at my feet...
Took all the maples by surprise,
And made the poplars clash and shiver,
And flung my hair about my eyes,
And sprang and blackened on the river.

> ARCHIBALD LAMPMAN, "The wind's word", *Independent*, July 26, 1894.

There paused to shut the door
A fellow called the Wind,
With mystery before,
And reticence behind.

> BLISS CARMAN, "At the granite gate", 1895.

On wan dark night on Lac St. Pierre,
De win' she blow, blow, blow,
An' de crew of de woodscow "Julie Plante"
Got scar't an' run below —
For de win' she bow like hurricane
Bimeby she blow some more,
An' de scow bus' up on Lac St. Pierre
Wan arpent from de shore.

> WILLIAM H. DRUMMOND, "The wreck of the *Julie Plante*", 1897.

Beneath her sloping neck
Her bosom-gourds swelled chastely, white as spray,
Wind-tost — without a fleck —
The air which heaved them was less pure than they.

> CHARLES MAIR, "Innocence", 1901.

I am Wind, the Deathless Dreamer
Of the summer world;
Tranced in snows of shade and shimmer,
On a cloud scarp curled.

> WILFRED CAMPBELL, "The wind", 1905.

The Canada wind is the keen north wind,
The wind of the secret sea,
And quickens the soul of me.

> HELEN MERRILL, "The Canada wind", 1912.

The wind upon the hill has sweetest hush,
The day is melting into tenderest flame,

And from the valley, where the waters
rush,
Comes up the evensong of the lone
hermit-thrush.
> WILLIAM E. MARSHALL, "Brook-
> field", 1914.

And I have heard the wind awake
at nights
Like some poor mother left with
empty hands,
Go whimpering in the silent stubble
fields
And creeping through bare houses
without lights.
> FREDERICK LAIGHT, "Soliloquy",
> 1937.

WINNIPEG, MAN.

> (See also: CITIES AND TOWNS
> — NICKNAMES, etc.)

The city wants lifting into the air
ten or fifteen feet.
> GOLDWIN SMITH, *The Week*, Sept.
> 18, 1884, 659.

So far as Winnipeg is concerned it
is a discouraging place and always was,
but I would not fret about it. I think
it will come around all right. If it
does not we can always have the
satisfaction of consigning it to a warmer
place.
> SIR CLIFFORD SIFTON, letter to J. S.
> Willison, on the election, December,
> 1899.

WINTER.

> (See also: CLIMATE; SNOW)

The lank Canadian eager trims his
fire,
And all around their simpering stoves
retire.
> STANDISH O'GRADY, *The emigrant*,
> 1841.

Here the rough Bear subsists his
winter year,
And licks his paw and finds no better
fare.
> STANDISH O'GRADY, *The emigrant*,
> 1841.

Cold enough to freeze the hair off
a dog's back.
> THOMAS C. HALIBURTON, *Sam
> Slick's wise saws*, 1853, ch. XI.

The summers, the winters — I have
sometimes doubted whether there could
be a great race without the hardy influence of winters in due proportion.
> WALT WHITMAN, *Diary in Canada*,
> [1880], 1904.

What wonder we long for a breeze
from the islands —
The beautiful islands and blest of
the sea? —
Vine-lands or pine-lands, lowlands or
highlands,
So they be *summer* lands nought
care we!
> GEORGE FREDERICK CAMERON, "In-
> sulæ fortunatæ", 1882.

Canadian climate must have been
changeable ever since the world
begun,
One hour snowing, and the next
raining like fun,
Our blood sometimes thick, other times
thin,
This is the time colds begin.
> JAMES GAY, "Canadian climate",
> [1885?].

Sharp is the frost, the Northern Light
Flickers and shoots his streamers
bright;
Snow-drifts cumber the untracked
road;
Bends the pine with its heavy load;
Each small star, though it shines so
bright,
Looks half pinched with the cold
tonight.
> FRANCIS RYE, in, *Can. birthday
> book*, 1887, 384.

Lands that loom like spectres, whited
regions of winter,
Wastes of desolate woods, deserts of
water and shore;
A world of winter and death, within
these regions who enter,
Lost to summer and life, go to enter
no more.
> WILFRED CAMPBELL, "The winter
> lakes", 1889.

The winter comes one month before
the autumn.
> ABBÉ GEORGES DUGAS, *Un voyageur*,
> 1890, 97, on winter at Hudson's
> Bay. (trans.)

The windows of my room
Are dark with bitter frost,
The stillness aches with doom
Of something loved and lost.
> BLISS CARMAN, "A northern vigil",
> 1893.

The frost that stings like fire upon
my cheek,
The loneliness of this forsaken
ground,
The long, white drift upon whose
powdered peak
I sit in the great silence as one
bound.
> ARCHIBALD LAMPMAN, "Winter
> uplands", 1900.

There was an old man of Quebec,
Who was buried in snow to his neck.
When asked, "Are you friz?"
He replied, "Yes, I is,
But we don't call this cold in Quebec."
> RUDYARD KIPLING; attributed.

Were I not cold how should I come
to know
One potent pleasure of the sun's
sweet rays?
Or did I never breast the driving
snow
What bliss were sweetest kernel
of June days?
> WILSON MACDONALD, "A poet stood
> forlorn", 1918.

Beyond the dripping nose and tear,
Beyond the chilblain and the bite,
Beyond the scratchy underwere,
Beyond the eighty-below at night,
There still must lie — though drifts
conceal —
Some ridden good for man's desery,
Some secret bounty for his weal,
Which man should shovel out —
or try.
> P. G. HIEBERT, Sarah Binks, 1947.

WISDOM AND UNWISDOM.

> (See also: INTELLIGENCE;
> KNOWLEDGE; SIN; TRUTH)

Consait grows as natural as the hair
on one's head, but is longer in comin'
out.
> THOMAS C. HALIBURTON, Sam
> Slick's wise saws, 1853, ch. XVIII.

The philosophies of one age have
become the absurdities of the next,
and the foolishness of yesterday has
become the wisdom of tomorrow.
> SIR WILLIAM OSLER, Montreal med.
> jour. 1902, 684.

A man should be able to appreciate
a good thing even when it happens to
be his own.
> PETER MCARTHUR, To be taken
> with salt, 1903, 149.

The last great lesson is humility
before the unsolved problems of the
Universe.
> SIR WILLIAM OSLER, Intro., Life
> of Pasteur, 1911, by Vallery-Radot.

Doubt is the beginning, not the end,
of wisdom.
> GEORGE ILES, Canadian stories,
> 1918, 167.

Some people might just as well be
crazy for all the sense they have.
> ROBERT C. (BOB) EDWARDS, Cal-
> gary Eye Opener, May 11, 1918.

A man has to be as willing to forgive
himself, as to forgive other people.
> PETER MCARTHUR, (d. 1924) a
> favourite saying.

And never the body is free,
nor the heart,
nor the mind,
until it has mastered the law
that that which we hold, we must lose;
that willingly given away is our own.
> IRENE H. MOODY, "Jealousy", 1940.

WIT AND HUMOUR.

I've often observed it takes but a
very small joke to make a crowd larf.
They'll larf at nothin' amost.
> THOMAS C. HALIBURTON, Sam
> Slick, 1838, 96.

Your jokes hit, and hit pretty hard,
too. They make a man think as well
as laugh.
> THOMAS C. HALIBURTON, The
> attaché, 1844.

A joke, like an egg, is never no
good 'xcept it's fresh laid, — is it?
> T. C. HALIBURTON, The attaché,
> 2nd. ser., 1844, II, 4.

Wit in a woman is a dangerous thing,
like a doctor's lancet, it is apt to be

employed about matters that offend
our delicacy, or hurt our feelings.

> T. C. HALIBURTON, *Nature and
> human nature*, 1855, II, 95.

Grip still has a Sir John
But the Grand Old Face has gone.

> *Grip*, June 20, 1891, on the death
> of Sir J. A. Macdonald, who was
> often caricatured in its pages.

One of the blessings of being a
humorist is that all your mistakes pass
off as jokes.

> PETER MCARTHUR, *To be taken
> with salt*, 1903, 150.

Many a great man's reputation for
wit is due to his having been interviewed
by a bright reporter.

> ROBERT C. (BOB) EDWARDS, *Cal-
> gary Eye Opener*, Feb. 22, 1919.

WOLFE, JAMES.

> (See also: THE CONQUEST,
> 1759; MONTCALM)

Mat is he? mat? Well, by Gott,
I wish he would bite some of my other
chenerals.

> GEORGE III, 1758, answer to a
> remark made on the appointment
> of Wolfe by Pitt to command the
> expedition against Quebec.

He asks no one's opinion and wants
no advice.

> JAMES GIBSON, letter to Gov.
> Lawrence, Quebec, Aug. 1, 1759.

There is such a choice of difficulties
that I am at a loss how to determine.

> JAMES WOLFE, despatch to Pitt,
> Sept. 2, 1759.

Tell me, tell me how goes the battle
there?

> JAMES WOLFE, statement ascribed to
> him before his death, by James
> Henderson, letter, in *Can. hist. rev.*,
> IV, 54.

The world could not expect more
from him than he thought himself
capable of performing. He looked on
danger as the favourable moment that
would call forth his talents.

> HORACE WALPOLE, 1763, *Memoirs of
> George III*, 1845, 239.

England, with all thy faults I love
  thee still.
Time was when it was praise and
  boast enough
In every clime, and travel where we
  might,
That we were born her children.
  Praise enough
To fill the ambition of a private man
That Chatham's language was his
  mother's tongue
And Wolfe's great name compatriot
  with his own.

> WILLIAM COWPER, *The task*, book
> II, 1785.

Valour gave them a common death,
history a common fame, posterity a
common monument.

> JAMES C. FISHER; trans. of his
> Latin inscription on Wolfe-Mont-
> calm monument, Plains of Abraham,
> erected 1828: "Mortem virtus
> communem, famam historia, monu-
> mentum posteritas dedit".

Here died Wolfe victorious.

> Inscription on monument on Plains
> of Abraham, Quebec City, erected
> 1849.

"They run! they run!" — "Who
  run?" he cried,
As swiftly to his pallid brow,
Like crimson sunlight upon snow,
The anxious blood returned;
"The French! the French!" a voice
  replied,
When quickly paled life's ebbing
  tide,
And though his words were weak
  and low,
His eye with valour burned.
"Thank God! I die in peace," he
  said.

> CHARLES SANGSTER, "Death of
> Wolfe", 1860.

In days of yore, from Britain's shore
Wolfe, the dauntless hero came,
And planted firm Britannia's flag
On Canada's fair domain.
Here may it wave — our boast and
  pride,
And join in love together,
The Thistle, Shamrock, Rose entwine
The Maple Leaf forever!

> ALEXANDER MUIR, "The maple leaf
> forever", 1867, popular version.
> Muir wrote in a letter to the
> Toronto *Empire*, Sept. 8, 1894 that

the first two lines should be printed: "In days of yore the hero Wolfe/ Britain's glory did maintain." (See also: MAPLE)

WOLVES.

Wolves are scarce in Canada, but they afford the finest furs in all the country. Their flesh is white, and good to eat; they pursue their prey to the tops of the tallest trees.

> WILLIAM GUTHRIE, *Guthrie's geographical grammar*, 1807.

Wolves can't allure, they only skare their prey.

> T. C. HALIBURTON, *Sam Slick's wise saws*, 1853, II, 283.

Scriptur' don't warn us agin wolves, except when they have sheep's-clothin' on.

> T. C. HALIBURTON, *Sam Slick's wise saws*, 1853, II, 301.

Any man that says he's been et by a wolf is a liar.

> "SAM MARTIN" of Algoma, about 1910; attributed by J. W. Curran, in, *Wolves don't bite*, 1940, 212.

WOMEN.

(See also: MEN AND WOMEN)

The Frenchmen, who consider things in their true light, complain very much that a great number of the ladies in Canada have gotten into the pernicious custom of taking too much care of their dress, and squandering all their fortune and more upon it.

> PETER KALM, 1749, *Travels*, 1937, II, 525.

I always feel safe with these women folk, for I have always found that the road to a woman's heart lies through her child.

> THOMAS C. HALIBURTON, *Sam Slick*, 1836, ch. X.

The character and conduct of the mother is a sure and certain guarantee for that of the darter.

> T. C. HALIBURTON, *Sam Slick*, 1840, 124.

Rich gals and handsome gals are seldom good for nothin' else but their cash or their looks.

> T. C. HALIBURTON, *The attaché*, 2nd. ser., 1844, 63.

Women forgive injuries, but never forget slights.

> T. C. HALIBURTON, *The old judge*, 1849, ch. XV.

A really modest woman was never squeamish. Fastidiousness is the envelope of indelicacy.

> T. C. HALIBURTON, *Nature and human nature*, 1855, II, 188.

I do not know at what age one dare call a woman a spinster.

> SIR WILLIAM OSLER, *Nurse and patient*, 1897.

A bunch of the boys were whooping it up in the Malemute saloon;
The kid that handles the juke-box was hitting a jag-time tune;
Back of the bar, in a solo game, sat Dangerous Dan McGrew,
And watching his luck was his light-o'-love, the lady that's known as Lou.

> ROBERT W. SERVICE, "The shooting of Dan McGrew", 1907.

I am opposed by all the short-haired women and the long-haired men in the Province.

> SIR RODMOND ROBLIN, on the women's suffrage agitation, Manitoba, 1912.

Tact is the saving virtue without which no woman can be a success, as a nurse or not. She may have all the others, but without tact she is a failure. With most women it is an instinct, her protective mechanism in life. It is one of the greatest of human blessings that so many women are so full of tact. The calamity happens when a woman who has all the other riches of life just lacks that one thing.

> SIR WILLIAM OSLER, Commencement address to nurses, Johns Hopkins Univ., May 7, 1913.

It is the prime duty of a woman of this terrestrial world to look well. Neatness is the asepsis of clothes.

> SIR WILLIAM OSLER, Commencement address to nurses, Johns Hopkins Univ., May 7, 1913.

In point of morals the average woman is, even for business, too crooked.

STEPHEN B. LEACOCK, "The woman question". *Maclean's mag.*, Oct., 1915.

A woman is more influenced by what she suspects than by what she is told.

ROBERT C. (BOB) EDWARDS, *Calgary Eye Opener*, Nov. 3, 1917.

I say that the Holy Scriptures, theology, ancient philosophy, Christian philosophy, history, anatomy, physiology, political economy, and feminine psychology, all seem to indicate that the place of women in this world is not amid the strife of the political arena, but in her home.

J. J. DENIS, H. of C., *Debates*, 1918, 638.

Amorous creature of exquisite aura —
Marvel of dark glamorie.

TOM MACINNES, "Zalinka", 1923.

Then and now and always, wide away and the length of a span,
I gather that I must gather, by impulse, election:
In me only is attraction.
It alone can attract me.
So am I myself, and none other,
Myself — a mystery! a mouthpiece!

GRACE BLACKBURN, "Chant of the women", 1926.

Her thoughts were as pure as the dawn upon the sea,
But through those ugly eyes and mouth they couldn't get free —
And no one had a kinder heart anywhere about:
O, if God had only made her inside out!

WILSON MACDONALD, "Maggie Swartz", 1926.

WORDS.

(See also: QUOTATIONS; SPEECHES; TRUTH)

Not only the bitterest words, but the most direct and pointed personalities are justifiable in the exposure of public crime.

ROBERT GOURLAY, *Statistical account of U. C.*, 1822, ccxxxlv.

Thunderin' long words ain't wisdom.

T. C. HALIBURTON, *Sam Slick's wise saws*, 1853, I, 199.

To see harm in ordinary words betrays a knowledge, and not an ignorance of evil.

T. C. HALIBURTON, *Nature and human nature*, 1855, II, 188.

Once more I ask for definition; this is one of my fads.

JOHN S. EWART, speech, Canadian Club, Toronto, 1904.

I like those words that carry in their veins
The blood of lions. "Liberty" is one,
And "Justice", and the heart leaps to the sun
When the thrilled note of "Courage! Courage!" rains
Upon the sorely stricken will.

ETHELWYN WETHERALD, "Words", 1907.

It's as easy to recall an unkind word as it is to draw back the bullet after firing a gun.

ROBERT C. (BOB) EDWARDS, *Calgary Eye Opener*, Nov. 11, 1916.

Give me the words of a thinker,
When beauty has touched his pen,
That burn with the simple fervor.
That reaches the soul of men.

JAMES C. SINGER, "Foreword" to *Poems*, 1929.

Words still manifestly force the understanding, throw everything in confusion and lead mankind into vain and innumerable controversies and fallacies.

JOHN S. EWART, qu. in *Can. hist. rev.*, 1933, 137.

Candid words cannot compete with candied words.

R. J. MANION, *Life is an adventure*, 1936, 57.

The old eternal frog
In the throat that comes
With the words *Mother, sweetheart, dog*
Excites, and then numbs.

A. J. M. SMITH, "On reading an anthology of popular poetry", 1940.

WORK.

(See also: DEEDS AND DOING;
DUTY; LABOUR)

A trade won't be followed long that
ain't a profitable one, that's a fact.

T. C. HALIBURTON, *Sam Slick*,
1840, 91.

I'm a sort of Jack of all trades and
master of none.

THOMAS C. HALIBURTON, *Sam
Slick's wise saws*, 1853, ch. VII.

Work, for the night is coming!
Work through the sunny noon;
Fill the bright hours with labor;
Rest comes sure and soon.
Give every flying minute
Something to keep in store;
Work, for the night is coming,
When man works no more.

ANNA L. WALKER (COGHILL),
"Work for the night is coming",
hymn, in *Leaves from the back-
woods*, Montreal, 1861.

When it is understood that instead
of working and saving you may vote
yourself the earnings and savings of
other people, industry will lose some
of its charm.

GOLDWIN SMITH, *Canada and the
Can. question*, 1891, 33.

Not with vain noise
The great work grows,
Nor with foolish voice,
But in repose, —
Not in the rush
But in the hush.

CHARLES G. D. ROBERTS, "A song
of growth", 1893.

The joy of the hand that hews for
beauty
Is the dearest solace beneath the sun.

BLISS CARMAN, "Wanderer", 1893.

Not in perfection dwells the subtler
power
To pierce our mean content, but
rather works
Through incompletion, and the need
that irks,
Not in the flower, but effort toward
the flower.

CHARLES G. D. ROBERTS, "The cow
pasture", 1893.

Throw away, in the first place, all
ambition beyond that of doing the day's
work well.

SIR WILLIAM OSLER, "The army
surgeon", 1894.

Hem and Haw were the sons of sin,
Created to shally and shirk;
Hem lay 'round and Haw looked
on
While God did all the work,

BLISS CARMAN, "Hem and Haw",
1895.

The faltering restless hand of Hack,
And the tireless hand of Hew.

BLISS CARMAN, "Hack and Hew",
1896.

System, or as I shall term it, the
virtue of method, is the harness without
which only the horses of genius travel.

SIR WILLIAM OSLER, *Teacher and
student*, 1897.

In institutions the corroding effect
of routine can be withstood only by
maintaining high ideals of work; but
these become the sounding brass and
tinkling cymbals without corresponding
sound practice. ·

SIR WILLIAM OSLER, "Nurse and
patient", 1897.

The work of the world has been done
by men who had not reached *la crise
de quarante ans*.

SIR WILLIAM OSLER, "Importance of
post-graduate study", in *Lancet*,
1900.

The effective, moving, vitalizing work
of the world is done between the ages of
twenty five and forty   these fifteen
golden years of plenty, the anabolic or
constructive period, in which there is
always a balance in the mental bank
and the credit is good.

SIR WILLIAM OSLER, "The fixed
period", address Feb. 22, 1905, at
Johns Hopkins Univ.

No man does as much today as
he is going to do tomorrow.

ROBERT C. (BOB) EDWARDS, *Calgary Eye Opener*, Mar. 23, 1912.

No mind however dull can escape the
brightness that comes from steady
application.

SIR WILLIAM OSLER, address,
"The way of life", April 20, 1913.

A French Canadian will accomplish as much with an ax as a man of any other race with a full outfit of tools.

HENRY M. AMI, *Canada and Newfoundland*, 1915, 334.

Grant me dear Lord, the alchemy of toil.

ALAN SULLIVAN, "Suppliant".

We are all born lazy. Some of us get impressions, vivid impressions, which call for our industry; industry leads to facility, and everything becomes easy.

SIR WILLIAM VAN HORNE, qu., Macnaughtan, *My Can. memories*, 1920, 97.

I've done no work. Work consists of doin' somethin' you don't want to do — yet I've always been as busy as a cow's tail in fly-time.

JACK MINER, from his *Philosophy*.

If you want work well done, select a busy man — the other kind has no time.

ROBERT C. (BOB) EDWARDS, in his *Annual*, 1922, 63.

THE WORLD.

The world is wiser than its wisest men,
And shall outlive the wisdom of the gods,
Made after man's own liking.

CHARLES MAIR, *Tecumseh*, 1886.

This is yet the childhood of the world, and a supine credulity is still the most charming characteristic of man.

SIR WILLIAM OSLER, Address, "Recent advances in medicine", Baltimore, Feb. 22, 1891.

Oh keep the world for ever at the dawn,
Ere yet the opals, cobweb-strung have dried;
Ere yet too bounteous gifts have marred the morn,
Or fading stars have died.

MARJORIE PICKTHALL, "Dawn", submitted to Toronto *Mail and Empire*, 1900.

When Earth was mostly vapour
It was a dizzy spot;

Small comets cut a caper,
And everything was hot.

JOHN C. MURRAY, "History".

The world has drifted far from its old anchorage and no man can with certainty prophesy what the outcome will be.

SIR ROBERT BORDEN, Nov. 11, 1918, in his diary, *Memoirs*, 1938.

WORRY.

To carry care to bed is to sleep with a pack on your back.

THOMAS C. HALIBURTON, *Sam Slick's wise saws*, 1853, ch. XX.

Taking things philosophically is easy if they don't concern you.

ROBERT C. (BOB) EDWARDS, *Calgary Eye Opener*, April 3, 1915.

Worry is a circle of futile thought, revolving on a pivot of fear.

PETER MCARTHUR, (d. 1924) a favourite saying.

WRITERS.

(See also: AUTHORS; CRITICS)

It appears to me that I could write a book in favor of myself and my notions, without writin' agin any one, and if I couldn't I wouldn't write at all.

T. C. HALIBURTON, *Sam Slick*, 1836, ch. XXIV.

Writin' only aggravates your opponents, and never convinces them.

T. C. HALIBURTON, *Sam Slick*, 1836, ch. XXIV.

Style! I have no style, I merely wait till the mud settles.

GOLDWIN SMITH to Arnold Haultain, qu., Haultain, *Goldwin Smith*, 129.

The less there is happening the more a truly great writer finds to write about.

PETER MCARTHUR, *To be taken with salt*, 1903, 154.

The writers of Canada are its first line of patriots, and the fact is established by the mortality tables. If it be true that the righteous are never forsaken there must be few of the righteous among Canadian authors.

Sir John Willison, in, *Willison's monthly*, Mar., 1927, 369.

We are too young a people apparently for our writers to indulge in irony.

F. H. Underhill, in *Can. hist. rev.*, 1945, 69.

Y

YOUTH.

Youth is the time for improvement.

T. C. Haliburton, *Sam Slick*, 1836, ch. XIV.

And now we are aged and grey, Maggie,
The trials of life nearly done,
Let us sing of the days that are gone, Maggie,
When you and I were young.

George W. Johnson, "When you and I were young, Maggie", in his *Maple leaves*, Hamilton, 1864.

Was it a year or lives ago
We took the grasses in our hands,
And caught the summer flying low
Over the waving meadow lands,
And held it there between our hands?

Bliss Carman, "Low tide on Grand Pré", 1889.

Somewhere he failed me, somewhere he slipped away —
Youth, in his ignorant faith and his bright array.
The tides go out; the tides come flooding in;
Still the old years die and the new begin;
But Youth? —
Somewhere we lost each other, last year or yesterday.

Theodore G. Roberts, "The lost shipmate", *Canadian mag.*, April 1913.

The good don't die young; they simply outgrow it.

Robert C. (Bob) Edwards, *Calgary Eye Opener*; attributed.

Fellows, come and ride with me
Swiftly now to the edge of the end!
Holding the Stars of Joy in fee! —
Youth is a splendid thing to spend.

Tom MacInnes, "Ballade of youth remaining", 1918.

Still as the land, without a sigh,
Dark images, uncouth,
We stand against a light May sky —
The living-dead of youth.

Alan Creighton, "Unemployed", 1936.

YUKON.

I am the land that listens, I am the land that broods;
Steeped in eternal beauty, crystalline waters and woods.
Long have I waited lonely, shunned as a thing accurst,
Monstrous, moody, pathetic, the last of the lands and the first.

Robert W. Service, "The law of the Yukon", 1907.

This is the law of the Yukon, that only the Strong shall thrive;
That surely the Weak shall perish, and only the Fit survive.
Dissolute, damned and despairful, crippled and palsied and slain,
This is the Will of the Yukon, — Lo, how she makes it plain!

Robert W. Service, "The law of the Yukon", 1907.

There's a land where the mountains are nameless
And the rivers all run God knows where;
There are lives that are erring and aimless,
And death that just hangs by a hair;
There are hardships that nobody reckons;
There are valleys unpeopled and still;
There's a land — oh, it beckons and beckons,
And I want to go back —— and I will.

Robert W. Service, "The spell of the Yukon", 1907.

INDEX